THE
OFFICIAL
ACT
SCIENCE GUIDE

THE
OFFICIAL
ACT

SCIENCE GUIDE

ACT

WILEY

Contents

Introduction

So you want to do well on the ACT science test. That's a good goal to have! Whether you've already taken the test once or are planning to do so in the near or even distant future, this book will help you achieve your goal. There are three major factors that will determine how well you do on the ACT science test:

- Focus
- Effort
- Guidance

You need to be focused and diligent in your studies and preparation for the ACT science test. There is no getting around that. You need to put the time and effort into fully practicing the skills the test will be looking for. If you are reading this guide, it can be assumed that you are focused on achieving your goal of success and that you are willing to put the necessary time and effort into making it happen.

The third factor, guidance, is where this guide comes into play. Guidance is difficult to supply to yourself. Each time you take the ACT science test you don't know what is going to be on it, or the way the questions are structured, or the content that is going to be covered. Maybe you wonder how all science can be distilled down into a test that lasts only 35 minutes and has only 40 questions on it. There are so many facts, figures, formulas, theories, and everything else you've covered in school and have seen elsewhere. The great thing is that you aren't expected to know every single fact, figure, and theory you've ever been taught when taking the ACT science test. This book will provide you with the guidance you need to succeed by telling you what you need to study, sharing details on how to prepare, and offering a lot of practice questions.

In chapters 1–3, you'll see examples of the three types of passages on the science test. Knowing how to handle and approach each of these passages is essential to accurately getting through the science section in the time allowed. Each passage type presents you with scientific information in a different format: perhaps a series of graphs and tables, a description of an experiment with different trials and results, or several contrasting hypotheses regarding some premise or data set. The examples will provide you with strategies for how to best approach and conquer each passage type.

In chapters 4–6, you're going to see detailed explanations of the three reporting categories on the ACT science test and strategies for how to best approach each one in your studies. A science reporting category is ACT's way of breaking down the science test into smaller, more understandable subsections. Each reporting category is different and focuses on a specific area of science. You'll also be given official ACT science test sample questions tied directly to each reporting category so that you will know exactly what to expect when you take the test.

In chapter 7 you'll get into more specifics about what you should do to review for success on the ACT science test. Remember: you don't need to remember everything you've ever learned in your science classes, just a few specific things. More important is that you need to have a solid overall grasp of the *idea* of science and how to perform and interpret scientific investigations. In this chapter you'll start by exploring what the scientific method is, and then you'll learn how to formulate a hypothesis, design an experiment, draw conclusions from the results, and make predictions based on those results. Again, all of this will be shown through explanations of official ACT science test sample items.

In chapter 8 you'll get to review how to assess graphs and charts. The chapter starts with the basics of how to read a graph and moves on from there. A major focus is to help you not get overwhelmed by the different kinds of data presented. The chapter will help you learn how to pick out what you need from a graph or chart through provided examples and ignore the excess information given to you. The ACT science test is filled with graphs and charts of all kinds so having a solid understanding of how to read them is absolutely essential.

After reviewing the graphs and charts you'll come to realize just how important and prevalent numbers and measurements are in science. Chapter 9 provides an in-depth review of the major types of measurements and units you might encounter when taking the ACT science test, such as what the metric system is, how prefixes are used, and a detailed discussion of many of the most commonly used SI units. You aren't expected to become an expert on every type of measure and unit. This chapter just helps you gain some familiarity with the measurements you might see on the ACT science test, increasing your confidence when taking the test.

In the same way, understanding and being comfortable with the vocabulary of science is paramount to succeeding on the test. No one resource can prepare you for the number of content-specific terms when reading science material. However, this book will help you become familiar with the most commonly used terms on the ACT science test for each of the major scientific disciplines. It will point out which words are important and which are not. Most important, chapter 10 will show you how to deal with words that you have never seen before and don't know what they mean. You don't need to understand every term on the test, but you'll want to know how to approach those unknown words. This way, when you encounter a science word you aren't familiar with on the test you won't have to waste time trying to figure out what it means. You'll just be able to keep right on going without any loss of time or focus.

In chapters 11 and 12, you're provided with a large set of ACT science test questions. Each question provides a thorough breakdown of the solution. This section will prove invaluable because each question is tied directly to the specific reporting category and provides detailed solutions. Practice is essential to success in any endeavor in life, and test taking is not any different, so use these questions to prepare yourself for the ACT science test.

You definitely want to pick up the other ACT subject guides, and you'll eventually want to take at least one full-length practice exam from *The Official ACT Prep Guide*, but this is a good start for the science. You can and will succeed with your goal of doing well on the ACT science test. You provide the focus and the effort, and this book will provide the guidance. So read on and let's get started.

Chapter 1: Data Representation Passages

This chapter is the first of three that focuses on the different passage types found on the ACT science test. It initially discusses passages briefly and then focuses on the data representation passage type. The chapter provides some basic suggestions and tips for how to best approach the data representation section. It then walks you through an official ACT sample data representation passage while providing guidance on what is important to focus on in each passage.

Passages on the ACT Science Test

There are three types of passages that you are going to encounter in the ACT science section. Each passage type presents some information in a different format that you will need to use to answer the questions. These passages are usually a combination of written description and graphical information. The written portion usually informs you, the test taker, about the data represented in the passage and can provide descriptions of experiments or differing scientific viewpoints. This graphical information might be in the form of one or more graphs, tables, or charts.

In general, science passages can be a bit intimidating to students if they are not totally comfortable with science as a subject. As the test taker it is your job to analyze all of the information in the passage and figure out the answer. The questions require critical thinking and the ability to see trends and predict future results based on the information presented, all while making sure you don't get bogged down in one confusing passage or question and your time doesn't run out.

The ACT science test measures your ability to understand and interpret scientific experiments and results. It is not asking you to remember the meaning of vocabulary words or specific topics. It is important to remember that if you need to understand a scientific concept presented to you in a test passage on the ACT science test it will be explained to you somewhere. Either the passage itself will provide you with the meaning and understanding necessary to use the information or it will be provided in the question asking about a specific piece of information.

Before getting into the specifics of each passage type there are a few general pieces of advice about how to best approach the passages on the ACT science test.

Tip 1: Approach the Science Test with the Right Mind-Set

First, you need to have the right mind-set for the ACT science test. Know that you will face some challenging questions in each passage and will probably see some very specific science concepts that you might not have heard about before. You might find some of the graphs intimidating and challenging to understand at first glance, more so than in other sections of the ACT. In the other ACT sections you will see paragraphs of words, numbers, and equations all separately, but in the science section you'll see all that information combined together into one passage. It is what makes science unique. Have the mind-set that you are not going to let anything make you feel ill at ease.

Tip 2: Have a Strategy for Answering Science Passages

Second, you want to have the right approach to dealing with passages on the ACT science test. What is the right approach? It is a general plan for how you are going to deal with the passages and questions you see to best succeed when you take the test. For some other sections of the ACT test, you have may have heard that the best way to approach each section is by jumping around from question to question, answering all of the simple ones first or perhaps reading each question first before you even look at the passage provided for those questions. This can prove useful in other sections and is not bad advice, but it is not the best approach for the science test specifically.

Why isn't it the right way to go about taking the ACT science test? Most of the experiments and data are complex and not something simple that you can easily glance at and have an in-depth understanding of. If you skip reading the passage on the science test you are just going to be wasting your time. Each squestion is going to ask you for specifics about the passage you see; it isn't asking about themes or broad strokes. If you read the questions first you are just going to end up going back and reading, and re-reading, the passage for each and every question. It isn't going to be an efficient use of your time.

Instead, actually read the passage first. You don't need to study it in grand detail but a good initial reading will go a long way to helping you work through the science test faster. Get an initial idea about what the passage is covering, what data are presented, and what research method is used. The better initial idea you have, the easier and faster it will be to answer each question. Once you have the initial knowledge about the passage, you'll be able to read each question and have a good idea of where you should look to find the specific information you need. Your general approach to each passage should be to read it and underline important terms or other information that you think will be useful and relevant to the questions. If you are taking the online version be sure to use the annotation tools to their fullest extent and actually make some notes in the passage. Don't go overboard though; you'll end up with the entire passage underlined, which won't help you easily find the important details to answer the questions.

Each of the passage types is unique in its own way, and they all present their own unique challenges when reading them and answering the questions associated with them. As you read these first three chapters there will be some specific tips about how to initially read each passage type and what you should be looking for when you make that first read through. Plus you will see an in-depth description of an official ACT science sample passage and a breakdown of all the questions that go along with that type of passage.

What You Can Expect from a Data Representation Passage

The first type of passage that we will be looking at is data representation. As you can probably guess this section involves looking at data and interpreting meaning from that data. The passages will generally consist of charts, graphs, tables, and diagrams presenting data to you. There will usually be some amount of scientific text that goes along with the data providing any necessary background information you might need to understand and interpret the information represented.

Something you'll want to do before proceeding with any passage is to make sure you are able to recognize which type of passage it is. Make sure that you do not get a data representation passage type confused with a research summaries passage type. They can look similar in that both sometimes have graphs or tables displayed throughout the passage. The key difference between the two is that the research summaries passages contain a focused description of an experiment or multiple experiments instead of a more general description of a scientific concept or process. If you see a mention of multiple trials or of multiple experiments you are definitely looking at a research summaries passage and not a data representation passage.

Remember when approaching a data representation passage that you are not expected to understand everything it is talking about. There is a chance that you will look at this background information and have little to no knowledge of the exact scientific information it is talking about.

You don't need to be an expert on whatever topic it might be discussing, not even close. The data representation passages will provide you with all the information you need to understand and correctly interpret the graphs and tables you see in any given passage. You simply need to be able to read it in a timely fashion and use the information provided to you in the appropriate way to answer the questions.

The next thing you need to remember is to not get overwhelmed when you first look at each of these passages. There is a lot of information shown to you in these passages, and the graphs and tables can look very intimidating at first glance. You don't need to use all of this information. The ACT is not expecting you to take it all in and divine meaning from each and every piece of data you see. You are going to be asked specific questions about the data and it is going to be up to you to focus on those questions and determine the best answer to each of them. If you can stay focused on the goal and not get overwhelmed by the avalanche of data you see in each passage then you will be fine.

With that in mind, before getting into the examples, we suggest you focus on performing a few specific steps each time you encounter a data representation passage.

- **First, read through whatever background information is presented in the passage.** When you are reading this passage make sure that you don't get bogged down by words or phrases that you don't fully understand. Just get through it so you have a general idea about the data the passage is referring to. There are usually going to be at least one or two scientific terms or names in each of these passages that you might not know. Don't be worried about them yet. If they are truly important more information will be provided as you read the passage. Don't spend a large amount of time trying to figure out what a particular word means. You'll want to conserve your time when you do the science section, so you want to make sure your actions are always focused and forward thinking.

- **Second, look at each graph, table, or data representation and determine how each is labeled.** Once you have identified the name or title of each graph and how it will be referred to in the questions circle it, underline it, or do whatever you need to make it stand out in your mind. The questions in the ACT science section regularly make reference to the graphs and tables found in the passages by a specific name. Usually it is Figure 1, Figure 2, and so on; however, there can be different names associated with each graph or table. No two passages are exactly alike in that regard. It is vitally important when you are reading the questions associated with the passage that you know which graph is being referred to in the discussion. This will help you save time and stay focused on exactly the information you need to answer each question.

- **Third, look at the graphs and tables and try to make some meaning out of the data you see.** The better your understanding of the data before you tackle the questions, the better off you will be when it comes to problem-solving and reasoning. This is not to say that you should take a long time and thoroughly study each graph in detail. It simply means that you should look at each graph or table and try to get a general idea about what it is saying. Look at each axis and see what it represents, how it is labeled, and what units it uses to show the data. Each of these pieces of information is important, and overlooking it can lead to you potentially to not fully understanding a relationship the graph might be trying to show. (If you need to brush up on how to read graphs and identify what axis is what, make sure you look at chapter 8, which covers graph reading in detail.) Once you've identified how the data are being represented you should try to make some meaning out of the data. Try to determine what type of relationship each graph or table is showing in regards to the data. At the most basic level this could be an increase shown on one axis and a corresponding increase or decrease on the other axis. Perhaps as one value increases there is a corresponding decrease in another. This can be challenging because each graph is different. Make sure you spend your time wisely and don't get bogged down in trying to create a trend or meaning where there simply might not be one. Take a quick look, get a general idea of the graph, and move on to the questions.

These are, of course, just a basic guide for how you can best approach each data representation passage. No two are exactly alike, and each passage presents its own unique and interesting challenge. The most important thing you can do is to not get overwhelmed by what you see. Focus on the data in front of you and what it is trying to show you, nothing more.

Trying Your Hand at a Data Representation Passage

Now that we've covered some basic tips it is time to tackle an official ACT science data representation passage. In the following section you will see a data representation passage along with the entire question set that goes with the passage. First there will be a detailed breakdown of the passage itself. You'll see a discussion related to the concept it covers along with a basic analysis of the graphics associated with the passage.

After that you will see the entire question set associated with this passage. Each question will be discussed in detail, and you will be provided with the thought process explaining how you should go about solving each question. This will go into more depth than simply explaining which answer choice is right and wrong. Instead there will be a discussion of what the question is looking for, what you should know in advance, and what information you can pick up from the question itself. Each question will also have a detailed breakdown of the correct answer and how you can reach that answer the fastest.

So, now take a moment and read the sample passage to yourself and answer the sample questions that follow it. Look at the graphs and the relationships they show. Try to determine the answers before moving on and looking at the analysis provided. In any of these sections it is always important that you read each question and sample passage thoroughly before moving on to the analysis presented here. Simply seeing someone tell you the right answer or explanation to an idea or concept is not as useful if you have not considered the material yourself first.

Example Passage and Questions

Passage XIV

Tiny marine organisms build shells from *calcite* ($CaCO_3$) dissolved in seawater. After the organisms' death, the shells sink. Some shells dissolve before they reach the seafloor, but some form layers of *calcareous ooze* ($CaCO_3$-rich sediment). Figure 1 shows how seawater's degree of saturation with respect to $CaCO_3$ and the rate at which $CaCO_3$ dissolves change with depth. The *$CaCO_3$ compensation depth* (CCD) represents the depth beneath which $CaCO_3$ dissolves faster than it precipitates. Figure 2 shows typical depths at which various seafloor sediments are found. Figure 3 shows the percent coverage for two seafloor sediments in three oceans.

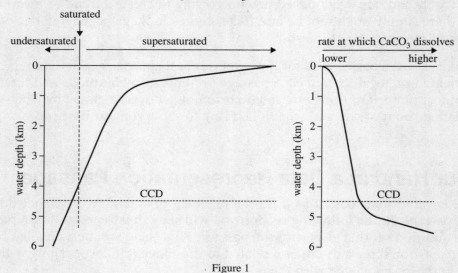

Figure 1

Figure 1 adapted from J. Andrews, P. Brimblecombe, T. Jickells, and P. Liss, *An Introduction to Environmental Chemistry.* ©1996 by Blackwell Science, Ltd.

Figure 2

Figure 2 adapted from M. Grant Gross, *Oceanography*, 6th ed. ©1990 by Macmillan Publishing Company.

Figure 3

Figure 3 adapted from Harold Thurman, *Introductory Oceanography.* ©1991 by Macmillan Publishing Company.

Sample Question 1

Assume that the Arctic Ocean seafloor has an average depth of 4.9 km. According to Figures 2 and 3, the Arctic Ocean seafloor is most likely covered with:

F. calcareous ooze only.

G. nearly the same areas of calcareous ooze and red clay.

H. a greater area of calcareous ooze than of red clay.

J. a greater area of red clay than of calcareous ooze.

Sample Question 2

The data in Figure 2 support which of the following statements about the relative thickness of marine organism shells and the depths at which calcareous oozes composed of those shells are found? Calcareous oozes formed mainly from thick-shelled organisms are found:

A. at shallower depths than those formed mainly from thin-shelled organisms.

B. at greater depths than those formed mainly from thin-shelled organisms.

C. over the same depth range as those formed mainly from thin-shelled organisms.

D. in the same areas of a given ocean as those formed mainly from thin-shelled organisms.

(continued)

Passage XIV (*continued*)

Sample Question 3

$CaCO_3$ often precipitates out of seawater in areas where the seawater is shallow (less than 1 km deep). According to Figure 1, this most likely occurs because seawater in those locations:

F. is undersaturated with respect to $CaCO_3$.

G. is saturated with respect to $CaCO_3$.

H. is supersaturated with respect to $CaCO_3$.

J. contains no $CaCO_3$.

Sample Question 4

According to Figure 1, above what maximum depth is seawater supersaturated with respect to $CaCO_3$?

A. 3.0 km

B. 3.5 km

C. 4.0 km

D. 4.5 km

Sample Question 5

Figure 1 shows that the rate at which $CaCO_3$ dissolves increases the most between which of the following depths?

F. Between 3.5 km and 4.0 km

G. Between 4.0 km and 4.5 km

H. Between 4.5 km and 5.0 km

J. Between 5.0 km and 5.5 km

Analyzing the Example Passage and Questions

Now that you have read the passage and have given some thought to what you see let's begin our analysis.

This passage discusses calcite ($CaCO_3$) saturation in the ocean at various depths. It provides you with some background information on the process by which calcite dissolves, and it makes mention of small marine organisms that use the calcite to build their shells. As we've mentioned you are not expected to know what calcite is or how it dissolves in the ocean at various depths. You just need to look at the data presented and interpret it as the questions require. Everything you need to know to answer the questions that go along with this passage is presented in the passage itself.

There are a few specific scientific vocabulary words that you could potentially get hung up on if you don't fully understand them. Specifically, in this passage there are several mentions of *dissolving*. If you have no idea what *dissolving* means (a solid breaking apart in a liquid to form a solution) this could present a problem. The passage also clearly uses the chemical formula, $CaCO_3$, and the name of calcite interchangeably. The great thing about this passage though is that nowhere does it require or expect you to understand what the chemical formula means beyond simply being used as an identifier for calcite. You just have to recognize that $CaCO_3$ is being used as an identifier and nothing more.

After the paragraph with the background information, this passage then provides you with three figures that show data regarding calcite and its ability to dissolve at different depths. Let's talk about each figure now and see what information each is trying to show you:

- **Figure 1** shows you two line graphs dealing with calcite dissolving. The graph on the left shows you the level of calcite saturation at various depths. It shows clearly that the saturation of calcite is much greater near the ocean surface compared to deeper waters. The graph on the right shows you the rate calcite dissolves at different ocean depths. It shows clearly that calcite dissolves faster as you move deeper in the ocean. These graphs can be a little tricky due to the fact that the zero, the origin point, is on the top left instead of the bottom left. This makes sense though when you consider the fact that these graphs are representing ocean depth and zero should be on top in that case. However, this inverts the graph compared to the way you traditionally are taught and shown graphs in school. Do not let this bother you. Carefully look at each axis and each graph and find the meaning and the relationship shown.

  Another potential issue here is your understanding of the term *saturation*. If you have no idea what *saturation* means this graph might be of very little use to you. If you are struggling with any term, a suggestion is to look at whatever other information is provided to you. If you look at the other two figures you should be able to make a connection to the idea that as depth increases the level of calcite dissolved decreases. This should give you a clue that saturation is a measure of how dissolved or concentrated something is in a solution. Are you required to go to this level of analysis in each passage and figure? No, you aren't, but it's included here to show you that there is almost always a path to discovering meaning in each passage. Even if there is a word or two you don't understand there is almost always a way to figure it out from the information given to you if you will truly need it.

- **Figure 2** shows a graph that provides detail on the concentration of calcareous ooze at different depths of the ocean. Figure 2 clearly shows how the concentration of calcareous ooze is higher at lower depths. As you progress deeper into the ocean Figure 2 shows how the percentage of calcareous ooze decreases, and toward the bottom it shows that you mainly begin to observe red clay. It also shows a pattern that as depth increases the shell thickness of organisms in the ooze increases.

- **Figure 3** shows a comparison of the seafloor covered by calcareous ooze and red clay in three of the four oceans throughout the world. You'll notice that red clay is not mentioned in the paragraph above the graphs at all, yet it appears in Figure 2 and also in Figure 3. You should notice a clear relationship between the Atlantic Ocean and the Indian Ocean in terms of their similar depths. This corresponds to a similar distribution of seafloor coverage in regards to calcareous ooze when compared to red clay.

The hope is now, after a detailed look at each figure, you can see a very real and distinct relationship shown by each graph in the passage: that as the ocean depth increases, the amount of calcite dissolved in water, as represented by the calcareous ooze, decreases. That should be the major take away from your initial reading of this passage. Beyond that you shouldn't perform any more analysis without first approaching the questions associated with the passage. Next we will look at a few official ACT sample questions associated with this passage in detail and discuss how to best answer each one.

Sample Question 1

Assume that the Arctic Ocean seafloor has an average depth of 4.9 km. According to Figures 2 and 3, the Arctic Ocean seafloor is most likely covered with:

F. calcareous ooze only.

G. nearly the same areas of calcareous ooze and red clay.

H. a greater area of calcareous ooze than of red clay.

J. a greater area of red clay than of calcareous ooze.

This question refers to Figures 2 and 3 in the passage. It clearly tells you those are the two figures you should be looking at when answering this question. It presents you with a data point about the depth of the Arctic Ocean and asks you to determine from the figures what the probable composition of the seafloor is based on that depth.

First look at Figure 2. According to the question the Arctic Ocean has an average depth of 4.9 km. According to the graph in Figure 2 this should correspond to a low concentration of calcareous ooze (below 20%). It tells you that in this range you have red clay present. You can also look at Figure 3 and see a trend from the three oceans regarding their depth and their seafloor composition. The first two oceans, the Atlantic and the Indian, both show a higher concentration of calcareous ooze compared to red clay. They also share a similar depth. As you move deeper into the Pacific Ocean the concentration shifts toward there being more red clay then calcareous ooze. Because the average depth listed for the Arctic Ocean is shown to be lower than the Pacific Ocean you can extrapolate the seafloor coverage of the Arctic will be even more heavily weighted toward red clay.

This question illustrates that sometimes there are multiple pathways to the solution you need. Either one of the figures shows the data you need to determine the answer. For the sake of time, once you've established your answer with confidence, move to the next question. There is no need to check both Figures 2 and 3 if you are able to determine the correct answer by simply looking at one of them. **The correct answer is J.**

Sample Question 2

The data in Figure 2 support which of the following statements about the relative thickness of marine organism shells and the depths at which calcareous oozes composed of those shells are found? Calcareous oozes formed mainly from thick-shelled organisms are found:

A. at shallower depths than those formed mainly from thin-shelled organisms.

B. at greater depths than those formed mainly from thin-shelled organisms.

C. over the same depth range as those formed mainly from thin-shelled organisms.

D. in the same areas of a given ocean as those formed mainly from thin-shelled organisms.

Sample question 2 asks you to specifically look at Figure 2. It doesn't require you to look at any other figure or the introductory paragraph. When you see a question that is straightforward like this be sure you don't overthink it and try to include other data charts that aren't required. Because you only need to look at one graph you shouldn't spend time looking at multiple data sets. Just look at what you need to and save as much time as you can while working to get the correct answer.

In this case the question asks you to look at the shell thickness associated with calcareous ooze at different depths. It begins by saying "Calcareous oozes formed mainly from thick-shelled organisms are found:" and you are expected to pick the answer that best finishes this statement based on Figure 2. Specifically, it gives you four statements and you must determine which of the them best matches what Figure 2 shows about shell thickness at various depths.

In looking at Figure 2 you should notice that at the depths closer to the surface the calcareous ooze is found to be composed of mostly thin-shelled organisms. As you move deeper down into the ocean the ooze is found to be composed of thick-shelled organisms. So you need to determine which answer choice explains that thicker-shelled organisms are found at greater depths than thin-shelled organisms. **Clearly choice B explains and supports that statement, and it is the correct answer.**

Sample question 2 is a great example of a very straightforward question. You will see several of these in each test and usually at least one in each data representation passage question set. These are the type of questions that you should take advantage of when working through the test to save you time. They ask a very simple statement question that wants you to find support data from a single graph. There is no extrapolation or comparisons between data sets required here.

Sample Question 3

$CaCO_3$ often precipitates out of seawater in areas where the seawater is shallow (less than 1 km deep). According to Figure 1, this most likely occurs because seawater in those locations:

F. is undersaturated with respect to $CaCO_3$.

G. is saturated with respect to $CaCO_3$.

H. is supersaturated with respect to $CaCO_3$.

J. contains no $CaCO_3$.

Sample question 3 is a great example of a question that appears to require that you have some specific knowledge of a scientific concept but, in reality, it doesn't require any to answer the question. In this case the concept of precipitation is mentioned immediately at the beginning of the question. Precipitation in regards to this question is not the same as what happens when it rains outside. Something is said to precipitate when a dissolved substance in a solution returns to its solid state in the liquid. This occurs when a solution becomes saturated, which means that the liquid cannot have anything more dissolved into it. Depending on conditions, sometimes a solution can become supersaturated and hold even more dissolved solid.

All of this detail is important and can help you to better understand this question and answer it quickly. However, none of it is required to actually determine the right answer to this question. You can figure everything out you need to answer the question from the graph presented and nothing more.

Sample question 3 clearly refers to only Figure 1. This means you are not expected to reference either one of the other figures presented in this passage. It mentions the idea of precipitation, as discussed, yet that isn't actually very meaningful to the question. It never says you are looking at shallow water less than 1 km deep and that that information is important to the question. This question is simply asking you what level of saturation is shown at a depth of less than 1 km. Looking at the trend line, you can see that as the depth of the water decreases the saturation level of $CaCO_3$ increases. You just need to read the graph and see what level of $CaCO_3$ saturation is present around and above 1 km. The area you should be focused on is circled in Figure 1 to the right. **That shows the answer to question 3 is clearly choice H.**

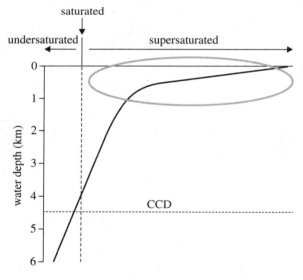

Figure 1

Sample Question 4

According to Figure I, above what maximum depth is seawater supersaturated with respect to $CaCO_3$?

A. 3.0 km

B. 3.5 km

C. 4.0 km

D. 4.5 km

Sample question 4 ties in closely to sample question 3, and you will see this type of connection from time to time on the ACT. Sometimes there will be questions asking about very similar concepts in succession on the ACT science portion and especially in the data representation section. Try to take advantage of the familiarity with these related questions and use your time wisely. This is another straightforward data analysis question that asks you to pick out a specific point on the graph and nothing more. It doesn't require specific knowledge of any of the concepts mentioned.

To approach this question, you need to determine how the graph in Figure 1 identifies supersaturation and how it separates this from saturation. In this graph there is a dashed vertical line marked with an arrow indicating where the saturation point is in regards to $CaCO_3$. Once the graph moves to the right of this, the x-axis shows that water is now supersaturated. So the correct place to identify where supersaturation begins is from the intersection point of the saturation curve line and the dashed saturation point line. Your task is to now determine where on the y-axis this point is. **The correct answer is C.**

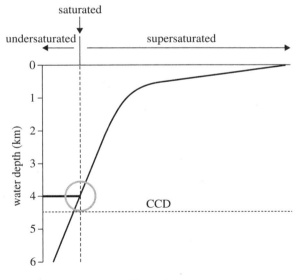

Figure 1

If it helps you to determine the answer feel free to physically draw a horizontal line from that intersection point to the y-axis and determine what depth you see. However, if you do plan on drawing a physical line like this, be sure that it is straight. Generally, if you are going to be asked a question like this on the ACT science section you will usually see specific measurement markers called *graduations* that indicate the potential answer choices you might need. In this question you can clearly see that there are graduations on this graph every 1 km. Such graduations on passage graphs can help you determine a potential intersection point or other numerical prediction you need to make.

Sample Question 5

Figure 1 shows that the rate at which $CaCO_3$ dissolves increases the most between which of the following depths?

F. Between 3.5 km and 4.0 km

G. Between 4.0 km and 4.5 km

H. Between 4.5 km and 5.0 km

J. Between 5.0 km and 5.5 km

Sample question 5 refers you again to Figure 1. This time, however, it expects you to look at the graph to the right. The previous two questions have been in reference to the graph on the left so when you first see this question it is natural to refer to Figure 1 and think for a moment that it only consists of the graph on the left regarding saturation. You might look at it and realize it has no mention of the rate at which dissolving takes place. The other graph in the figure does show the rate at which $CaCO_3$ dissolves.

Figure 1

In this case the question is asking you to focus on the rate at which $CaCO_3$ dissolves in comparison to the depth of water. It wants you to identify the depth range where the rate increases the most. Each of the ranges provided has the rate of dissolving increasing so it is up to you to determine where the rate increases the most. You can see on the graph that as you move down there is a slow but steady increase in the rate of dissolving. However, after you move past the line labelled *CCD* (which the paragraph above identifies as the $CaCO_3$ compensation depth) you begin to see a dramatic move higher in the rate of dissolving. The change begins somewhat slowly after you cross the CCD line and then shoots up higher after it crosses the 5 km depth mark. **The correct answer to the question is J.** Even though the rate begins increasing after the 4.5 km depth mark it goes higher faster as you move below the 5 km depth line.

Summary

So now that you've gone through an entire data representation passage and looked at each question, there should be some conclusions you can make regarding the section. The first thing to do is read the passage thoroughly. When you are reading be sure that you don't get hung up on any confusing or tricky scientific vocabulary words you don't understand. A detailed understanding of the content vocabulary words is more than likely not required to answer the questions successfully so don't worry if you don't understand a few of the words. They either will be explained or you don't have to worry about them. Once you've read the text be sure to look at the figures presented and try to determine a general meaning behind them then move on to the questions.

When working on the questions be sure to focus specifically on what they want you to answer and nothing else. Don't waste time trying to find relationships or meaning in the data that isn't required. Focus on only the figures each question refers to in the text. Do not become so focused on a specific figure or part of a figure that you overlook important information. It is easy to become hyper-focused on only one part of a graph and sometimes overlook some other meaningful data presented in another portion of that graph.

Finally, as always, practice is essential to succeeding. This chapter presented you with a detailed breakdown of one data representation passage; however, no two are quite alike. Each can present its own unique challenges, and the more you have reviewed the better off you will be when you take the real ACT.

To review more official ACT data representation passages and sample questions please see chapter 11.

Chapter 2: Research Summaries Passages

This chapter is going to discuss the research summaries passage type you will encounter when taking the ACT science portion. The chapter will provide some basic suggestions for how to recognize a research summaries passage type and some strategies for how to best approach them. It will then focus on walking you through an entire official ACT research summaries passage broken down in detail along with all of the questions associated with the passage.

What You Can Expect from a Research Summaries Passage

The research summaries passage type is focused on the scientific process and experimental results. These passages generally expect you to look at a scientific experiment and the data generated by that experiment. Research summaries passages sometimes can look very similar to data representation passages, but if you pay careful attention to the details presented you shouldn't have any trouble determining the correct passage type.

Research summaries passages generally begin by providing you with one or more written paragraphs describing an experiment. This introductory text can describe how the experiment was designed, some background on the concept the experiment or study is based on, the method by which the experiment was carried out, what the purpose of the experiment was, or anything else related to the experiment. Depending on the experiment itself you might also see an image or diagram depicting the actual physical experimental setup. This will generally then be followed with several graphs or charts indicating the results from the experiment.

Differences between research summaries passages and data representation passages are mentions of multiple experimental trials, headers in the passage titled "Experiment 1, Experiment 2, and so on," "Study 1, Study 2, and so on," or anything else that makes direct mention of an experiment taking place. If you see any text along those lines you are looking at a research summaries question. However, if all you see is introductory text describing a phenomenon or concept and then some data charts related to the concept without any mention of any related experiment or trials, you are looking at a data representation passage.

How You Should Approach a Research Summaries Passage

Once you've identified a research summaries passage, the next step is knowing how to best approach it and what you should be looking for on your initial reading. As with data representation passages, you are not expected to be an expert on the experiment you read about. You may encounter a passage discussing various flood plateaus or a study comparing how different phases of matter expand when exposed to heat. Your first instinct might be to get a little nervous about the fact that you are not an expert on thermal expansion or flood plateaus yet you need to remember that anything you need to know about the topic will be presented to you in the question. If you need to know something specific about thermal expansion, the passage will describe it to you and provide any background knowledge you require. Your task is to be able to look at the method and purpose behind the experiment along with the data presented and understand the results shown to you. If you can do that, you'll do very well on research summaries passages.

One thing that can help dramatically with research summaries passages is a concrete understanding of the scientific method and scientific experimentation in general. If you are a little rusty in that area it might help to brush up on it in chapter 7, which is entirely focused on the scientific method and the process of science.

Now let's go over a few tips that you should focus on when reading each research summaries passage for the first time:

1. **Attempt to identify the driving question and/or hypothesis of the experiment.** As you read through the initial description portion of the passage and then read through the different results sections you should be asking yourself the question, "What is the point of this experiment?" Specifically ask yourself why the topic is being researched. You should be looking for a sentence or two somewhere that specifically states the purpose of the research or clearly explains what the

researcher was looking into when he or she began the experiment. It might be in the form of a question the researcher is investigating or it might be presented in the form of a hypothesis, which is a proposed answer to the research question. If you find that sentence or two be sure to underline it or circle it so that you can reference it later. Do not be afraid to mark your test up and write important things down. If you are taking the test online you will have a highlighting tool available within the test program along with scrap paper. Use them. Just because the online test is on a screen instead of paper shouldn't change your strategy. You will need to move through the materials quickly and read a lot of information, so you will benefit if you can help yourself remember important facts or statements by marking on your test or using your highlighter tool and the scrap paper.

2. **Determine how the experiment was conducted, specifically, what method was used to perform the research.** A method is the physical process by which the scientist performed the experiment. It is a designed and written plan created before the research began to investigate the question and hypothesis the experiment is based on. It will probably be spelled out clearly in a few sentences somewhere in the introductory information presented in the passage.

3. **Determine the independent variable: what is changed during the course of the experiment by the researcher.** Look at the data presented to you, either in the initial write-up or in the data tables or graphs, and identify what experimental variables were manipulated (changed) by the researcher. The variables determined by the researcher that are not otherwise changed as a result of the experiment are called the *independent variables.* The conditions of the experiment that are changed could be incredibly varied depending on the design of the experiment so there is no one set thing to look for here. Instead look at all the information presented and see what was intentionally changed by the researcher. Examples might include the researcher changing the temperature of the experiment, the time given for trials, the type of solution used, the location of the experiment, the starting point of the experiment, and so on. There are so many possible elements that can be changed in an experiment it is impossible to present you with every option here. You just need to carefully read the information presented and make your determination.

4. **Determine the dependent variable: what happens as a result of the experiment.** Look at the data results shown and see what happened when the independent variables were changed. The result of this change is called the *dependent variable.* It is dependent on the conditions of the experiment and changes accordingly. It is the data the researchers are looking for to determine the results of their experiment and draw conclusions. Whatever it is, it will probably vary as the independent variable is changed. These are only brief descriptions of variables in an experiment.

5. **Look at the data presented and determine the results of the experiment and draw conclusions.** Once you've identified the purpose of the experiment, the method, and the variables, the final step is to analyze the data quickly and draw

a few simple conclusions about the results. Look for simple trends or patterns in the results. Is there a clear change that occurs when the independent variable is altered? Can you draw a conclusion from the results you see? If so, it might help to underline or circle the data points you see that can help you draw the conclusion you are making.

Trying Your Hand at a Research Summaries Passage

So now you have a general idea of how to approach a research summaries passage. The next step is walking through an official ACT research summaries passage in detail. This portion of the chapter will analyze the passage in depth to help you better grasp how you might go about looking at any research summaries passage you encounter. In addition, all of the questions associated with the research summaries passage will be answered and their solutions discussed in significant detail. The purpose of all of this is to help you get better and work quicker when approaching a research summaries passage.

Before you move on to the summary of the passage and the explanation of the questions be sure to read the passage and attempt to answer the questions yourself. Again, this is not a self-quiz or check for understanding; instead, it will help you to understand the explanations provided. Being familiar with the material is always better than just skipping to the answers in hope of them making sense. This advice is a bit different compared to what you might see in other sections of the test, which tell you to first look at the questions before reading the passage. The ACT science test provides you with a lot of information in a passage. Most of the experiments presented are detailed in nature and not something simple that you have a serious familiarity with.

As said in chapter 1 on data representation, if you try to skip reading the passage on the science test you are just going to waste your time. Each of the questions are going to ask you for detailed specifics about the passage or the data you are presented with. There are no general questions about the general feel or the overall structure of anything. If you read the questions first you are just going to end up going back and reading, and re-reading, the passage for each and every question. It isn't going to be an efficient use of your time. Read the following passage carefully and attempt to answer the questions to the best of your ability.

Example Passage and Questions

Passage IX

Carbon monoxide gas (CO) is toxic in air at concentrations above 0.1% by volume. Cars are the major source of atmospheric CO in urban areas. Higher CO levels are observed during colder weather. A group of students proposed that cars emit more CO at colder air temperatures than at warmer air temperatures during the first 15 minutes after they are started. The students did the following experiments to investigate this hypothesis.

Experiment 1

A hose was connected to the tailpipe of a car. The engine was started and the exhaust was collected in a plastic bag. A 1 mL sample of the exhaust was taken from the bag with a syringe and injected into a *gas chromatograph,* an instrument that separates a mixture of gases into its individual components. Comparisons of the exhaust with mixtures of known CO concentrations were made to determine the percent by volume of CO in the exhaust. Exhaust was collected at two-minute intervals. Samples of exhaust from each of four cars were tested at an external temperature of −9°C. The results are shown in Table 1.

Table 1				
Time after starting (min)	Percent of CO in the exhaust at −9°C:			
	1978 Model X	1978 Model Y	1996 Model X	1996 Model Y
1	3.5	3.2	1.2	0.3
3	4.0	3.7	1.0	1.2
5	4.5	7.5	1.5	2.5
7	3.6	10.0	1.0	3.0
9	3.2	9.1	0.5	2.6
11	3.1	8.0	0.5	2.0
13	3.0	7.0	0.5	2.0
15	2.9	7.0	0.4	1.8

Experiment 2

The same four cars were tested at a temperature of 20°C using the procedure from Experiment 1. The results are shown in Table 2.

Table 2				
Time after starting (min)	Percent of CO in the exhaust at 20°C:			
	1978 Model X	1978 Model Y	1996 Model X	1996 Model Y
1	2.0	0.8	0.3	0.2
3	2.8	2.0	0.5	1.0
5	3.4	6.0	0.5	1.5
7	1.5	7.0	0.3	0.8
9	1.3	7.0	0.3	0.5
11	1.0	6.5	0.1	0.3
13	1.0	5.0	0.1	0.3
15	0.9	4.8	0.1	0.2

(continued)

Passage IX (*continued*)

Sample Question 1

Do the results from Experiment 1 support the hypothesis that, at a given temperature and time, the exhaust of newer cars contains lower percents of CO than the exhaust of older cars?

F. Yes; the highest percent of CO was in the exhaust of the 1996 Model Y.

G. Yes; both 1996 models had percents of CO that were lower than those of either 1978 model.

H. No; the highest percent of CO was in the exhaust of the 1978 Model Y.

J. No; both 1978 models had percents of CO that were lower than those of either 1996 model.

Sample Question 2

A student, when using the gas chromatograph, was concerned that CO_2 in the exhaust sample may be interfering in the detection of CO. Which of the following procedures would best help the student investigate this problem?

A. Filling the bag with CO_2 before collecting the exhaust

B. Collecting exhaust from additional cars

C. Injecting a sample of air into the gas chromatograph

D. Testing a sample with known amounts of CO and CO_2

Sample Question 3

Based on the results of the experiments and the information in the table below, cars in which of the following cities would most likely contribute the greatest amount of CO to the atmosphere in January? (Assume that the types, numbers, and ages of cars used in each city are approximately equal.)

City	Average temperature (°F) for January
Minneapolis	11.2
Pittsburgh	26.7
Seattle	39.1
San Diego	56.8

F. Minneapolis

G. Pittsburgh

H. Seattle

J. San Diego

Sample Question 4

In Experiment 1, which of the following factors varied?

A. The method of sample collection

B. The volume of exhaust that was tested

C. The year in which the cars were made

D. The temperature at which the engine was started

Sample Question 5

Many states require annual testing of cars to determine the levels of their CO emissions. Based on the experiments, in order to determine the maximum percent of CO found in a car's exhaust, during which of the following times after starting a car would it be best to sample the exhaust?

F. 1–3 min

G. 5–7 min

H. 9–11 min

J. 13 min or longer

Sample Question 6

How would the results of the experiments be affected, if at all, if the syringe contents were contaminated with CO-free air? (The composition of air is 78% N_2, 21% O_2, 0.9% Ar, and 0.1% other gases.) The measured percents of CO in the exhaust would be:

A. higher than the actual percents at both –9°C and 20°C.

B. lower than the actual percents at –9°C, but higher than the actual percents at 20°C.

C. lower than the actual percents at both –9°C and 20°C.

D. the same as the actual percents at both –9°C and 20°C.

Analyzing the Example Passage and Questions

This passage begins by introducing carbon monoxide gas to you and the fact that it is toxic above a certain concentration. Carbon monoxide is a gas that you probably have a little familiarity with. You might have seen a carbon monoxide detector on the wall somewhere or heard that it is bad to breathe. It isn't necessary for you to actually have any background knowledge of carbon monoxide to answer this question though. A passing familiarity might make you feel more comfortable with the passage but it won't help you answer the questions any better than if you had never heard the term before.

After introducing carbon monoxide, the passage then says that cars are the major atmospheric producer of it in urban areas. It states that at colder temperatures there are higher concentrations of atmospheric carbon monoxide. This is useful background information that helps you put the research being done in this passage into context.

In the case of this passage the researchers are students. The students speculate that the larger concentration of carbon monoxide is due to cars putting out more carbon monoxide during colder weather. They specifically said that they believe there is more carbon monoxide expelled during the first 15 minutes of the car engine running in cold weather compared to warmer weather. This statement is the hypothesis of the experiment. You should underline it. As you read further the next sentence confirms it is the hypothesis by stating "The students did the following experiments to investigate this *hypothesis*." Sometimes the passages are helpful like this and will very clearly identify the hypothesis. Other times they are not as clear. It is up to you to make sure you are able to determine it in either case.

After the initial description the passage introduces Experiment 1. The beginning of this description is used to explain the method of the experiment. This is something you will see from time to time. The method of the experiment is not always discussed before the "trials" or "experiments" are brought into the passage. In this case you see that Experiment 1 describes the method in some depth. It says that a hose was connected to the tail pipe of a car and exhaust gas collected into a bag. The students then took a 1 ml sample every two minutes at a specific temperature. The samples were analyzed with a gas chromatograph to determine the percent by volume of carbon monoxide in the exhaust. This is the method of the experiment. It might help to underline or circle the 1 ml sample, two-minute intervals, percent by volume, and the gas chromatograph. Each of those are important factors in the method of the experiment.

Table 1 provides you with all of the results of Experiment 1, which is performed at −9°C. Something interesting to note that has not been mentioned anywhere else in the passage to this point is how the students tested two car models from different years. This is another variable to account for when you look at the experimental data, so keep it in mind. In your initial look at the data presented in Table 1 the carbon monoxide exhaust generally seems to be relatively stable across the models and years as you move down in time after starting. There is some variation but in general the numbers are somewhat grouped. One fact that should clearly stand out is there is less carbon monoxide put out by the newer model cars when compared to the older model cars. This makes sense when you consider manufacturing and engine technology has improved dramatically over the years.

Experiment 2 performs the same procedure as described in Experiment 1, but it clearly informs you that the temperature has now been raised to 20°C. The data are presented in Table 2. The first thing you can do is look at Table 2 and draw some basic conclusions. You can see again that the newer year models produce less carbon monoxide than the earlier models. In addition, the carbon monoxide production of all the car models is relatively stable, though the 1978 Model Y shows a significant increase after the initial data points. To really draw significant conclusions, though, you need to look at the data from both experiments together. A good way to compare data in research summaries is to find a common point across the experiments and see how the data are different.

First, make sure that when you are comparing data presentation to never take for granted that the tables and graphs you are looking at match up. Look at the headings, titles, and data points to ensure they are the same when you compare data. Just because they are formatted the same doesn't mean they are exactly the same. It is very easy to overlook a different unit or value, yet it can completely skew your interpretation of the graph and the results. In this case, however, thankfully, the data are laid out exactly the same and the collecting time frames are the same. So you can use these two tables to compare the results from the cold temperatures to the warmer temperatures.

Across all models from all years the biggest conclusion you can draw, in general, is that cars do produce more carbon monoxide in colder weather during the first 15 minutes of their run time. The simplest way to determine this is to pick a couple of time measurements and compare the carbon monoxide readings of the different car models and years from Table 1 to Table 2. As a specific example look at 5 minutes after starting the engine in Tables 1 and 2.

Table 1				
Time after starting (min)	Percent of CO in the exhaust at −9°C:			
	1978 Model X	1978 Model Y	1996 Model X	1996 Model Y
1	3.5	3.2	1.2	0.3
3	4.0	3.7	1.0	1.2
5	4.5	7.5	1.5	2.5
7	3.6	10.0	1.0	3.0
9	3.2	9.1	0.5	2.6
11	3.1	8.0	0.5	2.0
13	3.0	7.0	0.5	2.0
15	2.9	7.0	0.4	1.8

In this case you can clearly see that each of the car models in Table 1 at 5 minutes after starting the engine shows a higher level of carbon monoxide than the corresponding car model in Table 2 at 5 minutes after starting the engine.

Table 2				
Time after starting (min)	Percent of CO in the exhaust at 20°C:			
	1978 Model X	1978 Model Y	1996 Model X	1996 Model Y
1	2.0	0.8	0.3	0.2
3	2.8	2.0	0.5	1.0
5	3.4	6.0	0.5	1.5
7	1.5	7.0	0.3	0.8
9	1.3	7.0	0.3	0.5
11	1.0	6.5	0.1	0.3
13	1.0	5.0	0.1	0.3
15	0.9	4.8	0.1	0.2

However, just looking at one data point usually isn't enough to confirm a trend so be sure to look at several and make the comparisons. There might even be a point or two that doesn't follow the trend but don't let an outlier throw off your analysis or change your overall conclusion. If all but one or two of the data points support the conclusion that engine exhaust contains more carbon monoxide at lower temperatures, then that is a fair and accurate conclusion to make.

Sample Question Answers and Analysis

Sample Question 1

Do the results from Experiment 1 support the hypothesis that, at a given temperature and time, the exhaust of newer cars contains lower percents of CO than the exhaust of older cars?

F. Yes; the highest percent of CO was in the exhaust of the 1996 Model Y.

G. Yes; both 1996 models had percents of CO that were lower than those of either 1978 model.

H. No; the highest percent of CO was in the exhaust of the 1978 Model Y.

J. No; both 1978 models had percents of CO that were lower than those of either 1996 model.

Sample question 1 provides you with a hypothesis about the data from Experiment 1. The hypothesis basically states that the exhaust from newer cars has less carbon monoxide than older cars. The question presents you with two tasks. First, it wants you to look at Experiment 1 and determine whether or not the hypothesis presented is accurate. Yet if you look at the answer choices it doesn't want a simple yes or no. The second task is for you to pick which statement is correct after the yes or no.

So you can approach this question in two parts. First, you need to determine if the basic hypothesis is true or not. Do newer model cars emit less carbon monoxide? It appears clearly from the chart in Experiment 1 that, yes, the newer model cars emit less carbon monoxide. If you look at Model X or Model Y in 1996 you can clearly see that during the entire time measurement period all of the emissions were lower than the models from 1978. This supports the hypothesis that newer cars produce less carbon monoxide. The first part of the question must say yes. You've now narrowed the question down to two possible answers. The next thing you have to do is determine which statement is the most accurate between the two yes options. The first statement says that the highest amount of carbon monoxide was present in the 1996 Model Y. This is clearly not accurate because you can look at it and compare it to the models from 1978 and see that both produced far more carbon monoxide. If you look at the other yes option it clearly confirms that yes, both newer model cars produce lower carbon monoxide than either of the older models. **The answer to this question is G.**

Sample Question 2

A student, when using the gas chromatograph, was concerned that CO_2 in the exhaust sample may be interfering in the detection of CO. Which of the following procedures would best help the student investigate this problem?

A. Filling the bag with CO_2 before collecting the exhaust

B. Collecting exhaust from additional cars

C. Injecting a sample of air into the gas chromatograph

D. Testing a sample with known amounts of CO and CO_2

Sample question 2 presents you with a potential problem regarding the gas chromatograph. It says it might not be detecting CO concentration correctly due to contamination from CO_2. The best thing to remember about this question is that it doesn't require you to have any specific knowledge regarding a gas chromatograph. If you look back in the initial passage you can see the gas chromatograph is used to measure the concentration of carbon monoxide in a sample of gas. Beyond that you don't need to know anything about it. You just need to think about the problem presented to you and how to best solve it. In this case you need to determine if the gas chromatograph is reading CO levels correctly. The entire experiment is focused on the CO levels so you want to ensure that is correct. You are presented with several options that could potentially let you determine if it is accurately working.

In a case like this, if you aren't entirely sure how to determine the answer, you can work by eliminating answer choices. Choice **A** (filling the bag with CO_2 before collecting the exhaust) doesn't in anyway help you determine if the CO readings are accurate. How can a bag filled with CO_2 have anything to do with determining the correct CO readings? Choice **B** (collecting exhaust from additional cars) is much the same in that it doesn't help you ensure your CO measurements are correct. You would be able to gather more data about CO production but it doesn't help you to determine if the values you get from the gas chromatograph are correct. Choice **C** (injecting a sample of air into the gas chromatograph) may seem tempting because air has CO_2 present in it at some concentration. Yet this wouldn't help you to know if the readings for CO are correct. Choice **D** (testing a sample with known amounts of CO and CO_2) is the only choice that makes sense. If you test a sample with a known quantity of carbon monoxide gas present, along with carbon dioxide, you will be able to determine if the gas chromatograph is accurately determining concentration levels. You would simply perform your test and compare it to the known value of your sample and see if it matches. If it matches the machine is working right; if not, the CO_2 is causing a problem. **The correct answer to this question is D.**

Sample Question 3

Based on the results of the experiments and the information in the table below, cars in which of the following cities would most likely contribute the greatest amount of CO to the atmosphere in January? (Assume that the types, numbers, and ages of cars used in each city are approximately equal.)

City	Average temperature (°F) for January
Minneapolis	11.2
Pittsburgh	26.7
Seattle	39.1
San Diego	56.8

F. Minneapolis

G. Pittsburgh

H. Seattle

J. San Diego

Sample question 3 presents you with a chart that gives you four cities and their average January temperatures. It asks you to determine in which of the cities would cars contribute the greatest amount of CO to the atmosphere during January. The question also helps you to remove many of the possible variables that would potentially have an impact on your answer. In this case it says you can ignore the type, number, and age of the cars. This means when you look at the data from Experiments 1 and 2 you can focus only on the difference in temperature and not worry about anything more. This is a good example of the reasoning behind why you should carefully look at all of the information and data presented to you before you begin doing the questions. If you have familiarized yourself with the experiments and have drawn some basic conclusions about the data this question becomes very easy and quick to answer. You should have already determined that more CO is produced in colder temperatures than warmer temperatures. Based on this conclusion you can look at the chart and see that Minneapolis has the lowest average January temperature. This would correspond to the city that should see the most CO production from cars due to the experimental results that show colder temperatures lead to more CO production. **The correct answer is F.**

Sample Question 4

In Experiment 1, which of the following factors varied?

A. The method of sample collection

B. The volume of exhaust that was tested

C. The year in which the cars were made

D. The temperature at which the engine was started

Sample question 4 asks you to look at Experiment 1 and determine which factors were changed. It is a very straightforward question, especially if you familiarized yourself with the passage beforehand. To determine which factor was changed you can look at the paragraph explaining the method and look at the data table presenting the results. The initial discussion of the experiment outlines the method of sample collection (using a plastic bag). It says that a 1 ml sample (the volume) was analyzed each time and that the procedure was done at a temperature of $-9°C$ for every measurement. This rules out answer choices **A, B,** and **D.** Just to confirm, though, you can look at Table 1 and see clearly there are only two things changed during Experiment 1: the model type and the year. The model type is not an answer choice but the year the car was made is a choice so it is the correct answer. **The correct answer is C.**

Sample Question 5

Many states require annual testing of cars to determine the levels of their CO emissions. Based on the experiments, in order to determine the maximum percent of CO found in a car's exhaust, during which of the following times after starting a car would it be best to sample the exhaust?

F. 1–3 min

G. 5–7 min

H. 9–11 min

J. 13 min or longer

Sample question 5 starts by discussing state testing for CO emissions in cars. This is relevant because it provides background to the question but it isn't necessary in terms of solving the question in any way so don't get distracted by it being there. Instead keep reading and you'll see the question wants you to identify the time range when CO emissions were highest for the cars in Experiments 1 and 2. The question words it in a slightly more complex fashion, but if you focus specifically on what it asks, you will see that the majority of the wording is not needed for this question. You just need to identify the time range when the most CO is being put out by the cars. The best way to do this is to go down each model number and year until you clearly see a pattern developing. If you are short of time you can probably be confident that if you see the pattern in two of the models then this is likely to be the answer, but it is always best to confirm with all of the data if possible.

First look at Experiment 1 and you will see that each model from both years show the single highest output of CO at either the 5-minute mark or the 7-minute mark. This is an obvious pattern and at this point you should be comfortable selecting the 5- to 7-minute range as your answer. To ensure there aren't any unanswered questions there are a few concepts you will want to potentially look at. Specifically, in the 1978 Model Y you can see that the second highest output comes at the 9-minute mark and the 1978 Model X has the second highest output appearing at the 3-minute mark. The highest output is still in the 5- to 7-minute range but these second highest values could lead to confusion. You could potentially argue that a range of 7–9 minutes would actually be the better measuring range based on that data. It isn't an answer choice though so it doesn't matter; you can safely ignore it and move on.

In Table 2 you have much the same issue. The highest CO output values can be found in either the 5-minute range or the 7-minute range for each model and year. There are again outliers that would potentially correspond to a slightly different time frame, like 7–9 minutes. Yet again, though, that isn't an answer choice so you don't need to worry about. Once you have the correct answer, go with it and move on. Don't waste time wondering why an answer choice isn't there. **The correct answer to this question is G.**

Sample Question 6

How would the results of the experiments be affected, if at all, if the syringe contents were contaminated with CO-free air? (The composition of air is 78% N_2, 21% O_2, 0.9% Ar, and 0.1% other gases.) The measured percents of CO in the exhaust would be:

A. higher than the actual percents at both –9°C and 20°C.

B. lower than the actual percents at –9°C, but higher than the actual percents at 20°C.

C. lower than the actual percents at both –9°C and 20°C.

D. the same as the actual percents at both –9°C and 20°C.

Sample question 6 is the most challenging of this set. It says that you are going to be adding CO-free air to syringe contents you are testing, and it also gives you the percentages of the gases that are found in air. It asks you to determine how this will change the CO exhaust measurements. The first thing you can do is ignore the percent composition of the gases found in air. Beyond telling you that air does not contain CO (which is already stated in the question) the percentages presented to you play no role in determining the correct answer. Nowhere in this question does knowing the percentage of argon, oxygen, or nitrogen found in air matter.

What this question does require is for you to do some analysis and consideration beyond what is simply shown to you in the passage. No amount of reading or staring at the passage information by itself will get you to the correct answer here. You are going to need to consider the situation presented and attempt to determine how it changes accordingly. The passage does provide you with a lot of hints, though, and will point you in the right direction if you analyze it closely. If you refer back to the passage and some of the information you underlined or circled you will see that the gas chromatograph is measuring the percent by volume of CO in the exhaust. This is your key to starting on the path to the right answer. You need to consider how adding more air to the syringe would affect the percent by volume of CO in the sample. This is a situation in which a passing familiarity with volume and concentration would be helpful. The best way to start is by visualizing what is happening. You begin with a sample of CO gas in the syringe and then add air to that syringe. Nowhere does it say that you will be adding more CO to the syringe. So you now need to consider this from the perspective of the concentrations of gas in the syringe. By increasing the amount of air present you increased the total volume of gas in the syringe, but you did not increase the amount of CO present in the syringe. This means that when the gas chromatograph measures the percent by volume of CO in the sample it will be lower than it otherwise should. This result will hold for either temperature because you are altering the sample the same way regardless of temperature. **The correct answer is C.**

Summary

Research summaries passages are focused on the process of science and the results of a specific experiment. They are generally going to expect you to look at a scientific experiment, the procedure by which the experiment was conducted, and the results of that experiment. It is your job to analyze all of that and answer the questions as best you can. You aren't expected to understand these experiments in depth but you do need to be comfortable with the process of science that is described in each of the passages. The scientific method and the process of science is covered in detail in chapter 7.

A research summaries passage will generally begin by providing you with a description of an experiment and then the results of that experiment. There will likely be more than one trial or experimental result presented to you in the passage. This data will likely be in the form of one or more graphs and/or tables.

When you recognize a research summaries passage you should remember to follow a few key steps:

1. Attempt to identify the driving question and/or hypothesis of the experiment.

2. Determine how the experiment was conducted, specifically, what method was used to perform the research.

3. Determine the independent variable: what is changed during the course of the experiment by the researcher.

4.   Determine the dependent variable: what happens as a result of the experiment.

5.   Look at the data presented and determine the results of the experiment and draw conclusions.

You don't need to overanalyze each research summaries passage but a quick yet thorough analysis of the passage that is focused on these thought processes will make it far easier for you to answer the questions quickly and accurately.

To review more official ACT research summaries passages and sample questions please see chapter 11.

3

Chapter 3: Conflicting Viewpoints Passages

This chapter discusses the conflicting viewpoints passage type you will encounter when taking the ACT science section. The chapter provides some basic suggestions for how to best approach and read this passage type. You will then be walked through an official ACT sample of conflicting viewpoints passage along with all of the questions that go along with the passage.

What You Can Expect from a Conflicting Viewpoints Passage

The final type of passage that you will find in the ACT science section science section is the conflicting viewpoints passage. There is always one conflicting viewpoints passage found in the ACT science section. The major goal of a conflicting viewpoints passage is exactly what you would expect based on the title of the passage. You will be presented with two different views, commentaries, or opinions related to a scientific idea or experiment. The expectation and the focus of the questions will be on getting you to identify the similarities and differences found between the opinions.

Conflicting viewpoints passages are usually the easiest to identify when taking the test. Whereas the data representation and research summaries passages can have some similarities in that they both include some amount of data, the conflicting viewpoints passages are usually very clear in their identity. The passages begin with some amount of scientific text discussing an idea, a phenomenon, or an experiment. Then you will clearly see two different viewpoints presented that relate to the introductory information. They will usually be labeled along the lines of Scientist 1 and Scientist 2 or some variation along those lines.

If you see a mention of multiple experiments or studies, you are looking at a research summaries passage instead of a conflicting viewpoints passage. If you see an introductory paragraph followed by one or more graphs or tables with no mention of viewpoints or experiments, you are looking at a data representation passage. Be sure you are confident in your ability to identify different passage types so that you will have a good idea how to proceed no matter what you encounter.

Once you've identified a conflicting viewpoints passage the next step is to analyze the passage. Here are a few basic steps you should follow each time you encounter one.

- **First, read the introductory passage carefully.** This is seemingly an obvious one but it is very important when dealing with a conflicting viewpoints passage. The questions associated with these passages expect you to be familiar with specific details regarding the scientific concept and opinions presented. Skimming is always a useful and good strategy to save time but in the case of these passages it is best to read them in detail. As with the other types of science passages, remember not to get bogged down by scientific words or concepts you don't understand. The world of science is incredibly vast and large and there is no one person anywhere who could read all of the passages and have a detailed understanding of each concept discussed. If there is a concept that you are expected to understand to answer questions, it will be explained in the reading.

- **Second, determine what scientific concept or idea is being presented by the passage.** If it helps, you can underline whatever you might want to make it easier for you to reference later. Having a basic idea of the concept being presented will help you when it comes to understanding the different viewpoints that will be presented.

- **Third, read each of the viewpoints in detail and identify the basic argument or theory presented from each viewpoint.** A good goal after your initial reading is to understand the major difference between the viewpoints presented. Usually the major conflict or disagreement is easy enough to spot but other times you may have to pay a little more attention to the details of the arguments. The best place to look when trying to determine the initial conflict is the introductory sentence of each viewpoint. The first sentence will usually contain the overall argument of the viewpoint. After your initial read it is a good idea to compare the first sentence from each of the viewpoints and see what is different about them. That will be your easiest and simplest path to figuring out the major conflict between the viewpoints. It might help to underline this first sentence so you can go back and reference it easily if the questions require you to.

- **Fourth, determine the supporting evidence presented for each viewpoint.** As you are reading each viewpoint, circle or underline any evidence you find that clearly is used to support the main argument. Be sure to look at any specific details presented in the argument or statement. This way if a question references something specific you will have an easier time going back and finding it in the viewpoint.

So now you have some basic suggestions for how to best approach any conflicting viewpoints passage. Clearly no two are exactly alike but these suggestions will go a long way toward helping you to quickly and efficiently work through any passage you encounter. The most important thing to remember is to not get stuck when reading these passages. Keep focused and don't dwell on any one sentence or word you encounter.

Trying Your Hand at a Conflicting Viewpoints Passage

Now we are going to examine a conflicting viewpoints passage and question set in detail. You will see an analysis of the passage first and then a detailed explanation of each question and how to determine the answer. First, though, as in the previous two chapters, it is strongly encouraged that you read the passage and attempt to answer the questions yourself. It is always better to be familiar and have spent a few minutes thinking about a passage yourself before looking at the detailed description.

Example Passage and Questions

Passage XIII

A *polypeptide* molecule is a chain of amino acids. A *protein* consists of one or more polypeptides. A protein's shape is described by three or four levels of structure.

1. The *primary structure* of a protein is the sequence of amino acids in each polypeptide.

2. The *secondary structure* of a protein is the local folding patterns within short segments of each polypeptide due to *hydrogen bonding* (weak chemical bonds).

3. The *tertiary structure* is the folding patterns that result from interactions between amino acid *side chains* (parts of an amino acid) in each polypeptide. These folding patterns generally occur across greater distances than those associated with the secondary structure.

4. The *quaternary structure* is the result of the clustering between more than one folded polypeptide.

A protein can adopt different shapes, and each shape has a relative energy. Lower-energy shapes are more stable than higher-energy shapes, and a protein with a relatively high-energy shape may *denature* (unfold) and then *renature* (refold), adopting a more stable shape. A protein that is almost completely denatured is called a *random coil.* Random coils are unstable because they are high-energy shapes; however, some can renature, adopting more stable shapes.

(continued)

Passage XIII (*continued*)

Two scientists discuss protein shape.

Scientist 1

The *active shape* (the biologically functional shape) of a protein is always identical to the protein's lowest-energy shape. Any other shape would be unstable. Because a protein's lowest-energy shape is determined by its primary structure, its active shape is determined by its primary structure.

Scientist 2

The active shape of a protein is dependent upon its primary structure. However, a protein's active shape may also depend on its *process of synthesis,* the order (in time) in which the amino acids were bonded together. As synthesis occurs, stable, local structures form within short segments of the polypeptide chain due to hydrogen bonding. These local structures may be different than the local structures associated with the protein's lowest-energy shape. After synthesis, these structures persist, trapping the protein in an active shape that has more energy than its lowest-energy shape.

Sample Question 1

According to the passage, protein shapes with relatively low energy tend to:

A. be random coils.

B. lack a primary structure.

C. become denatured.

D. maintain their shape.

Sample Question 2

The information in the passage indicates that when a protein is completely denatured, it still retains its original:

F. primary structure.

G. secondary structure.

H. tertiary structure.

J. quaternary structure.

Sample Question 3

Scientist 2's views differ from Scientist 1's views in that only Scientist 2 believes that a protein's active shape is partially determined by its:

A. quaternary structure.

B. amino acid sequence.

C. process of synthesis.

D. tertiary folding patterns.

Sample Question 4

A student has 100 balls. The balls are various colors. The student chooses 15 balls and aligns them in a row. The spatial order in which the balls were placed corresponds to which of the following levels of structure in a protein?

F. Primary structure

G. Secondary structure

H. Tertiary structure

J. Quaternary structure

Sample Question 5

Suppose proteins are almost completely denatured and then allowed to renature in a way that allows them to have their lowest-energy shapes. Which of the following statements about the proteins is most consistent with the information presented in the passage?

A. If Scientist 1 is correct, all of the proteins will have their active shapes.

B. If Scientist 1 is correct, all of the proteins will have shapes different than their active shapes.

C. If Scientist 2 is correct, all of the proteins will have their active shapes.

D. If Scientist 2 is correct, all of the proteins will have shapes different than their active shapes.

Sample Question 6

Which of the following diagrams showing the relationship between a given protein's shape and its relative energy is consistent with Scientist 2's assertions about the energy of proteins, but is NOT consistent with Scientist 1's assertions about the energy of proteins?

Analyzing the Example Passage and Questions

Now that you've read the passage and the questions let's move on to the analysis.

This passage discusses protein folding and the relative energy related to different protein shapes. It begins by outlining some very basic facts about what a protein is and how it is composed. It discusses that a polypeptide molecule consists of a chain of amino acids and that a protein consists of one or more polypeptide chains. If you don't know what a polypeptide is, or a protein, or an amino acid, don't worry. The question just told you everything you need to know about those concepts. Proteins are made of polypeptide and polypeptides are made from a chain of amino acids. That's all you need. If there was more expected of you it would be included. Simply underline the vocabulary words or make a mental note about it and keep reading.

The passage then goes on to describe the different structural levels of a protein and how those levels define the shape of the protein. There are again multiple vocabulary words such as *primary structure, secondary structure, hydrogen bonding, tertiary structure, side chains,* and *quaternary structure* that you may have heard at one point or another but probably aren't very familiar with. The great thing about this question, again, is that you don't need to know anything beyond what the question tells you about each concept.

The passage discusses the various energy states of a protein relative to their shapes, with lower-energy protein shapes corresponding to a more stable protein and higher-energy shapes corresponding to a more unstable protein. It describes that higher-energy protein shapes can lead to a protein denaturing (unfolding) and then renaturing (refolding) leads to a more stable low-energy shape.

Finally, the passage presents the conflicting scientific viewpoints. Sometimes you can tell from the very first sentence where the opinions differ. It might be spelled out very clearly, and if it is, that's great. Sometimes you have to look more carefully to determine where the conflict in the viewpoints arises. This passage is definitely of the second variety.

Scientist 1 makes a statement in their initial sentence that "The *active shape* (the biologically functional shape) of a protein is always identical to the protein's lowest-energy shape." The scientist then explains that any other shape is unstable. The final sentence in the opinion is an example of why you need to pay careful attention to the logical pathway taken. It explains that because the lowest-energy shape is determined by the primary structure, the active shape is determine by the primary structure. Understanding this final sentence requires you to connect the first sentence to this third sentence. Sentence 1 basically states that the active shape is equal to the lowest-energy shape. Sentence 2 says clearly, no other shape can be the active shape, because it would be unstable. Sentence 3 then says that because the low-energy shape determines the primary shape the active state determines the primary structure.

It can be confusing to follow this logic through the short paragraph when you are reading about protein and energy shapes, so perhaps a more symbolic visual explanation might help you see the relationship. Let's break down the statement sentence by sentence focusing on the ideas of active protein shape, energy shape, and primary structure. You can clearly see the use of the transitive property in this paragraph when you look at the following:

Sentence 1: active shape = lowest energy protein shape

Sentence 2: Provides a statement saying sentence 1 is correct.

Sentence 3: lowest energy protein shape = primary structure

active shape = lowest energy protein shape = primary structure

active shape = primary structure

The hope is that looking at it written out like this helps to illustrate the relationship between each sentence. Now this explanation is quite in-depth for a single viewpoint but there is a reason it is being explained to you like this. The hope is that you are able to see the line of reasoning in the viewpoint and that you can formulate your approach to reading through these ideas quickly. The quicker you can orient yourself to the viewpoint's line of reasoning the better of you will be when reading these passages.

Scientist 2's line of reasoning is a bit less clear. The scientist begins by stating "The active shape of a protein is dependent upon its primary structure." So far that agrees with the conclusion of Scientist 1, and you may be tempted to save time by assuming the rest of the paragraph will say something along the same line and therefore to skip reading it. Do not do that. The best advice for each passage is to read the entire thing and not skip anything. This is called a *conflicting viewpoints passage* for a reason. There should be some level of disagreement between the statements. As you read on in the passage you can see that Scientist 2 does disagree with Scientist 1. Scientist 2 introduces the idea of the process of synthesis and goes on to describe what that term means. The scientist says, in the final sentence, that this process sometimes leads to there being an active shape that has more energy than the lowest-energy shape. It is in this final sentence that you can clearly see the contradiction to Scientist 1.

So, in summary, Scientist 1 thinks the active shape of a protein depends on its primary structure, which is the lowest-energy shape. Scientist 2 agrees that the active shape of a protein is dependent on its primary structure. However Scientist 2 thinks the active shape is not always the lowest-energy shape due to the process of synthesis.

Now that we've analyzed the passage lets walk through each sample question and discuss the correct answer and suggested strategies for solving each one.

Sample Question 1

According to the passage, protein shapes with relatively low energy tend to:

A. be random coils.

B. lack a primary structure.

C. become denatured.

D. maintain their shape.

Sample question 1 is a factual question that doesn't require you to provide a comparison between the scientists' viewpoints.

The question isn't as straightforward as it appears, however. Nowhere does the question bluntly state that low-energy proteins maintain their shape. It does lay out enough information for you to determine the right answer though. The introductory passage states that lower-energy shapes are more stable and higher-energy shapes are more likely to denature and unfold then refold into stable shapes. This implies that the higher-energy shapes are unstable. It also says that a denatured protein is called a *random coil,* which is unstable. From that you can look at the answer choices and eliminate two answers quickly. Low-energy protein shapes are not random coils and they will not denature.

The one fact that isn't directly mentioned in the initial paragraph is the lack of a primary structure. However, in Scientist 1's statement you can follow the logic that proteins with low-energy shapes have a primary structure. In addition, if you have a solid base in biology you will remember that a protein cannot exist without having a primary structure. The primary structure is the basic order of amino acids that makes the protein up. If you somehow were to disrupt that, the protein would cease to be a protein. Yet you are not required to use that knowledge to solve the question. The knowledge definitely helps, but it isn't required. The idea that low-energy protein shapes will maintain their shapes is clearly the correct answer. **The correct answer to this question is D.**

Sample Question 2

The information in the passage indicates that when a protein is completely denatured, it still retains its original:

F. primary structure.

G. secondary structure.

H. tertiary structure.

J. quaternary structure.

Sample question 2 is another factual question that requires you to determine the answer from the reading without comparing the viewpoints of the two scientists. Just like sample question 1, if you have a solid background in biology, this is a very simple question to answer. You can just look at it and know that a denatured protein loses all of its structure except for the primary order of amino acids. But what if you don't know that? There is a good chance that while taking the test you might not remember it or you simply never got that information in the first place. If that is the case you just need to carefully read the information given to you to figure out what's right.

The place to begin here is focusing on what *denatured* means. You might know from your own studies or you might not. In either case, the passage says that when a protein denatures it unfolds. *Unfold* is a key term you need to understand to be able to answer the question. Denatured means a protein is unfolding. Once you've got that, the next part is to figure out which structure of a protein can't unfold. The place to go to find that is the clearly numbered portion of the passage dealing with each of the structures and answer choices.

Your approach should be to reread each of the structure descriptions and see what jumps out at you in terms of protein folding being mentioned. The primary structure description makes no mention of protein folding. Yet the other three structures all make some mention of protein folding. That means they can be disrupted when a protein denatures. The primary structure involves no folding of any kind though, so it is not affected when a protein denatures, making it the correct answer. **The correct answer to this question is F.**

Sample Question 3

Scientist 2's views differ from Scientist 1's views in that only Scientist 2 believes that a protein's active shape is partially determined by its:

A. quaternary structure.

B. amino acid sequence.

C. process of synthesis.

D. tertiary folding patterns.

Sample question 3 requires you to look at both scientists' views and determine how they differ in regards to determining a protein's active shape. Your initial analysis of the two views should help you make this a quick and efficient question to answer. You want to focus on what is different between their statements. Scientist 1 states the active shape is determined by the lowest energy shape, which corresponds to the primary structure. Scientists 2 states the active shape of a protein is dependent upon the primary structure. However, Scientist 2 says, due to the process of synthesis, the active shape is not the lowest-energy shape possible. **This supports the correct answer being C.**

If you are struggling you can look at the other answer choices and perform a process of elimination. Neither scientist's viewpoint mentions the other three answer choices in any way. There is no discussion of quaternary structure, the amino acid sequence, or tertiary folding patterns in either of their statements. You can say logically that if those three items are not even mentioned in either viewpoint then there can be no way that the difference of opinion is based on those terms. The only one that is mentioned is the process of synthesis so it must be the cause of the difference.

Sample Question 4

A student has 100 balls. The balls are various colors. The student chooses 15 balls and aligns them in a row. The spatial order in which the balls were placed corresponds to which of the following levels of structure in a protein?

F. Primary structure

G. Secondary structure

H. Tertiary structure

J. Quaternary structure

Sample question 4 requires you to analyze an example presented to you that represents a protein. It gives you the analogy of 15 balls being lined up and connected together and wants you to determine which level of a protein that organization represents.

Your first task when approaching a question like this should be to determine what the balls represent in this example. To do that you should go back to the beginning of the passage and re-read exactly what a protein is and what makes it up. If you do, you will see that a protein consists of a chain of amino acids. Even if you have no idea what an amino acid represents you should be able to put together that the amino acid is an object that is organized into a chain. It says that the sequence of the amino acids determines a protein's primary structure. It would seem that a chain of balls could very likely represent amino acids and their primary structure sequence.

As you read on to the other structures you really don't see any mention of things that could represent a sequence of balls. There are mentions of hydrogen bonding, side chains, and lots of talk about folding, yet nothing that specifically discusses anything that could be 15 balls put together in order. **So based on that the correct answer is F.**

Sample Question 5

Suppose proteins are almost completely denatured and then allowed to renature in a way that allows them to have their lowest-energy shapes. Which of the following statements about the proteins is most consistent with the information presented in the passage?

A. If Scientist 1 is correct, all of the proteins will have their active shapes.

B. If Scientist 1 is correct, all of the proteins will have shapes different than their active shapes.

C. If Scientist 2 is correct, all of the proteins will have their active shapes.

D. If Scientist 2 is correct, all of the proteins will have shapes different than their active shapes.

Sample question 5 is the type of question you want to make sure you have enough time to work through. This is why you want to efficiently and accurately get through the questions that require less analysis and more simple recall or recognition.

This question begins by telling you that proteins are denatured (unfolded) and then allowed to renature (refold) into their lowest-energy shapes. Based on that information you are given four statements and are tasked with determining which of those statements best matches the viewpoint of Scientists 1 or 2. It isn't asking you to determine which scientist is right, just that you need to pick the statement that best matches what one of the scientists says. The question states that a protein is completely denatured and then refolds into its lowest-energy shape. Once you've identified that, the best way to approach a question like this is go through the answer choices and see which choice matches with the viewpoint presented.

Choice **A** says that if Scientist 1 is correct, all of the proteins will have their active shapes. The question states that the protein has refolded into its lowest-energy state so your task is to determine if the lowest-energy state is also the active state based on the viewpoint of Scientist 1. You don't have to read further than the first sentence of Scientist 1's viewpoint to know that this is the correct statement. In the first sentence Scientist 1 clearly states, "The *active shape* (the biologically functional shape) of a protein is always identical to the protein's lowest-energy shape." So if Scientist 1 is correct then all proteins in their lowest energy shape will also be in their active shape. **This supports answer choice A, making it the correct answer.**

Answer choice **B** directly contradicts answer choice **A** so it is invalid based on the evidence just shown. Answer choices **C** and **D** are both wrong also, yet it might be a bit tougher to confidently say that on first reading the question. Go back and look at Scientist 2's view again. In it the scientist says that the active shape of a protein may be the lowest-energy state yet the scientist also says that it may not be due to the process of synthesis. There is no definitive statement made by Scientist 2, so any answer choice that deals with "all" proteins cannot be the correct choice.

Sample Question 6

Which of the following diagrams showing the relationship between a given protein's shape and its relative energy is consistent with Scientist 2's assertions about the energy of proteins, but is NOT consistent with Scientist 1's assertions about the energy of proteins?

Sample question 6 presents you with several possible graphical interpretations showing the relationship between relative energy and shape for three possible protein shapes. These questions can be intimidating because they take what you have read and turn it into a graph. You are now expected to analyze the information from the passage visually.

The best way to approach a question like this is to attempt to eliminate a couple of answer choices as quickly as possible so you can get a better focus on determining the correct answer. To do that you should try to pick some easily identifiable qualifier or data point that will enable you to perform the elimination. In this case you can look at the randomly coiled protein shape. Neither scientist's view mentions random coiling, yet it is presented in this bar graph. So before you go any further in comparing the views of the scientists you need to make sure that the randomly coiled shape graph is correct. The passage states "Random coils are unstable because they are high-energy shapes" so you need to find the graphs that correspond to random coils showing high relative energy. That enables you to eliminate the first two answer choices, graphs **F** and **G**. They both show random coils as having a lower relative energy, contradicting the passage.

Now that you've narrowed down the answer choices you can look at the difference between the two answer choices left. Graph **H** shows that the active shape and the most stable shape have the same relative energy. This corresponds to Scientist 1's viewpoint: "The *active shape* (the biologically functional shape) of a protein is always identical to the protein's lowest-energy shape. Any other shape would be unstable."

Graph **J** shows the active shape having more energy than the most-stable state. This corresponds to what Scientists 2 says at the end: "After synthesis, these structures persist, trapping the protein in an active shape that has more energy than its lowest-energy shape." **Going back to the question prompt you should choose J as the correct answer because you need to identify which graph best matches Scientist 2 and not Scientist 1.**

Summary

Conflicting viewpoints passages are the easiest to identify. They clearly present you with the opinions, theories, or statements of two scientists. Remember that the conflict probably won't be incredibly obvious, such as one saying the explanation is to go up and the other saying that the solution is to go down. There is generally a bit more nuance in the passages and their statements. When you recognize a conflicting viewpoints passage remember to follow these steps:

1. Read the introductory passage carefully.

2. Determine what scientific concept or idea is being presented by the passage.

3. Read each of the viewpoints in detail and identify the basic argument or theory presented from each viewpoint.

4. Determine the supporting evidence presented for each viewpoint.

Once you've made sure you understand the passage, go through and answer each question. Don't try to do more than the question asks, though; just find the answer and move on. If you follow these steps and prepare well, you'll be sure to do well on the conflicting viewpoints passage you encounter on test day.

To review more official ACT conflicting viewpoints passages and sample questions please see chapter 11.

Chapter 4:
Reporting Category:
Interpretation of
Data

The next three chapters will focus on covering the different types of reporting categories you are going to see on the ACT science test. Each chapter will break down the most important categories of question type you need to prepare for on the test. You will see a brief description of the category followed by official sample questions that are associated with each type of category.

Understanding What a Reporting Category Is

You might want a bit of clarification on what exactly is a reporting category and why should you care about it? It's a good question and an important one whose answer you need to understand. To provide the simplest definition possible, a reporting category is the content on which the questions are based. That is to say, the questions you see in each section of the ACT are based on the reporting categories with so many questions asking about Topic x, so many about Topic y, and so on.

The focus of the science reporting categories is likely not what you might be expecting though. When you think of science content you probably think of the science classes you've taken and their names, such as chemistry, biology, and physics. You would probably expect those to be the reporting categories you would see represented on the ACT science test but that is not the case. The ACT science test is not a science content–focused test. It is not going to ask you specifics about chemistry or biology and expect you to have some specific and specialized understanding of an obscure piece of content. It is more generalized than that.

Of course, because all of the questions and passages you will see on the ACT science test are science based, they will include content vocabulary words and descriptions of experiments that focus on science content areas. Understanding these content words and having a familiarity with the content areas will definitely make it easier for you to work quickly and more accurately through the test. Thankfully, though, it isn't a requirement that you have this background knowledge. It can help but you can still do it even if you haven't been the best science student over the past few years. The ACT science test focuses on the process and understanding of science as a discipline.

The reporting categories of the ACT science test, and in turn the questions themselves, are designed more on looking at scientific data and the experiments that generated that data rather than the science content behind them. It is your understanding of the process of science that is being tested rather than your understanding of the content of science. This is good because the amount of science content that exists, even at the most basic level of high school classes, is incredibly vast and varied. You won't be asked specifics about the content but there are some basic content areas of science that ACT draws its questions from, as shown in the following list, broken down by subject area:

Life Science: botany, cell biology, ecology, evolution, genetics

Physical Science: acids and bases, kinetics, properties of matter, thermochemistry

Physics: electromagnetism, fluids, mechanics, optics

Earth and Space Science: astronomy, environmental science, geology

This is simply a list of possible topic areas that ACT might use to draw its sample passages from. You will not be asked complex questions or expected to have an in-depth understanding of any of these topics. As always, remember, if you need to understand any of the specific science topics to answer a question, you will be given the information you need in the passage somewhere. You just have to find it.

Looking at this content list you can see how there would be no simple way to boil down chemistry, physics, biology, and all the other science classes into forty questions. It just isn't possible in any fair or balanced way that makes any sense. Yet in forty questions you can get a pretty good sense of whether you as a test taker have a good understanding of how the process of science happens and what it is used for.

Now that we've covered the idea behind the science reporting categories, why don't we take a look specifically at the three types of reporting categories present on the ACT science test. Each reporting category is broken down into different skill statements, and the questions found on the test are directly linked to each of these skill statements. Each reporting category has a different number of questions associated with it on the ACT science test. There is not a specific number represented on each test but rather a percentage given for each category. Following you will see the three types of reporting categories along with the official description of each given by ACT and the percentage representation of each category on the test:

Interpretation of Data 45%–55%

> Manipulate and analyze scientific data presented in tables, graphs, and diagrams (e.g., recognize trends in data, translate tabular data into graphs, interpolate and extrapolate, and reason mathematically).

Evaluation of Models, Inferences, and Experimental Results 25%–35%

> Judge the validity of scientific information and formulate conclusions and predictions based on that information (e.g., determine which explanation for a scientific phenomenon is supported by new findings).

Scientific Investigation 20%–30%

> Understand experimental tools, procedures, and design (e.g., identify variables and controls) and compare, extend, and modify experiments (e.g., predict the results of additional trials).

When you look at these categories you can see how there is no focus on specific science topics. Instead they are focused on the process of science and how scientists investigate. They expect you to be able to look at scientific information and draw conclusions or make predictions about experiments. You are expected to understand the ways in which experiments are conducted, how they are designed, and how they can be changed to look at new phenomenon. You will need to have the ability to look at data in graphic or table form and analyze in depth.

Each of these reporting categories is broken down into different skill statements describing specific skills you should be able to do within each reporting category. These skills can range from simple data retrieval to interpreting multiple models and predicting future outcomes based on information presented in a passage. Chapters 4, 5, and 6 of this book will each focus on the three reporting categories and the skill statements emphasized and tested the most. Each skill statement will include an example question or two that enables you to see the specific type of question associated with each skill. You may see some of these questions discussed later on in the chapters in specific passage types and in the science vocabulary chapter as well. When there is overlap, know that the question analysis you see here is specifically focused on the question and reporting category, and the latter chapters will focus on the question and the passage or the science content.

Interpretation of Data

The rest of this chapter is going to focus on the Interpretation of Data category. This is the most heavily weighted category on the ACT science test with a representation of 45%–55% of all of the questions. The broad focus of this category is as follows:

> Manipulate and analyze scientific data presented in tables, graphs, and diagrams (e.g., recognize trends in data, translate tabular data into graphs, interpolate and extrapolate, and reason mathematically).

The description sounds a lot like the title of the category. You are expected to interpret data. It's a pretty straightforward expectation. When you look at the description a bit more in depth though you should start to realize immediately that there is a lot more to it than just looking at a data table or graph and identifying information present.

Part of this category is looking at a graph or a chart and basically reading it and determining where a value or measurement falls on the graph. Some of it is that straightforward. You will need to read a graph and determine a numerical answer that matches the answer choices. That's it. There are always a few questions like that on the ACT science test. They are great questions because they are straightforward and they are fast. Yet, they are not the only questions you will see on the test from this reporting category.

When you look at the description of the reporting category you should see there is far more than basic identification that you will need to do. You are going to have to look at graphs and be able to identify patterns and relationships shown in the data represented on the graph. You will be expected to look at a table and compare it to data shown in a graph and back. You might need to look at a single graph and then compare it to the answer choices provided to find the best answer, or you might be given graphs as answer choices and expected to determine which graph best fits a table you see in the passage. There is a lot that the ACT science test expects you to do when looking at data presented in graphic or table form.

What you will see in the following sections of this chapter are the specific skills statements that you should focus on the most when preparing for the ACT science test. These are the ones that are most represented in the questions you will see on the test. Each of the skill statements has at least one official sample ACT science question included along with the passage it is associated with.

Skill Statement

Determine how the value of a variable changes as the value of another variable changes in a data presentation.

What Does It Mean?

You are going to be shown a graph or table with two or more sets of data. You will need to be able to determine a relationship between the two sets of data; for example, if one goes up, the other goes up.

Example Passage and Question

Passage I

Flood basalt plateaus are large areas of Earth's surface covered with thick hardened lava. It has been hypothesized that the huge outpourings of lava that formed these plateaus were produced by *plumes* of molten material rising from deep within Earth.

Study 1

A model of a typical plume was created using a computer. It was hypothesized that the "head" of the plume produced the flood basalt plateaus when its molten material reached the surface. Figure 1 shows the computer-generated plume, its diameter, and how long, in millions of years (Myr), it would take the head of the plume to reach the surface.

Figure 1

Figure adapted from R. I. Hill et al., *Mantle Plumes and Continental Tectonics.* ©1992 by the American Association for the Advancement of Science.

Study 2

Four flood basalt plateaus (A–D) were studied. The lava volume, in cubic kilometers (km³) was estimated for each plateau from the area of the plateau and the average thickness of the lava. The length of time lava was being produced at each plateau, and the rate of lava production, in km³ per year, were also estimated. The results are in Table 1.

			Table 1	
Plateau	Age (Myr)	Lava volume (km³)	Length of time lava was produced (Myr)	Rate of lava production (km³/yr)
A	60	2,000,000	1.6	1.25
B	67	1,500,000	1.3	1.2
C	135	1,440,000	1.2	1.2
D	192	2,125,000	1.7	1.25

Table adapted from Mark A. Richards et al., *Flood Basalts and Hot-Spot Tracks: Plume Heads and Tails.* ©1989 by the American Association for the Advancement of Science.

(continued)

Passage I (*continued*)

Study 3

Scientists found that three large extinctions of marine organisms had ages similar to those of the formation of three of the flood basalt plateaus; 58 Myr, 66 Myr, and 133 Myr. It was hypothesized that the production of large amounts of lava and gases in the formation of plateaus may have contributed to those extinctions.

(Note: All of these ages have an error of ± 1 Myr.)

According to Study 2, which of the following statements best describes the relationship, if any, between the age of a flood basalt plateau and the length of time lava was produced at that plateau?

F. As the age of a plateau increases, the length of time lava was produced increases.

G. As the age of a plateau increases, the length of time lava was produced decreases.

H. As the age of a plateau increases, the length of time lava was produced increases, and then decreases.

J. There is no apparent relationship between the age of a plateau and the length of time lava was produced.

The skill statement for this category expects you to look at two variables and compare how they change in a graph or table. In the case of this question those two variables are the *age* flood basalt plateau and the *length of time lava was produced*. The question asks you to examine if there is a relationship between two of these variables. It does include the words *if any,* which would imply that there might or might not be any relationship between the variables in the question. You need to look at Table 1, which shows the data, to determine the answer. Table 1 shows multiple pieces of data; plateau, age, lava volume, length of time lava was produced, and the rate of lava production. When you are answering a question for this category your focus should be on identifying the data you need, determining a relationship, and moving on.

Once you've identified the variables the next step is to see if there is a relationship between them. The word *relationship* in this context means that you are looking to see if a change in the age of the plateau leads to some noticeable change in the length of time lava was produced. As age increases does lava production increase? As age increases does lava production decrease? Or something else?

In the case of this question, when you look at the age data you can see it moves from 60 million years to 67 then 135 and finally 192. There is a clear trend toward older plateaus in the data. Yet when you look at the length of time lava was produced there is no discernable trend or pattern. It goes from 1.6 to 1.3 to 1.2 and finally 1.7 million years. There is no trend present. As the plateaus age nothing seems to happen in any specific fashion to the length of time lava is produced. **The answer to the question is J because there is no distinct relationship.**

Skill Statement

Compare data from a data presentation (e.g., find the highest/lowest value; order data from a table).

What Does It Mean?

You are going to be presented with a graph or table and expected to look at it and identify a specific piece of information presented in the graph. This is a pretty straightforward category in that there isn't any prediction or interpretation here. You are just reading a graph and determining an answer.

Example Passage and Question

Passage VIII

A team of researchers constructed a greenhouse, consisting of three artificially lighted and heated sections, to be used to grow food during a long space voyage. The researchers found the weekly average light intensity, in arbitrary units, and the weekly average air temperature, in degrees Celsius (°C), in each section. The results for the first six weeks of their measurements are given in Table 1 (weekly average light intensity) and Table 2 (weekly average air temperature).

Table 1			
	Weekly average light intensity (arbitrary units)		
Week	Section 1	Section 2	Section 3
1	289.3	84.4	120.7
2	305.5	79.2	80.8
3	313.4	76.2	77.0
4	314.9	73.6	69.4
5	304.5	68.8	74.6
6	311.1	68.5	68.4

Table 2			
	Weekly average air temperature (°C)		
Week	Section 1	Section 2	Section 3
1	19.68	19.10	18.66
2	20.12	19.22	18.47
3	20.79	19.21	18.61
4	20.98	19.49	18.95
5	21.04	19.91	19.09
6	21.13	19.60	18.59

The highest weekly average air temperature recorded during the first six weeks of the study was:

A. 18.47°C.

B. 21.13°C.

C. 120.7°C.

D. 314.9°C.

For this category you are expected to look at information from a data presentation (graph or table) and compare that information to determine a correct answer. In this question you are asked to look at weekly average air temperatures during the first six weeks of the study. This statement is a little misleading because it makes it seem like there might be more than six weeks of study data present but there isn't. The table only shows you six weeks of temperature data.

The question wants you to determine the highest average air temperature present during the six weeks shown in the graph. It doesn't specify which section it wants though. It just wants you to find the highest temperature recorded. This is the "comparing" instruction because you are going to be looking at all of the air temperatures for each section and determining the highest number present.

You would potentially think then that all you need to do is pick the highest number given in the answer choices and it would be the right answer, but that isn't the case. The answer choices given in the problem do not all specifically refer to the temperature from Table 2. Two of the answer choices, **C** and **D**, refer to the light intensity values presented in Table 1 but it shows them to you in the units of temperature. You can tell though when you look at Table 2 that those values clearly are not represented anywhere. Instead you are expected to look at Table 2 and determine which temperature is the highest of the valid answer choices. Because there are only two possible choices all you need to do is look at the highest value, 21.13°C, and see if it is present in Table 2 somewhere, which it is in the Week 6, Section 1 temperature. **B is the correct answer.**

This is a good strategy to follow when you see a question like this: be sure to look at all of the tables and graphs present in a passage when a question asks you about a specific piece of information but doesn't identify the specific figure, graph, or table you are supposed to use to find that piece of information. In this sample question you can tell when looking at the answer choices that there clearly are values from both tables present with units that are incorrectly labeled for two of the answer choices. You will see this from time to time on the ACT and you want to make sure it does not trip you up. Inspect all of the information you are given carefully when you are not specifically told what to look at to determine the correct answer.

Skill Statement

Compare data from two or more data presentations (e.g., compare a value in a table to a value in a graph)

What Does It Mean?

You are going to be shown multiple tables or graphs or both. You will need to look at both and compare the data shown on one of the tables or graphs to another to determine the correct answer.

Example Passage and Question

Passage XVII

The following experiments were performed to investigate the effects of adding various *solutes* (substances that are dissolved in a solution), in varying amounts, on the boiling points and freezing points of H_2O solutions. Pure H_2O freezes at 0°C and boils at 100°C at standard atmospheric pressure.

Experiment 1

A student dissolved 0.01 mole of sodium chloride (NaCl) in 100 g of H_2O. Each mole of NaCl produces 2 moles of solute particles (1 mole of sodium ions and 1 mole of chloride ions in solution). After the NaCl dissolved, the freezing point of the solution was determined. This procedure was repeated with different amounts of NaCl and table sugar (sucrose). Each mole of sucrose produces 1 mole of solute particles (sucrose molecule). The results are shown in Table 1.

	Table 1		
Solution	Substance added to H_2O	Amount added (mole)	Freezing point (°C)
1	NaCl	0.01	−0.3
2	NaCl	0.05	−1.7
3	NaCl	0.1	−3.4
4	NaCl	0.2	−6.9
5	sucrose	0.01	−0.2
6	sucrose	0.05	−1.0
7	sucrose	0.1	−2.1
8	sucrose	0.2	−4.6

Note: Freezing points were measured at standard atmospheric pressure.

Experiment 2

A student dissolved 0.01 mole of NaCl in 100 g of H_2O. After the NaCl dissolved, the boiling point of the solution was determined. The procedure was repeated using various amounts of NaCl. The results are shown in Table 2.

	Table 2	
Solution	Amount of NaCl added (mole)	Boiling point (°C)
9	0.01	100.1
10	0.05	100.5
11	0.1	101.0
12	0.2	102.0

Note: Boiling points were measured at standard atmospheric pressure.

(continued)

Passage XVII (*continued*)

According to the results of Experiments 1 and 2, which of the following conclusions can be made about the magnitudes of the changes in the boiling point and freezing point of H_2O solutions when 0.2 mole of NaCl is added to 100 g of H_2O? The freezing point is:

F. raised less than the boiling point is lowered.

G. raised more than the boiling point is raised.

H. lowered less than the boiling point is lowered.

J. lowered more than the boiling point is raised.

When you first see this question it might look intimidating a bit but once you identify all of the information you need, it's just determining which number is bigger. You are going to be looking at Experiments 1 and 2 to answer this question. You know that because the question refers to both. It asks you for a conclusion, which is just another way of asking which of the answers is right, nothing more than that. The one word it would help to recognize is *magnitude,* which in the context of this question means the largest numerical change in regards to freezing point or boiling point. If you have no idea what magnitude means, though, you can probably still determine what the question is asking by looking at the answer choices.

The question specifically tells you exactly which line to look at on each table so you shouldn't have much trouble identifying the information you need to compare. It says you need to look at the H_2O solutions that have 0.2 moles of NaCl added to them. Knowing that, find those specific solutions: in Table 1 it is solution 4 and in Table 2 it is solution 12. The final step is to determine which one has the greatest change in the freezing point or boiling point. If you read the passage you will see that the boiling point of water is 100°C and the freezing point of water is 0°C.

Now compare the freezing point of solution 4 to that of pure water. In this case it is −6.9°C to 0°C. That is a change of 6.9°C. Then compare the boiling point of solution 12 to the boiling point of pure water. It is 102°C to 100°C. That is a change of 2°C. The freezing point goes down more than the boiling point goes up. Now just find the answer choice that supports this. **For this question the answer choice is J.**

Skill Statement

Determine and/or use a mathematical relationship that exists between data (e.g., averaging data, unit conversions).

What Does It Mean?

You are going to need to look at some data and try to figure out a specific relationship. The exact type of relationship will depend on the question itself. The question might ask you to find an average of data, perhaps look at units, find a ratio, or otherwise see some relationship. You are not expected to solve some complex math operation on problems related to this statement. It should be relatively clear what you are expected to find and deal with.

Example Passage and Question

Passage XV

Students used two methods to calculate D, a car's *total stopping distance*; D is the distance a car travels from the time a driver first reacts to an emergency until the car comes to a complete stop.

In Method 1, R is the distance a car travels during a driver's assumed reaction time of 0.75 sec, and B is the average distance traveled once the brakes are applied. Method 2 assumes that D = initial speed in ft/sec × 2 sec. Table 1 lists R, B, and D for various initial speeds, where D was computed using both methods. Figure 1 contains graphs of D versus initial speed for Method 1 and Method 2.

Table 1					
Initial speed (mi/hr)	Initial speed (ft/sec)	Method 1			Method 2
		R (ft)	B (ft)	D (ft)	D (ft)
20	29	22	20	42	58
40	59	44	80	124	118
60	88	66	180	246	176
80	118	88	320	408	236

Figure 1

Table 1 and Figure 1 adapted from Edwin F. Meyer III, *Multiple-Car Pileups and the Two-Second Rule.* ©1994 by The American Association of Physics Teachers.

In Method 1, D equals:

F. R + B.

G. R − B.

H. R × B.

J. R ÷ B.

This question asks you to look at a data table to determine which answer choice shows the correct relationship between variables. It gives you four equations that could possibly equal D and wants you to figure out which of the equations is correct. The question itself is straightforward yet the data table presents you with one very easy-to-make mistake, it has two D variables listed. In a situation like this when you are hurrying, it is very easy to look at that and get the two mixed up. Look at the question, though: it says "In Method 1." That is your key to make sure you look at the D variable for Method 1 not the D for Method 2. Attention to this little detail will save you time from trying to determine a relationship that you aren't asked about.

The next step is to look at the relationship among R, B, and D. It doesn't matter which of the trials you pick because the relationship should be the same for all of them. Look at the one that has the smallest numbers and presents the easier mental math that you need to do. The first trial has an R value of 22 and B value of 20 with a D value of 42. 22 plus 20 is equal to 42. It is something that you can perhaps recognize quickly. If you can't, go through the process of elimination with the answer choices and see which is correct. Always try the simplest operations first. Look and see if you are required to use addition first if you see another question like this. If not, then try subtraction. You aren't going to be expected to do complex multiplication or division on these tests so those likely are not the answer. **In this case the answer is A.**

Skill Statement

Translate information into a table, graph, or diagram.

What Does It Mean?

This category expects you to look at some amount of data or information and identify a correct re-creation of that data in another format. You might be shown a graph with data and be expected to determine the correct tabular representation of that data. You might be shown a paragraph with an explanation of data and be expected to pick the correct graph representing that data.

Example Passage and Question

Passage XII

Some of the liquid in a closed container evaporates, forming a vapor that condenses, reforming the liquid. The pressure of the vapor at *equilibrium* (when the rates of evaporation and condensation are equal) is the liquid's *vapor pressure*. A liquid in an open container boils when its vapor pressure equals the *external pressure*. The following experiments were performed to study vapor pressures.

Experiment 1

The apparatus shown in Figure 1 was assembled except for the tubing. The flask was placed in a 20°C H_2O bath. After five minutes the manometer was connected, and 2 mL of hexane was added to the flask from the dropper. Some of the hexane evaporated. The vapor pressure was determined by measuring the height of the mercury (Hg) after the Hg level had stabilized. Additional trials were performed at different temperatures and with other liquids in the flask. The results are shown in Table 1.

Figure 1

Figure 1 adapted from Henry Dorin, Peter E. Demmin, and Dorothy L. Gabel, *Chemistry: The Study of Matter.* ©1989 by Prentice-Hall, Inc.

Table 1			
	Vapor pressure (mm Hg) at:		
Liquid	0°C	20°C	40°C
2-Butanone	35	75	200
Ethyl acetate	20	70	180
Hexane	40	110	250
Methanol	25	90	245
2-Propanol	9	35	100

Experiment 2

A test tube containing a thermometer and hexane was heated in an oil bath until the hexane boiled gently. The temperature was recorded. The external pressure was 760 mm Hg. This procedure was repeated in a chamber at pressures of 400 mm Hg and 100 mm Hg. The boiling points of other liquids were also determined. The results are shown in Table 2.

Table 2			
	Boiling point (°C) at external pressure of:		
Liquid	760 mm Hg	400 mm Hg	100 mm Hg
2-Butanone	79.6	60.0	25.0
Ethyl acetate	77.1	59.3	27.0
Hexane	68.7	49.6	15.8
Methanol	64.7	49.9	21.2
2-Propanol	82.5	67.8	39.5

(*continued*)

Passage XII (*continued*)

Which of the following bar graphs best represents the vapor pressures of the liquids from Experiment 1 at 20°C?

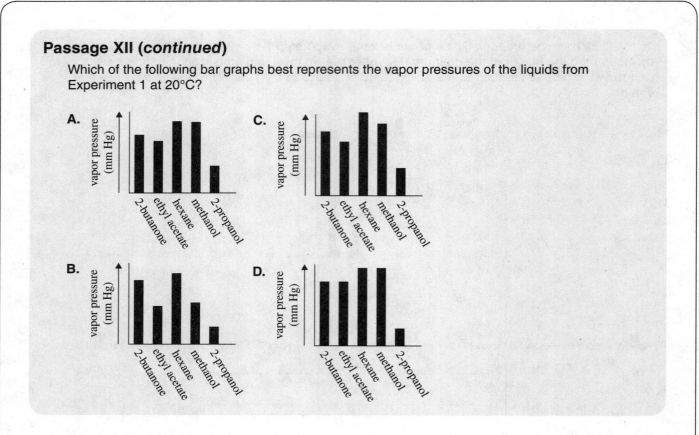

This question presents you with four possible graphs and tells you to pick the one that best represents the data shown to you in Experiment 1. It doesn't specifically say you need to look at Table 1, but that is where you will find the information. You can determine this because Table 1 is included directly after Experiment 1. Sometimes you might find some tricky information presented to you throughout the ACT science test, but you will not find the numbers of tables or graphs incorrectly labeled or placed out of order. That isn't something you need to worry about. Further, Experiment 2 does not deal with vapor pressure at all. It is focused on the boiling point of the liquids at different pressures so you know you are going to be looking at Table 1. Once you've made sure you are looking at the correct data table you now need to figure out where to look in it. In this case there are three data sets in Table 1 so you will need to specifically look at the 20°C column because that is what the question directs you to.

Once you've identified the correct data you need to turn into a graph, the next step is to look at the data and see how it should look in relation to the answer choice graphs. The graphs in the answer choices do not provide you with specific number intervals for the bars, so you are going to have to determine which one looks the closest to the data instead of which one matches exactly, because there is no way to determine that.

The bar graphs in the answer choices put the vapor pressure (measured in mm Hg) on the y-axis and the different liquids on the x-axis. The first thing you can look for on the answer graphs is to see if the highest and lowest numbers are represented correctly. Hexane should be the highest bar and 2-propanol should be lowest by a significant margin. 2-butanone and ethyl acetate should be very close to each other with 2-butanone being a bit higher and methanol should be somewhere between the high point of hexane and the middle area of 2-butanone and ethyl. With a question like this it is all about the proportion of one measurement to the next rather than the exact differences. The graph choices present you with several options but the only one that shows the correct order of vapor pressure with respect to the liquids and their values is graph **C,** the correct answer.

Skill Statement

Analyze presented data when given new information (e.g., reinterpret a graph when new findings are provided).

What Does It Mean?

This type of category will give you some piece of information that adds onto something mentioned in the passage. It might be a new fact or hypothesis related to one of the data sets or experiments. The questions will then ask you to look at one of the existing graphs or charts and see how the new information relates to them in regards to the answer choices presented. You'll have to think about the new information and use it to pick the correct choice.

Example Passage and Question

Passage I

Flood basalt plateaus are large areas of Earth's surface covered with thick hardened lava. It has been hypothesized that the huge outpourings of lava that formed these plateaus were produced by *plumes* of molten material rising from deep within Earth.

Study 1
A model of a typical plume was created using a computer. It was hypothesized that the "head" of the plume produced the flood basalt plateaus when its molten material reached the surface. Figure 1 shows the computer-generated plume, its diameter, and how long, in millions of years (Myr), it would take the head of the plume to reach the surface.

(continued)

Passage I (*continued*)

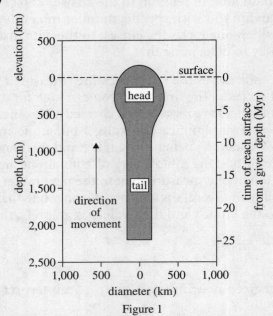

Figure 1

Figure adapted from R. I. Hill et al., *Mantle Plumes and Continental Tectonics.* ©1992 by the American Association for the Advancement of Science.

Study 2

Four flood basalt plateaus (A–D) were studied. The lava volume, in cubic kilometers (km^3) was estimated for each plateau from the area of the plateau and the average thickness of the lava. The length of time lava was being produced at each plateau, and the rate of lava production, in km^3 per year, were also estimated. The results are in Table 1.

			Length of time lava was produced (Myr)	Rate of lava production (km^3/yr)
Plateau	Age (Myr)	Lava volume (km^3)		
A	60	2,000,000	1.6	1.25
B	67	1,500,000	1.3	1.2
C	135	1,440,000	1.2	1.2
D	192	2,125,000	1.7	1.25

Table adapted from Mark A. Richards et al., *Flood Basalts and Hot-Spot Tracks: Plume Heads and Tails.* ©1989 by the American Association for the Advancement of Science.

Study 3

Scientists found that three large extinctions of marine organisms had ages similar to those of the formation of three of the flood basalt plateaus; 58 Myr, 66 Myr, and 133 Myr. It was hypothesized that the production of large amounts of lava and gases in the formation of plateaus may have contributed to those extinctions.

(Note: All of these ages have an error of ± 1 Myr.)

The scientists in Study 3 hypothesized that the larger the volume of lava produced, the larger the number of marine organisms that would become extinct. If this hypothesis is correct, the formation of which of the following plateaus caused the largest number of marine organisms to become extinct?

F. Plateau A

G. Plateau B

H. Plateau C

J. Plateau D

Something to note when looking at this passage in general, before considering the question, is that it involves some very specific science content you might not be familiar with. Specifically, the beginning part of the passage and the graph included after it focus on a the concept of a volcanic lava plume. A *plume* in this regard is a hot spot of lava rising through the earth that eventually leads to a release of pressure superheated gas causing an eruption. Understanding this concept of a plume is not essential to your success on the question but it might be a vocabulary word that trips you up for a moment. The question doesn't give you the definition of *plume* but it does present you with the graph that shows you a basic image of a volcanic plume rising through the surface of the earth. From that graph you should be able to infer some basic information about a plume to help you answer any questions.

The question begins by stating that in Study 3 scientists hypothesized that larger volumes of lava being produced correspond to there being a larger number of marine organisms becoming extinct. It then says that you are to assume this hypothesis is correct when answering this question. Then it wants you to analyze which flood basalt plateau formation corresponds to the largest extinction of organisms.

This question doesn't provide you with too much guidance in terms of where to look for the answers you are going to need. It says that Study 3 is where the hypothesis comes from, but there is no data presented in Study 3 that is useful to you in terms of the number of organisms that became extinct. To answer the question you need to make sure you know what information you are trying to find so you can get to the right answer. This is a good example of how you should always be able to find the information you need somewhere in a question. Conversely, if you think you need a specific piece of information to answer a question and you cannot find it anywhere in the passage then you don't need that piece of information. What you need to do, in a case like that, is go back and reevaluate what you should be looking for in the first place so you can reapply the information you already have to find the right answer.

In this case, the larger the lava production, the more organism extinction, according to the hypothesis, which is true (as stated in the question). That means you need to figure out which plateau corresponds to the highest amount of lava produced. The only place you're going to find that information in the passage is in Table 1. It shows you all the data you need to determine which plateau corresponds to the largest amount of lava. The best way to measure the amount of lava produced is by the volume, which the chart provides. It also provides you with the length of time of lava production and the rate. Each of these can play a factor in how much lava volume was produced but they are not the final determination. The volume is how much lava was produced, and that is what the question wants you to determine. So look at the chart and see that plateau D produced the largest volume. It should correspond to the greatest extinction. **The correct answer for this question is J.**

Summary

As you can see from each of the skill statements in this chapter the Interpretation of Data category is focused on interpreting the information you are shown in a passage. You need to look at data and use that data to find the right answer to a question. You are looking at numbers and values and using those numbers. You aren't going to be expected to analyze any of the scientific procedures or methods used in any of the research. You aren't going to need to analyze the data and draw conclusions about the validity of an experiment or on which opinion is correct. All that these questions expect you to do is look at a graph or table and correctly read the data they show in some way. They can be as simple as picking out a piece of data given at a specific interval or value on a graph or the problems can be as complex as taking a graph and turning it into a table. In the end though, remember, it is just data and you are just reading that data to find an answer.

5

Chapter 5: Reporting Category: Evaluation of Models, Inferences, and Experimental Results

This chapter is going to focus on the Evaluation of Models, Inferences, and Experimental Results reporting category. This is the second most heavily weighted category on the ACT science test with a representation of 25%–35% of all of the questions. The broad focus of this category is as follows:

> Judge the validity of scientific information and formulate conclusions and predictions based on that information (e.g., determine which explanation for a scientific phenomenon is supported by new findings).

This reporting category is the one that expects you to analyze information and draw conclusions from it. Where the Interpretation of Data category is focused on looking at data and picking out information presented in the passages, this category expects you to look at the information and draw conclusions from that information. You might be asked to look at a supplemental piece of information given in a question and see how that information ties into the experimental results shown in the passage; or you might need to look at multiple experimental models and decide which one best works to determine the outcome of the question. There are a lot of possible concepts this category can focus on.

What you will see in this chapter are five of the most-used skill statements from the Evaluation of Models, Inferences, and Experimental Results reporting category. Each statement will be shown to you and then broken down into a more understandable and relatable explanation of what you are going to have to do with questions from the category. Finally, each skill statement will have one or more official sample ACT questions that match the skill statement as coded by ACT along with the passage associated with the question. There will be a detailed answer that explains both how to interpret the question and how to best answer it in relation to the skill statement category it represents.

Evaluation of Models, Inferences, and Experimental Results

Skill Statement

Determine which hypothesis, prediction, or conclusion is or is not consistent with a data presentation or piece of information in text.

What Does It Mean?

You will be provided with some fact, statement, hypothesis, or piece of information in some way in these questions. Your job will be to look at that piece of information and compare it to what is in the passage. It says that you will be looking at a data presentation or a piece of information in the text so in the passage you might be looking at a graph, a table, or a portion of text. You'll need to determine whether the information provided in the question matches the information shown to you in the passage or not. It won't always be perfectly clear, so you will need to be flexible enough to interpret the question as needed. There is no single guideline for each of these reporting categories though certain skills, such as determining how consistent the data might be, are related to the categories. Specific step-by-step directions do not come with these categories and skills. One of the keys to success is to be flexible and able to adapt to what you are dealing with each time.

Example Passage and Question

Passage IV

Certain layers of Earth's atmosphere absorb particular wavelengths of solar radiation while letting others pass through. Types of solar radiation include X-rays, ultraviolet light, visible light, and infrared radiation. The cross section of Earth's atmosphere below illustrates the altitudes at which certain wavelengths are absorbed. The arrows point to the altitudes at which solar radiation of different ranges of wavelengths is absorbed. The figure also indicates the layers of the atmosphere and how atmospheric density, pressure, and temperature vary with altitude.

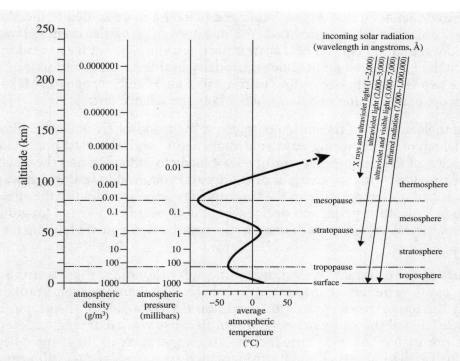

Figure adapted from Arthur Strahler, *The Earth Sciences.* ©1963 by Harper and Row.

Note: 1 Å = 1 × 10⁻¹⁰ meters.

The information provided in the figure indicates that the air temperature in the troposphere is LEAST likely to be influenced by which of the following wavelengths of energy?

F. 1,500 Å

G. 4,500 Å

H. 6,000 Å

J. 7,000 Å

In this question the piece of information you are given that you need to compare to the data in the passage is found in the answer choices. Each of the four answer choices you see is a possible piece of information, and you need to figure out which one fits into the graph properly based on the statement proposed in the question.

Before moving on though it is important for you to note the inclusion of some scientific terms that may or may not present you with something to consider. This question specifically asks you about the troposphere, which is a layer of atmosphere. The graph includes the names of many different layers of atmosphere. Neither the passage nor the question provide you with more information than the fact that you are dealing with layers of atmosphere so you as the test taker need to understand that you will not need to have a more in-depth understanding of the vocabulary words than what is provided. You just need to recognize them as layers of the atmosphere and use that to help you best answer the questions. Do not try to read into it more than you need. One other small point about vocabulary in this question and passage: you will notice there are two very similar-sounding words: *troposphere* and *tropopause.* Make sure you don't mix them up; pay attention to detail when taking the science test.

The key part of the question is "the air temperature in the troposphere is LEAST likely to be influenced by which of the following wavelengths of energy" with the most important parts being the air temperature of the troposphere, the one least likely to influence, and the wavelength of energy. You are provided with wavelengths of energy and you need to find which wavelength has the least influence on air temperature in the troposphere. Once you identify the specific need of the question then look at the graph and decide what the answer is. There is a lot going on in this graph, so make sure you pay careful attention to the information you are looking for and ignore everything else.

You can see that of the different types of incoming solar radiation, the lower the wavelength of energy, the less they penetrate into the atmosphere. The incoming solar radiation is represented by the four arrows angled downward on the right side of the graph. In addition, these arrows are labeled *incoming solar radiation.* Because you are trying to determine which wavelength of energy has the least influence on air temperature in the troposphere you need to use those arrows as a way to determine which type of solar radiation can reach the troposphere. If the solar radiation cannot reach the troposphere it won't have any impact on its temperature. In this case you can look at the arrows and see that the lower the wavelength of light, the less depth it penetrates into the atmosphere as noted on the *y*-axis of this graph. You can see the X-rays and ultraviolet light arrow is the shortest and penetrates the least into the atmosphere. There is also a numerical value range included for the X-rays and ultraviolet light arrow, which is what you will use to find your answer. **You can see that answer choice F is the correct answer.** It is the only choice which fits inside the range given by the X-rays and ultraviolet light arrow.

Atmospheric boundaries are at a higher than usual altitude above areas that get more direct solar radiation. Based on this information and the data provided, which of the following predictions about atmospheric boundaries would most likely be true if Earth received less solar radiation than it presently does?

F. The tropopause, stratopause, and mesopause would all increase in altitude.

G. The tropopause, stratopause, and mesopause would all decrease in altitude.

H. The tropopause and stratopause would increase in altitude, but the mesopause would decrease in altitude.

J. The tropopause would decrease in altitude, but the stratopause and mesopause would increase in altitude.

This question states in the first sentence that atmospheric boundaries are higher than normal in areas that receive more direct solar radiation. This is a piece of information you are going to need to use when answering this question. The question then presents you with a new statement that you need to analyze in the context of the question and the data. It says that you must consider the altitude (height) of the atmospheric boundaries if earth began receiving less solar radiation than it currently does.

The information you have now says that atmospheric boundaries are usually higher when receiving more direct radiation. You are supposed to determine what happens to the altitude of those boundaries when the amount of radiation decreases. The graph itself in this case is not going to be of that much use to figuring out the answer. The graph doesn't specifically address the issue of the height of atmospheric boundaries versus the amount of radiation received. It does show you the different atmospheric boundaries but it doesn't outline how they might change.

This is what can make this type of question challenging: you are required to mostly interpret the answer to the question from the information the question gives you. The best way to do this is to consider what you are told: atmospheric boundaries are usually higher when receiving more direct radiation. The question says you now must consider the exact opposite: what happens to atmospheric boundaries if radiation exposure goes down? This requires some logical thinking on your part and not just looking at the graph. In this case if more radiation raises the boundaries then it is logical to think that less radiation would lower the boundaries. It isn't information you will find on the graph, but it is an idea you can determine from the information given in the question. Once you've determined that you are looking for boundaries that are lower you just need to find the answer choice that supports that.

This is an example that really illustrates how you should focus on what each question is asking and nothing more. Don't get mixed up by the technical terms present in the question or passage. Focus on what you need and use your analytical skills to solve the question. There is no differentiation in the question's statement about altitude based on the type or name of atmospheric boundaries so all of the answer choices presented should do the same thing—decrease. You want to find the answer choice that matches this. **In this case the correct answer is G.**

Skill Statement

Determine which hypothesis, prediction, or conclusion is or is not consistent with two or more data presentations and/or pieces of information in text.

What Does It Mean?

This is a very similar statement to the previous one. It is almost identical except this requires you to look at two or more data presentations or pieces of information in text. So you'll be doing the same thing but you'll have to interpret and deal with more information. It won't just be from a single area of the passage or question; there'll be more that you have to look at to determine the answer.

Example Passage and Question

Passage I

Flood basalt plateaus are large areas of Earth's surface covered with thick hardened lava. It has been hypothesized that the huge outpourings of lava that formed these plateaus were produced by *plumes* of molten material rising from deep within Earth.

Study 1

A model of a typical plume was created using a computer. It was hypothesized that the "head" of the plume produced the flood basalt plateaus when its molten material reached the surface. Figure 1 shows the computer-generated plume, its diameter, and how long, in millions of years (Myr), it would take the head of the plume to reach the surface.

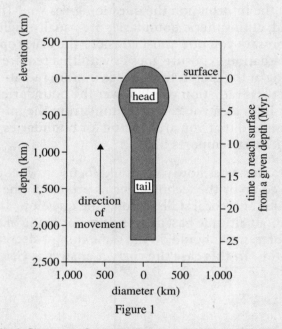

Figure 1

Figure adapted from R. I. Hill et al., *Mantle Plumes and Continental Tectonics.* ©1992 by the American Association for the Advancement of Science.

Study 2

Four flood basalt plateaus (A–D) were studied. The lava volume, in cubic kilometers (km^3) was estimated for each plateau from the area of the plateau and the average thickness of the lava. The length of time lava was being produced at each plateau, and the rate of lava production, in km^3 per year, were also estimated. The results are in Table 1.

| | Table 1 | | | |
Plateau	Age (Myr)	Lava volume (km^3)	Length of time lava was produced (Myr)	Rate of lava production (km^3/yr)
A	60	2,000,000	1.6	1.25
B	67	1,500,000	1.3	1.2
C	135	1,440,000	1.2	1.2
D	192	2,125,000	1.7	1.25

Table adapted from Mark A. Richards et al., *Flood Basalts and Hot-Spot Tracks: Plume Heads and Tails.* ©1989 by the American Association for the Advancement of Science.

Study 3

Scientists found that three large extinctions of marine organisms had ages similar to those of the formation of three of the flood basalt plateaus; 58 Myr, 66 Myr, and 133 Myr. It was hypothesized that the production of large amounts of lava and gases in the formation of plateaus may have contributed to those extinctions.

(Note: All of these ages have an error of ± 1 Myr.)

If the hypothesis made by the scientists in Study 3 is correct, evidence would most likely be found of another extinction of marine organisms that occurred around:

F. 77 Myr ago.

G. 192 Myr ago.

H. 250 Myr ago.

J. 314 Myr ago.

This question requires you to look at data from two different studies to determine the correct answer. It doesn't expect you to determine that out of the blue though. It provides you with the prompting that you should look at Study 3 first to determine the hypothesis.

When you look at Study 3 you see it is hypothesized that large extinctions of organisms took place at similar times to the formation of the three flood basalt plateaus discussed in Study 2. This is where you are expected to look at multiple pieces of data to determine the answer. You read the hypothesis in Study 3 and then you use the information presented to you in Study 3 to find the correct piece of data you need from Study 2. In this case you are trying to find out when another extinction event took place. To do this you need to match the data from Study 3 to the data in Table 1 found in Study 2. Each age value given in Study 3 is close to the age of a plateau presented in Table 1. 58 Myr (million years ago) corresponds to plateau A, 66 Myr corresponds to plateau B, and 133 Myr corresponds to plateau C. You are tasked with finding another age that corresponds to an extinction. The only plateau not discussed already is plateau D, which has an age of 192 Myr. You need to find an answer choice that is closest to that number. In this case the answer choice is exactly 192 Myr matching the number perfectly. **The right answer is G.**

Skill Statement

Determine which theoretical models support or contradict a hypothesis, prediction, or conclusion.

What Does It Mean?

This category expects you to look at a model (which will be anything that might describe or explain a scientific phenomenon) and determine whether a statement given to you in a question supports that model. It basically wants you to look at some science discussed in a passage and determine if a statement in the question agrees with it or generally doesn't. There are variations, of course, but you are mainly going to be drawing conclusions about the accuracy of a statement in the question or passage compared to other information given to you.

Example Passage and Question

Passage VI

Two students explain why the *smoke* (a mixture of gases and carbon particles) from burning wood in a fireplace rises up the chimney from the fireplace. They also discuss how chimney *efficiency* (the volume of smoke flowing out the top of the chimney per second for a given temperature difference between inside and outside the chimney) is related to chimney height.

Student 1

Smoke rises because the gases from burning wood are less dense than the air that surrounds the fireplace. Because the gases are hotter than the air, the gas molecules have a higher average speed than the air molecules. Consequently, the average distance between adjacent gas molecules is greater than the average distance between adjacent air molecules, and so the gas *density* is less than the air density. As a result, the upward *buoyant force* acting on the gases is stronger than the downward *force of gravity* acting on the gases, and the gases rise, carrying the carbon particles with them. The upward flow of smoke is maintained as new air enters the fireplace, causing more wood to burn.

As chimney height increases, efficiency increases. The taller the chimney, the greater the volume of hot gas, the stronger the buoyant force compared with the force of gravity, and the more rapidly smoke rises.

Student 2

Smoke rises because wind blows across the top of the chimney. When no wind is blowing, the air pressure at the bottom of the chimney is slightly higher than the air pressure at the top of the chimney. However, when air at the top of the chimney moves at a higher speed than air at the bottom of the chimney, the pressure difference between the bottom and the top of the chimney is so great that air is forced upward, carrying smoke with it. The departure of air from the bottom of the chimney, in turn, creates a pressure difference that forces new air into the fireplace, causing further burning and an upward flow of smoke.

As chimney height increases, efficiency increases. Generally, wind speed increases with altitude. The taller the chimney, the greater the difference in air speed, the greater the difference in air pressure, and the more rapidly smoke rises.

Based on Student 2's explanation, the reason the wings of an airplane keep the airplane up in the air is that air moves at a higher speed:

F. above the wings than below the wings.

G. below the wings than above the wings.

H. in front of the wings than behind the wings.

J. behind the wings than in front of the wings.

This question expects you to focus on the explanation Student 2 gives. It asks you to determine where the air flows around airplane wings to keep an airplane up in the air. The first thing you might notice is that Student 2's explanation about air flow is specific about the air in a chimney. There is no mention of an airplane anywhere in the passage. That is totally okay. The airplane itself is not important to the question or passage at all. You need to find the similarities between the question and Student 2's statement regarding airflow. All of the answer choices are focused on where the airflow goes around the wings of an airplane and the speed at which that air moves, because that is what you are trying to figure out.

You need to read the explanation to see how air flows around a chimney and the speed at which it moves. The first sentence of the explanation says, "Smoke rises because wind blows across the top of the chimney." It says a few sentences later, "However, when air at the top of the chimney moves at a higher speed than air at the bottom of the chimney, the pressure difference between the bottom and the top of the chimney is so great that air is forced upward." This is key. This is your answer to the question and what you need to be looking for. If you replace the idea of the chimney with an airplane, it matches what you are looking for exactly. It says that as the air moves faster above something than below it causes lift to take place. **This matches answer choice F, which states that air moves faster above the wings than below.**

Skill Statement

Determine which hypothesis, prediction, or conclusion is or is not consistent with two or more theoretical models.

What Does It Mean?

This category is very, very similar to the one in the previous example. The only difference is that this statement expects you to look at two or more theoretical models instead of one. This means you will be looking at some amount of information and comparing it to more than one portion of the passage. It will be a bit more involved in its expectation of your analysis.

Example Passage and Question

Passage XIII

A *polypeptide* molecule is a chain of amino acids. A *protein* consists of one or more polypeptides. A protein's shape is described by three or four levels of structure.

1. The *primary structure* of a protein is the sequence of amino acids in each polypeptide.

2. The *secondary structure* of a protein is the local folding patterns within short segments of each polypeptide due to *hydrogen bonding* (weak chemical bonds).

3. The *tertiary structure* is the folding patterns that result from interactions between amino acid *side chains* (parts of an amino acid) in each polypeptide. These folding patterns generally occur across greater distances than those associated with the secondary structure.

4. The *quaternary structure* is the result of the clustering between more than one folded polypeptide.

A protein can adopt different shapes, and each shape has a relative energy. Lower-energy shapes are more stable than higher-energy shapes, and a protein with a relatively high-energy shape may *denature* (unfold) and then *renature* (refold), adopting a more stable shape. A protein that is almost completely denatured is called a *random coil.* Random coils are unstable because they are high-energy shapes; however, some can renature, adopting more stable shapes.

Two scientists discuss protein shape.

Scientist 1

The *active shape* (the biologically functional shape) of a protein is always identical to the protein's lowest-energy shape. Any other shape would be unstable. Because a protein's lowest-energy shape is determined by its primary structure, its active shape is determined by its primary structure.

Scientist 2

The active shape of a protein is dependent upon its primary structure. However, a protein's active shape may also depend on its *process of synthesis,* the order (in time) in which the amino acids were bonded together. As synthesis occurs, stable, local structures form within short segments of the polypeptide chain due to hydrogen bonding. These local structures may be different than the local structures associated with the protein's lowest-energy shape. After synthesis, these structures persist, trapping the protein in an active shape that has more energy than its lowest-energy shape.

Suppose proteins are almost completely denatured and then allowed to renature in a way that allows them to have their lowest-energy shapes. Which of the following statements about the proteins is most consistent with the information presented in the passage?

A. If Scientist 1 is correct, all of the proteins will have their active shapes.

B. If Scientist 1 is correct, all of the proteins will have shapes different than their active shapes.

C. If Scientist 2 is correct, all of the proteins will have their active shapes.

D. If Scientist 2 is correct, all of the proteins will have shapes different than their active shapes.

This question presents you with a hypothetical statement about proteins being allowed to denature and then renature into their lowest-energy shapes. That is the initial information you are going to be using when you look at the passage to find the correct answer choice; your "hypothesis, prediction, or conclusion." You are then expected to look at the two models presented to you by Scientists 1 and 2 to determine which is correct.

To answer questions from this category you are going to have to do some critical analysis of the information presented to you. You are expected to do far more than just look at data and determine a correct answer or even look at one scientific model presented and pick which statements match it. You are going to need to evaluate both statements by the scientists to determine the right answer. That means you will need to analyze each of their descriptions given and see which best fits the idea of a protein denaturing and then renaturing into its lowest-energy shape.

In this case Scientist 1 states that all proteins in their lowest-energy shape are equal to their active state. This is a blanket statement and is the first sentence provided in that paragraph. Scientist 2 states that the lowest-energy state of a protein might be its active state but it also might not be due to the process of synthesis. Scientist 1 makes a clear statement that allows for no variation; the lowest-energy shape is the active state. Scientist 2 allows for variation in that the lowest-energy shape can be the active state but it also can potentially be another energy shape as well. With this information known you need to determine the correct answer choice that best matches this.

Make sure you don't get caught up in trying to figure out which scientist is right or wrong based on the information of the passage. Instead you are just trying to determine which scientist's statement, if right, matches the information given in the passage and question together. **In this case choice A is the right answer.** It confirms that if Scientist 1 is right then all proteins will have their active shapes exactly as the passage says.

Skill Statement

Explain why presented information or new information supports or contradicts a hypothesis or conclusion.

What Does It Mean?

Questions in this category are going to give you some amount of information in the question itself or be taken from the passage. There will also be a conclusion or statement provided and it will be your job to determine whether the information in the question or passage agrees with the conclusion or information given. The answer choices will potentially also ask you to support your choice by providing a yes or no answer multiple times but with different supporting reasoning. Pay attention to detail on these questions. It is very easy to pick the right yes or no, yet when going quickly, pick the wrong supporting explanation.

Example Passage and Question

Passage IX

Carbon monoxide gas (CO) is toxic in air at concentrations above 0.1 % by volume. Cars are the major source of atmospheric CO in urban areas. Higher CO levels are observed during colder weather. A group of students proposed that cars emit more CO at colder air temperatures than at warmer air temperatures during the first 15 minutes after they are started. The students did the following experiments to investigate this hypothesis.

Experiment 1

A hose was connected to the tailpipe of a car. The engine was started and the exhaust was collected in a plastic bag. A 1 mL sample of the exhaust was taken from the bag with a syringe and injected into a *gas chromatograph,* an instrument that separates a mixture of gases into its individual components. Comparisons of the exhaust with mixtures of known CO concentrations were made to determine the percent by volume of CO in the exhaust. Exhaust was collected at two-minute intervals. Samples of exhaust from each of four cars were tested at an external temperature of −9°C. The results are shown in Table 1.

Table 1				
Time after starting (min)	Percent of CO in the exhaust at −9°C:			
	1978 Model X	1978 Model Y	1996 Model X	1996 Model Y
1	3.5	3.2	1.2	0.3
3	4.0	3.7	1.0	1.2
5	4.5	7.5	1.5	2.5
7	3.6	10.0	1.0	3.0
9	3.2	9.1	0.5	2.6
11	3.1	8.0	0.5	2.0
13	3.0	7.0	0.5	2.0
15	2.9	7.0	0.4	1.8

Experiment 2

The same four cars were tested at a temperature of 20°C using the procedure from Experiment 1. The results are shown in Table 2.

Table 2				
Time after starting (min)	Percent of CO in the exhaust at 20°C:			
	1978 Model X	1978 Model Y	1996 Model X	1996 Model Y
1	2.0	0.8	0.3	0.2
3	2.8	2.0	0.5	1.0
5	3.4	6.0	0.5	1.5
7	1.5	7.0	0.3	0.8
9	1.3	7.0	0.3	0.5
11	1.0	6.5	0.1	0.3
13	1.0	5.0	0.1	0.3
15	0.9	4.8	0.1	0.2

Do the results from Experiment 1 support the hypothesis that, at a given temperature and time, the exhaust of newer cars contains lower percents of CO than the exhaust of older cars?

F. Yes; the highest percent of CO was in the exhaust of the 1996 Model Y.

G. Yes; both 1996 models had percents of CO that were lower than those of either 1978 model.

H. No; the highest percent of CO was in the exhaust of the 1978 Model Y.

J. No; both 1978 models had percents of CO that were lower than those of either 1996 model.

This question presents you with a very straightforward consideration: do new cars produce a lower percentage of CO compared to the exhaust of older cars? It says it wants you to look at the data from Experiment 1 only, so that is where you should focus. You don't need to worry about the reasoning behind the experiment or anything related to the temperature as discussed in the passage. It isn't part of the question. All you need to look at is which cars had lower CO percent emissions.

When you look at the data table you can see that both models from 1978 clearly had much higher levels of CO emissions than either of the 1996 models. At every time interval both older models had higher emissions than the newer models. There is no ambiguity or debate in that. The older is clearly higher than the newer models. So, yes, the exhaust from new cars contains lower percents of CO than older cars.

If you look at the answer choices though you will see that there are two yes choices. Be sure to pick the right one. The first yes choice (**F**) states that the highest percent of CO was in the exhaust of a 1996 model car. Although it is correct in its answer of yes, the supporting reasoning makes no sense because it completely contradicts the yes answer in the first place. This is a common theme that you sometimes see on ACT science questions. Two of the answer choices will have the right answer but only one of them will have the right explanation for the answer. Make sure you read the entire answer choice, always, before selecting it as the correct answer. **That is why the answer choice G is the right answer, as the supporting information backs up the correct answer.**

Summary

The questions found in this reporting category expect you to analyze information and think critically to determine an answer. The Interpretation of Data category discussed in chapter 4 is more focused on retrieval and identification of information. This category is far more focused on analyzing that information and drawing conclusions. Questions in the Evaluation of Models, Inferences, and Experimental Results category are going to expect you to look at information or models and determine if those things agree with other information provided to you. You are going to be comparing statements and analyzing which argument or hypothesis matches what you see in a passage. Make sure you always stay focused on what these questions are asking and don't overanalyze the information you see in a passage.

Chapter 6: Reporting Category: Scientific Investigation

This chapter is going to focus on the Scientific Investigation reporting category. This is the third most heavily weighted category on the ACT science test with a representation of 20%–30% of all of the questions. The broad focus of this category is as follows:

> Understand experimental tools, procedures, and design (e.g., identify variables and controls) and compare, extend, and modify experiments (e.g., predict the results of additional trials).

This reporting category is focused on the process of science. As you can tell by reading the general description, you are going to be looking at experiments and examining the many pieces that make those experiments up. You won't be looking at graphs and retrieving data or drawing conclusions about the research described in the different passages. Instead you'll be reading the description of the experiment presented in the passage and answering questions about the process by which the research was conducted. You might need to identify the variables you see in an experiment and how they might change if the conditions of the experiment changed. You might be asked about the actual design of an experiment and how it could be changed or modified to meet certain requirements or conditions.

On top of that you will likely be asked to look at an experiment presented in a passage and make a prediction about what would happen if you did more experimental trials. You may have to look at the results shown from the experiment and determine what the likely outcome would be if the experiment was run longer or if a certain specific variable was adjusted in some way. Being comfortable with the scientific method of research is important to doing well on these questions, so be sure to look at chapter 7 to brush up on the specifics of the scientific method.

What you will see in this chapter are five of the most-used skill statements from the Scientific Investigation reporting category. Each statement will be shown to you and then broken down into a more understandable and relatable explanation of what you are going to have to do with questions from the category. Finally, each skill statement will have one official sample ACT question that matches the skill statement as coded by ACT along with the passage associated with the question. There will be a detailed answer that explains how to interpret the question and best answer it in relation to the skill statement category it represents.

Scientific Investigation

Skill Statement

Understand the methods, tools, and functions of tools used in an experiment.

What Does It Mean?

This skill expects you to be able to look at an experiment and pick out some pieces of information from the experiment itself. It might be something simple like figuring out how a value was measured or the process by which a reaction was carried out. It might be more involved, such as asking you about the actual method of the experiment and how that method was used to get the data. The focus of this category is on the experiment itself and how it was conducted.

Example Passage and Question

Passage VIII

A team of researchers constructed a greenhouse, consisting of three artificially lighted and heated sections, to be used to grow food during a long space voyage. The researchers found the weekly average light intensity, in arbitrary units, and the weekly average air temperature, in degrees Celsius (°C), in each section. The results for the first six weeks of their measurements are given in Table 1 (weekly average light intensity) and Table 2 (weekly average air temperature).

Table 1			
	Weekly average light intensity (arbitrary units)		
Week	Section 1	Section 2	Section 3
1	289.3	84.4	120.7
2	305.5	79.2	80.8
3	313.4	76.2	77.0
4	314.9	73.6	69.4
5	304.5	68.8	74.6
6	311.1	68.5	68.4

Table 2			
	Weekly average air temperature (°C)		
Week	Section 1	Section 2	Section 3
1	19.68	19.10	18.66
2	20.12	19.22	18.47
3	20.79	19.21	18.61
4	20.98	19.49	18.95
5	21.04	19.91	19.09
6	21.13	19.60	18.59

According to Table 2, weekly average air temperatures were recorded to the nearest:

F. 0.01°C.

G. 0.1°C.

H. 1.0°C.

J. 10°C.

This question asks you to look at data gathered by the experiment and determine the accuracy at which it was collected. It is straightforward. In this category you will get some questions that just ask you to identify a piece of information about the experiment or research. When you see questions like this your first step should be to look at the information you need to identify and go from there. Don't overanalyze but also don't make mistakes by moving too quickly.

The question wants you to look at Table 2 specifically when answering this question so be sure to look at Table 2 only. Don't make the mistake of looking at Table 1 because it would lead to you making a mistake. Table 1 does not measure temperature but it is easy to miss that and just look at the numbers. If you do, you'll see that those measurements are made to the nearest 0.1, whereas Table 2 is measured to the nearest 0.01. This is a big difference and leads to you having a different answer. **Because you are looking at Table 2, you will see that the answer is F.**

Skill Statement

Predict the results of an additional trial or measurement in an experiment.

What Does It Mean?

You are going to be looking at an experiment and you will be expected to predict what a result would be if the experiment was continued in some way. It might involve measuring another object that has specific properties provided in the question, or it might involve predicting the result of another experimental trial conducted by the researcher. In any event you will need to look at the trends and patterns that you see in the data shown by the initial research to predict the results of future trials or measurements. You are going to need to think critically and be able to make your best guess about the future results to do well on questions in this category.

Example Passage and Question

Note: The following passage is used for multiple questions in this chapter. You may want to mark this page so you can find it easily when you are ready to answer those questions.

Passage IX

Carbon monoxide gas (CO) is toxic in air at concentrations above 0.1% by volume. Cars are the major source of atmospheric CO in urban areas. Higher CO levels are observed during colder weather. A group of students proposed that cars emit more CO at colder air temperatures than at warmer air temperatures during the first 15 minutes after they are started. The students did the following experiments to investigate this hypothesis.

Experiment 1

A hose was connected to the tailpipe of a car. The engine was started and the exhaust was collected in a plastic bag. A 1 mL sample of the exhaust was taken from the bag with a syringe and injected into a *gas chromatograph,* an instrument that separates a mixture of gases into its individual components. Comparisons of the exhaust with mixtures of known CO concentrations were made to determine the percent by volume of CO in the exhaust. Exhaust was collected at two-minute intervals. Samples of exhaust from each of four cars were tested at an external temperature of −9°C. The results are shown in Table 1.

Table 1				
Time after starting (min)	Percent of CO in the exhaust at −9°C:			
	1978 Model X	1978 Model Y	1996 Model X	1996 Model Y
1	3.5	3.2	1.2	0.3
3	4.0	3.7	1.0	1.2
5	4.5	7.5	1.5	2.5
7	3.6	10.0	1.0	3.0
9	3.2	9.1	0.5	2.6
11	3.1	8.0	0.5	2.0
13	3.0	7.0	0.5	2.0
15	2.9	7.0	0.4	1.8

Experiment 2

The same four cars were tested at a temperature of 20°C using the procedure from Experiment 1. The results are shown in Table 2.

Time after starting (min)	Percent of CO in the exhaust at 20°C:			
	1978 Model X	1978 Model Y	1996 Model X	1996 Model Y
1	2.0	0.8	0.3	0.2
3	2.8	2.0	0.5	1.0
5	3.4	6.0	0.5	1.5
7	1.5	7.0	0.3	0.8
9	1.3	7.0	0.3	0.5
11	1.0	6.5	0.1	0.3
13	1.0	5.0	0.1	0.3
15	0.9	4.8	0.1	0.2

Table 2

Based on the results of the experiments and the information in the table below, cars in which of the following cities would most likely contribute the greatest amount of CO to the atmosphere in January? (Assume that the types, numbers, and ages of cars used in each city are approximately equal.)

City	Average temperature (°F) for January
Minneapolis	11.2
Pittsburgh	26.7
Seattle	39.1
San Diego	56.8

F. Minneapolis

G. Pittsburgh

H. Seattle

J. San Diego

This question asks you to make a prediction about the continuation of the experiment. In this case the experiment is theoretically going to be continued in four different cities during the month of January. These cities each have different average temperatures so the temperature is what will be used to differentiate between the cities. You are provided a graph in the question that shows the average temperature of each of the cities. The question also says that you are to assume everything else about the experiment remains unchanged. That means that the age of the cars, the model, the sampling time, and so on will not be changed for this theoretical continuation.

Once you've established what you are looking at you now need to figure out exactly what you need to determine. You are asked to look at the question and figure out in which city cars will have the highest output of CO in January. Because you are going to be sorting this by temperature you will need to look back at the information given to you in Tables 1 and 2 to figure out what happens to CO production as temperature changes. In this case you can clearly see across all years and models that CO production is greater in colder temperatures compared to higher temperatures. That means in general it is safe to assume, according to the results shown, that cars will produce more CO emissions in colder temperatures than higher temperatures, regardless of location. Look at the chart given to you in the question and determine which city has the lowest average January temperature. **In this case it is Minneapolis, so the answer is F.**

Skill Statement

Understand an experimental design.

What Does It Mean?

This category expects you to look at the experiment shown in a passage and answer questions about the design of that experiment. In this case there are a lot of things you might be asked about. The most common will be something about the experimental factors and variables. You might need to look at the experiment and determine what variable changes between trials or which factor was changed by the researcher. It will require you to look at the passage and make sure you understand the process by which the experiment itself was conducted.

(Please refer to Passage IX on page 82 to answer the following question.)

In Experiment 1, which of the following factors varied?

A. The method of sample collection

B. The volume of exhaust that was tested

C. The year in which the cars were made

D. The temperature at which the engine was started

This question wants you to look at Experiment 1 and figure out what factors were varied by the researchers. That is, what is different about the data the researchers gathered and why. The answer choices present you with several options that you can consider. To be sure you have the right answer you will need to read the paragraph about the experiment and look at Table 1. As you read the paragraph you can get a sense of the process the researchers used to perform this experiment.

It clearly explains how they used a hose connected to the tailpipe of a car to collect emissions. They then sampled 1 mL of this exhaust emission from a bag using a syringe injected into a gas chromatograph and an analysis was done. This process is just generally described. There are no specifics saying this was done for some of the cars and not others. In addition, the exhaust was collected at two-minute intervals for each of the cars with no variation mentioned, and the external temperature for each measurement in Table 1 was −9°C.

So in the paragraph there is nothing noteworthy mentioned. Only when you look at the data in Table 1 do you notice that the cars used have different models and years. In this case there were two models of cars used, with each model having been made in two different years. Those are the only variations present specifically in Experiment 1. **In this case the only answer choice given that matches that is C, the years in which the cars were made.**

Don't mix up Experiments 1 and 2. The question specifically says it only wants you to look at Experiment 1. In Experiment 1 the only thing that is varied is the model and year of the cars used in the experiment. Yet if you broaden this analysis to include Experiment 2 you can see, because it is the entire point of the research, that the temperature is varied between Experiments 1 and 2. This is also one of the answer choices and you don't want to pick it by accident, so stick with what the question asks and don't get distracted or mix in more information than you need to.

Skill Statement

Determine the experimental conditions that would produce specified results.

What Does It Mean?

This category is going to require you to look at an experiment to do some critical thinking. It goes beyond some of what you've seen so far, such as identifying a basic variable in an experiment or picking out a simple measurement. For this category you'll need to analyze an experiment and make your best determination about when or how you could best achieve a desired result. That is, the question will pose some specific set of constraints or a specific type of information it wants, and it will expect you to determine how you could get that information out of the experiment described.

Example Passage and Question

(Please refer to Passage IX on pages 82–83 to answer the following question.)

Many states require annual testing of cars to determine the levels of their CO emissions. Based on the experiments, in order to determine the maximum percent of CO found in a car's exhaust, during which of the following times after starting a car would it be best to sample the exhaust?

F. 1–3 min

G. 5–7 min

H. 9–11 min

J. 13 min or longer

This question presents you with a specific need to determine the maximum amount of CO produced by a car due to emission testing requirements. It provides you with some extra information that you do not need to answer the question. The statement about states requiring annual testing for CO levels is completely unnecessary to find the right answer to the question, so do not get distracted by it. What you do need to find is when the maximum percent of CO is found in a car's exhaust, and nothing else.

To determine this you can look at Table 1, Table 2, or both if you want to be absolutely certain, but you will get the right answer in either case. You can see that Tables 1 and 2 both show that the highest amount of CO are produced in the middle of the measurement period, somewhere between 5 and 7 minutes. In each case, for each model and year, the highest peak of CO emission is either at the 5-minute or 7-minute interval so that will be your right answer. There is some overlap with the 9-minute interval but it is sporadic and does not correspond to the highest emission rate for each of the cars, so it is not the right answer and it does not fit in with the answer choices given either. **In this case the answer is G.**

Skill Statement

Predict the effects of modifying the design or methods of an experiment.

What Does It Mean?

This category might be one of the more challenging you face. It requires you to be able to look at the experiment as described in the passage and analyze how the results might change if you changed the experiment itself or one of the factors within the experiment. This is not always an easy task to do. It means you need to have a solid grasp on the variables present in the experiment so that you can understand how changing one of the might have an impact on the results. It also means you need to pay careful attention to the description of the experiment in the passage so you can be aware of how any changes to the design will potentially affect the final results.

Example Passage and Question

(Please refer to Passage IX on pages 82–83 to answer the following question.)

How would the results of the experiments be affected, if at all, if the syringe contents were contaminated with CO-free air? (The composition of air is 78% N_2, 21% O_2, 0.9% Ar, and 0.1% other gases.) The measured percents of CO in the exhaust would be:

A. higher than the actual percents at both –9°C and 20°C.

B. lower than the actual percents at –9°C, but higher than the actual percents at 20°C.

C. lower than the actual percents at both –9°C and 20°C.

D. the same as the actual percents at both –9°C and 20°C.

This question requires you to predict how the results of the experiment would potentially change if you altered the procedure of the research in a specific way. In this case it is asking you to consider how the results would change if you introduced CO-free air into the syringe used to gather the exhaust emissions. It is asking you to go back into the passage and reevaluate the procedure you see with this new and changed information.

To determine the answer, you need to figure out what happens when that air is introduced into the syringe. How might it change the results and why? When you add the air into the syringe that does not contain CO you are reducing the percentage of CO present in the sample you are measuring. There is more air and less CO. **Because the values shown in the chart are percentages of the CO present, this means they will be lower across all the experiments, so answer choice C is the correct answer.**

For a more detailed explanation and description of this passage and the four questions associated with it see chapter 2.

Summary

The Scientific Investigation reporting category requires you to really look at an experiment and see what is happening. As you can see in the skill statements this reporting category is entirely focused on the design, planning, method, and results of an experiment. These questions are not asking you to simply look at a table and pick out the right answer. Instead they expect you to be able to look at a description of a scientific experiment and answer questions based on the experiment. You will need to understand why experiments were conducted, how they were conducted, what variables were being tested, what the results show, and what might happen if you changed one of the variables or altered the procedure in some way. These questions require you to think critically about the process of science so you want to make sure you approach them in the right way: pay attention to detail and make sure you focus on the experiment described in the passage.

7

Chapter 7: The Scientific Method

This chapter is going to walk you through the process of science. To begin you will find a detailed explanation of the scientific method and the parts that make it up. This is an essential piece to any student's understanding of how science is conducted and how the ACT science test will expect you to analyze experimental procedures and data. In addition, the chapter will walk you through the process of identifying experimental variables and how to relate that to a specific ACT sample passage example.

Understanding What Science Is on the ACT

Science as a whole is split up into many different fields and disciplines. The number of things that could be considered "science" is amazing; the range of different topics and focuses is absolutely immense. From the smallest things that make up our universe to the largest forces that govern and control every action or movement you see, science is everywhere and it focuses on everything. Even if you narrow it down to the science you encounter only in your high school classes it is still an incredible range of material.

Biology is the study of life and everything related to that. Think about how varied life is and how wide-ranging the focus of biology can be. In biology you will talk about the smallest living things on the planet such as bacteria in great depth and then you will move on and discuss the existence of entire populations and ecosystems that make up huge swathes of our earth. In chemistry you will look at atoms, molecules, elements, and the reactions that they undergo. In physics you will look at the forces that make up and control our existence. These are all independent subjects that cover completely different content.

There is, of course, overlap between the sciences but there is a huge amount of specific and unique content that goes along with each and every subject. It can be overwhelming when you really think about it. The discipline of science is so large that no one person can possibly claim to be an expert on everything. Not even the smartest men or women can make that claim. It simply isn't possible to have such a wide breadth of knowledge.

Yet there is something that unifies all of the fields of science together completely. It isn't a fact or a topic or a specific area of content focus; it is the method by which that science is conducted. All science follows a basic method by which research and experiments are carried out. You've probably heard about it in one or more of your classes at some point; it's called *the scientific method.*

Understanding What the Scientific Method and the Process of Science Are

The scientific method is the basic process by which all disciplines of science conduct research and carry out investigations. There are variations and modifications to match the specific research of a topic but overall the basic idea is pretty much the same regardless of what you're doing. It is the process the ACT science test expects you to understand and work through. There is zero expectation that you as a student have in-depth knowledge of a multitude of content areas. It isn't a realistic expectation and it isn't something that can be tested in thirty-five minutes or with forty questions.

What is expected is that you are familiar with the process by which science is conducted; the "why" behind the way the experiment was designed, the "how" explaining the process by which the experiment was conducted, and the "what" explaining and informing the data generated by the experiment. You are expected to look at science and understand the process by which it was conducted. As has been said numerous times in this book, you will be told all of the specific content information you need to understand a question. You are just going to need to look at that question and understand the process the question discusses and the results the experiment shows. There are some basic science vocabulary terms and some subject-specific ones that are helpful to understand. For more practice on those, see chapter 10, which discusses some broad science terminology and some subject specific terminology.

The goal behind this chapter, though, is to remind you of what the scientific process is and how you can use that knowledge to help you on the ACT science test. Being familiar with the science behind all of the passages you see on the test describing scientific research and experiments will help you a great deal. It will enable you to more efficiently and quickly understand what you are reading and understand what the questions are asking you to do. It is an example of having a good background on a topic that you can use to quickly interpret and correctly answer any questions you see.

Steps of the Scientific Method

To begin with the process of science you need to focus on the scientific method and what that is. In general, the scientific method is a structured process by which scientific experiments are carried out. The simplest way to view the scientific method is through some basic steps. There are variations, of course, in how this is taught and how the steps are labeled, but the basic idea is always the same. If you want to investigate something, the scientific method is the process you should follow. Understanding this process and the steps that go into conducting research will definitely help you work through the ACT science test more accurately and more efficiently so refamiliarizing yourself with it is a good idea. The following sections describe the steps of the scientific method.

Ask a Question

To begin with you need to have a topic in mind that you plan on investigating. Once you have that idea, the first step in investigating it is to ask a question about the topic under investigation. What is it you are trying to figure out? What do you want to look into? This portion of the scientific method usually involves observation and research into your topic as well. You generally will start with an observation about something. Once you've observed it you'll ask a question about something you've observed. The more you understand a topic the better you will be able to formulate a question. Having a good question is important when you want to conduct good research. Performing some initial research and conducting quality initial observations is also very important for developing a hypothesis, which is the next step in the scientific method.

Formulate a Hypothesis

Formulating a hypothesis is a central and important focus to the scientific process. A hypothesis tries to answer the question you formed initially in the previous step. A hypothesis is not simply a prediction about what the answer is to your question. A hypothesis is a guess that is based on your observations and knowledge of the topic. It is an educated guess that tries to best predict what you think the answer will be to your question.

There are two major things a hypothesis should do. First, the hypothesis should relate two factors or variables to one another when making a prediction. The most basic and widely used example of this is the if-then statement, such as "If this happens then this will happen" with the factors that the hypothesis is relating being included in the statement. A hypothesis should not just say "this will happen" with no supporting statement or other factors listed. That is just a prediction, not a hypothesis.

The second essential part of a hypothesis is that it must be something that is testable. It must be something you can design your experiment around. A hypothesis can't be something that is impossible to test or not realistic to investigate. It must be something that any scientist anywhere could also do. Even with a good hypothesis it is usually hard to completely and utterly prove it beyond any doubt. There is a huge difference in an experiment's positive results between proving a hypothesis conclusively and just being able to confidently say that, yes, we can accept this hypothesis as being true for this experiment. The same goes for a negative experimental result. Just because an experiment does not agree with a hypothesis does not mean that the hypothesis has been proven to be false. It simply means the hypothesis as applied to the current experiment should be rejected (meaning the results of the experiment were not consistent with the proposed hypothesis).

Remember, there are many factors that usually play a role in the outcome of an experiment, so you must design your experiment intelligently to ensure that as many factors as possible are controlled for. The more you can lessen or eliminate the influence of factors outside of the variables in the experiment, the stronger your hypothesis will be if it is accepted or rejected based on the results.

Design and Conduct an Experiment

The next step in the scientific method is to conduct an experiment that is designed to prove or disprove your hypothesis. A good scientific experiment must be planned out in advance of the research actually being conducted. No scientist just goes and starts messing around with stuff in hopes of figuring out an answer to a question or a hypothesis. Planning an experiment requires a set procedure of steps and described measurements that will take place as the experiment is conducted.

The biggest key to a properly planned-out experiment that follows the scientific method is that the experiment is repeatable and the results reproducible. The great thing about science is that it is universal. There is no opinion that factors into scientific results, only hard facts and evidence. Any experiment that produces a specific result should be able to be conducted by any other scientist in the world to produce the exact same result. If that isn't the case, then something is wrong with the procedure or the results of the original experiment. Science must be repeatable.

What if someone makes a miraculous discovery when conducting an experiment and this result would change the world forever? That would be amazing and wonderful, but for that result to hold any weight or be valued by any other scientist it must be repeatable and reproducible. If other scientists carry out the same experiment and produce the same world-changing result, then the result has been validated and confirmed. If other scientists carry out the same procedure and end up with a different result, however, the initial world-changing result really doesn't hold any value or weight.

Science is only science if it can be done by anyone anywhere to produce the same result. That is the absolute key of any experiment. There must be a set procedure. There must be a plan in place for gathering data.

Data Analysis/Conclusion

The final piece of the scientific method involves looking at the data generated during the experiment to draw a conclusion. Your first thought when you hear *data* mentioned is to think of numbers. Most of the time, especially in the case of the ACT science test, you'll be right. A large amount of scientific data is quantitative in nature. *Quantitative* can be defined as a measurement related to the quantity of something, more generally meaning the data is made up of numbers. In most cases the quantitative data you see from experiments described on the ACT science test will be presented in graphs or tables that you need to interpret and use to figure out your answers.

Not all data is quantitative in nature. Sometimes you will see more qualitative data. *Qualitative* can be defined as a measurement or observation related to the quality of something instead of the numerical quantity. Qualitative data is not going to be based in numbers but instead will consist of word-based observations. Both are valid forms of data gathering. Again, on the ACT science test most of the data you see will be quantitative in nature. It is just the nature of the test and what the reporting categories expect out of you.

Once you've analyzed the data gathered in an experiment, the time has come to either accept your hypothesis or reject it. Science is all based on fact so this decision will be made entirely by the data collected from the experiment. There is no opinion that is allowed to be factored into this. If your data supports your hypothesis then the hypothesis is accepted; otherwise, it is rejected. In science there is no negative to having a hypothesis disproven. If a hypothesis was incorrect, there is no shame in that. Positive results and negative results are both useful. In the end, any conclusion that is drawn by scientists about their hypothesis will always have to be based on the results of the experiment. Scientists cannot just say they were right or wrong; they must say they were right *because* or wrong *because* of whatever the experiment showed.

This is the basis of the scientific method: make an observation, ask a question about what you've observed, form a hypothesis that tries to answer your question, perform a repeatable experiment on your hypothesis, and finally determine if your hypothesis is accepted or rejected based on the data collected. The key thing you see in the scientific method is that everything is focused on objective data collection and results. It is what makes the process so useful and why it is the accepted method of investigation across all scientific disciplines.

Having a good understanding of the scientific method will help you on the ACT science test, so making sure you are familiar with it is a useful way to spend some of your time. The easier you can look at an experiment and understand the process behind it, the better off you will be. Understanding the process of science is a bit like learning a foreign language. Once you begin to understand the basic structure of science and the basic rules that govern the process of science it will become much easier and faster to read descriptions about it and understand what the passages are describing. You might not understand the individual subject matter of each experiment, but you will understand the reasoning behind why the experiment was conducted and what information the experiment was trying to determine. This will make your life easier because it will enable you to focus on the specific details asked by each question instead of trying to wrap your mind around the description of the entire experiment and data that some passages will show you; you will read the passages quicker and you will understand them better.

Experimental Design

Now that you've reviewed the parts of the scientific method, the next thing to focus on is how experiments are designed. Understanding experimental design is an essential piece to doing well on the ACT science test. Beyond looking at the results of experiments there are many questions that ask you to look at the specifics behind the design of the experiments themselves. These questions will ask you to analyze the factors and variables found in the experiment and what might have happened if these were changed or altered in some specific way presented in the question. These questions can be challenging because they very much expect you to understand how and why experiments are designed. This section of the chapter is going to help remind you about the parts of an experiment and how they are designed in more detail.

The biggest goal when designing experiments is answering the specific question presented at the beginning of the scientific method process. The process works by first coming up with that question and then developing a hypothesis about the question. Remember, a hypothesis is your best educated guess attempting to answer your initial question. Any experiment you see will be designed based on accepting or rejecting the hypothesis as a potential answer to the question. All research is done with this in mind.

This is much easier said than done, however. There are generally many factors that can alter the results of an experiment. Sometimes these factors can have an impact on your results in a way that changes how you view your results. An experiment that is well designed will try to limit or control all factors that would affect its results, except for the specific variables the experiment is designed to investigate.

Understanding the Relationship between Variables

There are three specific variables that should be focused on when you consider an experiment and how it was designed:

- **Independent variable:** This is the variable or condition that is changed specifically to see what happens when it is changed. The scientist makes this change to see what it does to the other variables in the experiment. It is called *independent* because it is independent of anything else in the experiment; it does not rely on other variables. It is determined by the scientist and nothing else. There should be one independent variable in an experiment.

- **Dependent variable:** This is what the scientist is observing. It is the variable the scientist wants to look at and observe its change during the experiment. The change you see in the dependent variable should be based on the independent variable in the experiment. The dependent variable is named as such because it is entirely dependent on the independent variable. Whatever result the dependent shows should change as the independent variable is changed by the scientist. There should be one dependent variable in an experiment.

- **Control variable:** Control variables are very important in any scientific experiment. They are exactly as they sound: variables controlled by the scientist. A control variable is something else than what is being investigated in an experiment. It might be the ambient air temperature in a room, the amount of light allowed to hit the experiment, the number of animals used in a sample size, and so on. It is anything that the scientist thinks could alter the outcome of the experiment in a way that is not being tested. For every trial the control variables should all remain exactly the same. Let's say you are conducting an experiment looking at the amount of product produced when you combine one chemical substance with another. You want to see how the results change when you vary one of the compounds for each trial. If you conduct Trial 1 at 30°C then you would need to conduct all your trials at 30°C because temperature can play a role in the rate and yield of chemical reactions. You aren't specifically looking at the role of temperature in this reaction, so you want to ensure the temperature is the same for every trial. This is an example of a control variable. An experiment can have one control variable or many; it just depends on the conditions of the experiment.

General Experimental Design Example

To give a broad example of the relationship between experimental variables let's take a look at the idea of a gas and the properties and measurements of that gas, which is something you studied in chemistry. Don't worry: this isn't going to turn into a complex chemistry lesson. All that these are going to be used for is to show how experiments must account for all of the variables when they are designed.

With gases there are three factors that have a unique relationship to one another: the pressure of a gas, the temperature of a gas, and the volume of a gas. Any enclosed gas can have these three properties measured, and there has been proven to be a relationship among all three of them. If one of the factors (pressure, volume, temperature) is changed, the others will change in specific ways as well.

Suppose you are a scientist and your goal is to determine the relationship between two of the specific factors, how would you do it? In a scenario like this with three variables present you can't just change one of them and see what happens. For example, let's say you've spent some time researching gases and how they behave. You know that gas particles are always in constant motion; they just keep moving. You also know that the motion of gas particles is dependent on their temperature.

This interests you as a scientist. You want to investigate this relationship between gas particle motion and temperature. You also know that the pressure a gas is found at can be used to provide a rough estimate of the motion of gas particles. So you know there is supposedly a link between the temperature of a gas and the pressure of a gas. You want to see if changing the temperature of a gas changes the pressure of that gas and thus changes the motion of the particles. Yet there is one other factor you have to deal with: the volume of the gas itself. The volume of the gas plays a role in the temperature and the pressure of the gas as well. If you want to investigate the relationship between gas pressure and temperature, you can't allow the volume to become part of the investigation.

When conducting this experiment you will need to hold the volume of the gas constant, meaning, you do not let the volume change at all during the course of the experiment. You can then observe the relationship between the two variables you want. If you were to allow all three variables to change at once you would have no ability as a scientist to assign any type of relationship between just two of the variables. How would you know what caused what change?

Instead, let's keep the volume constant and raise the temperature of the gas and then observe what happens to the pressure of the gas. When you do this, you'll see that the pressure of the gas increases as you raise the temperature of the gas, showing a direct relationship: as one goes up the other goes up. Because you didn't allow volume to change, you can confidently conclude now that as gas temperature increases the pressure of the gas also increases. This is due to the motion of the gas particles increasing.

This example illustrates the importance of proper experimental design. It enables you to see how it is essential that an experiment accounts for and controls all possible variables that may influence the results of an experiment in a way that could make the data less reliable and accurate.

Now let's consider this example in terms of independent, dependent, and control variables specifically:

- The **independent variable** is the temperature of a gas. The experimenter specifically decides to raise the temperature of the gas. This is independent of anything else going on in the reaction, and it is entirely determined by the scientist.

- The **dependent variable** is the change in the pressure of the gas, which is dependent on how the temperature is changed by the experimenter. It depends on the temperature being increased to see how it changes. In this example the pressure of the gas was being used as a relatively simple method of measuring the motion of the gas particles to see if increasing the temperature of the particles leads to an increase in pressure. If the pressure, as the dependent variable, increases when the temperature increases then you as the researcher could say there is a relationship between the motion of gas particles and the temperature of the gas particles.

- The **control variable** is the volume of the gas. It is not changed in any way during the experiment. The scientist maintains the volume of the gas as the experiment is done so that the volume cannot affect the change observed in the dependent variable.

Official Sample Passage Example

Now let's consider this same idea by looking at a sample ACT science passage describing an experiment and the steps taken during the experiment. This is a research summaries passage and it is an example of the kind of passage that studying the scientific method will help the most with. Research summaries passages show you an experiment, describe the process, and present you with the results of that experiment. They really expect you to focus on the process of science, and having a solid understanding of the scientific method will help a great deal when you read over research summaries passages. The following passage is one you've seen several times throughout this book so we won't go over it in too much depth at this point. The focus this time is to analyze it to look for the different types of experimental variables found in the research description.

Passage IX

Carbon monoxide gas (CO) is toxic in air at concentrations above 0.1% by volume. Cars are the major source of atmospheric CO in urban areas. Higher CO levels are observed during colder weather. A group of students proposed that cars emit more CO at colder air temperatures than at warmer air temperatures during the first 15 minutes after they are started. The students did the following experiments to investigate this hypothesis.

Experiment 1

A hose was connected to the tailpipe of a car. The engine was started and the exhaust was collected in a plastic bag. A 1 mL sample of the exhaust was taken from the bag with a syringe and injected into a *gas chromatograph,* an instrument that separates a mixture of gases into its individual components. Comparisons of the exhaust with mixtures of known CO concentrations were made to determine the percent by volume of CO in the exhaust. Exhaust was collected at two-minute intervals. Samples of exhaust from each of four cars were tested at an external temperature of −9°C. The results are shown in Table 1.

Table 1				
Time after starting (min)	Percent of CO in the exhaust at −9°C:			
	1978 Model X	1978 Model Y	1996 Model X	1996 Model Y
1	3.5	3.2	1.2	0.3
3	4.0	3.7	1.0	1.2
5	4.5	7.5	1.5	2.5
7	3.6	10.0	1.0	3.0
9	3.2	9.1	0.5	2.6
11	3.1	8.0	0.5	2.0
13	3.0	7.0	0.5	2.0
15	2.9	7.0	0.4	1.8

Experiment 2

The same four cars were tested at a temperature of 20°C using the procedure from Experiment 1. The results are shown in Table 2.

Table 2				
Time after starting (min)	Percent of CO in the exhaust at 20°C:			
	1978 Model X	1978 Model Y	1996 Model X	1996 Model Y
1	2.0	0.8	0.3	0.2
3	2.8	2.0	0.5	1.0
5	3.4	6.0	0.5	1.5
7	1.5	7.0	0.3	0.8
9	1.3	7.0	0.3	0.5
11	1.0	6.5	0.1	0.3
13	1.0	5.0	0.1	0.3
15	0.9	4.8	0.1	0.2

The goal of the experiment is to determine the emissions of CO at different temperatures in the first 15 minutes of a car's engine being started. Because you've analyzed this passage several times before there is no need to go into depth about the experiment and the results presented. Instead this time let's focus specifically on the variables described in the experiment and presented in the tables you see:

- **Independent variable:** Remember, the independent variable is the factor changed by the experimenter. In the case of this experiment the independent variable is the temperature at which the CO emissions are measured. In Experiment 1 the temperature is −9°C. In Experiment 2 the temperature is 20°C. This is an intentional change made by the researcher to look at how temperature affects CO emission. Because that is the focus it makes sense to vary the temperature from low to high in Experiments 1 and 2. The temperature depends on nothing in the experiment except the conscious choice of the researcher.

- **Dependent variable:** The dependent variable depends on the independent variable. It is the result of the change the researcher makes to the independent variable. In this case the emission of CO from the car is the dependent variable. This is specifically what is being measured in both experiments at −9°C and at 20°C. The goal of this research is to see what the difference in CO emission is at different temperatures so it makes sense that the percent of CO emission is the dependent variable. It depends on the temperature at which the measurements are conducted. You can clearly see at colder temperatures there is a greater emission of CO when compared to warmer temperatures across all time interval measurements, years, and models of cars.

- **Control variables:** The control variables are specific experimental factors that are not changed during the course of the experiment or different trials. These are things that should always remain the same. Again, this is done to ensure the researcher is best able to determine the relationship between only the independent and dependent variables. In the case of this example there are many controlled variables just as there will be in most experiments. In the procedure there are several specific factors that are controlled across both experiments: the method of sampling, the size of the sample, and the time interval at which the sampling is conducted. This standardizes the procedure with the only change being the temperature at which the measurements are taken. There are, of course, other environmental factors that could potentially play a very small role in the results, such as air pressure, humidity, and so on, but overall this procedure does a very good job of minimizing the chance of errors in the results based on outside factors that are not controlled. Beyond the procedure itself the cars from which samples are taken are also a controlled variable. Specifically, both experiments use the same model and year of cars to conduct measurements with. There are four cars used but because the four are the same for both experiments they are part of the control variables. Controlling for cars made in different years also enables the researcher to see how the age of a car potentially plays a role in CO emission because you can clearly see that older cars have a higher output of CO when compared to newer cars across both temperature experiments.

Summary

Science is too big of a subject for you to be tested on your knowledge of individual science facts. It isn't feasible and it isn't done on the ACT. Instead, you need to be comfortable looking at the scientific process and the way in which experiments are designed and carried out. When you see an experiment described on the ACT science section the more comfortable you are with the scientific method the better off you will be in terms of accurately and quickly understanding the purpose of the experiment and the procedure with which it was carried out.

Remember, the scientific method begins by investigating a topic and formulating a question around it. Once there is an informed question based on research and observation, a hypothesis is then created that tries to best establish an answer to the question. An experiment designed to investigate the hypothesis is then conducted. This experiment should generate data, which is then analyzed to determine if the hypothesis is right or wrong.

A good experiment will clearly identify the experimental variables or factors that are being investigated and controlled. An experiment should have a well-defined independent variable, which is the factor chosen by the research to be intentionally changed to determine the results of that change. The results of that change can be observed by looking at the dependent variable in the experiment. Finally, all good experiments will involve multiple controlled variables that are constant from trial to trial or experiment to experiment. This is done to ensure that the researcher can investigate the relationship between only the independent and dependent variables.

Science covers a huge, absolutely massive, amount of topics and information. Yet at its core, all scientific subjects and experiments are based on the scientific method described in this chapter. Understanding that method and the process by which it is conducted will greatly help you on the ACT science test, especially the research summaries passages that you will see. As described in chapter 2, research summaries passages present you with a scientific experiment and expect you to analyze the results of the experiment, along with the procedure by which the experiment was conducted.

Being familiar with the scientific method means you'll be able to read through these passages quicker and that you will need to spend less time going over the information presented to you about each experiment. The hope is that this will make each passage sound a bit less like a foreign language and more like something you understand and comprehend. Even though each passage on the test will likely cover an unrelated topic to one another they will all be joined together at some level by their use of the scientific method and the process of science.

Chapter 8: Graphs and Charts on the ACT Science Test

The ACT science section involves a lot of graphical data representation. The largest representation of reporting category questions on the ACT science test is from the Interpretation of Data category. As you've seen, the Interpretation of Data category expects you to look at data and interpret the information in some way. It wants you to read a table or chart and understand what it is showing you or be able to pick some specific information out from the data set.

In reality it is a fancy way of saying there are going to be a lot of graphs and tables to be found on the ACT science test. A lot. Most passages will include at least one if not several graphs or charts so you have to be very good at reading them. It is essential that you are able to interpret the information presented to you on a graph or table and make meaning of it to answer the questions you'll see on the science test. This chapter is going to review some of the basic concepts of what makes up a graph and the different types of graphs and tables you'll see. It will also focus on the relationships you can see in the data shown on the graphs and tables.

Reading Graphs

Let's say you're conducting an experiment that is generating a lot of numerical data that is quite interesting. Yet when you look at all the numbers written down on your paper or in a spreadsheet it just doesn't look that appealing. What do you do to make all that data easier to understand and look at? You make a graph.

Graphs are used in science to show the results of experiments in a visual manner. They make it easier to see relationships or trends found in the data. Graphs can be used to illustrate a specific portion of data or to show an entire data set. They are very versatile and there are many types you can encounter.

The ACT science section uses a lot of graphs to display data in many ways. Some of the graphs presented in the science passages are quite complex and others are relatively straightforward. Before diving into some example graphs that you might see on the ACT test you need to make sure you are completely comfortable with the basics of reading a graph.

What Makes Up a Graph?

The best place to start is with a simple review of the general parts you might see on a graph:

- **Title/description:** The point of a graph is to convey information in an easily readable and accessible fashion. To do that the graph has to tell you what information it is showing you. If it doesn't clearly identify the information it is displaying, what use is it? All graphs should have a title or label of some sort that identifies what they are displaying. Some titles are more descriptive than others but in the end a title should convey the purpose of the graph.

   Reading the titles of graphs on the ACT science test is an important way to start. Because you are going to be pressed for time and trying to move through things quickly it will be important for you to identify the title to see what information each graph is showing you on the test. In many cases on the science test the title or description of a graph will be found within the passage itself. There might not be a separate label associated with each graph.

- **Legend/key:** Some graphs have a key. If so, it will be used to help you identify a specific area of the graph that has overlapping data points or lines. It is simply the graph maker's way of informing you of what information is represented by what notation on the graph. Not all graphs will have these because not all graphs convey multiple data sets in one graph.

- **Source of the information:** Generally, graphs will provide a small notation somewhere indicating the source of the information. In the case of the ACT science test the source of the graphs will generally be described in the passage itself, though not always. In many cases you will see an attribution at some point in the passage giving credit to the creator of the graph or the person who generated the information initially. Many times this is placed below the graph.

- **The x-axis:** The x-axis is the horizontal line across the bottom of a graph. It represents the values of the independent variable beginning with zero. The independent variable is the variable in the experiment that was determined by the experimenter. It is not dependent on anything and is specifically changed to allow the researcher to observe how the dependent variable changes in response.

- **The y-axis:** The y-axis is the vertical line located on the left-hand side of the graph. It represents the values of the dependent variable beginning with zero. The dependent variable in an experiment depends on the independent variable, hence, its name. It changes in accordance with the independent variable. In terms of data and the scientific method, it represents the results of the experiment that will be analyzed to determine a conclusion.

- **Labels and units:** Graphs will always label their axis to show what information is represented on each axis. Pay attention to the labels so you know what is what. Also, look at the units that the graph uses to display information. Do not ignore anything.

Identifying the parts of a graph is essential to understanding what that graph shows. If you don't bother to actually look at the information presented in a graph, how will you know what it's trying to show you? When you are reading a passage do not ignore the words on a graph. A lot of times students think that the only important portion of a graph is the actual trend line presented or the bars in a bar graph. They think the graphical portion is important and nothing else. That is not the case at all. If you don't read the words presented to you on a graph you will not know what the graph is showing you. Don't skip reading any description or identifying labels on a graph. In the end you'll have to go back and do that anyway because you won't have any success making meaning out of the graph if you don't.

Sample Passage and Graph Analysis

To help you identify the basic labels and parts of a graph here is a graph from an official ACT sample passage. Take a look at it and try to identify the different parts of the graph. Once you've done that try to draw some basic conclusions about the graph and the information presented. Included before the graph is the brief description of the graph given in the passage instead of the graph having a separate title.

Passage XI

A *blackbody* is an object that absorbs all of the radiation that strikes it. The blackbody also emits radiation at all wavelengths; the emitted radiation is called *blackbody radiation.* The brightness of blackbody radiation at a given wavelength depends on the temperature of the blackbody. A graph of brightness versus wavelength for a blackbody is called a *blackbody curve.* Blackbody curves for the same blackbody at three different temperatures are shown in the figure below.

(Note: 1 watt = 1 joule per second; joule is a unit of energy. At wavelengths above 25×10^{-6} m, the brightness of the blackbody at each temperature continues to decrease.)

A blackbody is an object that absorbs all radiation that strikes it, hence, it is called a blackbody. Yet according to the passage it also emits radiation at all wavelengths, though the brightness of the radiation is determined by the temperature of the blackbody. This graph is a blackbody curve according to the passage. Its purpose is to show the same blackbody at three different temperatures and enable you to compare the wavelength to the brightness of the light emitted.

To cover the basic parts of this graph let's break down what is represented here:

- **Title:** The title/description of the graph is given in the passage itself. There is no separate title, just a description of the passage as summarized. It tells you the purpose of the graph and the information it is attempting to show you.

- **Legend/key:** This graph shows three different data sets so it must include some way to indicate what is what. When you see a graph that shows multiple pieces of information or data sets at once, there will be a key or a distinct way to identify which information is which. In this case you are looking at a line graph with each line representing a different kelvin temperature of the blackbody. The solid line represents the blackbody at a temperature of 500 K, the larger dashed line represents it at 400 K, and the very small dashed line represents it at 300 K. This is not always standard for a line graph because there are many ways in which you can differentiate the lines. Sometimes you might see a symbol associated with each line or some other pattern used but in any case you should be able to tell the elements apart.

- **Source of the information:** In the case of this graph there is no specific source given for the information. You are simply told as the reader that this graph represents data about a blackbody at different temperatures. That is ok. If you needed to know more about the source of the information the test would tell you. This is not something you need to be worried about finding for every graph. In some cases you will see it listed but in other places you might not.

- **The x-axis:** The x-axis on this graph shows the wavelength of the light emitted by the blackbody. The axis is labeled with a unit as well: 10^{-6} m. This is a confusing unit to most students. It is saying that every number on the x-axis corresponds to that number $\times 10^{-6}$ m; for example, the 2 on the x-axis means 2×10^{-6} meters. This is not a very user-friendly notation for a graph but it is a way of not having to repetitively show the same notation on the axis. However, it is more than likely that the ACT will not expect you to deal with this unit when answering questions, so you don't have to worry too much about it. All you need to take away from it is that it is the unit used to measure the wavelength of the light emitted. The interval on the x-axis increases by 1 for each line of measure, though it only provides a numerical label for every even number.

- **The y-axis:** The y-axis on this graph measures the brightness of the light emitted by the blackbody. The units on this axis are measured in 10^6 watts per m^3. This is another unit that is not very clearly laid out or explained, so it more than likely will not be an essential piece of information you would need for any of the questions you see associated with this passage. The interval on the y-axis increases by 10 for each line of measure.

Now that you've identified the parts of the graph you can take a look at the graph and try to draw some meaning about what information the graph is showing you. The purpose of this graph is to compare the brightness of the wavelengths of light emitted by a blackbody at three different temperatures. Each line on the graph corresponds to a different temperature of the blackbody as shown in the key.

From looking at the three lines on the graph you can come to the conclusion that the higher the temperature of the blackbody, the higher the brightness of the emitted light will be. In addition, the peak brightness of the blackbody at each of the three temperatures occurs at lower wavelengths in the range of about 4×10^{-6} to 10×10^{-6} m (between 4 and 10 on the intervals shown on the x-axis). As the wavelength of the emitted light increases, the brightness significantly reduces down to where there is minimal differences between the temperatures.

Once you've identified this about the graph, along with all of the pieces of information already discussed, you are ready to deal with any questions you see. This might seem like a lot to go through in a short time when you are taking the ACT but it really shouldn't be once you've practiced enough. Your ability to interpret and read graphs will increase quickly.

Understanding Data Shown in Tables

A hugely important skill on the ACT science test is reading graphs and figuring out what you are being shown. You need to do this to interpret the information you see on the test. Yet there is more to that interpretation than just looking a graph and picking out the important parts you see. You are going to need to look at data in general and be able to quickly and efficiently interpret what that data show you. The graph is perhaps the most easily understandable of all the methods available for displaying data because it visually shows you a picture of the numbers behind the data.

The other very commonly used method for displaying a large amount of data in a concise manner is the table. You will see a large number of tables as you work through the ACT science test. They are everywhere and cannot be ignored. A table gives the researcher the ability to display a large amount of lab results or data in a short and easily readable manner.

There are some major differences between a graph and a table. The first and most obvious difference is that a table doesn't have the visual attractiveness of a graph. There is no distinct and obvious visual representation in a table to show the data. Instead a table labels all of the pieces of information you will see and then presents the information directly to you. Tables do what graphs generally don't in that they show you the actual numerical data behind the research. A graph shows you the general trend and result, yet it is hard to pick out specific numbers from a graph. You generally aren't going to be able to look at a graph and know the exact numerical value for a piece of information shown on that graph. A table shows you the exact values, the exact numbers.

A big part of the ACT is reading tables, just like it is reading graphs. Again, the largest representation of questions on the ACT science test is from the Interpretation of Data reporting category. You are going to have to look at data and read that data. Having looked at a graph in detail in the previous section we will now look at a table and discuss the major pieces that make one up.

What Are the Parts of a Table?

The major components of a table are as follows:

- **Name/title:** Just like a graph, a good table should have a name or title that provides you, the reader, with the necessary background knowledge to understand what the table is showing in the proper context. Sometimes in the ACT science test this background might be provided within the passage description rather than the specific table title or label. It will be somewhere, though, and you'll definitely want to find it and read it to understand the meaning of the table.
- **Rows and columns:** Tables use rows and columns to organize and display data. Rows are horizontal (across) in tables and columns are vertical (up and down).
- **Units/labels:** Tables will always have the data they are displaying labeled in some way along with what the numbers mean and the unit of measure. With any table you should be clearly able to find what the numbers you are seeing mean. The label for the data, which will generally consist of the unit, will be in the associated row or column for that data. Be sure to carefully identify what each column or row is showing you. Don't mix up the data or the units.
- **Captions/description:** Some tables will have a small amount of text added below them or included somewhere that will contain extra pertinent information about the data shown in the table. Not all tables have this, but every once in a while you will see it. If you do, use that information as necessary to understand the data you are seeing in the table.

Sample Table Analysis

Following is a table from an official ACT sample passage. The table is used to show the emission of CO in car exhaust across different years and model types. A full description and context for it is given in the text of this passage. If you would like to see the full text see page 82 for the passage in its entirety. Now let's look at the parts of this table in detail:

Time after starting (min)	Percent of CO in the exhaust at −9°C:			
	1978 Model X	1978 Model Y	1996 Model X	1996 Model Y
1	3.5	3.2	1.2	0.3
3	4.0	3.7	1.0	1.2
5	4.5	7.5	1.5	2.5
7	3.6	10.0	1.0	3.0
9	3.2	9.1	0.5	2.6
11	3.1	8.0	0.5	2.0
13	3.0	7.0	0.5	2.0
15	2.9	7.0	0.4	1.8

Table 1

- **Name/title:** This table is focused on the CO emissions of cars. It is titled Table 1 in the very first row. Tables on the ACT science test will not have fancy names, and they will generally be referred to as Table 1 or Table 2 and so on. You don't have to worry about dealing with odd names.
- **Rows/columns:** Directly below that you can see how the table begins to be separated into different rows and columns of information. The first column, furthest on the left, shows the time at which the emissions of CO were measured after starting the car engine. The units for the first column are labeled in *min,* which means minutes. Each row on the table corresponds to a different number of minutes since the engine was started. After the first column, the other four columns are used to show the different years and models of cars used in the study. In addition, above the four columns there is a general label associated with all four of the columns below. It says that each column represents the "Percent of CO in the exhaust at −9°C". This is the heading of the columns below it, and it also provides the unit of measure used in the columns below. In this case, the unit of measure is the percent of CO in the exhaust. There is no specific measured unit associated with these numbers, just a percent. Each column below is used to represent a different car model and year of manufacture. The first two columns show car Models X and Y from the year 1978. The third and fourth columns show car Models X and Y from the year 1996.
- **Units/labels:** There are two units used on this graph to display information. The first, in the column at the left, is the minutes at which measurements were conducted. The other unit in the four columns to the right of the graph is the percent of CO in exhaust. When you look at tables you will see that the unit of measure used in the table is rarely ever included with each numerical table value. Instead you will be given an overall label for a column indicating the unit of measure to be used for that entire data set.

Relationships Shown in Graphs and Data Sets

The next thing to look at is the relationships you will see in the data shown to you in tables and, more specifically, graphs. Many of the ACT science passages you see have data tables and graphs associated with them. Many of these questions will ask you to analyze the data you encounter to determine relationships shown in the graphs or tables. Looking at data and interpreting what you see is a major focus on the ACT. You are going to have to look at a visual display of data like a graph and be able to draw a basic conclusion about what a graph shows. It is just part of the expectation.

When doing this there are some terms you will encounter quite a bit. These are specific data analysis terms used to discuss, illustrate, or otherwise describe what you are seeing in the graph. To make sure you are familiar with these terms the following section provides a list of the most common data analysis terms you will see on the ACT science test. Where appropriate you will also see an example of a graph illustrating the concept. This is of course not the final word on data analysis but it is a good primer for you to look at and familiarize yourself with so you are never caught off guard when looking at data relationships.

Trends in Data

Trends in data is the general movement of data points in a graph or a chart showing a change toward a certain direction, outcome, or result. In more simplified terms a trend is data moving in a specific direction over time. You can see trends that show values increasing or decreasing over time. A trend might not even involve time on a graph; instead, it might involve a change over time between one experimental variable and another. It is important to note that trends are not perfect, however. To see a trend in data you do not need to have every single data point agree with the trend.

Example: Consider the stock market. It goes up and it goes down over the course of time. You might hear from time to time that the market is in an uptrend. Let's say specifically the market has been trending up for five years. This means that, in general, the market has moved up over the course of the past five years but it doesn't mean that it has always moved upward. In that five-year stretch the market also had times of moving down. A trend doesn't have to be perfect to be there; it just needs to be clearly identifiable that data are moving one way over a given period of time.

Relationships in Data

After looking at trends in data the next analysis point to discuss is the relationships you will see in data. There are two specific types you should be totally comfortable and familiar with when you take the ACT science test: direct relationship and inverse relationship.

Direct Relationship

A direct relationship between two variables or factors in an experiment is shown when they move in the same direction. If you see that variable x increases when variable y increases they have a direct relationship. If you see that variable x decreases when variable y decreases, would also have a direct relationship. A direct relationship just means that two variables will move in the same direction; they will increase or decrease.

Example: The graph below (Graph 1) shows a direct relationship between two variables. On the x-axis you have the corrected absorbance and on the y-axis you have the concentration of NO_2 in ppm (parts per million). The specifics behind the graph and what it is showing are not important to this example, so you don't have to worry about that right now. What you should focus on is that you can see how both variables increase in the same direction. They both go up together. As the corrected absorbance goes up in value, the concentration of NO_2 in ppm also moves up. This is a direct relationship.

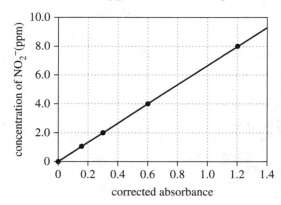

Graph 1 illustrating a direct relationship

Inverse Relationship

The second type of relationship you need to be able to identify is an inverse relationship. If two variables have an inverse relationship one of them will increase while the other decreases. In this case if variable x increases you would see that variable y decreases. When one goes up the other would do the opposite in the case of an inverse relationship.

Example: The following graph shows the volume of water measured on the y-axis compared to the day on the x-axis. Context is not essential to seeing the relationship shown by this graph so don't worry about it. Instead look at the graph to see the inverse relationship shown by the data here. As the number of days increases the volume of water measured or present decreases. This is a clear inverse relationship. As one value on the graph increases the other decreases.

Graph 1 illustrating an inverse relationship.

Other Data Analysis Terms

In addition to the relationships you will see in graphs there are a few other specific subject terms that it might not hurt to know about data and analysis. They are described in the next sections.

Correlation

You will notice that in the descriptions of direct and inverse relationships there is no mention of one variable causing the other variable to move. Instead, it is simply an observation that as one thing increases another decreases or that they both increase or decrease together. This is called a *correlation*.

Outlier

An *outlier* is a data point that does not fit into a clearly established trend or relationship in a data chart or graph. Sometimes when experiments are done there are data outliers. These can be the result of many different factors. In many cases if all of the data except for a single outlier follows a clear trend you can assume the outlier is not significant in the results. In short, don't let a single data point that goes against a clear trend change how you view the answer to a question. Thankfully when you are taking the ACT science test there will likely not be any tables or graphs that have an outlier present. The data you will see generally are clear and straightforward on the test. The test isn't designed to be confusing, so know that much about outliers isn't important, but it is safe to assume that you more than likely won't have to deal with any on the test.

Extrapolate

You may be asked to extrapolate what a future result of an experiment will be based on the data you are given. *Extrapolation* is making an informed prediction about future results based on trends in the data you are given. If you see that some value is regularly increasing over many measurements, then it is safe to extrapolate it will continue to increase in future measurements, or if all measurements under certain conditions yield a specific result, it is safe to assume that future measurements under the same conditions will yield similar results.

Example: Let's look at a data table and a question associated with that data table that expects you to extrapolate some information. You've seen in this book when discussing the reporting categories and passages. It is a great example of how you might be expected to extrapolate future results based on current information provided.

You are presented with two graphs that show the emission percent of CO in car exhaust at two different temperatures. Because you've been shown these tables before there is no need to discuss them in great depth beyond that.

Table 1				
Time after starting (min)	Percent of CO in the exhaust at −9°C:			
	1978 Model X	1978 Model Y	1996 Model X	1996 Model Y
1	3.5	3.2	1.2	0.3
3	4.0	3.7	1.0	1.2
5	4.5	7.5	1.5	2.5
7	3.6	10.0	1.0	3.0
9	3.2	9.1	0.5	2.6
11	3.1	8.0	0.5	2.0
13	3.0	7.0	0.5	2.0
15	2.9	7.0	0.4	1.8

Table 2				
Time after starting (min)	Percent of CO in the exhaust at 20°C:			
	1978 Model X	1978 Model Y	1996 Model X	1996 Model Y
1	2.0	0.8	0.3	0.2
3	2.8	2.0	0.5	1.0
5	3.4	6.0	0.5	1.5
7	1.5	7.0	0.3	0.8
9	1.3	7.0	0.3	0.5
11	1.0	6.5	0.1	0.3
13	1.0	5.0	0.1	0.3
15	0.9	4.8	0.1	0.2

The only difference between these two tables is the temperature at which the measurements were conducted. Everything else is the same. One of the questions associated with this passage presents you with four new locations and, more importantly, four new temperatures to consider.

City	Average temperature (°F) for January
Minneapolis	11.2
Pittsburgh	26.7
Seattle	39.1
San Diego	56.8

The question asks you to predict, based on the new temperatures, which location would show cars having the highest percent of CO emission in their exhaust. This is an example of extrapolation being required on the ACT science section. Usually it is associated with graphs and determining a trend line or a relationship and using it to predict future results yet it is something you can do with these charts as well. You specifically are extrapolating what the results will be of this measurement based on the temperature presented. It is a classic example of using results to predict future experimental results based on a new variable. In this case the lower temperature results show a higher percentage of CO emissions in the car exhaust. This would suggest that lower temperatures are correlated with higher CO emissions in car exhaust so the lowest-temperature city in the table would likely have the highest CO emissions in the cars.

Summary

So what is the importance of studying graphs in this section all on their own? Will you have an ACT question that specifically says, "Look at this graph and determine what the graph shows you"? No, you won't have something in such general terms like that, but you will need to look at the graphs and be able to determine the information it is showing you and the meaning of that information to answer certain questions.

In addition, reading a graph is an important skill that you need to practice to succeed on the ACT. You are going to see a large number of graphs when you take the ACT science test, and your comfort level and ability to interpret the information shown to you on those graphs will go a long way to determining how well you do on the test. Plus, it isn't just about how accurately you can read the graph. The efficiency and speed with which you read the graph is also very important. You need to be able to look at a graph and understand what it is trying to tell you in short order to succeed on the ACT science test. You can't spend a minute or two getting oriented with every graph you see. You need to look at it and quickly figure out the important parts of the graph and pick up what it is showing you.

Reading graphs is a skill that you need to practice. Treat it just like any other skill you need to work on and improve. If you want to become a better basketball player, you are going to spend a lot of time taking jump shots in a gym. People don't magically pick up something and understand it. So how can you practice your ability to read graphs more than what has already been covered in this chapter? Look through this book; there are graphs everywhere. Most of the passages you see have a graph or two. Look at the graphs and try to go through and identify the major points of the graph as discussed previously in this chapter:

- **Title/description**
- **Legend/key**
- **Source of the information**
- **The *x*-axis**
- **The *y*-axis**
- **Units/labels**

Once you've identified the points of the graph, look at the graph and try to draw some conclusions about the information you are seeing. It doesn't have to be in relation to a particular question. Just look at the graph and see what you see. The more you practice interpreting the data presented to you on the graph and drawing meaning about the information you see the easier it will become. So practice and you'll do great!

Chapter 9: Scientific Units and Measurements

In this chapter we are going to talk about the many different types of scientific measurements that you will encounter while taking the ACT science test. You will be introduced to the metric system and how it works along with common metric prefixes you can potentially expect to see. After that you will go through a review of many of the units and measurement types you may encounter.

Units in Science

In the scientific world there are so many types of measurements you can use that it can be very difficult to keep track of them. You can measure the length of something, the mass, the volume, the density, the velocity, the frequency, and so on. There are countless measurements that you can take. Each of these measurement types has a unit associated with it. In some cases these units might be something you are very familiar with, such as miles, in others you may have a passing familiarity with something, such as centimeters, or you many encounter a unit that you have never heard of, such as hertz (a measure of frequency).

The goal of this chapter is to provide you with a solid background on the most common potential units and measurements you may encounter on the ACT science test. When finished the hope is that you will feel relatively comfortable recognizing and understanding the meaning behind units that you otherwise might not have known. Yet this isn't all-encompassing, and there very well may be something not covered in this book that shows up on the ACT science test. That is okay. The hope is that after you read this chapter you will feel comfortable and be able to better deal with unfamiliar measurements.

One of the most challenging aspects of science for students is that any numbers they encounter have units associated with them. This is a major break from the way students see numbers presented in math class. In math class you are usually just dealing with numbers and those numbers often do not represent a physical quantity or measurement of something. In science numbers do represent something, and that is why they have units associated with them.

Understanding Why Units Matter for the ACT Science Test

What importance do units play in an ACT science question or passage? If you've done some previous reading about the ACT or taken the science portion before you probably know that you aren't really going to be expected to perform calculations based on any measurements you see. You just need to read the calculations and use them to better understand the passage and questions.

So why is there an entire chapter in this book dedicated to those units and measurements? Because being comfortable with units and measurements will make it much easier for you to understand their meaning when you do see them in problems. It will save you time on the test and help you keep your focus on the problems you are being asked to solve rather than on trying to figure out what a couple of seemingly random letters after a number mean.

The SI System of Units (Metric Units)

The place to start when discussing scientific measurements is a brief discussion of the International System of Units (the SI system), which you may know better as the metric system. The metric system is a system of measurement that is widely used in science and throughout the world. It is composed of seven different base units that enable you to measure the physical quantity or amount of a multitude of things. Table 9.1 details each of the metric base units and what they are used to measure.

Table 9.1 The Basics of Metric Base Units

Base Unit	Abbreviation	Description
Meter	m	The meter is the metric unit for **length**. Length can simply be defined as how long something is. The length of 1 meter exactly is defined as the length of the path light travels in a vacuum during 1/299,792,458 of a second. In your day-to-day existence you can see the length of a meter quite easily by looking at a meter stick (a ruler that measures 1 meter). Some of your teachers likely have a bunch of meter sticks in their room so don't hesitate to ask to see one.

Table 9.1 The Basics of Metric Base Units (*continued*)

Base Unit	Abbreviation	Description
Kilogram	**kg**	The kilogram is the metric unit for **mass**. Mass is the amount of matter in an object. It is independent of gravity. Do not confuse mass with weight, which is dependent on gravity. The exact definition of what a kilogram is has recently changed. One exact kilogram used to be determined by the mass of a solid chunk of platinum-iridium alloy. The definition recently changed to be based on a numerical constant value called the *Plank constant*. The definition is beyond the scope of this book so it will not be included here. However, if you want to get a general idea of what a kilogram is, go find a liter of water. One liter of water almost has an exact mass of 1 kilogram.
Second	**s**	The base unit for **time** is the second. The second is defined as the duration of 9,192,631,770 cycles of radiation corresponding to the transition between two hyperfine levels of the cesium-133 atom. You probably have some familiarity with what 1 second of time is. Don't let the very complicated scientific definition of a second confuse you at all. If you want to know about how long a second is, just say the number *one* out loud at pace that isn't too slow or too fast and you'll have just spent 1 second exactly.
Kelvin	**K**	The base unit for **temperature** measurements in the metric system is the kelvin. The definition of 1 kelvin is rather complex and will not be included here. The kelvin temperature scale is an absolute scale. There are no degrees associated with it like the other two major scales you are familiar with: Fahrenheit and Celsius. The kelvin temperature scale also does not go below zero. There is a theoretical bottom point to kelvin (called *absolute zero*) where there is no thermodynamic energy present. So there are no negatives in the kelvin temperature scale. To give you an idea of the kelvin scale compared to Fahrenheit and Celsius you can say that 273 K is about equal to 0 degrees Celsius or about 32 degrees Fahrenheit.
Ampere	**A**	The base unit for measuring **electric current** is the ampere. This is more commonly referred to as an *amp*. The definition of one ampere recently changed and is now based on the elementary charge. You do not need to concern yourself with any of that, however. Simply know that if you see *amp, A,* or *ampere* presented to you in a problem that it is in reference to electrical current in some form.
Candela	**cd**	The base unit for **luminous intensity** is called the *candela*. In simple terms luminous intensity just means the **light** given off by something. You will not encounter this metric base unit very often. However, it is one of the seven metric base units so it is included here. If you do see it know that it is simply referring to how much light is given off by an object. For a frame of reference: 1 candela is roughly equivalent to the light given off by a simple single-wick candle.
Mole	**mol**	The base unit for the **amount of a substance** that you have is called the *mole*. The mole is most commonly used when determining the quantity of particles, commonly atoms or molecules, you have in a substance. If you encounter it on the ACT it will be in reference to an amount of something.

These are the base units the metric system uses to measure everything. However, after reading through the chart you probably are asking yourself where some rather well-known commonly used units are. The first one that probably jumps out into your mind is the liter. It is a unit that has become common place to use throughout the world and even in the United States, though the metric system is not the primary system of measurement there.

You can go to the store and easily buy a two-liter bottle of pop (or soda) if you would like. It clearly says on the bottom of the bottle that the quantity of liquid inside is two liters. Yet liter is not mentioned anywhere as a metric base unit in the chart. There is a reason for that. The liter is a *derived* unit. A derived unit is a measurement derived from one or more of the metric base units. What does *derived* mean? In simple terms it means that when you combine one or more of the metric base units through a mathematical relationship you arrive at a derived unit.

To the say the least, there are a lot of derived metric units, far too many for this book to cover. Nor would it be useful for you to see hundreds of possible unit combinations. Instead in Table 9.2 you will see the most commonly used and referenced derived metric units along with a short explanation of what they mean and how they are used. This again, is not all-encompassing but it shows you the ones that you should be most familiar with.

Table 9.2 Derived Metric Units

Unit Name	Abbreviation	Description
Liters	L	**Liters** are used to measure volume. Volume is simply the physical space an object takes up. Volume can also be represented as a cubed length measurement, such as cm^3 or m^3.
Hertz	Hz	**Hertz** is a measure of frequency. Frequency is defined as the number of waves that pass a fixed point in a given amount of time. Frequency is often denoted as 1/S or S^{-1} with s representing seconds.
Newton	N	**Newton** is the derived unit in the SI/metric system that represents force. Force is defined as any interaction that can change the motion of an object.
Pascal	Pa	**Pascal** is the SI unit for pressure. Pressure is defined as the force applied per unit area by one substance on another. There are many units beyond pascal that are used to represent pressure in science, and they will be discussed later in this chapter.
Joule	J	**Joule** is the SI unit used to represent energy. Energy is defined as the ability to do work or heat an object. There are many types of energy such as kinetic, potential, chemical, thermal, and radiant.
Watt	W	**Watt** is the SI unit used to measure power. Power can be defined as the amount of energy delivered per unit time with the standard units of it being J/s.

There are many other named derived units that make up the metric system, however, these are the units you are most likely to encounter. Something to keep in mind when dealing with all of these units and reading through this chapter is that you are not going to be expected to perform calculations or conversions using these units. These units will be used to identify quantities in the graphs and tables you encounter. The reasoning for including this section, again, is to make it easier and faster for you to understand what quantities these units are representing when you see them in a problem.

It is hoped that after reading through this chapter if you see something measured in joules that you'll know it is referencing energy. It will definitely help speed up your reading and understanding of whatever concept is being presented.

Metric Prefixes and How to Use Them

This next section includes a breakdown of the possible metric prefixes you will encounter on the ACT science section. The metric system is based on multiples of ten. It uses the base units shown above along with prefixes that are added to the front of the base unit. These prefixes corresponded to different size measurements with each one representing a multiple of ten.

Some of the prefixes are very commonly used with certain base units and are more than likely familiar to you from school or your day-to-day life. Measurements such as centimeters, kilometers, milliliters, and kilograms are referenced often enough that you have probably seen them and maybe have even measured things in them. You might be less familiar with a hectometer or a dekagram, yet those prefixes are also regularly used when dealing with metric units.

In total there are twenty metric prefixes that can be applied to metric base units. Table 9.3 shows you all of them. Again, you are not going to be required to use these prefixes to perform metric conversions like you may have in school. These are simply included so that when you see something with a prefix such as *nano-* or *mega-* you will have a general idea of where it falls in terms of size.

Table 9.3 Twenty Metric Prefixes

Prefix name	Letter symbol of prefix	Value in exponential form	Value in words	Value in decimal form
yotta-	Y	10^{24}	Septillion	1000000000000000000000000
zetta-	Z	10^{21}	Sextillion	1000000000000000000000
exa-	E	10^{18}	Quintillion	1000000000000000000
peta-	P	10^{15}	Quadrillion	1000000000000000
tera-	T	10^{12}	Trillion	1000000000000
giga-	G	10^{9}	Billion	1000000000
mega-	M	10^{6}	Million	1000000
kilo-	k	10^{3}	Thousand	1000

(continued)

Table 9.3 Twenty Metric Prefixes (*continued*)

Prefix name	Letter symbol of prefix	Value in exponential form	Value in words	Value in decimal form
hecto-	h	10^2	Hundred	100
deka-	da	10^1	Ten	10
Base Unit		10^0	**One**	**1**
deci-	d	10^{-1}	Tenth	0.1
centi-	c	10^{-2}	Hundredth	0.01
milli-	m	10^{-3}	Thousandth	0.001
micro-	μ	10^{-6}	Millionth	0.000001
nano-	n	10^{-9}	Billionth	0.000000001
pico-	p	10^{-12}	Trillionth	0.000000000001
femto-	f	10^{-15}	Quadrillionth	0.000000000000001
atto-	a	10^{-18}	Quintillionth	0.000000000000000001
zepto-	z	10^{-21}	Sextillionth	0.000000000000000000001
yocto-	y	10^{-24}	Septillionth	0.000000000000000000000001

In looking at Table 9.3 you can see how there are numerical prefixes that you most likely will never encounter in your day-to-day life or even in your scientific studies. One thing in particular to notice from Table 9.3 is that all of the prefixes have normal letter abbreviations except for the prefix *micro-*. Micro uses the symbol μ- as a prefix. This is important to keep in mind because measurements like μl (microliters) or μm (micrometers) are seen somewhat commonly on the ACT science portion.

Also notice the capitalization of the letter abbreviations in the prefixes. Some are capitalized and some are not. When looking at metric prefixes capitalization matters. If you see a lowercase *m* it is in reference to the *milli-* prefix but if you see a capital *M* it is in reference to the *mega-* prefix. When you look at the chart you can see how mega- is quite a bit larger than milli- so it would not be good to get them mixed up!

Looking at a chart like Table 9.3 can be quite intimidating, especially if you are not comfortable with the numbers you are seeing. Thankfully you aren't going to be expected to deal with most of those prefixes often if ever. The most common range of metric prefixes that you will see is from milli- to kilo- on most things you encounter on the ACT science section and your day-to-day life.

To make it a little more palatable for you, take a look at Table 9.4. This one cuts off everything else and just shows you those specific prefixes. It might be helpful for you to look over this chart a little bit more carefully and try to commit it to memory. Again, it isn't a requirement for you in any way to do conversions on the ACT, but it really can make your life easier and your understanding of the problems faster once you are more comfortable with the metric prefixes, especially the most common and basic ones in Table 9.4.

Table 9.4 Most Common Metric Prefixes

Prefix name	Letter symbol of prefix	Value in exponential form	Value in words	Value in decimal form
kilo-	k	10^3	Thousand	1000
hecto-	h	10^2	Hundred	100
deka-	da	10^1	Ten	10
Base Unit		10^0	**One**	1
deci-	d	10^{-1}	Tenth	0.1
centi-	c	10^{-2}	Hundredth	0.01
milli-	m	10^{-3}	Thousandth	0.001

A common mistake to pay attention to specifically in these prefixes is the use of deka- and deci-. They both start with *d* yet the prefix for *deka-* is *da* and the prefix for *deci-* is *d.* It is a simple thing that trips many students up at some point or another.

Review of the Many Types of Units and Measures You May Encounter

Now that we've covered the SI/metric system in some depth it is time to look at some of the other common units you might encounter when taking the ACT science test. The metric system is very commonly used in all sciences, yet there are many other kinds of units that you will also see in science all the time. The goal of this section is to talk about and describe as many of those other units as possible for you.

Again, this is not a comprehensive list by any means, but it is hoped that it will give you a good foundation for anything you might encounter on the test. To do that, units have been grouped together based on what they measure. Some of the metric units will also be included in this section again just as a way of showing you their most common variations. This section will show you many common units used when performing basic measurements and the numerical conversions between those units. The conversions are included simply to give you a general idea regarding the relative size of each unit in comparison to one another.

Units of Length

What is length? Length is used to show the physical distance of an object from end point to end point. In simpler terms, length tells you how long something is. There are several common length measurements that you should be familiar with, and this section will explain each and show you any useful or meaningful conversions it might help to be familiar with.

Metric Length Units

The metric base unit for length is meters (m). Common prefixes used when dealing with meters are kilometers (km), centimeters (cm), and millimeters (mm).

To give you an idea of the relative size of each

> 1 km = 1000 m = 100000 cm = 1000000 mm.

Nonmetric Length Units

The other units of length that you are probably more familiar with are miles (mi), yards (yd), feet (ft), and inches (in), which are considered US customary units.

To give you an idea of the relative size of each here are a few helpful conversions:

> 1 mile (mi) = 1760 yards (yd) = 5280 feet (ft)
>
> 1 yd = 3 ft
>
> 1 ft = 12 inches (in)

One final conversion that you might be interested in is a conversion that enables you to compare the length of metric units to nonmetric units so here are a couple of common ones.

> 1 km = 1.6 miles
>
> 1 in = 2.54 cm

Units of Mass and Weight

What is mass? Mass is the amount of matter in an object. Mass can easily be confused with weight, which takes gravity into account when making measurements. However, this distinction is not really something you need to worry that much about on the ACT. If you see measurements for mass they will generally be in one of a few possible units.

Metric Mass Units

The metric base units for mass is the kilogram (kg). Other common prefixes and metric units used for measuring mass are gram (g) and milligram (mg).

To give you an idea of the relative size of each here are a few helpful conversions:

> 1 kg = 1000 g = 1000000 mg

Nonmetric Mass and Weight Units

There are other units you may be more familiar with in regards to weight and mass. When you stand on a scale the scale probably doesn't show your weight in kilograms. Instead it probably shows your weight in pounds (lb). This is a common enough unit that you've encountered before. In addition, you may have dealt with tons or ounces (oz).

To give you an idea of the relative size of each here are a few helpful conversions:

1 ton = 2000 lb

1 lb = 16 oz

Units of Volume

Volume is defined as the space an object takes up. It is something you should be somewhat familiar with based on filling up a gas tank or buying milk at the grocery store. Many things you encounter in your daily life deal with volume. There are metric volume units and nonmetric volume units.

Metric Volume Units

The metric base unit for volume is the liter (l). The other commonly used prefix with volume is the milliliter (ml).

For reference

1 liter (l) = 1000 milliliters (ml)

Nonmetric Volume Units

There are nonmetric units for volume but you will rarely, if ever, see them used in the sciences. In your day-to-day life they pop up but they are likely not going to be something you see on the ACT science section. For the sake of completeness though a couple that you probably are familiar with would be a gallon, a quart, or a pint.

Units of Time

Not to be overlooked is time. It is one of, if not *the* most, commonly measured things on this planet. You deal with time every single day. If you can honestly say there has been a day that has gone by where you have never once considered what time it is or how long something or other would take then consider yourself lucky.

The base unit for time is seconds (s). You are more than likely familiar with some of the other units used to measure time as well, such as hours (hr), days, years. Yet there may be a few time measurements that you are not familiar with but that you might see mentioned in one of the passages on the ACT science test. One in particular that is seen somewhat regularly is the nanosecond (ns).

1 second = 10^9 (1000000000) nanoseconds

Units of Temperature

Another unit that is used so regularly it might be taken for granted is temperature. The metric base unit for temperature is kelvin (k). The kelvin scale is an absolute temperature scale that has no degrees. It simply is kelvin. There is no below zero in the kelvin temperature scale. Why? It actually begins at zero and goes up from there. What is this zero that it begins at? The zero point is called *absolute zero*. It is the point at which an object would have zero thermal energy of any kind. It is the most commonly used measurement unit for temperature in the scientific community.

Yet when you check the temperature outside on your phone or see the weather report on the TV it more than likely isn't being reported in kelvin temperature. Instead it is reported in Fahrenheit (°F) or Celsius (°C) depending on where you are in the world. These temperature scales are the commonly used ones throughout the world. Neither is an absolute scale like the kelvin scale. Both can go below zero and are measured in degrees.

To give you a conversion among the three temperature scales you can look at a few commonly understood temperatures.

Boiling Water
100°C = 212°F = 373 K

Freezing Water
0°C = 32°F = 273 K

And now if you want to see what the coldest temperature attainable would be let's look at what absolute zero looks like in each temperature scale.

−273°C = −460°F = 0 K

Pressure Units

Pressure units are something you will encounter from time to time on the ACT science test. The metric base unit for pressure is the pascal (Pa). You may also encounter the kilopascal (kPa) from time to time as well. For your reference: 1 kPa = 1000 Pa.

There are a couple of other types of pressure units that you may encounter as well when looking at science data on the ACT. Perhaps the most commonly referenced in science materials after the pascal is atmospheres (atm). One atmosphere is roughly equivalent to the pressure exerted by the atmosphere at sea level. For reference 1 atm = 101.325 kPa.

Millimeters of mercury (mmHg) is another commonly referenced unit of pressure. It originated when pressure measurements were taken by measuring the height of a mercury column in barometers and manometers. For reference 760 mmHg = 1 atm.

Concentration Measurements

Concentration is a measure that shows the amount of a solute dissolved into a solvent. This can apply to many things, but it is best to look at it from the perspective of a solution. To give a quick example: imagine you are putting hot chocolate mix into water. The hot chocolate mix is the solute and the water is the solvent. The more hot chocolate mix (solute) you add to the water (solvent) without increasing the amount of water the more concentrated the solution. If you were to increase the water amount (solvent) without altering the amount of hot chocolate mix (solute) you would be making the solution more dilute.

The most commonly used concentration measurement that you will encounter is called molarity (M). The capitalization of the M is important as lowercase m represents another concentration called molality. Molarity is defined as the moles of solute over the liters of solution which can be written as mol/L or represented by M. So if you ever see something mention a molar concentration, molarity, or see a large M after a number you should know that it is in reference to concentration.

Density

Density is defined as the mass of a substance over the volume it takes up. Density is usually taught as a simple formula stating mass over volume. It is important to realize though when looking at density that because it is a ratio of mass to volume then it can have many possible units associated with it. Any mass unit over any volume unit is considered a density unit. The most common density units that you will see are g/ml, g/cm^3, or kg/l.

Units of Speed

Speed is another unit that you probably have some familiarity with. Perhaps you've driven in a car at some point or seen a speed limit posted on the side of a road. These are measurements of speed. They generally are a ratio based on the length you are moving over a unit of time it takes you to move across that distance. The most common measure of speed is miles per hour (mph) or miles/hr. If you see a sign on the side of the road indicating the speed limit is 70 miles/hour that means that your car is not supposed to travel more than 70 miles in 1 hour. The other common unit of speed that you may encounter is kilometers per hour (kph) or km/hr.

pH Measurements

pH is a measurement that is used to determine how acidic or basic a solution is based on the concentration of hydrogen ions present. It is a logarithmic scale that has a range of 0–14. Any solution with a low pH, in the range of 0–6, is considered to be acidic. An example from day-to-day life is Coca-Cola or lemon juice. Anything with a pH of 7 exactly is considered to be neutral and is neither an acid or a base. An example is pure water. Any solution with a pH in the range of 8–14 is considered to be basic. A common example is most soaps or cleaning solutions. For more on pH be sure to look at chapter 10 where pH and other science vocabulary words are discussed in more depth.

Conversion between Metric and Nonmetric Units

Sometimes you may be faced with a need to convert between metric units and nonmetric units. It isn't a common occurrence because most scientific measurements and units used are metric based but, every once in a while, it might be something you need to do. If nothing else, having some level of familiarity with the relative size of units will make it easier for you to visualize the units you are dealing with in the passages and problems.

Specifically, you might not have a real concrete understanding of what exactly a kilometer is in your own personal life experience. You might have never measured one out or ran one or really just considered how long a kilometer is. If you're not familiar with the kilometer, you probably do have some familiarity with a mile and probably have some idea of the actual distance that makes up a mile. This section is just here to enable you to contextualize and how certain units compare to others.

Table 9.5 shows some of the most common metric measurements along with a conversion to their equivalent nonmetric unit. You won't be expected to perform these conversions on the ACT science test but it is not a bad idea to just be aware of them. Anything that makes it easier for you to interpret the data and measurements you see in the passages and questions is good.

Table 9.5 Metric Units versus Nonmetric Units

Distance
1.6 kilometers (km) = 1 mile (mi)
2.54 centimeters (cm) = 1 inch (in)
0.91 meters (m) = 1 yard (yd)
Weight
1 kilogram (kg) = 2.2 pounds (lb)
28.3 grams (g) = 1 ounce (oz)
Volume
3.78 liters (L) = 1 gallon (gal)
0.95 liters (L) = 1 quart (qt)
Temperature
100 °C = 212 °F = 373 K
0°C = 32 °F = 273 K

Summary

After reading through this chapter you can tell there are quite a few scientific units and measurements. In fact, there are many that were not included in this review chapter. What you've seen presented here are the most commonly encountered units that you will see when taking the ACT science test. The best thing you can do with this information is to review it and familiarize yourself with the units presented. A strong understanding of the metric system, especially the most commonly used prefixes, is probably the singular best thing you could spend your time studying, but everything in this chapter might prove valuable.

You don't need a perfect understanding of any of this. Simply a familiarity with measurements and units in general will make your life easier on the ACT science test. It won't magically help you know the answer to any of the questions but it will make it easier and quicker for you to read the passages and understand them.

Chapter 10: Science Vocabulary

In this chapter we are going to talk about some of the common scientific vocabulary you will encounter when taking the ACT science test. There are a lot of science specific vocabulary words that you are going to encounter, and it helps to be a bit more familiar with them if possible. This chapter won't cover everything you might encounter, but the hope is it will get you prepared to understand or at least make meaning out of the science words you do see. This chapter will focus on the more basic scientific terms you might encounter first and then move into some subject-specific ones. In the hopes of it not reading like a glorified glossary, you will see some sections that just have definitions but others that elaborate in more detail on some of the words and concepts covered within.

The Vocabulary of Science

Science is a broad field. It covers a vast amount of information and content ranging from the natural life sciences, such as biology, to hard physical sciences, such as chemistry and physics.

Each subject contains its own unique knowledge base and content. Each has its own unique set of vocabulary terms and other material that you have to be familiar with to successfully answer questions and work with it.

It is safe to say that one of, if not, *the* most intimidating things when reading anything scientific is the sheer amount of unfamiliar and complicated vocabulary words that you encounter. If you are reading something about biology it will probably sound different than something written about chemistry or physics. Yet if you get even more specific there are so many subtopics that you could cover in chemistry, physics, biology, earth science, and more that the sheer weight of everything you might see can be downright bothersome.

The nice thing about the ACT science section is that it won't require you to have an in-depth understanding of the words you will see that are specific to some scientific experiment or another. If you need to know the definition of a specific vocabulary word in the science section it will be provided. For example, let's say you encounter a passage discussing the nesting habits of mole rats. The ACT is not going to expect that you are an expert on mole rats. Anything you need to know about the nesting habits of mole rats will be provided to you. You'll just need to read the passage carefully and make sure you pick up all of the information.

However, there is a good chance that the passage about mole rats will mention some other scientific terms or concepts that might not otherwise be defined for you. What if it says they are nocturnal or gives some other behavior traits? What if it mentions something about their nesting patterns based on climate? There are so many possibilities you might see. Again, if it is essential to answering the question it will be defined, but the speed at which you can process the question and take all of the information in can be increased substantially if you are comfortable with the wording. It can simply help to be able to read a passage and clearly know that certain words refer to the name of a species, that other words are behavioral traits, and that yet other words describe perhaps their food or nesting tendencies.

Simply having the knowledge that a scientific term fits into a broader category can help you out a lot. As you read this section the idea is for you to get more and more comfortable identifying what science words are and what they mean. You aren't going to become an expert on all science here but the hope is this chapter will give you a good background that will enable you to make decisions about the meaning and importance of science terms as you take the test. The less time you spend considering the meaning of a word is more time you can spend finding the answer to the question within the passage.

General Scientific Terms

First are some of the basic scientific vocabulary words that you may see on the ACT science test. There are quite a few words you might encounter that aren't subject-specific in science. They are based instead on the process of science, the scientific method, and data analysis. They can be equally likely to show up in any number of different questions and passages about any topic.

Terms Related to Experiments

These terms are ones that you will see quite a bit on the ACT science test. They have been mentioned throughout this book in other areas regarding the scientific method and the passage types but are all collected here for you to reference easily. It isn't all-encompassing but it covers the big ones that are very important to know. All of the definitions associated with these words are focused on how they pertain to scientific experiments.

Question: A **question** is generally the starting point of an experiment. It is the information the experiment is trying to determine and provide an answer to.

Hypothesis: A **hypothesis** is generally used to predict the outcome of an experiment based on the researcher's knowledge of the topic. The key difference between a hypothesis and a guess is that a hypothesis is an educated guess on the topic. It isn't completely speculative because it uses previous knowledge and intelligent informed prediction to try to determine the outcome of an experiment. In simplistic terms it is a guess that is made with sound scientific reasoning behind it.

Method: A research **method** is the process by which researchers go about answering a question or proving/disproving their hypothesis. Research methods need to be repeatable, meaning that any other scientist should be able to follow the same research process to get the same result as the original study. There are many types of research methods a scientist may use when performing an experiment.

Procedure: A **procedure** is the step-by-step process used by the scientist during the experiment. In your experience as a student it is the specific directions provided to you when doing a lab in science class.

Observation: In terms of an experiment, **observation** is something that occurs as a researcher watches or records some factor, variable, or other portion of the experiment.

Quantitative: **Quantitative** observation or data collection is a method that involves using numerical values or measured quantities.

Qualitative: **Qualitative** observation or data collection is a method that is based on observed, non-numerical factors. An easy way to remember the difference between quantitative and qualitative is that quantitative is based on quantities and qualitative involves the "quality" of an object instead of its quantity.

Variable: A **variable** is anything that can change or is changed during an experiment. It can be the temperature an experiment is conducted at, the location, the speed a reaction takes place at, or one of countless other possible experimental variations that can occur.

There are three types of variables you will encounter when dealing with experiments.

> **Control variable:** A **control variable** is something that is intentionally not changed throughout an experiment and is not a focus or active part of the experiment. It is held constant. This is usually something that is not actively a part of the experimental process but could have an impact if it is changed from trial to trial.

Independent variable: An **independent variable** is changed or altered specifically by the experimenter with the intention of seeing how it affects other variables that are being measured or observed.

Dependent variable: A **dependent variable** is something that is being observed. The researcher's main goal in an experiment is to see how the dependent variable changes based on the changes intentionally made to the independent variable. It is called a dependent variable because it is dependent on the independent variable. If that is changed, the dependent variables should change also.

The next thing to look at is the idea of there being different groups of subjects used during certain experiments.

Control group and experimental group: In some experiments the thing being tested is broken up into two groups. One group has a variable altered or changed in some specific way and one group does not have anything changed. Researchers observe what happens to the group with the changed variable and compare it to what happens in the non-altered group. The group that does not have anything changed is called the **control group.** The group that has some variable changed is called the **experimental group.** A good example is in drug research. This is simplified significantly, but if a scientist believes that a drug may help cure a disease, the best way to test it is to see if giving it to patients with the disease helps them get better. The way this is tested is by breaking patients up into two groups, a control group and an experimental group. The control group would not receive the new drug but the experimental group would. The scientist would then compare the results of the control group patients with the experimental group patients. This way they can say that if the experimental group patients got better but the control group patients did not then the new drug was the cause of the improvement. If there is no control group there would be no way for the scientist to confidently say the reason for the improvement was the drug.

Conclusion: A summation of the experiment that usually accepts or refutes the hypothesis initially presented. Generally a well-thought-out **conclusion** will support itself using data generated by the research. A scientist won't simply say my "hypothesis was right." Instead a scientist would say, "my hypothesis was right because the experiment showed x, y, and z."

Terms Related to Data and Data Analysis

The next set of terms you are going to see are related to data and data analysis. They are also included almost verbatim in the graphing and data analysis chapter but are included here as well for the sake of having a complete vocabulary chapter for easy reference.

Many of the ACT science passages have data tables and graphs associated with them. The questions will sometimes ask you to analyze the data and determine relationships shown in the graphs or tables. When the questions do this you will encounter some specific terms that you should know.

Trend: A **trend** is a general direction of data points in a graph a chart. A line graph that is clearly showing an increase in data measurement as time progresses would be considered an upward trend.

A trend is simply when you look at data and it moves in a specific direction. A trend, however, does not require that every data point in a graph or table support it completely. If thirteen out of fifteen data points show an upward movement in a measurement, that can be considered an uptrend. Even though there are two data points that go against the trend the overall result of the data show an uptrend.

Direct relationship: A **direct relationship** between two variables or factors in an experiment moves in the same direction. If you see that variable x increases when variable y increases the two have a direct relationship. If you see that variable x decreases when variable y decreases the two would also have a direct relationship. A direct relationship just means that two variables will move in the same direction: increase or decrease.

Indirect relationship: If two variables have an **indirect relationship,** one of them will increase while the other decreases. In this case if variable x increases you would see that variable y decreases. When one goes up the other would do the opposite in an indirect relationship.

Correlation: A **correlation** is simply an observation that as one thing increases another decreases or that they both increase or decrease together.

Outlier: An **outlier** is a data point that does not fit into a clearly established trend or relationship you see in a data chart or graph. Sometimes when experiments are done there can be data outliers. These can be the result of many different factors. In many cases if all of the data except for a single outlier follows a clear trend you can assume the outlier is not significant in the results. In short, don't let a single data point that goes against a clear trend change how you view the answer to a question. Outliers exist in data sometimes perhaps because a measurement was not done perfectly every trial, or there was some other source of error, maybe the chemical mixture used in the reactants was a bit off, and so on. There are so many potential reasons why you might have an outlier or two present in the data. If there is, again, don't let it bother you or change how you view the results.

Extrapolation: You may be asked to extrapolate what a future result of an experiment will be based on the data you are given. **Extrapolation** is making an informed prediction about future results based on trends in the data you are given. If you see that some value is regularly increasing over many measurements then it is safe to extrapolate it will continue to increase in future measurements.

Chemistry and Biology Terminology

After going through the terms focusing on the scientific method and process and data analysis, the next terms that you should review are some subject-specific vocabulary that you will potentially encounter on the ACT science test. There is no guarantee that you will see these but consider this a science primer on some of the most commonly covered and discussed content vocabulary in science.

In the following are vocabulary words that are specific to a certain science subject such as chemistry or biology. The terms have been grouped together by subject and the specific topics they refer to. An in-depth understanding of the concepts presented here is not required but a familiarity with each will definitely prove useful and let you move more efficiently through the ACT science test.

Instead of providing a word list for each topic, however, the subjects will be discussed in general terms with the vocabulary-specific words in bold. This way you don't have to just read yet another list of terms with little to no context. Some of this will be pretty basic review for you and if it is, that's great. It can never hurt though to brush up on science terms, and you even might see a few you aren't as familiar with. Plus, you are going to see official ACT science passages included in some of the content sections. These passages are included to show you how and where you might potentially see some of the science vocabulary being discussed in each of the sections. They are just there to give you some grounding for this information and how you might use it when you take the ACT science test. You aren't going to need to master these topics at all but a passing familiarity will make your test experience a bit easier.

Matter and Changes

The simplest definition of **matter** is anything that has mass and takes up space (has a volume). When you think about what fits that description you should quickly realize it is pretty much everything that physically exists except empty space. Matter exists most commonly in three phases, solid, liquid, and gas.

Solid: **Solids** are rigid, meaning they appear to not move. They maintain their shape and volume.

Liquid: A **liquid** is a free-flowing substance with the particles clearly able to move around one another. Liquids have a definite volume but no defined shape. They take the shape of whatever container you put them in.

Gas: A **gas** is composed of particles moving very quickly relative to a solid or liquid. Gases have no defined volume and no definite shape.

Once you've identified the three major phases of matter you now need to think about how matter can change between those phases. Some of these phase changes you are more than likely familiar with, but others you might not have spent much time thinking about. Table 10.1 provides you with the name of the associated phase change along with what happens.

Table 10.1 Phase Changes

Name of Phase Change	What happens?
Melting	Solid to Liquid
Freezing	Liquid to solid
Boiling/Evaporation	Liquid to gas
Condensation	Gas to liquid
Sublimation	Solid to gas
Deposition	Gas to solid

When you think of matter one of the things that might spring to mind is your chemistry class and the periodic table of elements. It isn't something you need to worry about for the ACT science test. As far as terminology goes, though, it would help to understand that an **element** is the simplest unique form of matter that you can have. The identity of an element is determined by its atomic number, which corresponds to the number of **protons** found in the **nucleus** of the **atom.**

An **atom** is the smallest unique particle of matter that exists. Atoms are composed of three **subatomic particles.** A subatomic particle is something that is smaller than an atom, hence the name *sub*atomic. The three subatomic particles are **protons, neutrons, and electrons.** Protons and neutrons are found in the **nucleus,** the middle of an atom, and electrons are found around the outer shell of an atom. Table 10.2 shows you each subatomic particle along with its location and charge.

Table 10.2 Subatomic Particle Locations and Charges

Name	Charge	Location
Proton	Positively charged (+)	Nucleus
Neutron	Neutral, no charge (0)	Nucleus
Electron	Negatively charged (−)	Outer shell of atom

Atoms are identified by their number of protons. If you could theoretically change the number of protons present in the nucleus of an atom, you would change the elemental identity of that atom. It would become a different element. In addition, sometimes different atoms of the same element have different properties. This occurs because they are isotopes.

Isotopes are atoms of the same element with different numbers of neutrons in their nucleus. The sum of the protons and neutrons in an individual atom is called the **mass number.** Sometimes isotopes are noted by their mass number using one of several possible notations.

There are two stable isotopes of carbon: one has a mass number of 12 and one has a mass number of 13. These can be written as follows: carbon –12 and carbon –13 or ^{12}C and ^{13}C. In both types of abbreviation, you have the mass number along with the name or symbol of the element. If you are dealing with isotopes it is important to remember that even though they may have different properties due to the number of neutrons being different they have the same number of protons because they are still the same element. To give an example of how isotopes can come up in the science test read the following research summaries passage and see how isotopes are used and mentioned throughout it.

Passage XVIII

The study of oxygen isotopes present in water can give us clues to the climate of a certain location. The ratio of the isotopes ^{18}O and ^{16}O in a sample of rain, snow or ice is compared to the $^{18}O/^{16}O$ ratio in a *standard sample*. A standard sample has a known value for the parameter being measured. The comparison of a sample's ratio to that of the standard is called the *O-18 index* ($\delta^{18}O$). The $\delta^{18}O$ is calculated using the formula:

$$\delta^{18}O = \frac{(^{18}O/^{16}O)_{sample} - (^{18}O/^{16}O)_{standard}}{(^{18}O/^{16}O)_{standard}} \times 1{,}000$$

Scientists conducted three studies to examine the $\delta^{18}O$ of glacial ice in Arctic and Antarctic locations and learn about the past climates there.

Study 1

Containers were placed on glaciers at 25 locations in the Arctic to collect snowfall. The containers' contents were collected every two weeks during a one-year period and analyzed for ^{16}O and ^{18}O. Figure 1 shows the calculated monthly $\delta^{18}O$ and air temperature averages.

Figure 1

Study 2

At the 25 Arctic locations from Study 1, a 500-m-deep vertical ice core was drilled. Each core represented the past 100,000 years of glacial ice accumulation at the site. Starting at the surface, samples were taken every 10 m along the length of the cores. These samples were analyzed for ^{18}O and ^{16}O. Larger $\delta^{18}O$ values indicate that a relatively warmer climate existed at the time the ice was formed than do smaller $\delta^{18}O$ values. The calculated average $\delta^{18}O$ values for the samples are shown in Figure 2.

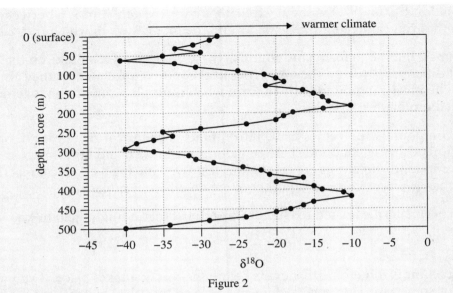

Figure 2

Study 3

The procedures of Study 2 were repeated at 25 Antarctic locations. The past 100,000 years of glacial ice accumulation at the site was represented by a 300-m ice core. The calculated average $\delta^{18}O$ values for the samples are shown in Figure 3.

Figure 3

In this example passage you can see there are multiple references to isotopes made throughout the introductory paragraph and studies presented. It clearly isn't essential to solving the problem but having that extra comfort with isotopes and the way they are written can make this question far easier to answer. If you have no idea what an isotope is you are potentially going to struggle identifying and dealing with the notation provided to you. You might not understand why there are numbers in front of an O and that those numbers and Os represent different isotopes of oxygen. The passage specifically does not use the word *oxygen* at any point. It just repeatedly uses the isotope notation ^{18}O and ^{16}O without explicitly saying oxygen. This is a perfect example why it is important that you can recognize elements and the many ways in which they can be written.

Sometimes atoms combine to form **compounds**. These compounds can take on their own unique properties that differ greatly from the properties of the individual elements they are made from. Some of these chemical compounds, which form when multiple atoms come together and form bonds, are called **molecules.**

When certain compounds/molecules come into contact, a **chemical reaction** can occur. A chemical reaction occurs when bonds between atoms are broken and new bonds are formed that create a new compound. No atoms are created or destroyed during a chemical reaction; instead, atoms simply change places with one another to create different molecules.

There are two specific terms related to chemical reactions that it might help to know: reactant and product.

Reactant: A **reactant** is something that exists before the reaction takes place. If you were watching a commercial for something showing a before and after picture, the reactants are the before.

Product: A **product** is a compound that is formed from the chemical reaction. Products are the after in a chemical reaction.

If you see a chemical reaction written out it will be written from left to right with the reactants on the left side and the products on the right side. There will be an arrow in the middle indicating a reaction is taking place.

$$CH_4 + O_2 \rightarrow CO_2 + 2H_2O$$

Products → Reactants

This particular reaction is the combustion of methane gas in oxygen. In simpler terms it is natural gas burning. Natural gas, which is called methane gas, is something that is used to heat hot water tanks, furnaces, and stoves in many homes. The reaction shows you the reactants and the products and enables you to see the general structure of a chemical reaction.

Following this you can see a small snippet of a passage from the ACT science test that involves a chemical reaction. It initially describes the reaction taking place and then proceeds to show you the written-out chemical equation. Knowing the reactants and the product compounds of this reaction can later help you understand the process being described in a question related to the passage. The passage is mostly focused on the H_2, hydrogen gas, production. Seeing the reaction enables you to place it in context easier.

Passage II

Aluminum water-based paints (AWPs) contain aluminum (Al) flakes that give surfaces a shiny, metallic appearance. If the flakes corrode, a dull coating of aluminum hydroxide forms on them:

$$2Al + 6H_2O \rightarrow 2Al(OH)_3 + 3H_2$$

Table 1 shows the volume of H_2 gas produced over time (at 25°C and 1 atm) from 100 mL samples of freshly made AWPs 1–3 in 3 separate trials. AWPs 1–3 were identical except that each had a different concentration of DMEA, an AWP ingredient that increases pH.

		Table 1			
		Volume (mL) of H_2 produced by:			
AWP	pH of AWP	Day 2	Day 4	Day 6	Day 8
1	8	4	33	81	133
2	9	21	187	461	760
3	10	121	1,097	2,711	4,480

If you look at this passage with no context and no knowledge of what the reaction is you very well could end up confused. You might assume it contains vital information to solving the problem even though it is there only for context, to support the word description of the reaction in the first paragraph. It will not be essential to solving the problem. If you don't recognize that it isn't essential, you might place more importance on it being present than you otherwise should.

So that's a brief look at matter and the basics behind how it changes. Make sure you understand after reading all of this that you do not need to become a master of all things chemistry related. This is simply meant to be a refresher and a reminder of a couple of reasonably important things about matter and how it changes. Nothing more than that. The reason behind this review is that you might see a mention of these vocabulary words or concepts somewhere in an ACT science passage or question. This way you will have some background knowledge on the concept. Remember though, if you are expected to understand the term and use it, then the ACT will provide you with the information you need about the vocabulary word or concept.

Evolution and Genes

The next major area of concentration to cover here is a quick review of the ideas behind evolution. There are commonly passages and questions on the ACT science section that discuss the ideas of evolution and natural selection so having a refresher on these topics is useful.

The basic idea of evolution is credited to Charles Darwin. He stated that species change over time based on the environment they live in, and this change can lead to new species being formed. These new species, although different and distinct, share a common ancestor. The process that drives this change is called natural selection. **Natural selection** occurs when organisms with more favorable survival **traits** survive and reproduce at a higher rate than organisms with less desirable survival traits. A species trait is simply a characteristic or quality that all organisms of a species share. It is said that organisms with a higher ability to reach reproductive age and produce offspring have a higher level of reproductive **fitness.**

Natural selection favors organisms that have traits best suited to survive in their environment. This leads to species changing over time to favor traits that help them survive in a given environment. Only traits that are heritable can be passed on from generation to generation. These traits are called **genes**. As these traits are passed from generation to generation the overall characteristics of a species change. Eventually, given a long enough period of time, organisms can change so much that they no longer resemble their ancestors enough to be classified as the same species. This is called **speciation,** when a new species is formed during the course of evolution.

Evolution takes place over a long period of time. It is not something that can happen over the course of a generation or two. It can take many generations of organisms to truly form a new species.

There are a few specific terms you should know regarding genes for the ACT. There is a good chance that you will see them at some point.

Genotype: Genotype is the genetic makeup of an organism. It is the total composition of all of the genes found in an organism.

Phenotype: Phenotype is the physical appearance or observable characteristics of an organism. Phenotypes are generally the physical expression of the genotype of an organism.

Alleles: Some genes can have multiple forms, each with a slight or large difference in how they are expressed. These multiple forms are called **alleles.** In many cases they are found in pairs.

Dominant: A **dominant** allele is a type of gene that will always produce a specific phenotype regardless of its pairing with another type of allele.

Recessive: A **recessive** allele is a type of gene that will only produce a specific phenotype when it is paired with another recessive allele. If it is paired with a dominant allele, the dominant allele will be expressed in the phenotype.

In the case of the following research summaries passage you can see how there is a mention and description of the genotype of an organism and how alleles can change that genotype.

Passage VI

Tomato plants grow poorly in high-salt environments. This effect is caused by 2 processes:

- A net movement of H_2O between the cytoplasm of the plants' cells and the environment via osmosis

- An increase in the cytoplasmic Na^+ concentration

The plant *Arabidopsis thaliana* carries a gene, *AtNHX1*. The product of this gene, *VAC*, facilitates uptake of cytoplasmic Na^+ by the plant's vacuoles.

A researcher created 4 genetically identical lines of tomato plants (L1–L4). An *AtNHX1* gene from *Arabidopsis thaliana* was isolated and 2 identical copies of this gene were incorporated into L1's genome. This process was repeated with L2 and L3 using a different *AtNHX1* allele for each line, so that L1, L2, and L3 had different genotypes for *AtNHX1*. The researcher then did an experiment.

This portion of the passage begins by describing tomato plants and the reason they grow poorly when placed in a high-salt environment. It then explains that there is a specific gene related to the uptake of Na in tomato plants. (This is also another example of a question that introduces an element, Na in this case, without stating its name. It just makes reference to Na and never specifically says what Na is, but if you remember your chemistry at all you will know that Na is the element sodium. Even if you don't remember the exact chemical symbol of Na you should at least be able to recognize that it is an element.)

The question then describes the process by which researchers develop four identical genetic lines of the plant and then says they alter those lines by adding a different type of allele to each of the four lines. It states that this creates a different genotype for each of the first three lines.

When you look at a passage like this you can see how understanding scientific terminology is important on the ACT science section. If you have no idea what genotype or allele means this might sound confusing. If you do understand the meaning, though, you are able to read this passage and remain focused on the actual experiment the researchers are performing instead of trying to determine the meaning behind some of the subject-specific words.

Species Classification

After discussing evolution, natural selection, and genes, the next subject to focus on is how species are named and classified. There is a very good chance you will see the scientific names of different organisms used as you read passages and questions on the ACT science test. These can be very intimidating if you don't understand how the names are created and how they should be read. They don't need to be though. They follow a specific pattern and don't deviate from that pattern at all. You will not be expected to know the scientific names of any specific organism when taking the ACT science section, but you may be required to recognize that a word is the scientific name of an organism. This section will help you with this.

There are two names by which organisms can be referred to: the common name and the scientific name. A common name is a simple name that is generally agreed on and used by all members of a community, location, language, and so on. They are easy to say and simple enough to remember. They are not universal, however. Living organisms in one area may not be referred to the same common name in another area of the world. In addition, common names are not specific enough to differentiate between individual species. Think about the tall plants you see in many areas of the word that have hard outer surfaces around their trunks and large branching leafy structures high in the air. These are generally called trees. They are a pretty well-known organism. Yet think about all of the types of trees there are. Just saying "tree" isn't specific enough. Even if you say "oak tree," that is still not very specific. There are about six hundred different species of oak trees that exist. The common name does a good job of identifying the organism for general conversation and discussion but it isn't specific enough to be used for scientific endeavors.

That is why the scientific naming and classification system exists. There is an entire system to classify all living organisms found on the planet. It is a branching system that helps narrow down where an organism fits into the grand scheme of existence. There isn't a need to go into the specific details of the entire classification system for this text because the ACT science test will not expect you to have any in-depth understanding of the hierarchy. It can be helpful, however, to have a reference for the classification system as a whole. Table 10.3 shows how a single organism, a bald eagle in this case, would be classified at every level of the scientific classification scale all the way to its specific species.

Table 10.3 Scientific Classification of a Bald Eagle

Kingdom	Animalia
Phylum	Chordata
Class	Aves
Order	Accipitriformes
Family	Accipitridae
Genus	Haliaeetus
Species	H. leucocephalus

Just glance at the chart but do not think there is any need to commit it to memory. Remember, the highest, most generalized, level is **kingdom** and the most specific being unique to the individual organism is **species.**

What you do need to focus on and prepare for, though, is the fact that you will see the names of many specific species presented to you in questions and passages. The goal of this section is to make sure you don't have any issue recognizing those names and dealing with them on the test.

Species are named using a binomial nomenclature system. There are two words that make up every scientific species name. The first word is the genus the species belongs to. **Genus** is one of the many parts of the taxonomic classification system used with organisms. The second part of a scientific name is the **species name** inside the genus for that organism.

The simplest example that you are perhaps familiar with is how humans are named:

The common name for a person is a human.

The scientific name is *Homo sapiens*.

Homo is the genus that humans belong to and *sapiens* is the specific species inside the genus that we belong to.

In terms of recognizing a scientific name you should, if nothing else, be able to look at how the word itself is structured and use that to identify the name of a species. The scientific name of a species is always italicized with the first letter of the genus, the first word, being capitalized. The second word is not capitalized. So if you see some very unfamiliar looking words italicized and structured like that you will realize the problem is referring to an organism of some kind.

Don't let the complexity of the name itself stop you from recognizing that it is just a name. The only thing you'll be required to do with these names is use them to help you contextualize a problem or analyze data that refers to the species by name.

You will see the names of many species on the ACT science test. Some will be common names but most will be their scientific names. If you see a scientific name, make sure you recognize it for what it is, the name of an organism, and use it accordingly. For an example of a scientific name used in a science passage look at passage VI in the previous section. You can see how the scientific name of the tomato plant *Arabidopsis thaliana* is used as part of the description of the experiment. Most people have probably never seen or spoken either of those words but as long as you can recognize it as referring to the tomato plant described in the passage you shouldn't have any issues.

DNA and RNA

After talking about evolution and natural selection the most fitting concept to look at next is DNA and what role it can play in how organisms pass on their genetic heritage from generation to generation.

DNA is the molecule responsible for carrying the genetic material for all of your, or any other, organisms. DNA stands for deoxyribonucleic acid. A level of information stored in a DNA molecule is incredibly complex, yet the method of information storage itself is relatively simple.

DNA is composed of four chemical bases: **adenine (A)**, **guanine (G)**, **cytosine (C)**, and **thymine (T)**. A DNA molecule is a long chain of these bases organized into a double helix with each strand of the DNA being a mirror image of the other on the opposite side of the helix (Figure 10.1). The order of the bases in the DNA molecule is how all genetic information is stored and then passed on. The bases in DNA are organized into **codons**. Every three bases on the DNA strand represent a single codon. A codon represents a small portion of the genetic code stored in DNA. When they are all used together, in the order found within the DNA molecule, this information is incredibly complex and essential to all life.

DNA Replication

DNA is able to copy itself during **cell replication**. Each DNA molecule splits into two strands of DNA with the original strand serving as a template strand for the creation of the new DNA strand (see Figure 10.1).

Figure 10.1 Double Helix

When DNA is replicating there are many mechanisms in place to ensure it is copied correctly and accurately yet sometimes there are errors that take place during the replication cycle. Sometimes these errors are minor and have little or no impact on the organism as a whole. Every once in a great while, though, an error in replication occurs that leads to a functional mutation in the DNA replication. A **mutation** occurs when the structure of a gene is changed by altering the DNA. Mutations, if not fatal to the organism, can be transferred by reproduction to offspring. Sometimes these mutations are beneficial to an organism. This is one way by which evolution and the process of natural selection can take place and how the fitness of an organism can change over the course of many generations.

Transcription and Translation

Another important aspect of DNA is how its stored information is expressed in the organism. This process occurs through two pathways: transcription and translation.

Transcription is the process that occurs when a DNA strand is copied into a strand of **mRNA, messenger RNA.** mRNA is one of the three types of **RNA** molecules that are used to help DNA successfully express the genetic information stored within it. RNA stands for ribonucleic acid. It is far less lengthy than DNA because it is used only to carry portions of information stored within the DNA molecule and it is only single-stranded. Transcription of DNA into mRNA takes place in the **nucleus** of a cell. (We will be discussing the parts of the cell a little bit later in this chapter.)

The mRNA molecule is then transferred out of the nucleus of the cell to an organelle called a **ribosome,** a cellular organelle used to make proteins. The ribosome is composed of rRNA, ribosomal RNA. The process by which the ribosome creates a protein out of the mRNA is called **translation.** The mRNA is translated into **tRNA, transfer RNA**, another type of RNA molecule that transfers the information stored in the mRNA to the ribosome for protein synthesis.

Each tRNA molecule corresponds to one codon of genetic information from the DNA. Most codons from the tRNA correspond to an **amino acid,** the building blocks of proteins. The ribosome uses the information conveyed by the tRNA molecules to construct a chain of amino acids linked together in the order specified by the DNA, the mRNA, and finally the tRNA. This chain of amino acids is called a **polypeptide chain.** It is the most basic structure of a protein.

This process can continue with many polypeptide chains being formed and folded together to form a much more complex protein molecule with multiple structural layers. This folding process that proteins undergo is incredibly important to their functioning. If a protein doesn't properly fold into its necessary structure it will not be able to function as intended. The structure and shape of a protein is essential to the protein working properly. The conditions in which a protein can fold properly are specific though. Sometimes a protein is exposed to unfavorable conditions, such as extreme heat, and the protein can lose its shape and unfold. When a protein does this it is called **denaturing.** A denatured protein has lost its shape and will not function as intended. Whatever specific use the protein had is lost when it loses its shape and structure. The only way it can regain that is to **renature,** refold, and regain its shape.

Take a look at the following sample ACT conflicting viewpoints passage. You will see that this is a conflicting viewpoints passage in its entirety. It specifically concerns protein synthesis to a degree and the process by which proteins fold and denature.

Passage XIII

A *polypeptide* molecule is a chain of amino acids. A *protein* consists of one or more polypeptides. A protein's shape is described by three or four levels of structure.

1. The *primary structure* of a protein is the sequence of amino acids in each polypeptide.

2. The *secondary structure* of a protein is the local folding patterns within short segments of each polypeptide due to *hydrogen bonding* (weak chemical bonds).

3. The *tertiary structure* is the folding patterns that result from interactions between amino acid *side chains* (parts of an amino acid) in each polypeptide. These folding patterns generally occur across greater distances than those associated with the secondary structure.

4. The *quaternary structure* is the result of the clustering between more than one folded polypeptide.

A protein can adopt different shapes, and each shape has a relative energy. Lower-energy shapes are more stable than higher-energy shapes, and a protein with a relatively high-energy shape may *denature* (unfold) and then *renature* (refold), adopting a more stable shape. A protein that is almost completely denatured is called a *random coil.* Random coils are unstable because they are high-energy shapes; however, some can renature, adopting more stable shapes.

Two scientists discuss protein shape.

Scientist 1

The *active shape* (the biologically functional shape) of a protein is always identical to the protein's lowest-energy shape. Any other shape would be unstable. Because a protein's lowest-energy shape is determined by its primary structure, its active shape is determined by its primary structure.

Scientist 2

The active shape of a protein is dependent upon its primary structure. However, a protein's active shape may also depend on its *process of synthesis,* the order (in time) in which the amino acids were bonded together. As synthesis occurs, stable, local structures form within short segments of the polypeptide chain due to hydrogen bonding. These local structures may be different than the local structures associated with the protein's lowest-energy shape. After synthesis, these structures persist, trapping the protein in an active shape that has more energy than its lowest-energy shape.

This passage discusses protein folding in some depth as well as the structural make up of proteins. It explains what a polypeptide chain is and goes into significant depth regarding the different levels of protein structure that exist due to folding. The passage then describes how the shape of a protein can denature and renature and describes the stability of these proteins.

Even though the passage provides a basic definition of words such as polypeptide, denature, and renature it still doesn't provide a clear explanation of the entire process by which proteins are created and then folded. Having that background of how protein synthesis takes place, how polypeptide chains are made, and how proteins are folded will make it easier and faster for you to work through the passage and enable you to avoid any confusion over the meaning or use of the words.

*   *   *

Included here is a portion of a sample passage that shows how proteins, lipids, and carbohydrates might be used or mentioned in the ACT science test.

Passage V

Some oceanic shrimp are vertical migrators. For vertically migrating species, most of the population is found at the bottom of their depth range during the day and at the top of their depth range at night. Table 1 shows the depth ranges and water, protein, lipid, and carbohydrate content of three vertically migrating (vm) species of shrimp and three non-migrating (nm) species of deep-sea shrimp. Figure 1 shows water temperature and oxygen partial pressure at various ocean depths.

Table 1					
			% ash-free dry weight		
Species	Depth range (m)	Water content (% wet weight)	protein	lipid	carbohydrate
vm 1	300–600	77.5	62.8	23.8	0.7
vm 2	10–400	76.6	53.4	16.4	0.8
vm 3	75–400	79.5	60.5	14.7	0.7
nm 1	500–1,100	75.9	36.9	36.1	0.5
nm 2	500–1,000	76.7	41.5	31.5	0.8
nm 3	650–1,100	72.8	35.8	49.0	0.5

After looking at the paragraph and table you can see that percentages of proteins, lipids, and carbohydrate macromolecules found in shrimp species are examined at various depths. There is a lot going on in Table 1 in the passage. There are multiple species of shrimp shown along with various water depths. The percentage of water content found in the shrimp along with their percentage of protein, lipid, and carbohydrate are displayed. Having a familiarity with the macromolecule names can be useful here. You can probably determine that the water content of an organism is simply how much water that organism has present within its body. Yet if you lack a familiarity with a term such as lipid you might struggle to understand how it can be part of an organism's makeup.

Parts of a Cell

After discussing the process of transcription and translation of DNA the next focus should be on the location that it all takes place: the cell. In this section you will see a brief description of what a cell is, the types of cells you will find, and a description of a couple of specific components found inside cells. Cellular biology can be incredibly complex and detailed. With that in mind this chapter is going to review only a few of the most important cell organelles and cell types. There is no need to have an in-depth knowledge of the biology of all cells when taking the ACT science test, but a good quick refresher on the basics of cell biology will make reading passages and answering questions easier and quicker for you.

A **cell** is the basic unit of life. It is the smallest functional unit of any organism. The basic idea of a cell is an enclosed structure that is usually very, very small (though not always). The first thing to know is that not all cells are exactly alike. Clearly there are differences in the life found all over this planet, and the cells that make up that life have differences as well. There are two major types of cells that exist throughout the world: prokaryotic cells and eukaryotic cells.

Prokaryotic Cells

Prokaryotic cells are entirely self-contained, single-celled organisms. They are not like animals or plants, which are made up of millions and billions of cells working together. That means that a single prokaryotic cell by itself is a living organism all by itself. The most commonly known prokaryotic organism is bacteria. All bacteria cells are prokaryotic cells.

Prokaryotic cells have some specific properties unique to them. The biggest characteristic of a prokaryotic cell is that they do not have a nucleus. In prokaryotic cells the cellular DNA is not contained in a nucleus but instead can be found in a region called the **nucleoid.** In addition, prokaryotic cells do not contain any membrane organelles. This means that prokaryotic cells do not have any of the traditional cellular organelles you have studied before. This is not a big deal for bacteria or any other prokaryotic cell but it severely limits their size. Though most cells are microscopic, prokaryotic cells are significantly smaller than eukaryotic cells, which contain organelles.

Eukaryotic Cells

Eukaryotic cells are more complex and much larger than prokaryotic. Eukaryotic cells are what make up all multicellular organisms. Your body and all the living things around you that you can see with your eyes are composed of eukaryotic cells. Even though they are larger than prokaryotic cells, eukaryotic cells are still generally microscopic.

Eukaryotic cells contain **organelles,** specialized structures or objects that perform a certain function or have a specific purpose for the functioning of the cell. There are many types of organelles that can be found in cells and each one has a different function. Here you will find a very quick breakdown of some of the key cellular organelles. Not every cell has all of these organelles, and this list is not definitive by any means. There are many very specialized cellular structures found throughout cells but these are the basics.

Nucleus: The **nucleus** is often referred to as the brain of the cell. It is an enclosed area of the cell that is surrounded by its own barrier called the nuclear envelope. The nucleus is the location where cellular DNA is stored in chromosomes. The nucleus is responsible for sending out signals to the rest of the cell telling it what to do, such as making proteins or dividing and reproducing.

Plasma membrane: The **plasma membrane** is the barrier that surrounds the entire cell. It is semi-permeable, meaning that some things can pass through the membrane but others cannot. The membrane is mostly composed of molecules called **phospholipids** that do not like water very much. This means that water cannot freely flow through a plasma membrane. Other objects can and do move through the plasma membrane with regularity though because one of the jobs of the plasma membrane is to control the flow of molecules into and out of the cell.

Cell wall: The **cell wall** is a specialized structure only found in specific types of cells. It is a rigid structured barrier that surrounds the entire cell, including the plasma membrane.

Cytoplasm: The **cytoplasm** is simply the inside portion of the cell that isn't made up of organelles. It is mostly composed of water and another gel like fluid called cytosol.

Mitochondria: **Mitochondria** are often referred to as the powerhouse of the cell. The mitochondria organelle takes food energy consumed by the organism and turns it into energy the cell can use. It does this by synthesizing ATP (adenosine triphosphate) molecules.

Vacuole: The **vacuole** is a membrane-enclosed space inside the cytoplasm of a cell that is used to store or temporarily contain specific nutrients, chemicals, or liquids. Vacuoles can also perform many other functions in the cell depending on the needs placed on it, such as structural support and waste disposal.

Ribosome: The **ribosome** is the organelle responsible for protein synthesis. The ribosome uses the information provided by mRNA molecules from the nucleus to bind amino acids together into polypeptide chains.

Endoplasmic reticulum: The **endoplasmic reticulum** is an organelle found near the nucleus of the cell. There are two types: rough and smooth. It has many functions but the one that it is mostly thought of is the ability to move and fold proteins into their proper structures.

Types of Macromolecules

The term *molecule* is broad and widely used to define elements combined into a compound. Molecules can be very small such as hydrogen gas, H_2, or water, H_2O. Yet there are other molecules that are not small when compared to a water or hydrogen molecule. These molecules are called **macromolecules**, which can be defined as molecules composed of a large number of atoms. They are bigger than a basic molecule and far more complex. In the grand scheme of existence, though, they are still incredibly tiny. For the ACT science test there are three specific organic macromolecules you should be aware of and familiar with. Following is a list of the three along with some specific characteristics related to each.

Carbohydrates: **Carbohydrates** are something you probably have some familiarity with because they are regularly discussed in regards to food. Sugars and starches, such as that found in pasta, are composed of carbohydrate molecules. The most basic building block of a carbohydrate is the simple sugar glucose. This simple sugar, the most basic form of a carbohydrate, is called a **monosaccharide**. When you put many monosaccharides together into a chain you create a more complex carbohydrate molecule called a **polysaccharide**. A polysaccharide is a type of **polymer,** which is a molecule consisting of a chain of similar, smaller components called **monomers** bonded together.

Lipids: **Lipids** are found mostly associated with fatty acids. Lipids are found in foods that are associated with fat such as oil or grease. Lipids as a molecule are very **hydrophobic**, meaning they do not like water or, more specifically, will not dissolve in water. That is why oil and water don't mix. The lipids found in the oil will not dissolve or mix into the water due to their polarity. In addition, lipids are the major component found in the membrane of cells and are also used as a means by the body to store excess food energy.

Proteins: **Proteins** are large biological molecules used in many components of living things. A protein is a type of polymer, which is made up of a chain of amino acids. The order of the amino acids determines the function and structure of the protein. For more detail on proteins see the "Transcription and Translation" section earlier in this chapter focusing on their synthesis.

Physics Terminology

After taking a look at some basic chemistry and biology concepts, the next subject-specific vocabulary terms we should look at are some physics concepts. Physics is an incredibly wide-ranging subject with some very, very complex theories. At the basic level, physics mainly focuses on things and forces you experience in your everyday life.

Density: **Density** is the mass of something divided by its volume. It is a ratio between the amount of matter something is composed of and how much space that matter takes up. The more matter you can stuff into an area of space without increasing the space itself, the more dense that object will be. If you decrease the amount of matter in a given volume, the density of an object will decrease.

Gravity: **Gravity** is a force of nature that is responsible for there being an attraction between all physical objects. It is the force that causes objects to fall toward the earth instead of floating away. Gravity is the cause behind objects having weight on earth. When you get on a scale it is weighing how much gravity is pulling you down toward the scale. If you got on a scale on the moon your weight would be lower because the gravitational pull of the moon is less.

Speed: **Speed** is the distance an object travels during a given rate of time. In simpler terms it is how fast something is moving. You are probably most familiar with the physics definition of speed in your day-to-day life. When drivers get in a car and go somewhere, one of the most important things to be aware of is the speed they are travelling because there are set speed limits for each road. Those speed limits, in the United States, use the distance-to-time ratio of miles per hour, which is probably the most common measure of speed that is used. If a speed limit is seventy miles per hour, that means you should not go faster than seventy miles in one hour of travel.

Velocity: In **physics**, velocity is a function of speed and direction. The velocity of an object is equal to the speed that object is moving and the direction it is moving in. It is important to note that velocity and speed are different measurements. Speed is a measure of how fast something is moving regardless of direction. Velocity is focused on both speed and direction of an object. If you say a plane is flying at 400 miles an hour that is a speed. If you say a plane is flying northwest at 400 miles an hour that is a velocity.

Inertia: In the simplest terms possible, **inertia** is an object's ability to resist changes to its velocity. Generally, inertia is associated with mass; the greater the mass of an object the greater its inertia will be. This means, in a general sense, that a large, heavy object moving in one direction will have a greater inertia than a smaller, lighter object moving at the same speed.

Momentum: **Momentum** is used regularly when talking about sports, especially teams competing. If a team gets on a roll the announcers may say that the team now has all the momentum. Momentum is the term used to describe matter in motion. If something has mass and a velocity, it has momentum. If you get up from your desk and begin walking down the hallway, you have momentum. If you then begin to run, you have a greater momentum.

Kinetic energy: **Kinetic energy** is the energy of motion. The faster something moves the more kinetic energy it has. Particles or objects that are at rest have less kinetic energy than objects that are moving.

Potential energy: **Potential energy** is the energy that an object possesses based on its position relative to other objects in a given situation. A ball sitting on top of a hill near the edge, ready to roll down that hill, possesses a great deal of potential energy. Once the ball begins to roll down the hill, that potential energy has been converted to kinetic energy, the energy of motion. Once the ball is at the bottom of the hill and has ceased moving, it has far less potential energy.

Lens: **Lens** is a term you will see regularly when dealing with physics topics. A lens is a transparent (having the ability to allow light through) curved object that is used to refract light. **Refract** is a fancy way of saying that a lens causes light to change direction. The most common use of lenses is for magnification. Glasses and contact lenses are used by millions and millions of people throughout the word to help magnify and adjust the light so they see a clear image.

Following is a conflicting viewpoints sample passage in its entirety that shows how you might see physics concepts and terms. It discusses smoke and the forces that cause smoke to rise up a chimney.

Passage VI

Two students explain why the *smoke* (a mixture of gases and carbon particles) from burning wood in a fireplace rises up the chimney from the fireplace. They also discuss how chimney *efficiency* (the volume of smoke flowing out the top of the chimney per second for a given temperature difference between inside and outside the chimney) is related to chimney height.

Student 1

Smoke rises because the gases from burning wood are less dense than the air that surrounds the fireplace. Because the gases are hotter than the air, the gas molecules have a higher average speed than the air molecules. Consequently, the average distance between adjacent gas molecules is greater than the average distance between adjacent air molecules, and so the gas *density* is less than the air density. As a result, the upward *buoyant force* acting on the gases is stronger than the downward *force of gravity* acting on the gases, and the gases rise, carrying the carbon particles with them. The upward flow of smoke is maintained as new air enters the fireplace, causing more wood to burn.

As chimney height increases, efficiency increases. The taller the chimney, the greater the volume of hot gas, the stronger the buoyant force compared with the force of gravity, and the more rapidly smoke rises.

Student 2

Smoke rises because wind blows across the top of the chimney. When no wind is blowing, the air pressure at the bottom of the chimney is slightly higher than the air pressure at the top of the chimney. However, when air at the top of the chimney moves at a higher speed than air at the bottom of the chimney, the pressure difference between the bottom and the top of the chimney is so great that air is forced upward, carrying smoke with it. The departure of air from the bottom of the chimney, in turn, creates a pressure difference that forces new air into the fireplace, causing further burning and an upward flow of smoke.

As chimney height increases, efficiency increases. Generally, wind speed increases with altitude. The taller the chimney, the greater the difference in air speed, the greater the difference in air pressure, and the more rapidly smoke rises.

After reading this passage you can see it discusses quite a few physics terms and understanding them can very much help your comprehension. Gravity and density are both addressed by Student 1, who uses the concepts of density and gravity to explain why smoke rises in the chimney. Both of those words are defined in the passage. Yet there is also another specific physics term used that is not defined in the section above: buoyant force.

This is an example of a passage in which you encounter a subject-specific word that you might not know the meaning of. As stated there are just too many science vocabulary words to list in a single book, so you are definitely going to see a few here and there that you don't know. The important thing to remember when you encounter an unknown word is that the passage or problem should provide some background on the meaning of the word. In this case, it does that, but not in the most obvious way. Sometimes the passage or question will very clearly spell out that "this word" means "this exact definition."

This passage tells you the meaning of the vocabulary term in the same sentence that it is introduced in. This is why it is important to read carefully and examine the passage in detail. Skipping through it quickly will lead to you potentially missing important points like this. The passage states, "As a result, the upward *buoyant force* acting on the gases is stronger than the downward *force of gravity* acting on the gases." The only description you get of buoyant forces is the word *upward,* yet that should be enough. The passage proceeds to describe that gravity is the "downward" force acting on the smoke, though you probably had some idea of what gravity is already.

In this passage, if you had no idea what a *buoyant force* was you can figure out that a buoyant force causes something to rise or it acts in the opposite manner of gravity. If gravity causes something to go down, buoyancy makes it go up. That's all you need to understand about it in regards to this passage. Is the full description of it more complicated than that? Of course, but that doesn't matter for this passage.

This is the mind-set you should have when you read ACT science passages and questions: if you see a word you don't understand, figure out what its meaning is to the specific passage or question and that is all. Do not try to reason out the full and complex meaning of the term. Determine its usefulness and move on. In some cases there will be science words that are of little to no use for you in answering the question. If the passage doesn't give you a description of the word in any way then it probably is not something you need to worry about at all.

Properties of a Wave and the Electromagnetic Spectrum

Waves in physics and chemistry curriculum help describe **electromagnetic radiation**, which is visible light and other energy that travels through space as a wave. Such concepts might appear in the ACT science test. Humans can only see a small portion of the whole spectrum of electromagnetic radiation that exists. Some of the types of radiation you probably are already familiar with and use every single day: X-rays, radio waves, microwaves, and so on. Figure 10.2 shows the entire electromagnetic spectrum. There is no need to memorize or even study this very thoroughly but it can be helpful for you to be familiar with the different names used in association with the various types of radiation.

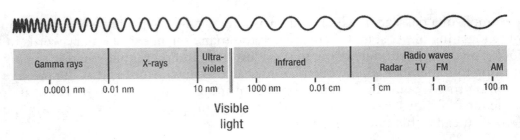

Figure 10.2 The Electromagnetic Spectrum

In looking at the electromagnetic spectrum chart you see that it provides two ways to classify the waves: **frequency** and **wavelength**, which are are two measurements that are used to describe the properties of a wave. You can see a diagram of a wave in Figure 10.3.

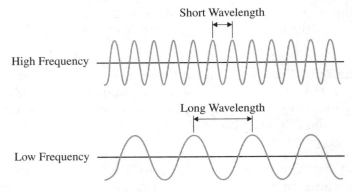

Figure 10.3 Diagram Showing High Frequency and Low Frequency Waves

The first property of a wave that you can observe from the diagram is the **wavelength**, which is represented by the symbol, λ. In simple terms the wavelength is the length of a wave. A more specific definition is the distance from peak to peak or any two successive points on a wave. It is generally the most easily identifiable property of a wave because you can visually observe it in a diagram. It is also the simplest property to understand because the measurement itself is exactly as the name says. It is just the length of the wave.

The next important wave property is the **frequency**, which is represented by the symbol v. The frequency of a wave can be defined as the number of times a wave passes a given point in one second. Frequency is measured in hertz (Hz) and it is something that is discussed in chapter 9 on scientific units. The frequency and wavelength of a wave have an indirect (inverse) relationship. As the wavelength of a wave increases the frequency of a wave decreases. That means waves with bigger wavelengths have shorter frequencies and vice versa. This relationship can clearly be observed above in Figure 10.3.

There is a good chance you will see waves represented somewhere on the ACT science test. There are many passages that make reference to them in some way, so understanding them is important. Wavelength is probably the most commonly referenced wave property, yet all wave concepts can be integrated into passages or questions. Following is a data representation passage that discusses electromagnetic radiation passing through the earth's atmosphere.

Passage IV

Certain layers of Earth's atmosphere absorb particular wavelengths of solar radiation while letting others pass through. Types of solar radiation include X-rays, ultraviolet light, visible light, and infrared radiation. The cross section of Earth's atmosphere below illustrates the altitudes at which certain wavelengths are absorbed. The arrows point to the altitudes at which solar radiation of different ranges of wavelengths is absorbed. The figure also indicates the layers of the atmosphere and how atmospheric density, pressure, and temperature vary with altitude.

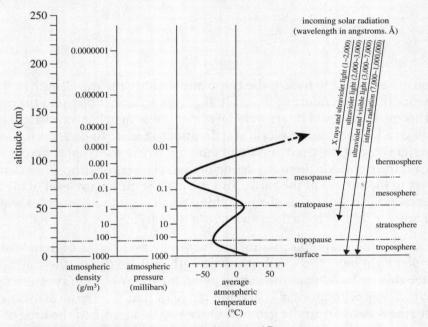

Figure adapted from Arthur Strahler, *The Earth Sciences.* ©1963 by Harper and Row.

Note: 1 Å = 1 × 10⁻¹⁰ meters.

This passage and chart show the altitude that different wavelengths of solar radiation are absorbed based on the density of the atmosphere. The introductory paragraph describes the different types of solar radiation that are absorbed by the atmosphere and gives a bit of background on the process. The graph is where everything is happening in this passage.

Wavelength is used to differentiate between the different types of radiation on the right side of the graph. If you see a wavelength it will always be accompanied by some type of distance measurement. In this case the distance of the wave is measured in angstroms, Å. This is a commonly used unit for measuring the wavelength of light waves. For context 1 Å is equal to 10⁻¹⁰ meters. The question never explains what the symbol Å is nor does it explain that it is the distance by which wavelengths are measured in the question. This is why it is useful to have a solid understanding of the properties of waves.

This is further illustrated by the following question. This question is a sample question associated with the previous passage.

> The information provided in the figure indicates that the air temperature in the troposphere is LEAST likely to be influenced by which of the following wavelengths of energy?
>
> **F.** 1,500 Å
>
> **G.** 4,500 Å
>
> **H.** 6,000 Å
>
> **J.** 7,000 Å

In this question you are expected to look at the graph and identify the wavelength of light that is least likely to influence the temperature of the air in the troposphere. It provides the answers to you in angstroms, Å. This question could be answered without knowing what wavelength is or how it is measured but it will go a lot faster and easier if you do understand it. To determine the answer, you need to look at the right side of the chart and first figure out where the troposphere is located on the graph. You can see on the right side there is a listing of several layers of atmosphere with troposphere being the one closest to the surface of the earth. This means it is the lowest level of the atmosphere presented by the question. Knowing that. the next thing you'll want to figure out is which wavelength represented by the answer choices is furthest away from the surface.

If you look at the area of the graph discussing the varying wavelengths of light you can see that X-rays and ultraviolet light have the smallest wavelength and are the furthest away from the surface. You can see this by looking at the values given for the Å of each type of radiation. The question also provides you with an easy visual reference in that the arrow associated with them is the shortest and furthest away from the ground. Once you've identified the area of the spectrum that has the lowest wavelength of light that is absorbed furthest from the surface you just need to find the answer choice that best matches that region. Based on what you've identified you want to find the answer choice that has the smallest, shortest wavelength. In this case that is answer choice **A,** 1500 Å. All of the other choices show wavelengths of light that can be absorbed in or near the troposphere so they clearly have some effect on the temperature of the air there. The question wants the thing with the least impact so it will not be those.

The previous question and the passage are an example of how there can be many areas of science brought into one passage and question. This example deals with wavelength, yet if you read the question and look at the graph included you also see there is a significant focus on the different levels of the atmosphere. This is another one of those scientific concepts that it might help to glance over and have a passing familiarity with. You definitely don't need to memorize the order or names of the atmospheric levels, but again, being familiar with those levels and the fact that they exist can make it easier for you to understand questions and passages like this. Figure 10.5 shows the major layers of the atmosphere along with their names.

Table 10.4 Layers of Atmosphere

Exosphere	440 to 6,200 miles above Earth
Thermosphere	50 to 440 miles above Earth
Mesosphere	31 to 50 miles above Earth
Stratosphere	7 to 31 miles above Earth
Troposphere	0 to 7 miles above Earth

After looking at the previous question and passage focusing on wavelength, with that short detour into the levels of atmosphere, let's look at another passage and question on wavelength. This is a full research summaries passage looking at the results of activities performed with a microscope. Initially you might wonder what a microscope has to do with wavelengths of light, but then you should consider that light is what allows you to see through a microscope. Pay special attention to Activity 3 in this passage, because that is where wavelength is discussed.

Passage X

A student performed three activities with a microscope that had four objective lenses.

Activity 1

The student viewed four slides (A, B, C, and D) through each objective lens. Each slide had two thin lines painted on it. For each objective lens, the student determined whether she could see the lines as separate or whether they blurred into one image. The results appear in Table 1.

Table 1

Slide	Objective Lens: 1	2	3	4
A	|	|	|	|
B	|	|	|	||
C	|	|	||	||
D	|	||	||	||

Note: \|\| indicates lines appeared separate; \| indicates lines blurred together.

Activity 2

The student was given a prepared slide with a line on it that was 0.1 mm in length. This length was defined as the *object size*. Next, she viewed the slide with each objective lens, estimating how long the line appeared. This estimated length was called the *image size*. Finally, she calculated the magnification (M) associated with each objective lens from the following formula:

$$M = \text{image size} / \text{object size}.$$

(continued)

Passage X (*continued*)

The data appear in Table 2.

Table 2		
Objective Lens	Image size (mm)	M
1	4	40
2	10	100
3	20	200
4	40	400

Activity 3

The *numerical aperture* (NA) of each objective lens was printed on the microscope. NA determines how much detail can be seen and is related to *resolution* (R). R is defined as the smallest distance separating two objects such that the objects appear separate. Thus an objective lens with a small R shows a sample more clearly than does an objective lens with a large R. R is calculated from the following formula:

$$R = \lambda / 2(NA)$$

where λ is the wavelength of the light, in nanometers (nm), used to view the objects.

The student calculated R for each objective lens, assuming a λ of 550 nm. The data appear in Table 3.

Table 3		
Objective Lens	NA	R (nm)
1	0.10	2,750
2	0.25	1.100
3	0.40	688
4	0.65	423

The third activity can look daunting because it presents you with numerical data and a formula associated with it. The passage also includes a specific scientific term that you may or not be familiar with: **aperture**, which, in the case of a microscope, is the small opening through which light is allowed to pass. Changing the size of the aperture changes the amount of light that can enter the microscope. It isn't essential to your understanding of the question but it is yet another example of a vocabulary word that would be helpful for you to know to save time instead of trying to reason out its meaning.

The passage states that a specific wavelength of 550 nm was used to obtain the data in Table 3 but it doesn't say wavelength when doing this; instead, it uses the λ symbol. Of course, two sentences previously it had just told you that λ is the symbol for wavelength, but it is easy to miss that or overlook it during a test that you are trying to finish in a very short amount of time.

Let's examine a sample question associated with the passage.

Which of the following equations correctly calculates R (in nm) for Objective Lens 2, using light with a wavelength of 425 nm?

A. R = 425 / 2(0.10)

B. R = 425 / 2(0.25)

C. R = 0.10 / 2(425)

D. R = 0.25 / 2(425)

This question expects you to use the formula given in Activity 3. It doesn't expect you to solve the equation but it does want you to plug in values from the data table and apply them. It very clearly says to focus on Objective Lens 2 so you should only be looking at that specific data. Once you've identified that the next focus should be on determining the easiest way to identify which equation is correct.

The equation R = λ / 2(NA) refers to wavelength and NA as the two variables that you can use to identify the correct equation. The question tells you that the λ is 425 nm, so the correct answer to the equation must have a λ of 425. The answer choices do not include units in the equation so you don't need to worry about them. In addition, the NA for objective lens 2 is 0.25 so you'll need to find the equation that has NA = 0.25.

It really comes down to **A** and **B** as possible answers because they are the only ones that show a λ of 425. But only one equation, choice **B**, has the correct NA of 0.25. If you catch onto that first when looking at the answer choices then it is the only variable you need because it enables you to eliminate all other answer choices.

Concentration, pH, and Acid-Base Chemistry

The final area to cover here is pH and concentration. This section will have some overlap with the scientific unit chapter but pH is important enough in the ACT that it should be discussed here as well.

Before talking about pH, though, you should do a quick review of solutions. The solutions that are discussed here are liquid. A **solution** is composed of a smaller quantity of matter, the **solute**, which is dissolved uniformly in a larger amount of liquid, the **solvent.** Solutions are **homogeneous** in nature, meaning they are uniform (the same) throughout. Homogeneous solutions look the same throughout and the distribution of particles found in the solution is spread out evenly throughout the entirety of the solution. Make sure that you don't confuse solutions with a **heterogeneous** mixture, which is a mixture of two or more compounds that don't have a uniform distribution of particles throughout.

Solutions are usually described using the term **concentration**, which is just another way of saying the amount of solute in a given quantity of the solvent or the solution as a whole. There are many units that are used to measure concentration, but they all concern the amount of solute in some amount of solvent or solution.

A simple and easy way of viewing concentration and how it can change is to think about a drink you order at a restaurant. Assume you go out and order a Coke with ice in it. Initially that Coke probably tastes pretty good, but if you let it sit for a while and the ice melts, then it tastes less good. You would probably say that the drink has become watered down by the ice melting and that statement is correct. What occurs when the ice melts in a glass of coke is called **diluting a solution**. It is the process by which more solvent is added to the solution without changing the solute. In the case of the Coke, the flavoring syrup used to make the soda pop is the solute. The amount of that syrup is not changed as you drink it or let it sit and the ice melts. The solvent in the solution is the water. Over the course of time as the ice melts the amount of water in the solution increases, which means the amount of solvent in the solution increases. When you increase the quantity of solvent without also increasing the solute you are diluting the solution and lowering the overall concentration. If you want to increase the concentration of a solution you can either increase the amount of solute or decrease the amount of solvent.

Passage XVII

The following experiments were performed to investigate the effects of adding various *solutes* (substances that are dissolved in a solution), in varying amounts, on the boiling points and freezing points of H_2O solutions. Pure H_2O freezes at 0°C and boils at 100°C at standard atmospheric pressure.

Experiment 1

A student dissolved 0.01 mole of sodium chloride (NaCl) in 100 g of H_2O. Each mole of NaCl produces 2 moles of solute particles (1 mole of sodium ions and 1 mole of chloride ions in solution). After the NaCl dissolved, the freezing point of the solution was determined. This procedure was repeated with different amounts of NaCl and table sugar (sucrose). Each mole of sucrose produces 1 mole of solute particles (sucrose molecule). The results are shown in Table 1.

Table 1			
Solution	Substance added to H_2O	Amount added (mole)	Freezing point (°C)
1	NaCl	0.01	−0.3
2	NaCl	0.05	−1.7
3	NaCl	0.1	−3.4
4	NaCl	0.2	−6.9
5	sucrose	0.01	−0.2
6	sucrose	0.05	−1.0
7	sucrose	0.1	−2.1
8	sucrose	0.2	−4.6

Note: Freezing points were measured at standard atmospheric pressure.

Experiment 2

A student dissolved 0.01 mole of NaCl in 100 g of H_2O. After the NaCl dissolved, the boiling point of the solution was determined. The procedure was repeated using various amounts of NaCl. The results are shown in Table 2.

Table 2		
Solution	Amount of NaCl added (mole)	Boiling point (°C)
9	0.01	100.1
10	0.05	100.5
11	0.1	101.0
12	0.2	102.0

Note: Boiling points were measured at standard atmospheric pressure.

From the results of Experiment 2, what would one hypothesize, if anything, about the effect of the number of solute particles dissolved in H_2O on the boiling point of a solution?

A. The more solute particles that are present, the higher the boiling point.

B. The more solute particles that are present, the lower the boiling point.

C. No hypothesis can be made because only one solute was tested.

D. The number of solute particles produced does not affect the boiling point.

Solutions and concentration are mentioned and used regularly when dealing with the **pH level** of acids and bases. **pH** is a measure of the amount of dissolved hydrogen ion found in a solution compared to pure water. It is one of the ways to classify substances as acidic or basic. Sometimes you will see basic solutions referred to as **alkaline solutions**. The more hydrogen ion that is dissolved in the solution, the more **acidic** a solution is considered to be. If a solution has less hydrogen ion dissolved in it than pure water, it is said to be **basic** (alkaline).

The molar concentration of hydrogen ions in acidic and basic solutions is generally very, very small, so small, in fact, that the concentrations can prove difficult to work with on their own. This is why the concentrations are expressed using pH instead. pH is a logarithmic scale developed to express the concentration of hydrogen ion in a useful and easy-to-read way. One can look at a pH value and quickly identify if a solution is acidic or basic solely by the pH value.

The **pH scale goes from 0–14** with 0 being the most acidic and 14 being the most basic. The middle of the scale, 7, represents a solution of pure water and nothing else. Pure water is important to keep in mind because most of the water you deal with is definitely not pure in the scientific sense. Tap water, rain water, lake water, and so on all have dissolved solutes in them to some extent that alter the pH level of water. Only pure water, which contains nothing else in it, can be used to determine a true **neutral** pH of 7.

You aren't going to be expected to be incredibly familiar with acid-base chemistry on the ACT science section. You may though be asked to predict how the pH of a solution might change based on information provided in a question or passage. Having a familiarity with the pH scale can prove very useful for that type of question. Remember that as you decrease the pH you are making a solution more acidic. If you increase the pH of a solution you are making it more basic (alkaline).

One other thing to know about acids and bases is that some solutions resist changes in pH. These are called **buffers**. A buffered solution is generally a mixture of an acid and a base together with certain other elements added in that help the solution resist a pH change. That is to say, if you had a buffer and added a quantity of acidic solution to it, the pH of the buffered solution would not increase as you would expect it to because you are adding acid to the solution. The buffer is designed to resist a change in pH. Of course, if you overwhelm a buffer solution with enough acid or base the pH will change accordingly, but overall, these solutions can be very effective at resisting that change. The most well-known buffered solution is a pretty important thing to you and everyone else on this planet: blood. It is essential to human survival that the pH of blood be within a given specific range between 6.8 and 7.8 at all times, though a true healthy blood pH is right about 7.4. The body and your blood are designed to always maintain this pH by being a buffered system and resisting pH change.

When dealing with acids and bases sometimes you are tasked with determining the concentration of an unknown solution. That means you have a solution of some chemical but you don't know the concentration of the solution and you need to figure it out. What do you do with the solution? You **titrate** the unknown solution with a solution of known concentration. It might sound a bit complicated but it really doesn't need to be. A **titration** is a technique used in chemistry to determine the concentration, in molarity, of an unknown solution. It is something you may see mentioned on the ACT in a passage or in a question, so being familiar with the process is worth your time.

The basic process of performing a titration is relatively standard. To begin, a defined volume of the unknown solution is measured out into a beaker or flask and an **indicator** is added to the unknown solution. An indicator causes the solution to change color when the pH of the solution reaches a specified point. This color change is used to signal the end of the reaction that takes place during the titration. Once you have your unknown sample you then add some amount of a solution with known concentration, called the **titrant,** to a device called a **burette**. A burette is a long glass tube with measured graduations that enable you to accurately add small quantities of the titrant to the flask containing the unknown solution.

Generally, if the unknown solution is a base then the titrant being added is an acid and vice versa. The titrant, known solution, and the unknown solution will undergo a reaction that slowly changes the pH of the unknown solution. This will continue until the pH reaches the value at which the indicator will change color. When the color change appears you stop and measure the amount of titrant that has been added to the unknown solution. Using the chemical equation enables you to perform a calculation that determines the concentration of the unknown solution.

Now this might sound pretty complicated, and in reality titrations are a more complex topic in chemistry. Thankfully though on the ACT science test you aren't going to have to do any of these calculations nor are you going to have to physically perform a titration. However, you might see a question or a passage that deals with titrations, so having the basic background knowledge of what a titration is and what they are used for may prove useful to you. If you encounter a research summaries passage detailing how a scientist used a titration to measure the unknown concentration of a solution you'll now have a little bit more background knowledge on what was going on during that experiment.

This should always be the goal when you go from passage to passage and question to question on the ACT science test. You should be comfortable enough with science concepts so that you don't get stuck on the vocabulary or the process described and can instead focus on what the questions are asking you. Remember though, if there is a term or process that is essential to answering a question or understanding a passage it will be described to you somewhere. All the information you need is in every question and passage; you just need to find it.

Summary

This chapter presented you with a summary of some of the main scientific concepts and vocabulary words you might see on the ACT science test. In a research summaries passage the research or data in it could be from any branch of science covering any possible topic. When you see a data representation passage you will encounter graphs from many potential categories.

It would be helpful to be familiar with the vocabulary words and concepts presented in this chapter. There is no guarantee you will see them on the test but you will likely encounter at least a few of the topics covered. Being familiar with them will make answering questions easier and faster for you. It is always easier to analyze data or examine an experiment when you have some background knowledge about the data you are seeing or the experimental procedure.

Remember that the ACT will not expect you to understand a scientific concept unless it explains it specifically in the passage. You will not be expected to remember how protein synthesis occurs in detail on your own, but you might see a passage that discusses protein synthesis and that passage might describe some of the processes behind protein synthesis. If it does, the questions you encounter might ask about it. Anything the questions ask though will be from the passage or can be understood from reading the passage.

If you see a complex science word you don't know, it is described somewhere in the passage. If you see a concept you don't understand and can't find an explanation somewhere, you won't be asked about it in the questions. The most important thing you can do when taking the ACT science test, as has been said throughout this book, is to maintain your focus and never get worried about something you might not understand. The information is always there for you; you just have to know how to find it and how to use it.

Chapter 11: Practice Questions

This chapter contains a wide variety of sample ACT science passages and the questions associated with them. These are all official ACT passages and sample questions so be sure to look over them in detail.

Some of these passages and questions are ones that you have seen throughout the rest of the book, but don't skip them just because you've seen them already. The more you practice the better off you will be on the test.

Finally, this chapter is not set up like a practice test so don't feel as though you need to go through each set of questions in sequential order or on a timed basis. Simply read through the passages and answer the questions to the best of your ability. Be sure to look at the answer key, which provides a detailed explanation or solution to each problem.

Passage I

Two measures of water quality are the number of *Escherichia coli* bacteria present and the *biotic index*, BI (a numerical value based on the type, diversity, and pollution tolerance of aquatic invertebrate animals). Both of these measures can be affected by water flow.

E. coli levels that are above 100 colonies formed per 100 mL of water indicate reduced water quality. Figure 1 shows the *E. coli* levels on 5 collection days at Sites 1 and 2 in a river.

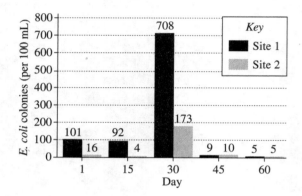

Figure 1

Table 1 shows how water quality rating varies with BI. Table 2 shows the average BI of each site during the collection period.

Table 1	
BI	Water quality rating
≥ 3.6	excellent
2.6 to 3.5	good
2.1 to 2.5	fair
1.0 to 2.0	poor

Table 2	
Location	Average BI
Site 1	6.3
Site 2	2.5

Figure 2 shows the water flow at each site on the 5 collection days.

Figure 2

Figures adapted from Stephen C. Landry and Michele L. Tremblay, "State of the Upper Merrimack 1995–1997: A River Quality Report." ©2000 by Upper Merrimack River Local Advisory Committee.

1. If an *E. coli* level of over 400 colonies formed per 100 mL of water is unsafe for swimming, on which of the following collection days and at which site would it have been unsafe to swim?

   A. Day 1 at Site 1
   B. Day 30 at Site 1
   C. Day 1 at Site 2
   D. Day 30 at Site 2

2. Based on Figures 1 and 2, consider the average water flow and the average *E. coli* level for Site 1 and Site 2 over the collection period. Which site had the higher average water flow, and which site had the higher average *E. coli* level?

	Higher water flow	Higher *E. coli* level
F.	Site 1	Site 1
G.	Site 1	Site 2
H.	Site 2	Site 1
J.	Site 2	Site 2

3. According to Table 1, what is the relationship between water quality and biotic index?

   A. As water quality improves, biotic index increases.
   B. As water quality improves, biotic index remains the same.
   C. As water quality degrades, biotic index increases.
   D. As water quality degrades, biotic index remains the same.

4. As water quality improves, the number of *stone fly larvae* (a type of aquatic invertebrate) increases. Students hypothesized that more stone fly larvae would be found at Site 1 than at Site 2. Are the data presented in Table 2 consistent with this hypothesis?

   F. Yes; based on BI, Site 1 had a water quality rating of good and Site 2 had a water quality rating of poor.
   G. Yes; based on BI, Site 1 had a water quality rating of excellent and Site 2 had a water quality rating of fair.
   H. No; based on BI, Site 1 had a water quality rating of poor and Site 2 had a water quality rating of good.
   J. No; based on BI, Site 1 had a water quality rating of fair and Site 2 had a water quality rating of excellent.

5. Which set of data best supports the claim that Site 1 has *lower* water quality than Site 2 ?

   A. Figure 1
   B. Figure 2
   C. Table 1
   D. Table 2

6. Suppose large amounts of fertilizer from adjacent fields begin to enter the river at Site 1. The BI of this site will most likely change in which of the following ways? The BI will:

   F. increase, because water quality is likely to increase.
   G. increase, because water quality is likely to decrease.
   H. decrease, because water quality is likely to increase.
   J. decrease, because water quality is likely to decrease.

Passage II

Aluminum water-based paints (AWPs) contain aluminum (Al) flakes that give surfaces a shiny, metallic appearance. If the flakes corrode, a dull coating of aluminum hydroxide forms on them:

$$2Al + 6H_2O \rightarrow 2Al(OH)_3 + 3H_2$$

Table 1 shows the volume of H_2 gas produced over time (at 25°C and 1 atm) from 100 mL samples of freshly made AWPs 1–3 in 3 separate trials. AWPs 1–3 were identical except that each had a different concentration of DMEA, an AWP ingredient that increases pH.

AWP	pH of AWP	Volume (mL) of H_2 produced by:			
		Day 2	Day 4	Day 6	Day 8
1	8	4	33	81	133
2	9	21	187	461	760
3	10	121	1,097	2,711	4,480

Table 1

The AWP 3 trial was repeated 4 times, but for each trial, the sample had the same concentration of 1 of 4 corrosion inhibitors (see Figure 1).

Key
- gluconic acid
- citric acid
- EDTA
- cupferron

Figure 1

Figure 1 adapted from Bodo Müller, "Corrosion Inhibitors for Aluminum." ©1995 by Division of Chemical Education, Inc., American Chemical Society.

7. Based on Table 1, which of the following graphs best shows how the volume of H_2 produced by AWP 2 changed over time?

8. Based on Table 1, if the volume of H_2 produced by Day 10 from the AWP 1 sample had been measured, it would most likely have been:

F. less than 133 mL.
G. between 133 mL and 461 mL.
H. between 461 mL and 760 mL.
J. greater than 760 mL.

9. According to Table 1, what volume of H_2 was produced by AWP 1 from the time the volume was measured on Day 6 until the time the volume was measured on Day 8 ?

A.   52 mL
B.   81 mL
C.   133 mL
D.   214 mL

10. In the trials represented in Table 1 and Figure 1, by measuring the volume of H_2, the experimenters were able to monitor the rate at which:

F. H_2O is converted to Al.
G. Al is converted to H_2O.
H. Al is converted to $Al(OH)_3$.
J. $Al(OH)_3$ is converted to Al.

11. Based on the passage, is DMEA most likely an acid or a base?

   A. An acid, because DMEA decreases pH.
   B. An acid, because DMEA increases pH.
   C. A base, because DMEA decreases pH.
   D. A base, because DMEA increases pH.

12. Consider the volume of H_2 produced by Day 2 from the AWP 3 sample that contained no corrosion inhibitor. Based on Table 1 and Figure 1, the AWP 3 sample containing EDTA produced approximately the same volume of H_2 by which of the following days?

   F. Day 1
   G. Day 4
   H. Day 7
   J. Day 10

Passage III

Students studied forces by using 2 identical platform scales, Scale A and Scale B, one of which is shown in Figure 1.

Figure 1

The weight of the platform of each scale was insignificant. When a force (such as that produced by a weight) was exerted on the surface of the platform, the hand rotated clockwise away from the zero point on the dial. The amount of rotation was directly proportional to the strength of the force.

Study 1

Prior to each of Trials 1–3, the students set the dial readings of both Scales A and B to zero. In each of these 3 trials, Scale A was stacked on top of Scale B (see Figure 2). In Trial 1, no weight was placed on the platform of Scale A; in Trial 2, a 5.0 newton (N) weight was placed on the platform of Scale A; and in Trial 3, a 10.0 N weight was placed on the platform of Scale A. The dial readings for the 3 trials are also shown in Figure 2.

Figure 2

Study 2

The students placed a pencil on the platform of each scale and positioned on top of the pencils a board that spanned the 0.40 m distance between the 2 scales. Prior to each of Trials 4–6, the students set the dial readings of Scales A and B to zero (see Figure 3).

Figure 3

In each of these 3 trials, a 10.0 N weight was placed on the board at various distances from the pencil on Scale B (see Figure 4). In Trial 4, the weight was 0.10 m from the pencil; in Trial 5, the weight was 0.20 m from the pencil; and in Trial 6, the weight was 0.30 m from the pencil. The dial readings for the 3 trials are also shown in Figure 4.

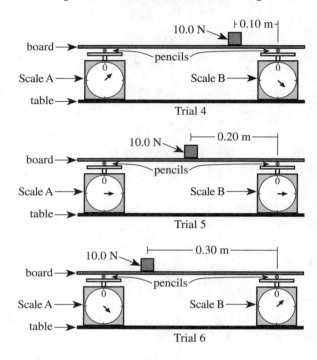

Figure 4

13. In which of the trials in Study 2, if any, was the force of the 10.0 N weight equally distributed between Scales A and B ?

    A. Trial 4
    B. Trial 5
    C. Trial 6
    D. None of the trials

14. Based on the results of Trials 1 and 2, Scale A and Scale B each weighed:

    F. 2.5 N.
    G. 5.0 N.
    H. 7.5 N.
    J. 10.0 N.

15. Assume that whenever a weight was placed on a scale's platform, a spring inside the scale was compressed. Assume also that the greater the added weight, the greater the amount of compression. Was the amount of potential energy stored in Scale A's spring greater in Trial 1 or in Trial 3 ?

   A. In Trial 1, because the amount of weight on the platform of Scale A was greater in Trial 1.
   B. In Trial 1, because the amount of weight on the platform of Scale A was less in Trial 1.
   C. In Trial 3, because the amount of weight on the platform of Scale A was greater in Trial 3.
   D. In Trial 3, because the amount of weight on the platform of Scale A was less in Trial 3.

16. In a new study, suppose Scale A were placed upside down atop Scale B, so that the platform of Scale A rested directly on the platform of Scale B. Which of the following drawings best represents the results that would most likely be obtained for this arrangement?

   F.

   G.

   H.

   J.

17. The main reason the pencils were placed on the scales in Study 2 was most likely:

   A. so that the line of contact between each pencil and its platform could be used as a reference line for distance measurements.
   B. so that the board would roll from side to side, rather than sliding from side to side over the scales' platforms.
   C. to add additional weight to the scales.
   D. to provide extra room for air above each scale's platform, so that the air pressure would be the same above and below the platform.

18. In Study 2, as the distance between the 10.0 N weight and the pencil on Scale B increased, the amount of force exerted on the surface of Scale B's platform:

   F. remained the same.
   G. increased only.
   H. decreased only.
   J. varied, but with no general trend.

19. Which of the following statements most likely describes an important reason for setting the dial readings of both scales to zero after Study 1, prior to each of Trials 4–6 ?

   A. To add the weights of the scales to each weight measurement
   B. To add the weights of the board and pencils to each weight measurement
   C. To subtract the weights of the scales from each weight measurement
   D. To subtract the weights of the board and pencils from each weight measurement

Passage IV

The *octane number* of a fuel is a measure of how smoothly the fuel burns in a gasoline engine. Lower octane fuels *knock* (explode) when burned, which lowers fuel efficiency and can cause engine damage. Heptane knocks considerably when burned and is given an octane number of 0. Isooctane knocks very little and is given an octane number of 100.

Different proportions of heptane and isooctane were mixed to obtain mixtures with octane numbers between 0 and 100 (see Table 1).

Table 1		
Volume of heptane (mL)	Volume of isooctane (mL)	Octane number
0	100	100
10	90	90
25	75	75
50	50	50
90	10	10
100	0	0

Experiment 1

A sample of each fuel mixture listed in Table 1 was burned in a test engine at an engine speed of 600 revolutions per minute (rpm). The number of knocks per minute was determined for each mixture. This was done so that an octane number could be assigned to any fuel by measuring its knock rate.

Experiment 2

Adding tetraethyllead (TEL) to a fuel changes its octane number. Different amounts of TEL were added to 1,000 mL samples of isooctane. Each fuel mixture was tested under the same conditions used in Experiment 1, and the measured knock rate was used to determine the octane number (see Figure 1).

Figure 1

Experiment 3

The *engine octane requirement* (EOR) is the minimum octane number of a fuel required for an engine to operate without becoming damaged. Fuels A and B were burned separately in an engine at different speeds. Table 2 shows the octane number determined for each fuel at each engine speed and the known EOR of the engine at each speed.

Table 2			
Engine speed (rpm)	EOR	Octane number in engine of:	
		Fuel A	Fuel B
1,500	97.4	98.4	96.7
2,000	95.3	96.6	96.1
2,500	93.5	95.0	95.4
3,000	91.9	92.3	93.8
3,500	90.6	90.9	92.5

20. Based on Experiment 3, as engine speed increases, the minimum octane number of fuel required for an engine to operate without becoming damaged:

    F. increases only.
    G. decreases only.
    H. increases, then decreases.
    J. decreases, then increases.

21. Suppose a trial had been performed in Experiment 3 at an engine speed of 2,200 rpm. At this engine speed, which of the following sets of octane numbers would most likely have been determined for Fuel A and Fuel B ?

	Fuel A	Fuel B
A.	95.0	95.4
B.	96.1	95.8
C.	96.6	96.1
D.	97.6	96.4

22. Which of the following expressions is equal to the octane number of each fuel mixture listed in Table 1 ?

    F. $\dfrac{\text{volume of isooctane}}{\text{volume of heptane}} \times 100$

    G. $\dfrac{\text{volume of heptane}}{\text{volume of isooctane}} \times 100$

    H. $\dfrac{\text{volume of isooctane}}{(\text{volume of heptane} + \text{volume of isooctane})} \times 100$

    J. $\dfrac{\text{volume of heptane}}{(\text{volume of heptane} + \text{volume of isooctane})} \times 100$

23. Based on Table 1 and Experiment 2, if 3 mL of TEL were added to a mixture of 100 mL of heptane and 900 mL of isooctane, the octane number of the resulting fuel would most likely be:

    A. less than 55.
    B. between 55 and 90.
    C. between 90 and 125.
    D. greater than 125.

24. Which of the 2 fuels from Experiment 3 would be better to use in an engine that will run at all engine speeds between 1,500 rpm and 3,500 rpm ?

    F. Fuel A, because its octane number was lower than the EOR at each of the engine speeds tested.
    G. Fuel A, because its octane number was higher than the EOR at each of the engine speeds tested.
    H. Fuel B, because its octane number was lower than the EOR at each of the engine speeds tested.
    J. Fuel B, because its octane number was higher than the EOR at each of the engine speeds tested.

25. Based on Table 1, if 2 mL of heptane were mixed with 8 mL of isooctane, the octane number of this mixture would be:

    A. 2.
    B. 8.
    C. 20.
    D. 80.

26. Suppose that 1 mL of TEL is added to 1,000 mL of heptane. Based on Experiment 2, one would predict that the octane number of the TEL/heptane mixture would be:

    F. higher than the octane number of pure heptane, but lower than 115.
    G. higher than the octane number of pure heptane, and higher than 115.
    H. lower than the octane number of pure heptane, but higher than 115.
    J. lower than octane number of pure heptane, and lower than 115.

Passage V

Introduction

Comets are complex mixtures of ices and dust that orbit the Sun. They can be classified by orbital period as either *long-period comets* or *short-period comets*.

Long-period comets have orbital periods of more than 200 yr and originate within our solar system in the *Oort Cloud*, a spherical shell of many icy bodies located at an average distance of 40,000 A.U. from the Sun (1 A.U. = average distance of Earth from the Sun). Long-period comets approach the Sun from all directions.

Short-period comets have orbital periods of 200 yr or less, and their orbital planes have *inclinations* 30° or less with respect to the *ecliptic plane*, the plane of Earth's orbit around the Sun. Portions of these planes are shown in Figure 1.

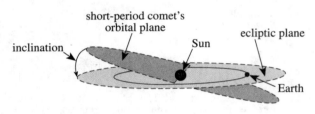

Figure 1

Two scientists present their viewpoints about the origin of short-period comets.

Scientist A

Short-period comets in our solar system originate within a thin ring-shaped region called the *Kuiper Belt* (KB). The KB has a small inclination with respect to the ecliptic plane and is located in the solar system between 30 A.U. and 50 A.U. from the Sun. The KB contains billions of icy bodies with diameters between 10 km and 30 km. These comet-size objects are too small to be clearly discerned at that distance with telescopes located on Earth's surface. Such telescopes have gathered indirect evidence, but not clear images, of much larger icy bodies that are part of the KB. The small inclinations of short-period comets' orbital planes with respect to the ecliptic plane are consistent with an origin in the KB. It has been discovered that other nearby stars have similar regions of icy bodies surrounding them.

Scientist B

The KB does not exist. Short-period comets were once long-period comets. Some long-period comets pass close enough to the giant planets (for example, Jupiter) to be influenced by the gravitational fields of the giant planets and are forced into orbits with orbital periods less than 200 yr. These altered orbits have orbital planes that have small inclinations with respect to the ecliptic plane. Also, most of the studied short-period comets have orbital planes with small inclinations with respect to the orbital planes of the giant planets, which, in turn, have small inclinations with respect to the ecliptic plane.

27. Which of the following generalizations about comets is most consistent with Scientist B's viewpoint?

    A. Long-period comets cannot become short-period comets.
    B. Short-period comets cannot become long-period comets.
    C. Long-period comets can become short-period comets.
    D. No long-period comets or short-period comets orbit the Sun.

28. Scientist A would most likely suggest that a new telescope more powerful than previous telescopes be used to search which of the following regions of space for objects in the KB ?

    F. The region 100,000 A.U. beyond our solar system
    G. The region 30 A.U. to 50 A.U. from the Sun at an angle of 90° with respect to the ecliptic plane
    H. The region 30 A.U. to 50 A.U. from the Sun at angles of 0° to 30° with respect to the ecliptic plane
    J. The region closely surrounding the planet Jupiter

29. Given the information about short-period comets in the introduction, which of the following inclinations with respect to the ecliptic plane would most likely NOT be observed for the orbital planes of short-period comets?

    A. 5°
    B. 15°
    C. 30°
    D. 45°

30. According to Scientist B, which of the following planets in our solar system is most likely capable of changing the orbit of a long-period comet over time?

    F. Mercury
    G. Earth
    H. Mars
    J. Saturn

31. Comet Halley currently has an orbital period of 76 yr. According to the information provided, Scientist B would most likely currently classify Comet Halley as a:

    A. short-period comet that originated in the Oort Cloud.
    B. short-period comet that originated in the KB.
    C. long-period comet that originated in the Oort Cloud.
    D. long-period comet that originated in the KB.

32. Based on Scientist A's viewpoint, the "much larger icy bodies" in the KB most likely have diameters of:

    F. less than 10 km.
    G. between 10 km and 20 km.
    H. between 20 km and 30 km.
    J. greater than 30 km.

33. Suppose a study of 1 nearby star revealed that it had no spherical shell of material similar to the Oort Cloud surrounding it. How would this discovery most likely affect the scientists' viewpoints, if at all?

    A. It would weaken Scientist A's viewpoint only.
    B. It would strengthen Scientist B's viewpoint only.
    C. It would strengthen both scientists' viewpoints.
    D. It would have no effect on either scientist's viewpoint.

Passage VI

Tomato plants grow poorly in high-salt environments. This effect is caused by 2 processes:

- A net movement of H_2O between the cytoplasm of the plants' cells and the environment via osmosis

- An increase in the cytoplasmic Na^+ concentration

The plant *Arabidopsis thaliana* carries a gene, *AtNHX1*. The product of this gene, *VAC*, facilitates uptake of cytoplasmic Na^+ by the plant's vacuoles.

A researcher created 4 genetically identical lines of tomato plants (L1–L4). An *AtNHX1* gene from *Arabidopsis thaliana* was isolated and 2 identical copies of this gene were incorporated into L1's genome. This process was repeated with L2 and L3 using a different *AtNHX1* allele for each line, so that L1, L2, and L3 had different genotypes for *AtNHX1*. The researcher then did an experiment.

Experiment

Fifty seedlings from each of the 4 lines were grown in 10 L of nutrient solution for 80 days. The 10 L nutrient solution contained H_2O, 12 g of fertilizer, and 3 g of NaCl. The nutrient solution was replaced every 5 days. After 80 days, average height, average mass (without fruit), and average fruit mass (per plant) were measured (see Table 1).

Table 1			
3 g of NaCl/10 L nutrient solution			
Line	Height (cm)	Mass (kg)	Fruit mass (kg)
L1	124	1.2	2.1
L2	128	1.2	2.0
L3	120	1.2	2.1
L4	124	1.2	2.0

This process was repeated except the 10 L nutrient solution contained 60 g of NaCl instead of 3 g of NaCl (see Table 2).

Table 2			
60 g of NaCl/10 L nutrient solution			
Line	Height (cm)	Mass (kg)	Fruit mass (kg)
L1	119	1.1	1.9
L2	121	1.1	1.9
L3	61	0.4	1.1
L4	63	0.5	1.0

The process was repeated again except the 10 L nutrient solution contained 120 g of NaCl instead of 3 g of NaCl (see Table 3).

Table 3			
120 g of NaCl/10 L nutrient solution			
Line	Height (cm)	Mass (kg)	Fruit mass (kg)
L1	118	1.0	1.8
L2	115	1.0	1.7
L3	34	0.2	0
L4	36	0.3	0

Tables 1–3 adapted from Hong-Xia Zhang and Eduardo Blumwald, "Transgenic Salt-Tolerant Tomato Plants Accumulate Salt in Foliage But Not in Fruit." ©2001 by Nature Publishing Group.

34. One plant produced no fruit and had a height of 21 cm. Which of the following most likely describes this plant?

   F. It was from L2 and was grown in a 10 L nutrient solution containing 60 g of NaCl.

   G. It was from L2 and was grown in a 10 L nutrient solution containing 120 g of NaCl.

   H. It was from L4 and was grown in a 10 L nutrient solution containing 60 g of NaCl.

   J. It was from L4 and was grown in a 10 L nutrient solution containing 120 g of NaCl.

35. During osmosis, water migrates through a semipermeable barrier. The osmosis referred to in the passage occurs through which of the following structures?

   A. Chromosomes

   B. Nuclear envelope

   C. Cell membrane

   D. Rough endoplasmic reticulum

36. For each line, as the concentration of salt in the nutrient solutions increased, average plant mass:

   F. increased only.

   G. decreased only.

   H. increased, then decreased.

   J. decreased, then increased.

37. Which of the following was an independent variable in the experiment?

   A. Whether a line received *AtNHX1*

   B. Whether a tomato plant was used

   C. Plant mass without fruit

   D. Plant height

38. Which of the following best characterizes the genotype of L1 for *AtNHX1* after L1 was genetically modified?

   F. It was heterozygous, since its 2 *AtNHX1* alleles were different.

   G. It was heterozygous, since its 2 *AtNHX1* alleles were identical.

   H. It was homozygous, since its 2 *AtNHX1* alleles were different.

   J. It was homozygous, since its 2 *AtNHX1* alleles were identical.

39. Suppose the data for all of the plants were plotted on a graph with height on the *x*-axis and mass (without fruit) on the *y*-axis. Suppose also that the best-fit line for these data was determined. Which of the following would most likely characterize the slope of this line?

   A. The line would not have a slope, because the line would be vertical.

   B. The slope of the line would be zero.

   C. The slope of the line would be negative.

   D. The slope of the line would be positive.

40. The researchers included 1 of the 4 lines to serve as a control. This line was most likely which one?

   F. L1

   G. L2

   H. L3

   J. L4

Passage VII

Flood basalt plateaus are large areas of Earth's surface covered with thick hardened lava. It has been hypothesized that the huge outpourings of lava that formed these plateaus were produced by *plumes* of molten material rising from deep within Earth.

Study 1

A model of a typical plume was created using a computer. It was hypothesized that the "head" of the plume produced the flood basalt plateaus when its molten material reached the surface. Figure 1 shows the computer-generated plume, its diameter, and how long, in millions of years (Myr), it would take the head of the plume to reach the surface.

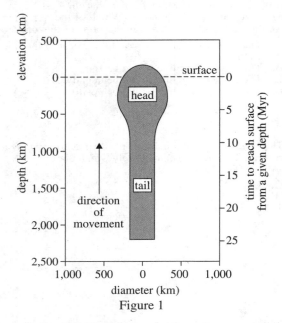

Figure adapted from R. I. Hill et al., *Mantle Plumes and Continental Tectonics.* ©1992 by the American Association for the Advancement of Science.

Study 2

Four flood basalt plateaus (A–D) were studied. The lava volume, in cubic kilometers (km³) was estimated for each plateau from the area of the plateau and the average thickness of the lava. The length of time lava was being produced at each plateau, and the rate of lava production, in km³ per year, were also estimated. The results are in Table 1.

Table 1				
Plateau	Age (Myr)	Lava volume (km³)	Length of time lava was produced (Myr)	Rate of lava production (km³/yr)
A	60	2,000,000	1.6	1.25
B	67	1,500,000	1.3	1.2
C	135	1,440,000	1.2	1.2
D	192	2,125,000	1.7	1.25

Table adapted from Mark A. Richards et al., *Flood Basalts and Hot-Spot Tracks: Plume Heads and Tails.* ©1989 by the American Association for the Advancement of Science.

Study 3

Scientists found that three large extinctions of marine organisms had ages similar to those of the formation of three of the flood basalt plateaus; 58 Myr, 66 Myr, and 133 Myr. It was hypothesized that the production of large amounts of lava and gases in the formation of plateaus may have contributed to those extinctions.

(Note: All of these ages have an error of ± 1 Myr.)

41. If the plume model in Study 1 is typical of all mantle plumes, the scientists would generalize that the heads of plumes are:

A. approximately half the diameter of the tail.
B. approximately twice the diameter of the tail.
C. the same diameter as the tail.
D. half as dense as the tail.

42. The scientists in Study 3 hypothesized that the larger the volume of lava produced, the larger the number of marine organisms that would become extinct. If this hypothesis is correct, the formation of which of the following plateaus caused the largest number of marine organisms to become extinct?

F. Plateau A
G. Plateau B
H. Plateau C
J. Plateau D

43. Based on the results of Study 2, a flood basalt plateau that produced lava for a period of 1.8 Myr would most likely have a lava volume

A. between 1,440,000 km³ and 1,500,000 km³.
B. between 1,500,000 km³ and 2,000,000 km³.
C. between 2,000,000 km³ and 2,125,000 km³.
D. over 2,125,000 km³.

44. According to Study 2, which of the following statements best describes the relationship, if any, between the age of a flood basalt plateau and the length of time lava was produced at that plateau?

    F. As the age of a plateau increases, the length of time lava was produced increases.

    G. As the age of a plateau increases, the length of time lava was produced decreases.

    H. As the age of a plateau increases, the length of time lava was produced increases, and then decreases.

    J. There is no apparent relationship between the age of a plateau and the length of time lava was produced.

45. Which of the following graphs best represents the relationship between the age of a flood basalt plateau and the rate of lava production?

A.

B.

C.

D.

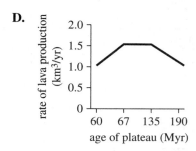

46. If the hypothesis made by the scientists in Study 3 is correct, evidence would most likely be found of another extinction of marine organisms that occurred around:

    F. 77 Myr ago.
    G. 192 Myr ago.
    H. 250 Myr ago.
    J. 314 Myr ago.

Passage VIII

Succession refers to the change in species composition in a given area over ecological time.

Table 1 shows the bird species, the *dominant* (most common) plants, and the successional time in years (yr) on plots of abandoned farmland studied in Georgia.

The estimated changes in *net productivity* (grams of organic mass produced per square meter per year [$g/m^2/yr$]) and biomass (kilograms of organic material per square meter [kg/m^2]) of plants on abandoned farmland in New York appear in Figures 1 and 2, respectively. Successional time is divided into three stages based on the dominant plants.

Table 1									
Bird species / Successional time (yr)	1	3	15	20	25	35	60	100	150
Dominant plants	Weeds	Grasses	Shrubs		Pines				Oaks
Grasshopper sparrow	■	■							
Eastern meadowlark		■	■						
Yellowthroat			■	■					
Field sparrow			■	■	■				
Yellow-breasted chat				■					
Rufous-sided towhee					■	■	■	■	
Pine warbler					■	■	■	■	
Cardinal						■	■	■	
Summer tanager						■	■	■	
Eastern wood pewee							■	■	■
Blue-gray gnatcatcher							■	■	
Crested flycatcher								■	■
Carolina wren								■	■
Ruby-throated hummingbird								■	■
Tufted titmouse								■	■
Hooded warbler								■	■
Red-eyed vireo								■	■
Wood thrush									■

Note: Shaded areas indicate bird species was present at a density of at least 1 pair per 10 acres.

Figure 1

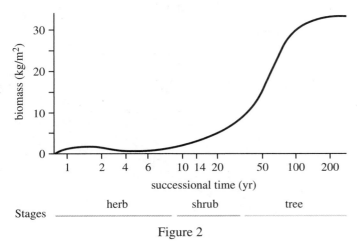

Figure 2

Figures and table adapted from William T. Keeton and James L. Gould, *Biological Science.* ©1986 by W.W. Norton & Company, Inc.

47. According to Figure 1, at the end of Year 50 the net productivity of the land was closest to:

    A. 15 g/m²/yr.
    B. 50 g/m²/yr.
    C. 425 g/m²/yr.
    D. 1,125 g/m²/yr.

48. Based on the data in Figures 1 and 2, the researchers should make which of the following conclusions about the overall change in net productivity and biomass over the 200 years studied?

    F. Both net productivity and biomass increased.
    G. Both net productivity and biomass decreased.
    H. Net productivity increased and biomass decreased.
    J. Net productivity decreased and biomass increased.

49. According to Figure 1, total net productivity increased the most during which of the following time periods?

    A. From the end of Year 2 to the end of Year 4
    B. From the end of Year 4 to the end of Year 14
    C. From the end of Year 14 to the end of Year 50
    D. From the end of Year 50 to the end of Year 200

50. Which of the following conclusions about net productivity is consistent with the results shown in Figure 1?

    F. Net productivity was lowest when shrubs were the dominant plants.
    G. Net productivity was lowest when trees were the dominant plants.
    H. Net productivity was highest when herbs were the dominant plants.
    J. Net productivity was highest when trees were the dominant plants.

51. A student learned that a particular plot of abandoned farmland in Georgia supported eastern meadowlarks, yellowthroats, and field sparrows at a density of at least one pair per 10 acres. Based on Table 1, the student would predict that the dominant plants on this plot of land were most likely:

    A. weeds.
    B. grasses.
    C. shrubs.
    D. pines.

Passage IX

Solids, liquids, and gases usually expand when heated. Three experiments were conducted by scientists to study the expansion of different substances.

Experiment 1

The apparatus shown in Diagram 1 was used to measure the linear expansion of wires of the same length made from different metals. In each trial, a wire was connected to a voltage source, run through a series of pulleys, then attached to a weight. The temperature of the wire was varied by changing the amount of voltage applied. The amount of expansion is directly proportional to the rotation of the final pulley. The results are shown in Figure 1.

Diagram 1

Figure 1

Experiment 2

A sample of liquid was placed in a stoppered test tube fitted with a graduated capillary tube and the test tube was then placed in a temperature-controlled water bath (Diagram 2). The rise of the liquid in the capillary tube was then measured at different temperatures. The results for three liquids are shown in Figure 2.

Diagram 2

Figure 2

Experiment 3

A 20 mL sample of a gas in a gas syringe at room temperature (20°C) was placed in a temperature-controlled water bath (Diagram 3). Changes in gas volume as the temperature increased were measured for three gases. The results are shown in Figure 3.

Diagram 3

Figure 3

52. In Experiment 2, at which of the following temperatures did all of the liquids tested have the same volume?

F. 20°C
G. 30°C
H. 40°C
J. 50°C

53. A scientist has hypothesized that as the temperature of a gas is increased at constant pressure, the volume of the gas will also increase. Do the results of Experiment 3 support his hypothesis?

A. Yes; the volume of all of the gases tested in Experiment 3 increased as temperature increased.
B. Yes; although air decreased in volume when the temperature increased, nitrogen and methane volumes both increased.
C. No; the volume of all of the gases tested in Experiment 3 decreased as temperature increased.
D. No; although air increased in volume when the temperature increased, nitrogen and methane volumes both decreased.

54. Based on the results of Experiment 1, if an engineer needs a wire most resistant to stretching when it is placed under tension and heat, which of the following wires should she choose?

F. Aluminum
G. Brass
H. Iron
J. Nickel

55. Based on the results of Experiment 3, if a balloon was filled with air at room temperature and placed on the surface of a heated water bath, as the temperature of the water increased, the volume of the balloon would:

A. increase only.
B. decrease only.
C. decrease, then increase.
D. remain the same.

56. The scientists tested a copper wire of the same initial length as the wires tested in Experiment 1. At 80°C, the linear expansion of the wire was 0.12 mm. Based on the results of Experiment 1, which of the following correctly lists five wires by their length in the apparatus at 80°C from *shortest* to *longest*?

F. Aluminum, brass, copper, iron, nickel
G. Aluminum, copper, brass, iron, nickel
H. Nickel, iron, copper, brass, aluminum
J. Nickel, iron, brass, copper, aluminum

57. If Experiment 1 had been repeated using a heavier weight attached to the brass wire, which of the following figures best shows the comparison between the results of using the heavier weight and the original weight on the brass wire?

A.

B.

C.

D.

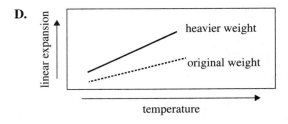

Passage X

Certain layers of Earth's atmosphere absorb particular wavelengths of solar radiation while letting others pass through. Types of solar radiation include X-rays, ultraviolet light, visible light, and infrared radiation. The cross section of Earth's atmosphere below illustrates the altitudes at which certain wavelengths are absorbed. The arrows point to the altitudes at which solar radiation of different ranges of wavelengths is absorbed. The figure also indicates the layers of the atmosphere and how atmospheric density, pressure, and temperature vary with altitude.

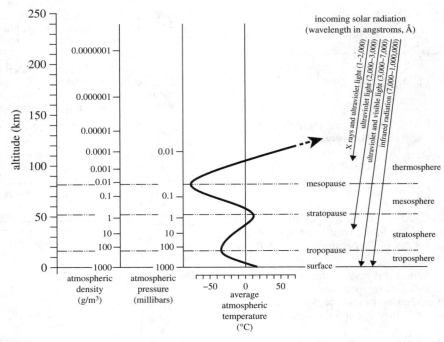

Figure adapted from Arthur Strahler, *The Earth Sciences.* ©1963 by Harper and Row.

Note: $1 \text{ Å} = 1 \times 10^{-10}$ meters.

58. According to the data provided, at what altitude is the upper boundary of the thermosphere located?

F. 150 km
G. 200 km
H. 250 km
J. The upper boundary is not included on the figure.

59. The ozone layer selectively absorbs ultraviolet radiation of 2,000–3,000 Å wavelengths. According to this information and the data, which atmospheric layer contains the ozone layer?

A. Troposphere
B. Stratosphere
C. Mesosphere
D. Thermosphere

60. The information provided in the figure indicates that the air temperature in the troposphere is LEAST likely to be influenced by which of the following wavelengths of energy?

F. 1,500 Å
G. 4,500 Å
H. 6,000 Å
J. 7,000 Å

61. On the basis of the information in the figure, one could generalize that atmospheric pressure in each atmospheric layer increases with:

A. decreasing temperature.
B. increasing temperature.
C. decreasing altitude.
D. increasing altitude.

62. Atmospheric boundaries are at a higher than usual altitude above areas that get more direct solar radiation. Based on this information and the data provided, which of the following predictions about atmospheric boundaries would most likely be true if Earth received *less* solar radiation than it presently does?

F. The tropopause, stratopause, and mesopause would all increase in altitude.
G. The tropopause, stratopause, and mesopause would all decrease in altitude.
H. The tropopause and stratopause would increase in altitude, but the mesopause would decrease in altitude.
J. The tropopause would decrease in altitude, but the stratopause and mesopause would increase in altitude.

Passage XI

Some oceanic shrimp are vertical migrators. For vertically migrating species, most of the population is found at the bottom of their depth range during the day and at the top of their depth range at night. Table 1 shows the depth ranges and water, protein, lipid, and carbohydrate content of three vertically migrating (vm) species of shrimp and three non-migrating (nm) species of deep-sea shrimp. Figure 1 shows water temperature and oxygen partial pressure at various ocean depths.

			% ash-free dry weight		
Species	Depth range (m)	Water content (% wet weight)	protein	lipid	carbohydrate
vm 1	300–600	77.5	62.8	23.8	0.7
vm 2	10–400	76.6	53.4	16.4	0.8
vm 3	75–400	79.5	60.5	14.7	0.7
nm 1	500–1,100	75.9	36.9	36.1	0.5
nm 2	500–1,000	76.7	41.5	31.5	0.8
nm 3	650–1,100	72.8	35.8	49.0	0.5

Table 1

Key
— temperature
—□— oxygen partial pressure

Figure 1

63. Based on the information in Table 1, one would conclude that vertically migrating shrimp have a higher percent content of:

A. protein than lipid.
B. lipid than protein.
C. carbohydrate than lipid.
D. carbohydrate than protein.

64. On the basis of the information given, one would expect that, compared to the vertically migrating shrimp species, the non-migrating shrimp species:

F. have a greater water content.
G. have a lower percent lipid content.
H. can tolerate higher water temperatures.
J. can tolerate lower oxygen partial pressures.

65. Assume that shrimp of a newly discovered species of vertically migrating shrimp were captured at night at a minimum depth of 200 m. Assume that only temperature limits the range of this species. Based on the information in Figure 1, one would predict that the maximum water temperature these shrimp could survive in would be:

A. 3.5°C.
B. 7.5°C.
C. 12.5°C.
D. 15.5°C.

66. Protein is a major component of muscle. Assume that shrimp that are strong swimmers tend to have a higher protein:lipid ratio than do shrimp that are weaker swimmers. On the basis of Table 1, one would conclude that which of the following shrimp species is the strongest swimmer?

F. vm 2
G. vm 3
H. nm 1
J. nm 3

67. Assume that only oxygen partial pressure limits the range of the shrimp species shown in Table 1. Accordingly, which of the following pieces of information supports the hypothesis that vm 2 and vm 3 cannot tolerate oxygen partial pressures below 25 mm Hg?

A. They are not able to tolerate temperatures above 10°C.
B. They have unusually high water contents.
C. They are not found below a depth of 400 m.
D. They are not found above a depth of 100 m.

Passage XII

Two students explain why the *smoke* (a mixture of gases and carbon particles) from burning wood in a fireplace rises up the chimney from the fireplace. They also discuss how chimney *efficiency* (the volume of smoke flowing out the top of the chimney per second for a given temperature difference between inside and outside the chimney) is related to chimney height.

Student 1

Smoke rises because the gases from burning wood are less dense than the air that surrounds the fireplace. Because the gases are hotter than the air, the gas molecules have a higher average speed than the air molecules. Consequently, the average distance between adjacent gas molecules is greater than the average distance between adjacent air molecules, and so the gas *density* is less than the air density. As a result, the upward *buoyant force* acting on the gases is stronger than the downward *force of gravity* acting on the gases, and the gases rise, carrying the carbon particles with them. The upward flow of smoke is maintained as new air enters the fireplace, causing more wood to burn.

As chimney height increases, efficiency increases. The taller the chimney, the greater the volume of hot gas, the stronger the buoyant force compared with the force of gravity, and the more rapidly smoke rises.

Student 2

Smoke rises because wind blows across the top of the chimney. When no wind is blowing, the air pressure at the bottom of the chimney is slightly higher than the air pressure at the top of the chimney. However, when air at the top of the chimney moves at a higher speed than air at the bottom of the chimney, the pressure difference between the bottom and the top of the chimney is so great that air is forced upward, carrying smoke with it. The departure of air from the bottom of the chimney, in turn, creates a pressure difference that forces new air into the fireplace, causing further burning and an upward flow of smoke.

As chimney height increases, efficiency increases. Generally, wind speed increases with altitude. The taller the chimney, the greater the difference in air speed, the greater the difference in air pressure, and the more rapidly smoke rises.

68. According to Student 1, which of the following quantities is less for the gases from burning wood than for the air that surrounds the fireplace?

F. Average speed of the molecules
G. Average distance between adjacent molecules
H. Density
J. Temperature

69. When wood was burned in two fireplaces that differ only in the height of their chimneys (keeping the same temperature difference between inside and outside each chimney), Chimney Y was found to be more efficient than Chimney X. What conclusion would each student draw about which chimney is taller?

A. Both Student 1 and Student 2 would conclude that Chimney X is taller.
B. Both Student 1 and Student 2 would conclude that Chimney Y is taller.

C. Student 1 would conclude that Chimney X is taller; Student 2 would conclude that Chimney Y is taller.
D. Student 1 would conclude that Chimney Y is taller; Student 2 would conclude that Chimney X is taller.

70. Which student(s), if either, would predict that smoke from burning wood will rise up the chimney from a fireplace on a day when the air at the top of the chimney is NOT moving?

F. Student 1 only
G. Student 2 only
H. Both Student 1 and Student 2
J. Neither Student 1 nor Student 2

71. When wood is burned in a fireplace, air in the fireplace, as well as gases from the burning wood, rises up the chimney. Student 1 would most likely argue that the air in the fireplace rises because the air is:

A. hotter than the gases from the burning wood.
B. cooler than the gases from the burning wood.
C. hotter than the air that surrounds the fireplace.
D. cooler than the air that surrounds the fireplace.

72. When the air inside a particular hot-air balloon cooled, the balloon and its inside air descended. Based on Student 1's explanation, the reason the balloon and its inside air descended is most likely that the:

F. downward buoyant force acting on the balloon and its inside air was stronger than the upward force of gravity acting on the balloon and its inside air.
G. upward buoyant force acting on the balloon and its inside air was stronger than the downward force of gravity acting on the balloon and its inside air.
H. downward force of gravity acting on the balloon and its inside air was stronger than the upward buoyant force acting on the balloon and its inside air.
J. upward force of gravity acting on the balloon and its inside air was stronger than the downward buoyant force acting on the balloon and its inside air.

73. Based on Student 1's explanation, if the gases from burning wood lose heat while rising up a chimney, which of the following quantities pertaining to the gases simultaneously increases?
A. Density of the gases
B. Temperature of the gases
C. Average speed of the gas molecules
D. Average distance between adjacent gas molecules

74. Based on Student 2's explanation, the reason the wings of an airplane keep the airplane up in the air is that air moves at a higher speed:

F. above the wings than below the wings.
G. below the wings than above the wings.
H. in front of the wings than behind the wings.
J. behind the wings than in front of the wings.

Passage XIII

Salts containing nitrite ions (NO_2^-) are often added to meats to prevent discoloration caused by air and bacterial growth. Use of NO_2^- is controversial because studies have linked NO_2^- with cancer. Students performed two experiments to measure NO_2^- levels.

Experiment 1

Four solutions, each containing a different amount of $NaNO_2$ (a salt) in H_2O were prepared. A coloring agent was added that binds with NO_2^- to form a purple compound that strongly absorbs light of a specific wavelength, and each solution was diluted to 100 mL. A *blank* solution was prepared in the same manner, but no $NaNO_2$ was added. A *colorimeter* (a device that measures how much light of a selected wavelength is absorbed by a sample) was used to measure the *absorbance* of each solution. The absorbances were corrected by subtracting the absorbance of the blank solution from each reading (see Table 1 and Figure 1).

Table 1		
Concentration of NO_2^- (ppm*)	Measured absorbance	Corrected absorbance
0.0	0.129	0.000
1.0	0.282	0.153
2.0	0.431	0.302
4.0	0.729	0.600
8.0	1.349	1.220
*ppm is parts per million		

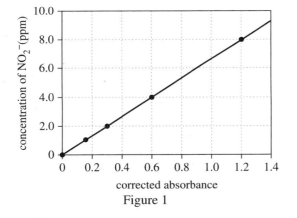

Figure 1

Experiment 2

A 100 g meat sample was ground in a blender with 50 mL of H_2O and the mixture was filtered. The blender and remaining meat were then washed with H_2O, these washings were filtered, and the liquid was added to the sample solution. The coloring agent was added and the solution was diluted to 100 mL. The procedure was repeated for several meats, and the absorbances were measured (see Table 2).

Table 2		
Meat	Corrected absorbance	Concentration of NO_2^- (ppm)
Hot dog	0.667	4.4
Bologna	0.561	3.7
Ground turkey	0.030	0.2
Ham	0.940	6.2
Bacon	0.773	5.1

75. Based on the results of Experiment 1, if the concentration of NO_2^- in a solution is doubled, then the corrected absorbance of the solution will approximately:

   A. remain the same.
   B. halve.
   C. double.
   D. quadruple.

76. A sample of pastrami was also measured in Experiment 2 and its corrected absorbance was determined to be 0.603. Which of the following correctly lists bologna, bacon, and pastrami in *decreasing* order of NO_2^- concentration?

   F. Bologna, bacon, pastrami
   G. Pastrami, bacon, bologna
   H. Bologna, pastrami, bacon
   J. Bacon, pastrami, bologna

77. Based on the results of Experiment 1, if a solution with a concentration of 1.5 ppm NO_2^- had been tested, the corrected absorbance would have been closest to which of the following values?

   A. 0.15
   B. 0.23
   C. 0.30
   D. 0.36

78. If Experiments 1 and 2 were repeated using a different coloring agent that produces a different color when it binds with NO_2^-, then which of the following changes in procedure would be necessary?

   F. The new coloring agent should be added to the blank solution, but not to the sample solutions.
   G. Both of the coloring agents should be added to the blank solution and to all of the samples.
   H. The absorbance of the blank solution made with the new coloring agent should be added to the measured absorbances.
   J. The colorimeter should be set to measure at a different wavelength of light.

79. Based on the results of Experiments 1 and 2, if the measured absorbances for the meats tested in Experiment 2 were compared with their corrected absorbances, the measured absorbances would be:

   A. higher for all of the meats tested.
   B. lower for all of the meats tested.
   C. lower for some of the meats tested; higher for others.
   D. the same for all of the meats tested.

80. If some of the water-soluble contents found in all of the meats tested in Experiment 2 absorbed light of the same wavelength as the compound formed with NO_2^- and the coloring agent, how would the measurements have been affected? Compared to the actual NO_2^- concentrations, the NO_2^- concentrations apparently measured would be:

   F. higher.
   G. lower.
   H. the same.
   J. higher for some of the meats, lower for others.

Passage XIV

A team of researchers constructed a greenhouse, consisting of three artificially lighted and heated sections, to be used to grow food during a long space voyage. The researchers found the weekly average light intensity, in arbitrary units, and the weekly average air temperature, in degrees Celsius (°C), in each section. The results for the first six weeks of their measurements are given in Table 1 (weekly average light intensity) and Table 2 (weekly average air temperature).

Table 1			
	Weekly average light intensity (arbitrary units)		
Week	Section 1	Section 2	Section 3
1	289.3	84.4	120.7
2	305.5	79.2	80.8
3	313.4	76.2	77.0
4	314.9	73.6	69.4
5	304.5	68.8	74.6
6	311.1	68.5	68.4

Table 2			
	Weekly average air temperature (°C)		
Week	Section 1	Section 2	Section 3
1	19.68	19.10	18.66
2	20.12	19.22	18.47
3	20.79	19.21	18.61
4	20.98	19.49	18.95
5	21.04	19.91	19.09
6	21.13	19.60	18.59

81. The highest weekly average air temperature recorded during the first six weeks of the study was:

A. 18.47°C.
B. 21.13°C.
C. 120.7°C.
D. 314.9°C.

82. According to Table 2, weekly average air temperatures were recorded to the nearest:

F. 0.01°C.
G. 0.1 °C.
H. 1.0°C.
J. 10°C.

83. A plot of weekly average air temperature versus weekly average light intensity for Section 1 is best represented by which of the following graphs?

A.

B.

C.

D.

84. Which of the following statements best describes the changes in the weekly average air temperature in Section 1 during Weeks 1 through 6?

F. The weekly average air temperature increased between Weeks 1 and 3 and decreased between Weeks 4 and 6.

G. The weekly average air temperature decreased between Weeks 1 and 3 and increased between Weeks 4 and 6.

H. The weekly average air temperature always increased.

J. The weekly average air temperature always decreased.

85. Suppose the *efficiency of illumination* is defined as the intensity of light absorbed by the plants divided by the intensity of light provided to the plants. Based on the data, would one be justified in concluding that the efficiency of illumination was higher in Section 1 than in the other sections?

A. Yes, because the illumination provided to the plants was highest in Section 1.

B. Yes, because the amount of light not absorbed by the plants was highest in Section 1.

C. No, because the amount of light absorbed by the plants was lowest in Section 1.

D. No, because the information provided is insufficient to determine efficiency of illumination.

Passage XV

Carbon monoxide gas (CO) is toxic in air at concentrations above 0.1% by volume. Cars are the major source of atmospheric CO in urban areas. Higher CO levels are observed during colder weather. A group of students proposed that cars emit more CO at colder air temperatures than at warmer air temperatures during the first 15 minutes after they are started. The students did the following experiments to investigate this hypothesis.

Experiment 1

A hose was connected to the tailpipe of a car. The engine was started and the exhaust was collected in a plastic bag. A 1 mL sample of the exhaust was taken from the bag with a syringe and injected into a *gas chromatograph,* an instrument that separates a mixture of gases into its individual components. Comparisons of the exhaust with mixtures of known CO concentrations were made to determine the percent by volume of CO in the exhaust. Exhaust was collected at two-minute intervals. Samples of exhaust from each of four cars were tested at an external temperature of −9°C. The results are shown in Table 1.

Table 1				
Time after starting (min)	Percent of CO in the exhaust at −9°C:			
	1978 Model X	1978 Model Y	1996 Model X	1996 Model Y
1	3.5	3.2	1.2	0.3
3	4.0	3.7	1.0	1.2
5	4.5	7.5	1.5	2.5
7	3.6	10.0	1.0	3.0
9	3.2	9.1	0.5	2.6
11	3.1	8.0	0.5	2.0
13	3.0	7.0	0.5	2.0
15	2.9	7.0	0.4	1.8

Experiment 2

The same four cars were tested at a temperature of 20°C using the procedure from Experiment 1. The results are shown in Table 2.

Table 2				
Time after starting (min)	Percent of CO in the exhaust at 20°C:			
	1978 Model X	1978 Model Y	1996 Model X	1996 Model Y
1	2.0	0.8	0.3	0.2
3	2.8	2.0	0.5	1.0
5	3.4	6.0	0.5	1.5
7	1.5	7.0	0.3	0.8
9	1.3	7.0	0.3	0.5
11	1.0	6.5	0.1	0.3
13	1.0	5.0	0.1	0.3
15	0.9	4.8	0.1	0.2

86. Do the results from Experiment 1 support the hypothesis that, at a given temperature and time, the exhaust of newer cars contains lower percents of CO than the exhaust of older cars?

   F. Yes; the highest percent of CO was in the exhaust of the 1996 Model Y.
   G. Yes; both 1996 models had percents of CO that were lower than those of either 1978 model.
   H. No; the highest percent of CO was in the exhaust of the 1978 Model Y.
   J. No; both 1978 models had percents of CO that were lower than those of either 1996 model.

87. A student, when using the gas chromatograph, was concerned that CO_2 in the exhaust sample may be interfering in the detection of CO. Which of the following procedures would best help the student investigate this problem?

    A. Filling the bag with CO_2 before collecting the exhaust
    B. Collecting exhaust from additional cars
    C. Injecting a sample of air into the gas chromatograph
    D. Testing a sample with known amounts of CO and CO_2

88. Based on the results of the experiments and the information in the table below, cars in which of the following cities would most likely contribute the greatest amount of CO to the atmosphere in January? (Assume that the types, numbers, and ages of cars used in each city are approximately equal.)

City	Average temperature (°F) for January
Minneapolis	11.2
Pittsburgh	26.7
Seattle	39.1
San Diego	56.8

    F. Minneapolis
    G. Pittsburgh
    H. Seattle
    J. San Diego

89. In Experiment 1, which of the following factors varied?

    A. The method of sample collection
    B. The volume of exhaust that was tested
    C. The year in which the cars were made
    D. The temperature at which the engine was started

90. Many states require annual testing of cars to determine the levels of their CO emissions. Based on the experiments, in order to determine the maximum percent of CO found in a car's exhaust, during which of the following times after starting a car would it be best to sample the exhaust?

    F. 1–3 min
    G. 5–7 min
    H. 9–11 min
    J. 13 min or longer

91. How would the results of the experiments be affected, if at all, if the syringe contents were contaminated with CO-free air? (The composition of air is 78% N_2, 21% O_2, 0.9% Ar, and 0.1% other gases.) The measured percents of CO in the exhaust would be:

    A. higher than the actual percents at both −9°C and 20°C.
    B. lower than the actual percents at −9°C, but higher than the actual percents at 20°C.
    C. lower than the actual percents at both −9°C and 20°C.
    D. the same as the actual percents at both −9°C and 20°C.

Passage XVI

A student performed three activities with a microscope that had four objective lenses.

Activity 1

The student viewed four slides (A, B, C, and D) through each objective lens. Each slide had two thin lines painted on it. For each objective lens, the student determined whether she could see the lines as separate or whether they blurred into one image. The results appear in Table 1.

Table 1				
	Objective Lens:			
Slide	1	2	3	4
A	|	|	|	|
B	|	|	|	||
C	|	|	||	||
D	|	||	||	||

Note: \|\| indicates lines appeared separate; \| indicates lines blurred together.

Activity 2

The student was given a prepared slide with a line on it that was 0.1 mm in length. This length was defined as the *object size*. Next, she viewed the slide with each objective lens, estimating how long the line appeared. This estimated length was called the *image size*. Finally, she calculated the magnification (M) associated with each objective lens from the following formula:

$$M = \text{image size} / \text{object size}.$$

The data appear in Table 2.

Table 2		
Objective Lens	Image size (mm)	M
1	4	40
2	10	100
3	20	200
4	40	400

Activity 3

The *numerical aperture* (NA) of each objective lens was printed on the microscope. NA determines how much detail can be seen and is related to *resolution* (R). R is defined as the smallest distance separating two objects such that the objects appear separate. Thus an objective lens with a small R shows a sample more clearly than does an objective lens with a large R. R is calculated from the following formula:

$$R = \lambda/2(NA)$$

where λ is the wavelength of the light, in nanometers (nm), used to view the objects.

The student calculated R for each objective lens, assuming a λ of 550 nm. The data appear in Table 3.

Table 3		
Objective Lens	NA	R (nm)
1	0.10	2,750
2	0.25	1.100
3	0.40	688
4	0.65	423

92. If the student had viewed the slide used in Activity 2 through a fifth objective lens and the image size with this objective lens was 30 mm, the M associated with this objective lens would have been:

   F. 30.
   G. 100.
   H. 300.
   J. 1,000.

93. Based on the results of Activity 2, the combination of which of the following lines and objective lenses would result in the greatest image size?

   A. A 0.7 mm line viewed through Objective Lens 1
   B. A 0.6 mm line viewed through Objective Lens 2
   C. A 0.5 mm line viewed through Objective Lens 3
   D. A 0.4 mm line viewed through Objective Lens 4

94. When viewing Slide C in Activity 1, the student was able to discern two distinct lines with how many of the objective lenses?

   F. 1
   G. 2
   H. 3
   J. 4

95. Which of the following equations correctly calculates R (in nm) for Objective Lens 2, using light with a wavelength of 425 nm?

   A. R = 425 / 2(0.10)
   B. R = 425 / 2(0.25)
   C. R = 0.10 / 2(425)
   D. R = 0.25 / 2(425)

96. Another student calculated the R of a fifth objective lens as described in Activity 3. He determined that for this fifth objective lens, R = 1,830 nm. Accordingly, the NA of this lens was most likely closest to which of the following values?

   F. 0.15
   G. 0.25
   H. 0.35
   J. 0.45

97. Activity 1 and Activity 2 differed in that in Activity 1:

   A. four different slides were used.
   B. four different objective lenses were used.
   C. the wavelength of the light was varied.
   D. the object sizes were greater than the image sizes.

Passage XVII

A *blackbody* is an object that absorbs all of the radiation that strikes it. The blackbody also emits radiation at all wavelengths; the emitted radiation is called *blackbody radiation.* The brightness of blackbody radiation at a given wavelength depends on the temperature of the blackbody. A graph of brightness versus wavelength for a blackbody is called a *blackbody curve.* Blackbody curves for the same blackbody at three different temperatures are shown in the figure below.

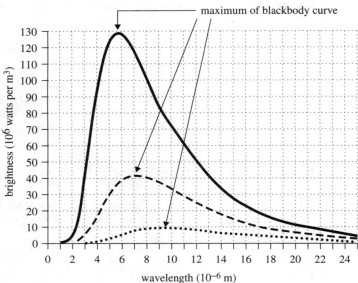

(Note: 1 watt = 1 joule per second; joule is a unit of energy. At wavelengths above 25×10^{-6} m, the brightness of the blackbody at each temperature continues to decrease.)

98. The area under each blackbody curve gives the total amount of energy emitted every second by 1 m² of the blackbody. Which of the following correctly ranks the three curves, from *greatest* to *least,* according to the total amount of energy emitted every second by 1 m² of the blackbody at the wavelengths shown?

   F. 300 K, 400 K, 500 K
   G. 300 K, 500 K, 400 K
   H. 400 K, 500 K, 300 K
   J. 500 K, 400 K, 300 K

99. Based on the figure, at a temperature of 300 K and a wavelength of 30×10^{-6} m, the brightness of a blackbody will most likely be:

   A. less than 5×10^6 watts per m³.
   B. between 5×10^6 watts per m³ and 40×10^6 watts per m³.
   C. between 41×10^6 watts per m³ and 130×10^6 watts per m³.
   D. greater than 130×10^6 watts per m³.

100. The radiation emitted by a star can be represented by the radiation from a blackbody having the same temperature as the star's visible surface. Based on the figure, which of the following sets of blackbody curves best represents stars of equal diameter with surface temperatures of 3,000 K, 6,000 K, and 9,000 K?

F.

G.

H.

J.

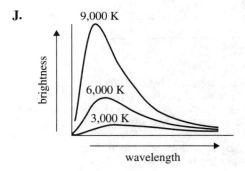

101. Based on the figure, the maximum of the blackbody curve will equal 75×10^6 watts per m^3 when the temperature of the blackbody is closest to:

A. 250 K
B. 350 K
C. 450 K
D. 550 K

102. The frequency of radiation increases as the radiation's wavelength decreases. Based on this information, over all wavelengths in the figure, as the frequency of the radiation from a blackbody increases, the brightness of the radiation:

F. increases only.
G. decreases only.
H. increases, then decreases.
J. decreases, then increases.

Passage XVIII

Some of the liquid in a closed container evaporates, forming a vapor that condenses, reforming the liquid. The pressure of the vapor at *equilibrium* (when the rates of evaporation and condensation are equal) is the liquid's *vapor pressure*. A liquid in an open container boils when its vapor pressure equals the *external pressure*. The following experiments were performed to study vapor pressures.

Experiment 1

The apparatus shown in Figure 1 was assembled except for the tubing. The flask was placed in a 20°C H_2O bath. After five minutes the manometer was connected, and 2 mL of hexane was added to the flask from the dropper. Some of the hexane evaporated. The vapor pressure was determined by measuring the height of the mercury (Hg) after the Hg level had stabilized. Additional trials were performed at different temperatures and with other liquids in the flask. The results are shown in Table 1.

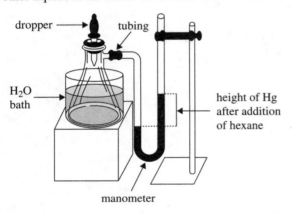

Figure 1

Figure 1 adapted from Henry Dorin, Peter E. Demmin, and Dorothy L. Gabel, *Chemistry: The Study of Matter.* ©1989 by Prentice-Hall, Inc.

Table 1			
	Vapor pressure (mm Hg) at:		
Liquid	0°C	20°C	40°C
2-Butanone	35	75	200
Ethyl acetate	20	70	180
Hexane	40	110	250
Methanol	25	90	245
2-Propanol	9	35	100

Experiment 2

A test tube containing a thermometer and hexane was heated in an oil bath until the hexane boiled gently. The temperature was recorded. The external pressure was 760 mm Hg. This procedure was repeated in a chamber at pressures of 400 mm Hg and 100 mm Hg. The boiling points of other liquids were also determined. The results are shown in Table 2.

Table 2			
	Boiling point (°C) at external pressure of:		
Liquid	760 mm Hg	400 mm Hg	100 mm Hg
2-Butanone	79.6	60.0	25.0
Ethyl acetate	77.1	59.3	27.0
Hexane	68.7	49.6	15.8
Methanol	64.7	49.9	21.2
2-Propanol	82.5	67.8	39.5

103. Which of the following bar graphs best represents the vapor pressures of the liquids from Experiment 1 at 20°C?

A.

B.

C.

D.
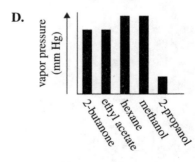

104. Which of the following figures best depicts the change in height of the Hg in the manometer in Experiment 1?

Hg height before liquid was added   Hg height after Hg level stabilized

F.

G.

H.

J.

105. A student hypothesized that, at a given external pressure, the higher a liquid's molecular weight, the higher the boiling point of that liquid. Do the results of Experiment 2 and all of the information in the table below support his hypothesis?

Liquid	Molecular weight (grams per mole)
2-Butanone	72
Ethyl acetate	88
Hexane	86
Methanol	32
2-Propanol	60

A. Yes; methanol has the lowest molecular weight and the lowest boiling point.
B. Yes; ethyl acetate has a higher molecular weight and boiling point than hexane.
C. No; the higher a liquid's molecular weight, the lower the liquid's boiling point.
D. No; there is no clear relationship in these data between boiling point and molecular weight.

106. According to the results of Experiment 2, as the external pressure increases, the boiling points of the liquids:

F. decrease only.
G. increase only.
H. decrease, then increase.
J. increase, then decrease.

107. Which of the following figures best illustrates the apparatus used inside the pressure chamber in Experiment 2?

A.

B.

C.

D.

108. Which of the following statements best explains why in Experiment 1 the experimenter waited 5 minutes before connecting the manometer to the flask with the tubing? The experimenter waited to allow:

F. all of the H_2O vapor to be removed from the flask.
G. time for the liquid in the flask to evaporate.
H. time for the height of the Hg in the manometer to stabilize.
J. the air in the flask to adjust to the temperature of the H_2O bath.

Passage XIX

A *polypeptide* molecule is a chain of amino acids. A *protein* consists of one or more polypeptides. A protein's shape is described by three or four levels of structure.

1. The *primary structure* of a protein is the sequence of amino acids in each polypeptide.
2. The *secondary structure* of a protein is the local folding patterns within short segments of each polypeptide due to *hydrogen bonding* (weak chemical bonds).
3. The *tertiary structure* is the folding patterns that result from interactions between amino acid *side chains* (parts of an amino acid) in each polypeptide. These folding patterns generally occur across greater distances than those associated with the secondary structure.
4. The *quaternary structure* is the result of the clustering between more than one folded polypeptide.

A protein can adopt different shapes, and each shape has a relative energy. Lower-energy shapes are more stable than higher-energy shapes, and a protein with a relatively high-energy shape may *denature* (unfold) and then *renature* (refold), adopting a more stable shape. A protein that is almost completely denatured is called a *random coil*. Random coils are unstable because they are high-energy shapes; however, some can renature, adopting more stable shapes.

Two scientists discuss protein shape.

Scientist 1

The *active shape* (the biologically functional shape) of a protein is always identical to the protein's lowest-energy shape. Any other shape would be unstable. Because a protein's lowest-energy shape is determined by its primary structure, its active shape is determined by its primary structure.

Scientist 2

The active shape of a protein is dependent upon its primary structure. However, a protein's active shape may also depend on its *process of synthesis,* the order (in time) in which the amino acids were bonded together. As synthesis occurs, stable, local structures form within short segments of the polypeptide chain due to hydrogen bonding. These local structures may be different than the local structures associated with the protein's lowest-energy shape. After synthesis, these structures persist, trapping the protein in an active shape that has more energy than its lowest-energy shape.

109. According to the passage, protein shapes with relatively low energy tend to:

  A. be random coils.
  B. lack a primary structure.
  C. become denatured.
  D. maintain their shape.

110. The information in the passage indicates that when a protein is completely denatured, it still retains its original:

  F. primary structure.
  G. secondary structure.
  H. tertiary structure.
  J. quaternary structure.

111. Scientist 2's views differ from Scientist 1's views in that only Scientist 2 believes that a protein's active shape is partially determined by its:

  A. quaternary structure.
  B. amino acid sequence.
  C. process of synthesis.
  D. tertiary folding patterns.

112. A student has 100 balls. The balls are various colors. The student chooses 15 balls and aligns them in a row. The spatial order in which the balls were placed corresponds to which of the following levels of structure in a protein?

  F. Primary structure
  G. Secondary structure
  H. Tertiary structure
  J. Quaternary structure

113. Suppose proteins are almost completely denatured and then allowed to renature in a way that allows them to have their lowest-energy shapes. Which of the following statements about the proteins is most consistent with the information presented in the passage?

  A. If Scientist 1 is correct, all of the proteins will have their active shapes.
  B. If Scientist 1 is correct, all of the proteins will have shapes different than their active shapes.
  C. If Scientist 2 is correct, all of the proteins will have their active shapes.
  D. If Scientist 2 is correct, all of the proteins will have shapes different than their active shapes.

114. Which of the following diagrams showing the relationship between a given protein's shape and its relative energy is consistent with Scientist 2's assertions about the energy of proteins, but is NOT consistent with Scientist 1's assertions about the energy of proteins?

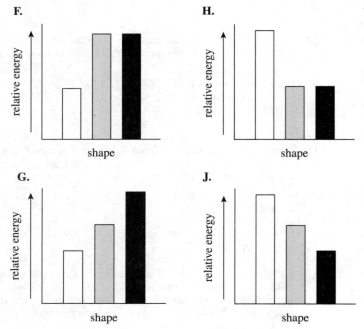

F.

H.

G.

J.

Key
☐ randomly coiled shape
▨ active shape
■ most stable shape

115. Scientist 2 says that a protein may be trapped in a moderately high-energy shape. Which of the following findings, if true, could be used to *counter* this argument?

A. Once a protein has achieved its tertiary structure, all of the folding patterns at the local level are stable.

B. Enough energy is available in the environment to overcome local energy barriers, driving the protein to its lowest-energy shape.

C. During protein synthesis, the secondary structure of a protein is determined before the tertiary structure is formed.

D. Proteins that lose their tertiary structure or quaternary structure also tend to lose their biological functions.

Passage XX

Tiny marine organisms build shells from *calcite* (CaCO₃) dissolved in seawater. After the organisms' death, the shells sink. Some shells dissolve before they reach the seafloor, but some form layers of *calcareous ooze* (CaCO₃-rich sediment). Figure 1 shows how seawater's degree of saturation with respect to $CaCO_3$ and the rate at which $CaCO_3$ dissolves change with depth. The *CaCO₃ compensation depth* (CCD) represents the depth beneath which $CaCO_3$ dissolves faster than it precipitates. Figure 2 shows typical depths at which various seafloor sediments are found. Figure 3 shows the percent coverage for two seafloor sediments in three oceans.

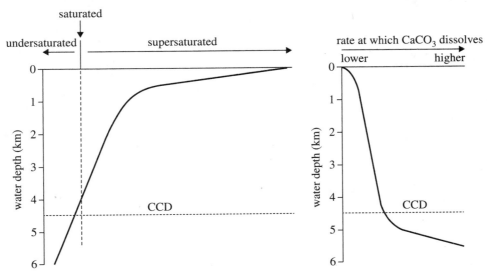

Figure 1

Figure 1 adapted from J. Andrews, P. Brimblecombe, T. Jickells, and P. Liss, *An Introduction to Environmental Chemistry.* ©1996 by Blackwell Science, Ltd.

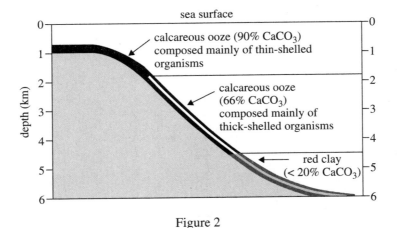

Figure 2

Figure 2 adapted from M. Grant Gross, *Oceanography*, 6th ed. ©1990 by Macmillan Publishing Company.

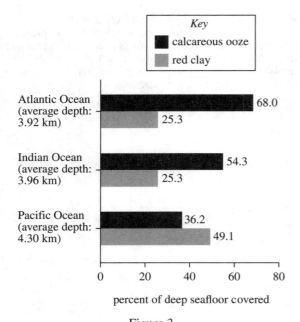

Key
■ calcareous ooze
▨ red clay

Atlantic Ocean
(average depth:
3.92 km) — 68.0 / 25.3

Indian Ocean
(average depth:
3.96 km) — 54.3 / 25.3

Pacific Ocean
(average depth:
4.30 km) — 36.2 / 49.1

percent of deep seafloor covered

Figure 3

Figure 3 adapted from Harold Thurman, *Introductory Oceanography.* ©1991 by Macmillan Publishing Company.

116. Assume that the Arctic Ocean seafloor has an average depth of 4.9 km. According to Figures 2 and 3, the Arctic Ocean seafloor is most likely covered with:

F. calcareous ooze only.
G. nearly the same areas of calcareous ooze and red clay.
H. a greater area of calcareous ooze than of red clay.
J. a greater area of red clay than of calcareous ooze.

117. The data in Figure 2 support which of the following statements about the relative thickness of marine organism shells and the depths at which calcareous oozes composed of those shells are found? Calcareous oozes formed mainly from thick-shelled organisms are found:

A. at shallower depths than those formed mainly from thin-shelled organisms.
B. at greater depths than those formed mainly from thin-shelled organisms.
C. over the same depth range as those formed mainly from thin-shelled organisms.
D. in the same areas of a given ocean as those formed mainly from thin-shelled organisms.

118. $CaCO_3$ often precipitates out of seawater in areas where the seawater is shallow (less than 1 km deep). According to Figure 1, this most likely occurs because seawater in those locations:

F. is undersaturated with respect to $CaCO_3$.
G. is saturated with respect to $CaCO_3$.
H. is supersaturated with respect to $CaCO_3$.
J. contains no $CaCO_3$.

119. According to Figure 1, above what maximum depth is seawater supersaturated with respect to $CaCO_3$?

A. 3.0 km
B. 3.5 km
C. 4.0 km
D. 4.5 km

120. Figure 1 shows that the rate at which $CaCO_3$ dissolves increases the most between which of the following depths?

F. Between 3.5 km and 4.0 km
G. Between 4.0 km and 4.5 km
H. Between 4.5 km and 5.0 km
J. Between 5.0 km and 5.5 km

Passage XXI

Students used two methods to calculate D, a car's *total stopping distance; D* is the distance a car travels from the time a driver first reacts to an emergency until the car comes to a complete stop.

In Method 1, R is the distance a car travels during a driver's assumed reaction time of 0.75 sec, and B is the average distance traveled once the brakes are applied. Method 2 assumes that D = initial speed in ft/sec × 2 sec. Table 1 lists R, B, and D for various initial speeds, where D was computed using both methods. Figure 1 contains graphs of D versus initial speed for Method 1 and Method 2.

Table 1					
Initial speed (mi/hr)	Initial speed (ft/sec)	Method 1			Method 2
		R (ft)	B (ft)	D (ft)	D (ft)
20	29	22	20	42	58
40	59	44	80	124	118
60	88	66	180	246	176
80	118	88	320	408	236

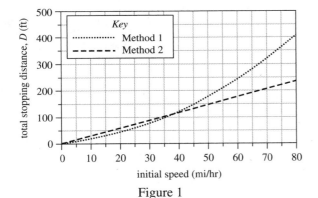

Figure 1

Table 1 and Figure 1 adapted from Edwin F. Meyer III, *Multiple-Car Pileups and the Two-Second Rule,* ©1994 by The American Association of Physics Teachers.

121. Compared to R at an initial speed of 20 mi/hr, R at an initial speed of 80 mile/hr is:

A. ¼ as great.
B. ½ as great.
C. 2 times as great.
D. 4 times as great.

122. In Method 1, D equals:

F. $R + B$.
G. $R - B$.
H. $R \times B$.
J. $R \div B$.

123. According to Figure 1, the two methods yield the same value for D when initial speed is closest to:

A. 20 mi/hr
B. 40 mi/hr
C. 60 mi/hr
D. 80 mi/hr

124. A driver was traveling 60 mi/hr when she spotted an accident and immediately applied her brakes. It took her 2 sec from the time she spotted the accident until she brought her car to a complete stop. According to Method 2, how far did her car travel during the 2-sec interval?

F. 58 ft
G. 118 ft
H. 176 ft
J. 234 ft

125. Based on Table 1 or Figure 1, if the initial speed of a car is 90 mi/hr, D, according to Method 2, will be:

A. less than 90 ft.
B. between 95 ft and 150 ft.
C. between 150 ft and 250 ft.
D. greater than 250 ft.

Passage XXII

Urine samples were collected from four students on one day at 8:00 A.M. and 8:00 P.M. The samples were then analyzed. Tables 1 and 2 show the volume, color, specific gravity, and the concentration of suspended solids of the 8:00 A.M. and 8:00 P.M. urine samples, respectively. *Specific gravity* was calculated as follows:

Specific gravity = (density of sample) / (density of water)

The normal range for the specific gravity of urine is 1.0001–1.0350.

Table 1				
8:00 A.M. urine samples				
Student	Volume (mL)	Color*	Specific gravity	Suspended solids (g/L)
A	100	8	1.028	74.48
B	260	5	1.016	42.56
C	270	4	1.027	71.82
D	385	2	1.006	15.96

*Note: Color was assigned using the following scale:
0 = very pale; 10 = very dark.

Table 2				
8:00 P.M. urine samples				
Student	Volume (mL)	Color*	Specific gravity	Suspended solids (g/L)
A	150	7	1.024	63.84
B	300	4	1.015	39.90
C	305	3	1.020	53.20
D	400	0	1.001	2.66

*Note: Color was assigned using the following scale:
0 = very pale; 10 = very dark.

126. Based on the information presented, which of the following urine samples most likely had the highest water content per milliliter?
    F. The 8:00 A.M. urine sample from Student A
    G. The 8:00 A.M. urine sample from Student B
    H. The 8:00 P.M. urine sample from Student C
    J. The 8:00 P.M. urine sample from Student D

127. Do the data in Tables 1 and 2 support the conclusion that as urine volume increases, urine color darkens?
    A. Yes, because urine samples with the greatest volumes had the highest color values.
    B. Yes, because urine samples with the greatest volumes had the lowest color values.
    C. No, because urine samples with the greatest volumes had the highest color values.
    D. No, because urine samples with the greatest volumes had the lowest color values.

128. Based on the results provided, as the concentration of suspended solids in urine increase, the specific gravity of the urine:
    F. increases only.
    G. decreases only.
    H. increases, then decreases.
    J. decreases, the increases.

129. One of the four students had the flu on the two days preceding the collection of the urine samples. During these two days, the student experienced a net fluid loss due to vomiting and diarrhea. Based on the information provided, the student with the flu was most likely:
    A. Student A.
    B. Student B.
    C. Student C.
    D. Student D.

130. A volume of 1 mL from which of the following urine samples would weigh the most?
    F. The 8:00 A.M. urine sample from Student B
    G. The 8:00 A.M. urine sample from Student D
    H. The 8:00 P.M. urine sample from Student A
    J. The 8:00 P.M. urine sample from Student C

Passage XXIII

The following experiments were performed to investigate the effects of adding various *solutes* (substances that are dissolved in a solution), in varying amounts, on the boiling points and freezing points of H_2O solutions. Pure H_2O freezes at 0°C and boils at 100°C at standard atmospheric pressure.

Experiment 1

A student dissolved 0.01 mole of sodium chloride (NaCl) in 100 g of H_2O. Each mole of NaCl produces 2 moles of solute particles (1 mole of sodium ions and 1 mole of chloride ions in solution). After the NaCl dissolved, the freezing point of the solution was determined. This procedure was repeated with different amounts of NaCl and table sugar (sucrose). Each mole of sucrose produces 1 mole of solute particles (sucrose molecule). The results are shown in Table 1.

Solution	Substance added to H_2O	Amount added (mole)	Freezing point (°C)
1	NaCl	0.01	−0.3
2	NaCl	0.05	−1.7
3	NaCl	0.1	−3.4
4	NaCl	0.2	−6.9
5	sucrose	0.01	−0.2
6	sucrose	0.05	−1.0
7	sucrose	0.1	−2.1
8	sucrose	0.2	−4.6

Table 1

Note: Freezing points were measured at standard atmospheric pressure.

Experiment 2

A student dissolved 0.01 mole of NaCl in 100 g of H_2O. After the NaCl dissolved, the boiling point of the solution was determined. The procedure was repeated using various amounts of NaCl. The results are shown in Table 2.

Solution	Amount of NaCl added (mole)	Boiling point (°C)
9	0.01	100.1
10	0.05	100.5
11	0.1	101.0
12	0.2	102.0

Table 2

Note: Boiling points were measured at standard atmospheric pressure.

131. A solution containing 100 g of H_2O and an unknown amount of NaCl boils at 104°C. Based on the results of Experiment 2, the number of moles of NaCl dissolved in the solution is closest to:

   A. 0.2
   B. 0.3
   C. 0.4
   D. 0.5

132. Which of the following factors was NOT directly controlled by the student in Experiment 2?

   F. The substance added to the H_2O
   G. The amount of H_2O used
   H. The amount of solute added to the H_2O
   J. The boiling points of the H_2O solutions

133. From the results of Experiment 2, what would one hypothesize, if anything, about the effect of the number of solute particles dissolved in H_2O on the boiling point of a solution?

   A. The more solute particles that are present, the higher the boiling point.
   B. The more solute particles that are present, the lower the boiling point.
   C. No hypothesis can be made because only one solute was tested.
   D. The number of solute particles produced does not affect the boiling point.

134. According to the results of Experiments 1 and 2, which of the following conclusions can be made about the magnitudes of the changes in the boiling point and freezing point of H_2O solutions when 0.2 mole of NaCl is added to 100 g of H_2O? The freezing point is:

   F. raised less than the boiling point is lowered.
   G. raised more than the boiling point is raised.
   H. lowered less than the boiling point is lowered.
   J. lowered more than the boiling point is raised.

135. Based on the results of Experiment 1, as the number of sodium particles and chloride particles in 100 g of H_2O increased, the freezing point of the solution:

   A. increased only.
   B. decreased only.
   C. decreased, then increased.
   D. remained the same.

136. $CaCl_2$ produces 3 moles of solute particles per mole when dissolved. Experiment 1 was repeated using a solution containing 100 g of H_2O and 0.1 mole $CaCl_2$. Assuming that $CaCl_2$ has the same effect on the freezing point of H_2O as does NaCl per particle produced when dissolved, the freezing point of the solution would most likely be:

   F. between 0°C and −2.1°C.
   G. between −2.1°C and −3.4°C.
   H. between −3.4°C and −6.9°C.
   J. below −6.9°C.

Passage XXIV

The study of oxygen isotopes present in water can give us clues to the climate of a certain location. The ratio of the isotopes ^{18}O and ^{16}O in a sample of rain, snow or ice is compared to the $^{18}O/^{16}O$ ratio in a *standard sample*. A standard sample has a known value for the parameter being measured. The comparison of a sample's ratio to that of the standard is called the *O-18 index* ($\delta^{18}O$). The $\delta^{18}O$ is calculated using the formula:

$$\delta^{18}O = \frac{(^{18}O/^{16}O)_{\text{sample}} - (^{18}O/^{16}O)_{\text{standard}}}{(^{18}O/^{16}O)_{\text{standard}}} \times 1{,}000$$

Scientists conducted three studies to examine the $\delta^{18}O$ of glacial ice in Arctic and Antarctic locations and learn about the past climates there.

Study 1

Containers were placed on glaciers at 25 locations in the Arctic to collect snowfall. The containers' contents were collected every two weeks during a one-year period and analyzed for ^{16}O and ^{18}O. Figure 1 shows the calculated monthly $\delta^{18}O$ and air temperature averages.

month
Figure 1

Study 2

At the 25 Arctic locations from Study 1, a 500-m-deep vertical ice core was drilled. Each core represented the past 100,000 years of glacial ice accumulation at the site. Starting at the surface, samples were taken every 10 m along the length of the cores. These samples were analyzed for ^{18}O and ^{16}O. Larger $\delta^{18}O$ values indicate that a relatively warmer climate existed at the time the ice was formed than do smaller $\delta^{18}O$ values. The calculated average $\delta^{18}O$ values for the samples are shown in Figure 2.

Figure 2

Study 3

The procedures of Study 2 were repeated at 25 Antarctic locations. The past 100,000 years of glacial ice accumulation at the site was represented by a 300-m ice core. The calculated average $\delta^{18}O$ values for the samples are shown in Figure 3.

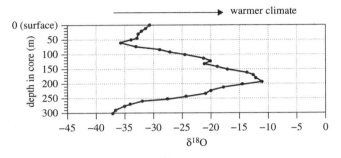

Figure 3

137. According to Study 1, average air temperatures in the Arctic were closest for which of the following pairs of months?

   A. January and March
   B. March and September
   C. May and September
   D. October and December

138. According to Study 1, which of the following best describes the relationship between the $\delta^{18}O$ of the Arctic snow samples and the average monthly air temperatures? As the average monthly air temperatures increased, then decreased, the $\delta^{18}O$:

   F. increased only.
   G. increased, then decreased.
   H. decreased only.
   J. decreased, then increased.

139. Which of the following statements best describes why sites in the Arctic and Antarctic were chosen for these studies? These sites had to have:

   A. average air temperatures below −25°C year-round.
   B. glaciers present at many different locations.
   C. several months during the year in which no precipitation fell.
   D. large areas of bare soil and rock present.

140. According to Study 2, the ice found in the Arctic core at depths between 150 m and 200 m was formed during a period when the climate in the Arctic was most likely:

   F. somewhat cooler than the present climate in the Arctic.
   G. the same as the present climate in the Arctic.
   H. the same as the present climate in the Antarctic.
   J. somewhat warmer than the present climate in the Arctic.

141. According to Studies 2 and 3, 100,000 years of ice accumulation was represented by a 500-m core in the Arctic and a 300-m core in the Antarctic. Which of the following statements best explains why the ice cores were different lengths? The average rate of glacial ice accumulation over that time period in the Arctic:

   A. was greater than the rate in the Antarctic.
   B. was the same as the rate in the Antarctic.
   C. was less than the rate in the Antarctic.
   D. could not be determined with any accuracy.

142. According to the information provided, a sample that had a calculated $\delta^{18}O$ of zero had a $^{18}O/^{16}O$ value that compared in which of the following ways to the $^{18}O/^{16}O$ value of the standard sample? The sample's $^{18}O/^{16}O$ ratio was:

   F. ½ of the $^{18}O/^{16}O$ ratio of the standard.
   G. the same as the $^{18}O/^{16}O$ ratio of the standard.
   H. 1½ times larger than the $^{18}O/^{16}O$ ratio of the standard.
   J. twice as large as the $^{18}O/^{16}O$ ratio of the standard.

Passage XXV

Lyme disease is caused by bacteria that are transmitted to humans by the bite of infected deer ticks. The first sign of Lyme disease is often a bull's-eye rash on the skin. Figure 1 shows the 2-year deer tick life cycle.

A study area adjacent to a forest was divided into 5 zones (A–E). People living in the study area were tested monthly for Lyme disease. The results are shown in Figure 2. For each zone, Table 1 shows the number of houses, mice, deer tick larvae per mouse, households that sighted deer daily, and the percent of households inhabited by at least 1 person infected with Lyme disease.

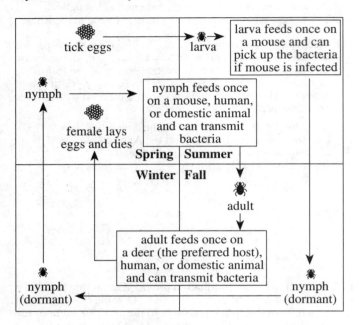

Figure 1

Figure 1 adapted from "Deer Tick Ecology." ©1998 by the American Lyme Disease Foundation, Inc.

Note: Bars on the graph are stacked.

Figure 2

Figure 2 and Table 1 adapted from Catherine C. Latavica et al., "Rapid Emergence of a Focal Epidemic of Lyme Disease in Coastal Massachusetts." ©1989 by The Massachusetts Medical Society.

Table 1				
	Number of:			Percent of households inhabited by at least 1 infected person
Zone	houses	mice	larvae/mouse	households that sighted deer daily	
A	12	300	50	12	75
B	13	203	19	10	62
C	13	128	23	8	54
D	13	108	67	4	38
E	14	93	20	6	36

143. Based on Table 1, as the number of mice found in a given zone increased, the number of larvae per mouse:

A. increased only.
B. decreased only.
C. decreased, then remained the same.
D. varied with no general trend.

144. Based on Figure 1, which organism is essential in maintaining the Lyme disease bacteria in the deer tick population?

F. Deer
G. Mice
H. Humans
J. Domestic animals

145. Based on Table 1, the average percent of households inhabited by at least 1 infected person in Zones A–E of the study area was closest to:

A. 30%.
B. 40%.
C. 50%.
D. 60%.

146. Suppose additional data had been obtained about the total number of infected deer tick larvae in each of the zones. Given Table 1, one would predict that the largest total of infected deer tick larvae would have been found in which zone?

F. Zone A
G. Zone B
H. Zone D
J. Zone E

147. According to Figure 2, the total number of new cases of Lyme disease was the same for both months in each of the following pairs of months EXCEPT:

A. March and September.
B. April and December.
C. May and October.
D. August and November.

Passage XXVI

Oxyfluorocarbons (OFCs) are oils composed of only carbon (C), fluorine (F), and oxygen (O). They are useful as lubricants in exposed mechanical systems on spacecraft. However, OFCs tend to decompose upon exposure to heated metal surfaces, which usually have a *metal oxide* (MO) outer layer (see Figure 1).

OFC (liquid) + MO (solid)

$\downarrow$ heat

COF_2 (gas) + CO_2 (gas) + M (solid) + liquid residue

Figure 1

When an oil decomposes, the mechanical systems stop working, crippling the spacecraft.

Chemists studied the decomposition of 2 OFCs (OFC1 and OFC2).

Experiment 1

In a chamber at 100°C and 0.01 atmospheres (atm) pressure, 1.5 g of OFC1 was mixed with 50 mg of powdered iron(III)oxide (Fe_2O_3), an MO. The gases produced by the decomposition of the OFC caused the pressure to increase. The *induction period* (the time for the pressure to rise to 0.20 atm) was measured. Shorter induction periods indicate more rapid decomposition. The procedure was repeated at different temperatures, and for OFC2 (see Table 1).

Table 1		
	Induction period (sec)	
Temperature (°C)	OFC1	OFC2
100	1,800	998
120	903	603
140	442	301
160	218	133
180	111	52
200	55	18
220	29	6

Experiment 2

The induction periods of OFC1 with various powdered Fe compounds were measured as in Experiment 1 at 180°C (see Table 2). Some of these compounds are hypothesized to exist on heated metal surfaces, or to form as minor by-products of the reaction shown in Figure 1.

Table 2		
Compound	Formula	Induction period (sec)
Iron(II)*oxide	FeO	5,784
Iron(III)fluoride	FeF_3	3
Iron(III)chloride	$FeCl_3$	48
Iron(III)carbonate	$Fe_2(CO_3)_3$	996
Iron(III)sulfate	$Fe_2(SO_4)_3$	998

*Roman numerals in parentheses indicate the amount of positive charge on the iron atom.

148. If, in Experiment 1, a trial had been done at 150°C, the induction periods (in sec) for OFC1 and OFC2 would most likely have been which of the following?

	OFC1	OFC2
F.	203	311
G.	311	203
H.	301	442
J.	442	301

149. Based on the results of Experiment 2, which compound produced the fastest decomposition of OFC1 at 180°C ?

A. FeO
B. FeF_3
C. $FeCl_3$
D. $Fe_2(CO_3)_3$

150. In which of the following ways was the design of Experiment 1 different from that of Experiment 2 ? In Experiment 1:

   F.   only OFC1 was studied; in Experiment 2, only OFC2 was studied.
   G.   only OFC2 was studied; in Experiment 2, only OFC1 was studied.
   H.   temperature was varied; in Experiment 2, temperature was always the same.
   J.   temperature was always the same; in Experiment 2, temperature was varied.

151. In Experiment 1, during the decomposition of OFC2 at 100°C, as time increased from 0 to 998 sec, the pressure in the chamber:

   A.   decreased from 0.20 atm to 0.01 atm.
   B.   decreased from 0.01 atm to 0.20 atm.
   C.   increased from 0.20 atm to 0.01 atm.
   D.   increased from 0.01 atm to 0.20 atm.

152. A chemist claimed that under identical conditions, OFC2 will always break down in the presence of an MO more quickly than will OFC1. Are the results of Experiment 1 consistent with her claim?

   F.   No; at each temperature tested, the induction period for OFC1 was less than that for OFC2.
   G.   No; at each temperature tested, the induction period for OFC1 was greater than that for OFC2.
   H.   Yes; at each temperature tested, the induction period for OFC1 was less than that for OFC2.
   J.   Yes; at each temperature tested, the induction period for OFC1 was greater than that for OFC2.

153. Based on the information in the passage, which of the following could be the chemical formula for an OFC ?

   A. $CF_3(CF_2O)_{25}CF_3$
   B. $CF_3(CH_2CF_2O)_{45}CF_3$
   C. $CF_3(CF_2CO_2)_{15}CCl_3$
   D. $CF_3(CF_2OCF_2)_{35}CH_3$

Passage XXVII

In *Zamia* (a genus of seed plants), males have pollen-producing cones, and females have seed-producing cones. Pollination requires the movement of pollen from inside a male cone to inside a female cone, where multiple *ovules* are located and pollinated. The ovules then develop into seeds. Two students discuss the pollination process.

Student 1

In *Zamia*, 90% of ovule pollinations result from insect pollination; 10% result from wind pollination. No other pollination mechanism exists.

Zamia have *mutualistic* (mutually beneficial) relationships with insects. *Weevils* (a type of beetle) swarm male *Zamia* cones when these cones are releasing pollen. Upon entering the cones, the weevils become covered with the plant's sticky pollen. The weevils then visit the female *Zamia* cones. In the absence of weevils, the percent of ovule pollination in *Zamia* is about 10%.

Wind pollination is infrequent because *Zamia* pollen is large and heavy. Additionally, the openings into the female cones are aligned horizontally, so wind-borne pollen must be blown horizontally to enter these cones.

Student 2

Wind pollination and insect pollination each cause 50% of pollination events in *Zamia* ovules. Without wind pollination, the percent of ovule pollination decreases by 50%. Likewise, without insect pollination, the percent of ovule pollination decreases by 50%. If neither of these processes occurs, the percent of ovule pollination decreases by 100%.

Wind tunnel experiments show that the shape of the female *Zamia* cones creates air currents that facilitate the horizontal movement of pollen into these cones. Additionally, male *Zamia* cones produce enormous quantities of pollen, a trait that is common only in wind-pollinated plants.

Experiments

The students proposed 3 experiments using a natural *Zamia* population in an area with weevils and in which the percent of ovule pollination is normally 99% (see the table).

Experiment	Procedure
1	Some female *Zamia* cones are covered with plastic bags that exclude insects and wind.
2	Some female *Zamia* cones are covered with mesh bags that exclude insects, but not wind.
3	Some female *Zamia* cones are covered with cylinders that exclude wind, but not insects.

154. Suppose Experiment 2 were performed as described. Based on Student 2's hypothesis, the percent of ovule pollination in the female *Zamia* cones that would be covered with mesh bags would be closest to:

    F. 0%.
    G. 10%.
    H. 50%.
    J. 99%.

155. Student 1 states that "wind-borne pollen must be blown horizontally to enter these cones." Which of the following describes how Student 2 responds to this statement? Student 2 argues that the shape of the:

    A. female *Zamia* cones creates air currents that decrease the likelihood that pollen will enter these cones.
    B. female *Zamia* cones creates air currents that increase the likelihood that pollen will enter these cones.
    C. male *Zamia* cones creates air currents that decrease the likelihood that pollen will enter these cones.
    D. male *Zamia* cones creates air currents that increase the likelihood that pollen will enter these cones.

156. Suppose an experiment were performed using a natural population of *Zamia* and that all of the male cones were covered with plastic bags that excluded insects and wind. Assuming that Student 1's hypothesis is correct, the percent of ovule pollination would most likely be closest to:

F. 0%.
G. 33%.
H. 67%.
J. 100%.

157. Student 1 would most likely agree with the statement that *Zamia* pollen is:

A. never present in the male *Zamia* cones.
B. not carried long distances by the wind.
C. produced in the female *Zamia* cones.
D. smaller than the pollen found in most plants.

158. With regard to the experiments described in the table, Students 1 and 2 would most likely agree that the percent of ovule pollination would be highest in female *Zamia* cones that are:

F. not covered with a bag or a cylinder.
G. covered with mesh bags that exclude insects.
H. covered with cylinders that exclude wind.
J. covered with plastic bags that exclude insects and wind.

159. Which of the following would most likely be used as a control group in Experiment 1 ?

A. Male *Zamia* cones that are covered with mesh bags
B. Male *Zamia* cones that are left uncovered
C. Female *Zamia* cones that are covered with mesh bags
D. Female *Zamia* cones that are left uncovered

160. Suppose the 3 experiments were performed as described. Student 2's hypothesis would be best supported if the percents of ovule pollination were the same for which of the following 2 groups of female *Zamia* cones?

F. Those in Experiment 1 that were covered with plastic bags and those in Experiment 1 that were not covered with plastic bags
G. Those in Experiment 1 that were covered with plastic bags and those in Experiment 2 that were covered with mesh bags
H. Those in Experiment 2 that were covered with mesh bags and those in Experiment 2 that were not covered with mesh bags
J. Those in Experiment 2 that were covered with mesh bags and those in Experiment 3 that were covered with cylinders

Passage XXVIII

Three studies were conducted to investigate factors that affect wind erosion.

Study 1

Samples of 3 different soils (A–C) were collected from a study area and each was analyzed for sand, silt, and clay particle content and water content (see Table 1).

Table 1			
Soil	Dry particle content (%)		Water content (%)
	sand	silt	clay	
A	79.8	11.7	8.5	2.9
B	67.1	18.1	14.8	6.8
C	17.6	33.2	49.2	21.3

Study 2

Another sample of each soil was dried in an oven for 24 hours, crushed, and passed through a screen with 0.84 mm openings. Each sample was used to fill its own 7 mm deep porous metal tray. Each tray was placed in a wind tunnel. A piece of white tape was placed at the downwind end of the tray (see Figure 1).

Figure 1

The wind speed was gradually increased until particles from the soil first began to collect on the white tape. This *threshold wind speed* was recorded for each sample.

The procedure described above was repeated, except that sand particles (an abrasive), which had been dyed green, were added at a constant rate to the moving air. The results are shown in Table 2.

Table 2		
Oven-dried Soil	Threshold wind speed (m/sec)	
	no sand added	sand added
A	0.31	0.22
B	0.30	0.21
C	0.31	0.21

Study 3

A third sample of each soil was prepared as in Study 2. Each tray was placed in shallow water for 24 hours to saturate the sample. Each tray was then placed in the wind tunnel and exposed to an 8.5 m/sec wind. Once the wind had dried the top of the soil sample sufficiently, soil particles began to appear on the white tape. At that time, the water content of the top 1 mm of the soil sample was determined. This procedure was repeated 3 more times: first adding dyed sand to the 8.5 m/sec wind, then using a 13 m/sec wind, without and then with added sand. The results are shown in Figure 2.

Figure 2

Tables and Figure 2 adapted from **A.** Selah and D. W. Fryrear, "Threshold Wind Velocities of Wet Soils as Affected by Wind Blown Sand." ©1995 by Williams and Wilkins.

161. It was hypothesized that soils with higher clay contents have typical water contents higher than those of soils with lower clay contents. Is this hypothesis consistent with the results of Study 1 ?

    A. Yes; as the clay content of the 3 soils increased, the water content decreased.
    B. Yes; as the clay content of the 3 soils increased, the water content also increased.
    C. No; as the clay content of the 3 soils increased, the water content decreased.
    D. No; as the clay content of the 3 soils increased, the water content also increased.

162. A fourth soil from the same study area was analyzed using the procedures described in Study 1 and was found to contain 73% sand, 15% silt, and 12% clay particles. A water content for that soil in which of the following ranges would be most consistent with the results of Study 1 ?

   F. Less than 2.9%
   G. Between 2.9% and 6.8%
   H. Between 6.8% and 21.3%
   J. Greater than 21.3%

163. Based on Study 1, the water content of Soil C immediately after being saturated for the 24 hours in Study 3 was most likely:

   A. less than 1%.
   B. between 1% and 5%.
   C. between 5% and 15%.
   D. greater than 15%.

164. Which of the following statements about the threshold wind speeds in the trials in which no dyed sand was added to the moving air is supported by the results of Study 2 for the 3 soils?

   F. The threshold speed for Soil A was twice as high as the threshold wind speeds for the other 2 soils.
   G. The threshold speed for Soil C was twice as high as the threshold wind speeds for the other 2 soils.
   H. The threshold speeds for all 3 soils were approximately the same.
   J. The threshold speeds for all 3 soils were all 0 m/sec.

165. Based on the results of Study 2 for a given soil, the addition of dyed sand to the moving air produced a threshold wind speed that was approximately:

   A. one-third lower than the threshold wind speed when no sand was added to the moving air.
   B. the same as the threshold wind speed when no sand was added to the moving air.
   C. half again as high as the threshold wind speed when no sand was added to the moving air.
   D. twice as high as the threshold wind speed when no sand was added to the moving air.

166. Suppose equal volumes of Soil A and Soil B were collected, thoroughly mixed, oven-dried for 24 hours, crushed, and passed through a screen as in Study 2. If this soil sample were then used in a repeat of Study 2 using added dyed sand, the threshold wind speed for this sample would most likely be between:

   F. 0.10 m/sec and 0.15 m/sec.
   G. 0.15 m/sec and 0.20 m/sec.
   H. 0.20 m/sec and 0.25 m/sec.
   J. 0.25 m/sec and 0.30 m/sec.

Passage XXIX

A *capacitor* is a device used to store electrical charge. *Capacitance* is the amount of charge a capacitor can hold at a given voltage.

A student used the circuit shown in Figure 1 to perform 3 experiments.

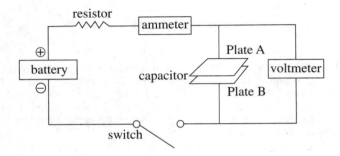

Figure 1

The *parallel-plate capacitor* consisted of 2 identical flat, parallel plates of copper, separated by a small distance (see Figure 2).

copper plates

Figure 2

Initially, each plate of the capacitor was *uncharged*. (That is, each plate contained an equal number of positive charges and negative charges.) When the switch in the circuit was closed, *electrons* (negatively charged particles) flowed from Plate A of the capacitor through the ammeter, resistor, and battery to Plate B. After an amount of negative charge (Q) equaling -1×10^{-8} coulomb flowed to Plate B, the switch was reopened, and the voltage (V) in volts, between the charged plates was measured. Finally, the capacitance (C) was calculated in farads (F).

Experiment 1

Two square copper plates, each 0.05 m × 0.05 m (surface area 2.5×10^{-3} m²), were separated by various thicknesses of air. The results are shown in Table 1.

Table 1		
Plate separation (10^{-4} m)	V (volts)	C (10^{-11} F)
1	45.2	22.1
5	227	4.4
10	455	2.2

Experiment 2

Three pairs of square copper plates, each pair having a different surface area, were tested. Each pair was separated by a 1×10^{-4} m thickness of air. The results are shown in Table 2.

Table 2		
Surface area of each plate (10^{-3} m²)	V (volts)	C (10^{-11} F)
1	112	8.9
3	37.6	26.6
5	22.6	44.2

Experiment 3

The square copper plates from Experiment 1 were separated by a 1×10^{-4} m thickness of various materials. The number K is related to each material's suitability for use in a capacitor. The results are shown in Table 3.

Table 3			
Material	K	V (volts)	C (10^{-11} F)
Mica	5.4	8.4	119
Water	80.4	0.56	1,780
Titanium dioxide	173	0.26	3,828

167. In Experiment 1, the voltage across the plates increased and the capacitance of the capacitor decreased as the:

- **A.** surface area of the plates increased.
- **B.** separation between the plates increased.
- **C.** separation between the plates decreased.
- **D.** number K of the material between the plates decreased.

168. In Experiment 2, the student varied which of the following properties of the capacitor?

- **F.** Number K of the material between the plates
- **G.** Surface area of the plates
- **H.** Separation between the plates
- **J.** Material composing the plates

169. Based on the results of the 3 experiments, the capacitor with which of the following combinations of separation, surface area per plate, and material will have the highest capacitance?

	Separation (m)	Surface area (m²)	Material
A.	1×10^{-4}	1×10^{-3}	mica
B.	1×10^{-4}	1×10^{-3}	titanium dioxide
C.	1×10^{-4}	2×10^{-3}	titanium dioxide
D.	2×10^{-4}	1×10^{-3}	water

170. Assume that as K decreases, a material's suitability for use between the plates of a capacitor decreases. Based on the results of Experiment 3, which of the following correctly lists mica, water, and titanium dioxide in order of decreasing suitability for use between the plates of a capacitor?

- **F.** Mica, water, titanium dioxide
- **G.** Mica, titanium dioxide, water
- **H.** Titanium dioxide, water, mica
- **J.** Titanium dioxide, mica, water

171. In each trial of Experiments 1–3, after the capacitor was charged and the switch opened, what was the charge on Plate A ?

- **A.** $+1 \times 10^{-8}$ coulomb
- **B.** $+2 \times 10^{-8}$ coulomb
- **C.** $+3 \times 10^{-8}$ coulomb
- **D.** $+4 \times 10^{-8}$ coulomb

172. To charge the capacitor as described in the passage, the student caused electrons to flow in the direction(s) indicated by which of the following figures?

F.

G.

H.

J.

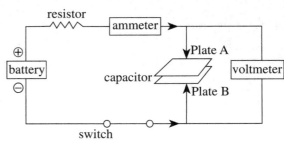

Passage XXX

When compounds dissolve in water, they either give off heat to, or absorb heat from, the solution. The transfer of heat (ΔH) is negative (*exothermic*) when heat is given off, or positive (*endothermic*) when heat is absorbed. Figure 1 shows the ΔH, in kilojoules per mole (kJ/mole, where 1 mole is 6×10^{23} molecules of any compound), when Compounds A or B dissolve in water at 25°C. *Solubility* is the maximum amount of a compound that will dissolve in a given volume of solvent. Figures 2 and 3 show how temperature affects the solubility (in moles/L) of Compounds A and B, respectively, in water.

Figure 1

Figure 2

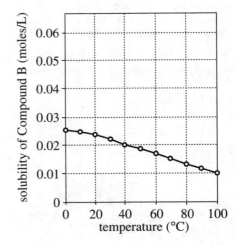

Figure 3

173. According to Figures 2 and 3, Compounds A and B have the same solubility at what temperature, if any?

    A.   0°C

    B.   35°C

    C.   55°C

    D.   The solubilities are not equal at any temperature shown in the figures.

174. A solution is made that has a concentration of 1 mole/L of Compound A and 0.5 mole/L of Compound B. According to the passage, the number of molecules of Compound A in the solution is:

    F.   half the number of molecules of Compound B in the solution.

    G.   equal to the number of molecules of Compound B in the solution.

    H.   twice the number of molecules of Compound B in the solution.

    J.   4 times the number of molecules of Compound B in the solution.

175. A chemist claimed that compounds that dissolve exothermically in water decrease in solubility as temperature increases. Is her claim supported by the data in Figures 1–3 ?

    A.   Yes; the solubility of Compound A decreased as temperature increased.

    B.   Yes; the solubility of Compound B decreased as temperature increased.

    C.   No; the solubility of Compound A increased as temperature increased.

    D.   No; the solubility of Compound B increased as temperature increased.

176. A chemist added either Compound A or Compound B to water at 25°C. The temperature of the solution decreased until the solution began to freeze. Based on the data in Figure 1, which compound did he most likely add to the water?

    F.   Compound A, because its ΔH is positive.

    G.   Compound A, because its ΔH is negative.

    H.   Compound B, because its ΔH is positive.

    J.   Compound B, because its ΔH is negative.

177. Ammonium nitrate is a compound that has a ΔH of +25.7 kJ/mole when it dissolves in water at 25°C. Based on the data in Figure 1, if 1 mole each of ammonium nitrate and Compound A are dissolved separately in equal amounts of water at 25°C, how will the transfer of heat compare?

    A.   Ammonium nitrate will absorb less heat from the solution than will Compound A.

    B.   Ammonium nitrate will absorb more heat from the solution than will Compound A.

    C.   Ammonium nitrate will give off less heat to the solution than will Compound A.

    D.   Ammonium nitrate will give off more heat to the solution than will Compound A.

Passage XXXI

Planets revolve around the Sun in elliptical orbits, as shown in Figure 1.

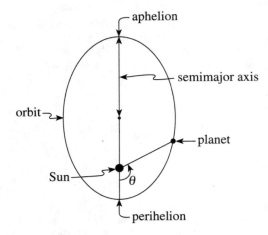

Figure 1

The *eccentricity* of an ellipse describes its elongation; the more elongated the ellipse, the greater its eccentricity. The semimajor axis is half the length of the ellipse.

Perihelion (Angle $\theta = 0°$) is the point on the orbit closest to the Sun; *aphelion* ($\theta = 180°$) is the point on the orbit farthest from the Sun. The speed of a planet varies with θ. The speed of a planet versus θ is shown in Figure 2 for orbits with various eccentricities and semimajor axes.

Figure 2

178. Consider a planet as it travels from $\theta = 0°$ to $\theta = 359°$ in an orbit with a semimajor axis of 1.5×10^8 km and an eccentricity of 0.10. Based on the data in Figure 2, how many times does the planet have a speed of 30 km/sec as it travels between those 2 angles?

    F. One time
    G. Two times
    H. Three times
    J. Four times

179. Based on the data in Figure 2, how does the speed of a planet change while it moves from perihelion to aphelion and while it moves from aphelion to perihelion?

	Perihelion to aphelion	Aphelion to perihelion
A.	speed increases	speed increases
B.	speed increases	speed decreases
C.	speed decreases	speed increases
D.	speed decreases	speed decreases

180. A planet will escape from the solar system if its orbital speed is greater than the *escape velocity*. Based on the data in Figure 2, if the semimajor axis is 1.5×10^8 km, the eccentricity is 0.10, and the escape velocity at perihelion is 44.2 km/sec, will the planet escape the solar system?

    F. Yes, because the planet's orbital speed at perihelion is greater than the escape velocity.
    G. Yes, because the planet's orbital speed at perihelion is less than the escape velocity.
    H. No, because the planet's orbital speed at perihelion is greater than the escape velocity.
    J. No, because the planet's orbital speed at perihelion is less than the escape velocity.

181. Based on the data in Figure 2, the orbital speed of a planet will most likely remain constant if the eccentricity of the planet's orbit is:

    A. exactly 0.
    B. between 0.1 and 0.5.
    C. between 0.5 and 0.9.
    D. exactly 1.

182. Based on the data in Figure 2, for a planet in an orbit around the Sun with a semimajor axis of 3.0×10^8 km and an eccentricity of 0.05, the speed at $\theta = 0°$ will be:

    F. less than 23 km/sec.
    G. between 23 km/sec and 26 km/sec.
    H. between 26 km/sec and 28 km/sec.
    J. greater than 28 km/sec.

Passage XXXII

Diploid human cells contain 46 chromosomes. Genes residing on the same chromosome are *linked*. Figure 1 shows the location of some genes in humans.

Figure 1 adapted from Susan Offner, "Human Chromosomes." ©1992 by Susan Offner.

Figure 1

Table 1 lists the biological process associated with some of the genes in Figure 1.

Table 1	
Biological process	Gene
Digestion	amylase gene trypsin gene chymotrypsin gene
Immune response	antibody light chain gene antibody heavy chain gene
Respiration	hemoglobin α chain gene hemoglobin β chain gene myoglobin gene
Protein synthesis	ribosomal RNA gene tRNA proline gene tRNA leucine gene tRNA threonine gene

Table 2 lists 7 genetic diseases, the chromosome associated with each disease, and the mode of inheritance for each disease.

Table 2		
Genetic disease	Chromosome	Mode of inheritance
Tay-Sachs disease	15	autosomal recessive
Neurofibromatosis	17	autosomal dominant
Familial hypercholesterolemia	19	autosomal dominant
Duchenne muscular dystrophy	X	X-linked recessive
Incontinentia pigmenti	X	X-linked dominant
Red-green color blindness	X	X-linked recessive
Hemophilia A	X	X-linked recessive

183. According to Figure 1 and Table 1, Chromosome 13 contains a gene associated with which of the following biological activities?

  A. Digestion
  B. Immune response
  C. Respiration
  D. Protein synthesis

184. Is the statement "The tRNA proline gene is linked to the hexokinase gene" supported by the information in Figure 1 ?

  F. No; the 2 genes are found on the same chromosome.
  G. No; the 2 genes are found on different chromosomes.
  H. Yes; the 2 genes are found on the same chromosome.
  J. Yes; the 2 genes are found on different chromosomes.

185. Table 1 lists 3 genes as being associated with digestion. According to Figure 1, these 3 genes are:

  A. on different chromosomes.
  B. on the same chromosome.
  C. linked to genes associated with immune response.
  D. linked to genes associated with respiration.

186. Based on the information presented, which of the following genes is linked to the neurofibromatosis gene?

  F. Amylase gene
  G. Growth hormone gene
  H. Myoglobin gene
  J. Rhodopsin gene

187. Based on the information presented, which of the following genes is typically present in human males, but not in human females?

  A. Amylase gene
  B. Hexokinase gene
  C. Ribosomal RNA gene
  D. TSPY gene

Passage XXXIII

G. soja (a wild soybean) produces γ-tocopherol (a type of vitamin E). It then converts some γ-tocopherol into α-tocopherol (another type of vitamin E). In G. soja, the enzyme TMT catalyzes this reaction:

$$\gamma\text{-tocopherol} \xrightarrow{\text{TMT}} \alpha\text{-tocopherol}$$

A. thaliana (a mustard plant) produces γ-tocopherol, but lacks TMT, so it produces only a small amount of α-tocopherol.

Because α-tocopherol is more effective at reducing cellular damage than is γ-tocopherol, a scientist tried to transfer G. soja's TMT gene into A. thaliana.

Experiment 1

Four versions of G. soja's TMT gene (TMT1–TMT4) were cloned. Each gene was incorporated into a *vector* (a biological structure that carries a gene and transfers it into the cells of an organism).

Six genetically identical lines of A. thaliana were developed (L1–L6). As shown in Table 1, L1–L4 were each exposed to a vector carrying 1 of the 4 cloned genes; L5 was exposed only to the vector; and L6 was left untreated.

Next, 10 plants from each line were grown. Table 1 gives the tocopherol concentration and the percent (%) by mass of the 2 types of tocopherol in the plants.

Experiment 2

Four genetically different strains of A. thaliana were grown (S1–S4). S1–S4 were each exposed to a vector carrying TMT1.

Next, 10 plants from each strain were grown. Table 2 shows the tocopherol concentration and the percent by mass of the 2 types of tocopherol in the plants.

Table 1				
Line	Treatment	Tocopherol concentration (mg/kg)	γ-tocopherol (%)	α-tocopherol (%)
L1	vector + TMT1	360	3	97
L2	vector + TMT2	360	3	97
L3	vector + TMT3	360	51	49
L4	vector + TMT4	360	2	98
L5	vector	360	99	1
L6	untreated	360	99	1

Table 2				
Strain	Treatment	Tocopherol concentration (mg/kg)	γ-tocopherol (%)	α-tocopherol (%)
S1	vector + TMT1	390	1	99
S2	vector + TMT1	360	3	97
S3	vector + TMT1	320	9	91
S4	vector + TMT1	310	99	1

Tables adapted from D. Shintani and D. DellaPenna, "Elevating the Vitamin E Content of Plants Through Metabolic Engineering." ©1998 by the American Association for the Advancement of Science.

188. At the end of Experiment 2, which of the 4 strains had the greatest amount of γ-tocopherol per kilogram of plant material?

   F. S1
   G. S2
   H. S3
   J. S4

189. One of the *A. thaliana* strains used in Experiment 2 was genetically identical to the *A. thaliana* used in Experiment 1. Based on the results of Experiments 1 and 2, this strain was most likely:

   A. S1.
   B. S2.
   C. S3.
   D. S4.

190. To determine whether exposure to the vector alone affected tocopherol concentration in Experiment 1, one should compare the results from which 2 lines?

   F. L1 and L2
   G. L2 and L4
   H. L3 and L4
   J. L5 and L6

191. The scientist believed that 1 of the 4 cloned genes in Experiment 1 produced an enzyme that was less efficient than the enzyme produced by the other 3 genes. Based on the results, this gene was most likely:

   A. TMT1.
   B. TMT2.
   C. TMT3.
   D. TMT4.

192. After reviewing the data from Experiment 2, the scientist concluded that the transfer of the TMT gene to 1 of the strains was unsuccessful. This strain was most likely:

   F. S1.
   G. S2.
   H. S3.
   J. S4.

193. Which of the following best explains why the scientist wanted to transfer the TMT gene from one organism to another?

   A. To increase the amount of α-tocopherol produced by some of the *G. soja* plants
   B. To increase the amount of α-tocopherol produced by some of the *A. thaliana* plants
   C. To decrease the amount of α-tocopherol produced by some of the *G. soja* plants
   D. To decrease the amount of α-tocopherol produced by some of the *A. thaliana* plants

Passage XXXIV

An elevated inclined plane makes an angle, θ, with a floor. Points A and B on the inclined plane are 0.50 m apart. Point B is at a height H above the floor (see Figure 1).

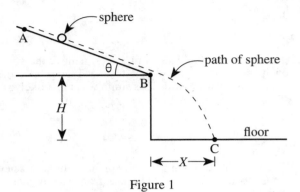

Figure 1

A solid metal sphere is released from rest at Point A and travels down the inclined plane to Point B. The sphere is in free fall between Points B and C and first hits the floor at Point C, a horizontal distance X from the bottom of the inclined plane.

Figure 2 shows how X varies with 0 for different H if the sphere *rolls* from Point A to Point B. Figure 3 shows how X varies with θ for different H if the sphere *slides* from Point A to Point B.

Key sphere rolls:	
symbol	H (m)
◇	1.0
×	1.5
○	2.0

Figure 2

Key sphere slides:	
symbol	H (m)
△	1.0
□	1.5
☆	2.0

Figure 3

194. Based on Figures 2 and 3, for the sphere either sliding or rolling down the inclined plane and for $H = 1.5$ m, as θ increases from 5° to 45°, X:

F. increases only.
G. decreases only.
H. increases, then decreases.
J. decreases, then increases.

195. For the sliding sphere at $\theta = 10°$, if $H = 0.5$ m, X would most likely be:

A. less than 0.56 m.
B. between 0.56 m and 0.68 m.
C. between 0.68 m and 0.79 m.
D. greater than 0.79 m.

196. For the sphere sliding down the inclined plane and $H = 2.0$ m, if X had been plotted every 2.5° instead of every 5° between $\theta = 5°$ and $\theta = 45°$, X would most likely have been greatest at which of the following θ ?

    F.   17.5°
    G. 22.5°
    H. 27.5°
    J.   32.5°

197. If $H = 2.0$ m for the rolling sphere and $\theta = 50°$, X will most likely be closest to which of the following?

    A. 0.50 m
    B. 0.65 m
    C. 0.80 m
    D. 0.95 m

198. Which of the following figures best shows how the sphere's kinetic energy varies with time as the sphere travels down the incline?

F.

H.

G.

J.
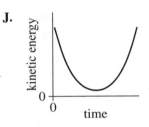

Passage XXXV

Using the circuit shown in Figure 1, students studied the variables that affect the electrical resistance, R, of a wire.

Figure 1

The students used the following procedure to find R for each test wire. They immersed the test wire in an oil bath and allowed the test wire to come to the temperature of the oil. Keeping the test wire in the oil bath (to control the temperature of the test wire), they then closed the switch and, using the *rheostat* (a variable resistor), adjusted the electrical current through the test wire until the ammeter indicated 0.80 amp. As soon as the ammeter indicated 0.80 amp, they measured the voltage, V, across the test wire. Finally, they used V and the current (0.80 amp) to calculate R.

Study 1

The students found R for test wires made of different metals. Each wire was at the same temperature and was 100 cm long and 0.130 mm² in cross-sectional area (see Table 1).

Table 1		
Metal	V (volts)	R (ohms)
Copper	0.11	0.14
Lead	1.36	1.7
Platinum	0.66	0.83
Tungsten	0.35	0.44

Study 2

The students found R for copper test wires of different lengths. Each wire was at the temperature of the test wires in Study 1 and was 0.130 mm² in cross-sectional area (see Table 2).

Table 2		
Length (cm)	V (volts)	R (ohms)
50	0.05	0.06
100	0.11	0.14
150	0.17	0.21
200	0.22	0.28

Study 3

The students found R for copper test wires of different cross-sectional areas. Each wire was at the temperature of the test wires in Study 1 and was 100 cm long (see Table 3).

Table 3		
Cross-sectional area (mm²)	V (volts)	R (ohms)
0.065	0.22	0.28
0.130	0.11	0.14
0.195	0.07	0.09
0.260	0.05	0.06

Study 4

The students varied the temperature of the oil. At each temperature, they found R for the copper test wire used in Study 1 (see Table 4).

Table 4		
Temperature (°C)	V (volts)	R (ohms)
20	0.11	0.14
60	0.13	0.16
100	0.14	0.18
140	0.16	0.20

199. Based on the results of Studies 1 and 4, the temperature of the test wire in Study 1 was most likely closest to which of the following?

   A.   5°C
   B. 10°C
   C. 20°C
   D. 60°C

200. The results of Study 3 are best represented by which of the following figures?

F.

H.

G.

J.

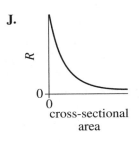

201. Which of the following correctly lists the wires tested in Study 1 in order of increasing electrical resistance?

   A. Copper wire, lead wire, platinum wire, tungsten wire
   B. Copper wire, lead wire, tungsten wire, platinum wire
   C. Copper wire, tungsten wire, lead wire, platinum wire
   D. Copper wire, tungsten wire, platinum wire, lead wire

202. Suppose that the length of the copper wire tested in Study 4 had been 200 cm instead of 100 cm. Based on the results of Study 2, when the temperature of the copper test wire was 60°C in Study 4, V would most likely have been closest to which of the following?

   F. 0.06 volt
   G. 0.16 volt
   H. 0.26 volt
   J. 0.36 volt

203. Based on Studies 2 and 3, a copper test wire at the temperature of the test wires in Studies 2 and 3 will have the greatest electrical resistance if the test wire has which of the following lengths and cross-sectional areas?

	Length (cm)	Cross-sectional area (mm^2)
A.	20	0.15
B.	20	0.30
C.	40	0.15
D.	40	0.30

204. Given the position of the ammeter in the circuit shown in Figure 1, which of the following assumptions about the electrical current were the students most likely making?

   F. Nearly all of the current went through the voltmeter.
   G. Nearly all of the current went through the test wire.
   H. Almost none of the current went through the test wire.
   J. Almost none of the current went through the rheostat.

Passage XXXVI

Rock types can often be differentiated by the rare earth elements (REEs) they contain. Table 1 shows the average concentration of 2 REEs, neodymium and samarium, in 4 igneous rock types (oceanic basalt, continental basalt, andesite, and granite) and also in 3 sedimentary rock types (shale, sandstone, and dolomite).

Table 1		
	Average concentration (ppm*) of:	
Rock type	neodymium	samarium
Igneous rocks		
oceanic basalt	10	3
continental basalt	50	8
andesite	30	7
granite	50	9
Sedimentary rocks		
shale	30	6
sandstone	15	3
dolomite	1	0.2
*ppm = parts per million		

Figure 1 shows the *relative concentration* of REEs in various igneous rock types and in sedimentary rocks taken as a group. Relative concentration is calculated using the following formula:

relative concentration of REE in rock type

$$= \frac{\text{average concentration of REE in rock type}}{\text{average concentration of REE in meteorites}}$$

Meteorites, taken as a group, are used to calculate the relative concentration because their composition is distinctly different from any Earth rock.

Figure 1

Figure adapted from S. Ross Taylor and Scott McLennan, "The Evolution of Continental Crust." ©1996 by Scientific American, Inc.

205. According to Figure 1, oceanic basalt and continental basalt differ the most in their relative concentrations of which of the following REEs ?

A. Cerium
B. Samarium
C. Holmium
D. Lutetium

206. A chemical analysis of another group of samples of 1 of the igneous rock types listed in Figure 1 revealed the following relative concentrations for 3 of its REEs:

REE	Relative concentration
Lanthanum	91
Europium	11
Ytterbium	10

According to Figure 1, to which rock type do these samples most likely belong?

F. Oceanic basalt
G. Andesite
H. Granite
J. Sodium granite

207. Which of the following statements comparing the average concentrations of neodymium and samarium in the rock types listed in Table 1 is true?

A. In each rock type, the average neodymium concentration is lower than the average samarium concentration.
B. In each rock type, the average neodymium concentration is higher than the average samarium concentration.
C. In some rock types, the average neodymium concentration is lower than the average samarium concentration; in other rock types, the average neodymium concentration is equal to the average samarium concentration.
D. In some rock types, the average neodymium concentration is higher than the average samarium concentration; in other rock types, the average neodymium concentration is equal to the average samarium concentration.

208. Based on Figure 1, the relative concentration of terbium for *limestone,* another rock type, would most likely be:

F. less than 10.
G. between 10 and 14.
H. between 15 and 20.
J. greater than 20.

209. In Figure 1, the plot of relative concentration versus atomic number covers the smallest range of relative concentrations for which of the following rock types?

A. Oceanic basalt
B. Continental basalt
C. Sodium granite
D. Sedimentary rocks

Passage XXXVII

Four billion years ago (4 BYA), the Sun was only 70% as bright as it is today. With sunlight that faint, Earth's average surface temperature should have been $-15°C$ and all surface water would have been frozen. However, isotope evidence from certain sedimentary rocks (rocks made of sediments deposited in liquid water) formed around that time indicates that Earth's surface temperature was well above freezing.

Scientists believe that 1 of 2 greenhouse gases, either ammonia (NH_3) or carbon dioxide (CO_2), was present in Earth's atmosphere at a concentration well above that of the respective gas in the atmosphere today. This gas trapped enough heat radiating from Earth's surface to keep the surface temperature above freezing.

Two scientists present their viewpoints.

Scientist 1

Four BYA, large quantities of NH_3 continuously entered Earth's atmosphere from ocean-floor hydrothermal vents and by other processes. NH_3 is a more efficient greenhouse gas than is CO_2, so a lower concentration of NH_3 is required to warm the atmosphere a given amount. Any NH_3 molecule entering the atmosphere would have been broken down in 5–10 days by UV radiation. However, methane (CH_4), another gas that was abundant in the atmosphere 4 BYA, combined with molecular nitrogen gas to produce organic compounds that blocked much of the incoming UV radiation and kept NH_3 molecules intact for much longer than 10 days. Continuous removal of CO_2 from the atmosphere by ocean water prevented CO_2 from accumulating in the atmosphere.

Scientist 2

Two carbon isotopes found in sedimentary rocks indicate a 75% higher concentration of CO_2 in Earth's atmosphere 4 BYA than the 360 parts per million (ppm) present today. Four BYA, large quantities of CO_2 continuously entered the atmosphere through widespread, long-term volcanic activity. Today, as in the past, much CO_2 is removed from the atmosphere as CO_2 becomes part of carbonates in rock and sediment on land. However, 4 BYA, there was 80% less dry land area on which to form and store carbonates, so CO_2 accumulated in the atmosphere.

The vast amounts of CH_4 that would be required to help preserve atmospheric NH_3 did not exist on Earth 4 BYA. Thus, atmospheric NH_3 was too short-lived to have been an effective greenhouse gas.

210. Which of the following diagrams is most consistent with Scientist 2's description of how CO_2 enters and is removed from Earth's atmosphere?

F.   atmosphere

G.   atmosphere

H.   atmosphere

J.   atmosphere

211. CH_4 is also a greenhouse gas. Scientist 1 would most likely agree that the presence of CH_4 in Earth's atmosphere 4 BYA:

A.   helped warm Earth's surface.
B.   helped cool Earth's surface.
C.   reduced the quantity of NH_3 present.
D.   increased the quantity of CO_2 present.

212. A given concentration of NH_3 in Earth's atmosphere can trap as much heat radiating from Earth's surface as can a CO_2 concentration 3 times higher. Given this information and Scientist 2's viewpoint, the present-day concentration of NH_3 that would trap an amount of heat equivalent to that trapped by the present-day concentration of CO_2 would be approximately:

F.   50 ppm.
G.   80 ppm.
H.   120 ppm.
J.   360 ppm.

213. The Sun was 30% dimmer 4 BYA than it is today. Assuming the relative proportions of all greenhouse gases in Earth's atmosphere have stayed constant, both scientists would most likely agree that the minimum total concentration of all greenhouse gases necessary to keep Earth's surface temperature above freezing 4 BYA was:

   A. more than the minimum total concentration necessary today.

   B. the same as the minimum total concentration necessary today.

   C. less than the minimum total concentration necessary today, but not zero.

   D. zero.

214. Suppose volcanic activity 4 BYA produced large quantities of CH_4. Which scientist would most likely use this information to support his/her viewpoint?

   F. Scientist 1, because it would explain how CH_4 entered Earth's atmosphere 4 BYA.

   G. Scientist 1, because it would explain how NH_3 entered Earth's atmosphere 4 BYA.

   H. Scientist 2, because it would explain how CH_4 entered Earth's atmosphere 4 BYA.

   J. Scientist 2, because it would explain how NH_3 entered Earth's atmosphere 4 BYA.

215. In order to protect NH_3 from incoming UV radiation, the organic compounds had to be located:

   A. below the elevation in the atmosphere where NH_3 was present.

   B. at or above the elevation in the atmosphere where NH_3 was present.

   C. on the ocean floor near where NH_3 was produced in hydrothermal vents.

   D. on land near where NH_3 was produced from carbonate deposits.

216. Scientist 2 would most likely agree that the concentration of CO_2 in Earth's atmosphere 4 BYA was closest to which of the following?

   F. 75 ppm

   G. 180 ppm

   H. 360 ppm

   J. 630 ppm

Passage XXXVIII

Students conducted experiments to study the effects of temperature on density.

In the experiments, each flask was filled to the top with either distilled water or salt (NaCl) water at 20°C. A rubber stopper with 2 holes—one fitted with a thermometer and the other fitted with glass tubing—was placed in the neck of the flask (see figure of apparatus).

The initial height of the liquid in the tubing was adjusted to 25 mm above the top of the stopper.

Experiment 1

A flask filled with distilled water was slowly heated. As the temperature of the water increased, the height of the water in the tubing increased. At 100°C, water and steam squirted out the top of the tubing.

Experiment 2

The body of a flask filled with distilled water was submerged in a cold bath at −6°C. As the temperature of the water in the apparatus decreased, the height of the water in the tubing decreased. At 4°C, the height of the water in the tubing stopped decreasing, and then began to increase. At 0°C, water and ice were forced out the top of the tubing. Eventually, the flask cracked in several places.

Experiment 3

Two saltwater solutions were prepared. Solution I had a lower salt concentration (in g/mL) than did Solution II. Two flasks containing Solutions I and II, respectively, were slowly heated. In both flasks, the salt water in the tubing rose and then squirted out the top of the tubing (at 102°C for Solution I and at 104°C for Solution II).

Two flasks containing Solutions I and II, respectively, were cooled as in Experiment 2. In both flasks, the height of the salt water in the tubing decreased until the temperature reached −6°C and then remained level (no freezing occurred).

217. Water in the upper part of a hypothetical 2-compartment container is at 10°C, and water in the lower part is at 80°C, as shown in the figure below.

If the barrier separating the 2 compartments could be removed without disturbing the water, what mixing, if any, would occur?

   A. No mixing would occur, because the water in the upper part of the container is more dense than the water in the lower part of the container.

   B. No mixing would occur, because the water in the upper part of the container is less dense than the water in the lower part of the container.

   C. Mixing would occur, because the water in the lower part of the container is more dense than the water in the upper part of the container.

   D. Mixing would occur, because the water in the lower part of the container is less dense than the water in the upper part of the container.

218. Based on the results of Experiments 1 and 3, 1 L of distilled water with which of the following quantities of NaCl added to it would most likely boil at the *lowest* temperature?

   F.   0 g
   G.   1 g
   H. 20 g
   J. 30 g

219. Which of the following graphs best shows how the volume of the liquid H_2O changed with temperature in Experiment 2 ?

A.

B.

C.

D.

220. Which of the following changes in the procedure of Experiment 3 would have provided the most information about the effect of decreasing temperature on the density of salt water?

F. Using a bath at −13°C to cool the flask
G. Using a bath at −3°C to cool the flask
H. Using a larger flask
J. Using a smaller flask

221. Suppose that equal volumes of Solutions I and II from Experiment 3 were mixed and the resulting solution was then tested as in Experiment 1. Salt water would most likely have started to squirt out of the top of the tubing when the temperature was:

A. less than 100°C.
B. between 100°C and 102°C.
C. between 102°C and 104°C.
D. greater than 104°C.

222. As the height of the water in the glass tubing decreased in Experiment 2, which of the following properties of the water in the apparatus also changed?

    I. Volume
    II. Mass
    III. Density

F. I only
G. I and II only
H. I and III only
J. I, II, and III

Passage XXXIX

Dimetrodon is a large, extinct, cold-blooded, carnivorous reptile (see figure below). Fossils show that *Dimetrodon* had fixed spines extending from its vertebrae that, when covered with skin, formed a large sail. Two scientists discuss the sail's function.

Scientist 1

The sail helped regulate body temperature. *Dimetrodon* needed to warm its body to the *activity temperature,* the temperature at which it was active enough to hunt. This could be achieved most rapidly by turning the broad side of the sail toward the morning sun. A mathematical model shows that a reptile with a sail would reach the activity temperature 3 times faster than a reptile without a sail. Rapid warming gave *Dimetrodon* a distinct advantage catching cold-blooded prey.

Grooves on the sail's spines held large blood vessels. Regulating the blood flow through these vessels during the heat of the day allowed the reptile to radiate heat away from its body and prevent overheating.

Four other cold-blooded reptile species from this same time and climate also had bony projections or sails on their back. Today, elephants regulate their body temperature by flapping their large ears.

Scientist 2

The sail was used for display. First, the sail made the reptile appear larger, thereby discouraging attacks from predators. Second, sails were smaller in female *Dimetrodon*s than in males, indicating the sails were used by the males for attracting mates. Modern lizards change their skin color and pattern to attract a mate. Similarly, *Dimetrodon*s controlled the appearance of the skin on the sail by regulating the blood supply to the sail.

Sphenacodon is a cold-blooded reptile that lived at the same time and in the same climate as *Dimetrodon*. *Sphenacodon* is a close relative of *Dimetrodon* and is identical in all details of its anatomy, except that it did not have a sail or any other projections on its back. If sails were needed for temperature regulation, *Sphenacodon* would have had one also.

Mathematical calculations show that as a *Dimetrodon* sail absorbed heat on the side facing the sun, it may have lost nearly as much heat from the side facing away from the sun.

223. According to the mathematical calculations mentioned by Scientist 2, a *Dimetrodon* that turned its sail toward the morning sun would experience:

   A. rapid overheating and death.
   B. little or no increase in body temperature.
   C. an increase in the length of the sail spines.
   D. a decrease in the blood supply to the sail.

224. If Scientist 1 is correct, exposing its sail to a strong wind would have which of the following effects on a *Dimetrodon*'s body temperature? Exposing its sail to a wind at a temperature less than the body temperature of *Dimetrodon* would:

   F. warm the sail and lower the body temperature.
   G. warm the sail and raise the body temperature.
   H. remove heat from the sail and lower the body temperature.
   J. remove heat from the sail and raise the body temperature.

225. According to Scientist 2, male *Dimetrodons* would control the blood supply to their sails in order to:

    A.   increase or decrease the spines' width.
    B.   reduce their body temperature.
    C.   change the sails' color or pattern.
    D.   raise or lower their sails.

226. Both scientists would most likely agree with which of the following statements about *Dimetrodons* and modern animals?

    F.   There are similarities between *Dimetrodons* and some modern animals.
    G.   There are no similarities between *Dimetrodons* and any modern animals.
    H.   There are no modern animals that are direct or indirect descendants of *Dimetrodons*.
    J.   There are many modern animals that look exactly like *Dimetrodons*.

227. According to Scientist 1, a cold-blooded, carnivorous reptile without a sail would have compared to a *Dimetrodon* of the same size in which of the following ways? This reptile without a sail would have:

    A.   reached the activity temperature more slowly than did *Dimetrodon*.
    B.   reached the activity temperature more quickly than did *Dimetrodon*.
    C.   been much easier to see than was *Dimetrodon*.
    D.   been less easily preyed upon than was *Dimetrodon*.

228. Both scientists would most likely agree with which of the following statements about *Dimetrodons* and their sails? *Dimetrodons* were able to:

    F.   raise and lower their sails at will.
    G.   shed and regrow their sails periodically.
    H.   control the blood supply to their sails.
    J.   regulate body temperature without their sails.

229. Based on the information in Scientist 1's viewpoint, which of the following figures best represents how a *Dimetrodon* would orient its sail with respect to the sun in order to *minimize* heating during late afternoon?

Passage XL

The *rate* of a chemical reaction can be measured as the change in the concentration of its products over a period of time. The following experiments were performed to investigate factors that influence the rate at which potassium permanganate ($KMnO_4$) reacts with oxalic acid ($H_2C_2O_4$) to form Mn^{2+} and other products.

Experiment 1

A 4.0 mL sample of 0.1 M (moles/liter) aqueous $KMnO_4$, which was purple in color, was measured with a clean graduated cylinder and poured into a test tube. A 4.0 mL sample of 1.0 M aqueous $H_2C_2O_4$ was then measured with a clean graduated cylinder and poured into a second test tube. The 2 test tubes were placed in a 25°C water bath. After 5 minutes the $H_2C_2O_4$ solution was mixed with the $KMnO_4$ solution and placed back in the water bath. The time until the purple color disappeared was recorded. This procedure was repeated at 3 other temperatures. The results are shown in Table 1.

	Table 1	
Trial	Temperature (°C)	Reaction time (sec)
1	25	210
2	35	105
3	45	48
4	55	25

Experiment 2

The procedure from Experiment 1 was repeated in every way except that 0.1 mg of manganous sulfate ($MnSO_4$), a *catalyst*, was added to each test tube containing $KMnO_4$ before the $H_2C_2O_4$ was added. Catalysts are substances that increase the rate of reactions without being used up. The results are shown in Table 2.

	Table 2	
Trial	Temperature (°C)	Reaction time (sec)
5	25	66
6	35	43
7	45	20
8	55	12

Experiment 3

The procedure from Experiment 1 was repeated at a constant temperature of 25°C and various concentrations of $H_2C_2O_4$. The results are shown in Table 3.

	Table 3	
Trial	Concentration of $H_2C_2O_4$ (M)	Reaction time (sec)
9	0.125	837
10	0.250	625
11	0.500	415

230. In Experiment 1, as the reaction temperature increased, the time until the purple color disappeared:

    F. remained the same.
    G. decreased only.
    H. increased only.
    J. increased, then decreased.

231. If the procedure described in Experiment 2 was repeated and a reaction time of 6 sec was measured, the temperature of the reaction was most likely:

    A. less than 25°C.
    B. greater than 25°C and less than 40°C.
    C. greater than 40°C and less than 55°C.
    D. greater than 55°C.

232. How is the experimental design of Experiment 1 different from that of Experiment 2? In Experiment 1:

    F. $MnSO_4$ was not added to the reaction; in Experiment 2 $MnSO_4$ was added.
    G. the concentration of $KMnO_4$ was less than that used in Experiment 2.
    H. reaction temperatures were varied; in Experiment 2 they remained constant.
    J. the concentration of $H_2C_2O_4$ was varied; in Experiment 2 it remained constant.

233. Each of the following factors was investigated in the experiments EXCEPT:

A. adding a catalyst to the reaction mixture.
B. changing the reaction solvent.
C. varying the reaction temperature.
D. changing the concentration of a reactant.

234. A student performed the procedure described in Experiment 1, mixing an $H_2C_2O_4$ solution at 45°C with a $KMnO_4$ solution at 40°C. Based on the results of Experiment 1, the reaction time was most likely:

F. less than 25 sec.
G. greater than 25 sec and less than 48 sec.
H. greater than 48 sec and less than 105 sec.
J. greater than 105 sec.

235. A student repeating Trial 9 unknowingly used a graduated cylinder that already contained 1.0 mL of H_2O to measure the $H_2C_2O_4$ solution. Based on the results of Experiment 3, the reaction time that she measured was most likely:

A. less than 415 sec.
B. greater than 415 sec and less than or equal to 625 sec.
C. greater than 625 sec and less than or equal to 837 sec.
D. greater than 837 sec.

Passage XLI

As a living cell's *surface area-to-volume ratio* (S/V) increases, so does the cell's ability to exchange substances with its environment.

To model this exchange process, different-sized cubes of gelatin were immersed in a dye for 1 minute. Table 1 lists the edge length, surface area, volume, S/V, and percent volume of gelatin that was dyed.

Table 1				
Edge length (mm)	Surface area (mm²)	Volume (mm³)	S/V (mm⁻¹)	Percent volume dyed
1	6	1	6	100
2	24	8	3	100
4	96	64	1.5	84
8	384	512	0.75	43
16	1,536	4,096	0.375	8

Figure 1 shows the S/V of certain rectangular solids and spheres.

(Note: For each rectangular solid, width = height = 1 mm.)

Figure 1

Figure 2 shows the volume of certain rectangular solids and spheres as a function of surface area.

(Note: For each rectangular solid, width = height = 1 mm.)

Figure 2

Table 2 lists the diameter and surface area of 5 types of spherical *ova* (egg cells).

Table 2		
Type	Diameter (mm)	Surface area (mm²)
Sea urchin	0.07	0.02
Human	0.1	0.03
Hummingbird	6	100
Hen	25	2,000
Ostrich	100	30,000

Table 2 adapted from Norman K. Wessells and Janet L. Hopson, *Biology.* ©1988 by Random House, Inc.

236. Ova with very large volumes tend to contain large amounts of nutrients that are used for growth by the embryo. Based on the information in Table 2 and Figure 2, which of the following ova most likely contain the greatest amount of nutrients?

F. Sea urchin ova
G. Human ova
H. Hummingbird ova
J. Hen ova

237. Based on the information in Table 1, a cube-shaped cell with which of the following edge lengths will have the greatest S/V ?

A. 20 mm
B. 40 mm
C. 60 mm
D. 80 mm

238. Which of the following best describes why the units for the S/V in Figure 1 are mm^{-1} ?

   F. The units for volume are mm and the units for surface area are mm^2.

   G. The units for volume are mm^2 and the units for surface area are mm^3.

   H. The units for surface area are mm and the units for volume are mm^2.

   J. The units for surface area are mm^2 and the units for volume are mm^3.

239. Based on the information in Figure 1, a spherical cell with a diameter of 6 mm will have an S/V closest to which of the following values?

   A. 0.1 mm^{-1}

   B. 1 mm^{-1}

   C. 2 mm^{-1}

   D. 10 mm^{-1}

240. Based on the information in Table 1, if a cube-shaped plant cell had an edge length of 0.5 mm, it would have an S/V of:

   F. 3 mm^{-1}.

   G. 6 mm^{-1}.

   H. 12 mm^{-1}.

   J. 18 mm^{-1}.

Passage XLII

Some students were interested in why antifreeze is mixed with the H_2O in a car's radiator. They knew that when a substance is dissolved in H_2O, the boiling points are elevated and the freezing points are lowered relative to H_2O. They performed the following experiments to investigate the effects of the addition of *ethylene glycol* ($C_2H_6O_2$), the active ingredient in most types of antifreeze, to H_2O.

Experiment 1

Six solutions of various concentrations of $C_2H_6O_2$ in H_2O were prepared. The mass of 10.00 mL of each solution was measured, and the density of each solution was calculated using the following formula:

$$\text{density} = \frac{\text{mass}}{\text{volume}}$$

The densities of 100% H_2O and 100% $C_2H_6O_2$ were also determined. The students found that as the concentration of $C_2H_6O_2$ increased, the density of the solution increased.

Experiment 2

A 20 mL sample of H_2O was placed in a flask containing a thermometer and the flask was heated. The temperature at which the H_2O first started to boil was recorded as the boiling point. This procedure was repeated with $C_2H_6O_2$ and the solutions prepared in Experiment 1 (see Figure 1).

Figure 1

Experiment 3

A 90 g sample of H_2O (freezing point = 0°C) and 10 g of $C_2H_6O_2$ (freezing point = –11.5°C) were placed in a cup containing a thermometer. The mixture was stirred as it was cooled in a low-temperature bath. The temperature at which ice crystals first began to appear was recorded as the freezing point. The procedure was repeated with different amounts of H_2O and $C_2H_6O_2$ (see Table 1).

Table 1		
Mass of $C_2H_6O_2$ (g)	Mass of H_2O (g)	Freezing point (°C)
10	90	–3.4
20	80	–7.9
30	70	–14.6
40	60	–23.8
50	50	–36.1
60	40	–51.2

241. If Experiment 2 were repeated with an aqueous solution containing 80% $C_2H_6O_2$ by mass, the boiling point of the solution would most likely be:

A. less than 100°C.
B. between 100°C and 110°C.
C. between 110°C and 115°C.
D. greater than 115°C.

242. Where the students live, the lowest temperature during the past year was –31°C. Based on the results of Experiment 3, which of the following percents, by mass, of $C_2H_6O_2$ in H_2O would have been necessary to be sure that the mixtures in car radiators in this area did not freeze?

F. 20%
G. 30%
H. 40%
J. 50%

243. Based on the results of Experiment 1, the mass of 10.00 mL of which of the following aqueous solutions would be the greatest?

A. 10% $C_2H_6O_2$
B. 20% $C_2H_6O_2$
C. 30% $C_2H_6O_2$
D. 40% $C_2H_6O_2$

244. A student repeating Experiment 3 placed an aqueous mixture containing 65% $C_2H_6O_2$ in the low-temperature bath. She did not observe the formation of any crystals. Which of the following statements best explains this observation?

F. The temperature of the low-temperature bath was exactly the same as the mixture's freezing point.
G. The temperature of the low-temperature bath was higher than the mixture's freezing point.
H. The temperature of the low-temperature bath was lower than the mixture's freezing point.
J. The mixture will not freeze and therefore has no freezing point.

245. Based on the results of Experiment 2, why would it be better to use a mixture of antifreeze and H_2O rather than pure H_2O in a car radiator during hot weather? The mixture has a:

A. higher boiling point than pure H_2O.
B. lower boiling point than pure H_2O.
C. higher freezing point than pure H_2O.
D. lower freezing point than pure H_2O.

246. Based on the passage and the results of Experiment 2, which of the following types of water would most likely have the *lowest* boiling point?

F. Lake water
G. Distilled water
H. Salt water
J. Tap water

Passage XLIII

Heat conduction is a process by which heat is transferred from a region at a higher temperature to a region at a lower temperature. Two regions that are in *thermal equilibrium* with each other are at the same temperature. No heat is transferred between regions in thermal equilibrium with each other.

A student studied the relationship between the length and diameter of a copper wire connecting 2 metallic blocks and the rate of heat conduction between the blocks.

Experiment 1

A small aluminum block, A, was heated to 100°C in boiling water, and an identical aluminum block, B, was cooled to 0°C in ice water. Both blocks were immediately placed on an *insulating* surface (a surface that does not conduct heat well) and connected by a given length of 1 mm diameter copper wire initially at room temperature so that the wire would conduct heat from Block A to Block B (see Figure 1).

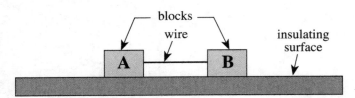

Figure 1

The temperature of each block was measured at regular time intervals for 3 minutes. The same procedure was done with different lengths of 1 mm diameter copper wire. The results are shown in Table 1.

Table 1						
Length of wire (cm)	Temperature (°C) of Block A after:			Temperature (°C) of Block B after:		
	1 min	2 min	3 min	1 min	2 min	3 min
10	79	66	54	18	25	31
20	88	80	72	9	15	19
30	91	85	78	6	10	14

Experiment 2

The procedure described in Experiment 1 was repeated using a copper wire with a diameter of 1.4 mm. The results are shown in Table 2.

Table 2						
Length of wire (cm)	Temperature (°C) of Block A after:			Temperature (°C) of Block B after:		
	1 min	2 min	3 min	1 min	2 min	3 min
10	61	45	40	34	45	40
20	79	65	53	17	25	35
30	85	75	66	12	16	20

247. The best way to test the hypothesis that the rate of heat conduction depends on the type of wire material used in the experiments would be to repeat the experiments using:

   A. silver wires and aluminum wires differing in size from the copper wires.
   B. silver wires and aluminum wires having the same sizes as the copper wires.
   C. copper wires each having a different diameter.
   D. copper wires each having a different length.

248. During Experiments 1 and 2, the 2 blocks reached thermal equilibrium when which of the following copper wires was used?

   F. The 10 cm long, 1 mm diameter wire
   G. The 30 cm long, 1 mm diameter wire
   H. The 10 cm long, 1.4 mm diameter wire
   J. The 30 cm long, 1.4 mm diameter wire

249. Based on Experiments 1 and 2, which of the following graphs best represents the relationship between the length of a copper wire of a given diameter and the temperature of Block A at a given time?

A.

B.

C.

D.

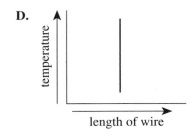

250. As *thermal conductivity* decreases, the ability to conduct heat decreases. Brass has a thermal conductivity one-third that of copper. If, in any of the experiments, a copper wire were replaced with a brass wire of the same length and diameter, which of the following outcomes would be most likely?

F. Block A would lose heat more slowly than when a copper wire was used.

G. Block A would lose heat at the same rate as when a copper wire was used.

H. Block B would gain heat at the same rate as when a copper wire was used.

J. Block B would gain heat more rapidly than when a copper wire was used.

251. In each of the 2 experiments, the amount of heat lost by Block A was greater than the amount of heat gained by Block B. The most probable explanation for this inequality is that:

A. Block A lost heat to the air.

B. the copper wire lost heat to Block A.

C. Block B lost heat to the copper wire.

D. the air lost heat to Block B.

252. Suppose, after 4 minutes, the temperature of Block A was 64°C and that of Block B was 23°C. According to the results of the experiments, which of the following copper wires was most likely being used to connect the blocks?

F. A 1 mm diameter wire, 10 cm long

G. A 1 mm diameter wire, 20 cm long

H. A 1.4 mm diameter wire, 10 cm long

J. A 1.4 mm diameter wire, 20 cm long

Passage XLIV

Air at its *dew point temperature* (or *dew point*) is saturated with water vapor. Air temperature usually decreases with increasing altitude. When air cools to its dew point, the water vapor in the air can begin to condense and form clouds.

Air temperatures and dew points were measured every 600 m from the surface (0 m) to an altitude of 3,000 m at 4 cities (A–D). Data, including the altitude of the cloud base over each city, were taken at 2 P.M. on every summer day that clouds were present. Figures 1–4 show the average air temperatures, the average dew points, and the average cloud-base altitudes at each city.

Figure 3

City A

Figure 4

Figure 1

Figure 2

253. A pilot flying a plane at 1,200 m altitude notices that there are cloud layers both above and below her, but none at her current altitude. Which of the following statements about the weather conditions at or near her altitude is supported by the information provided?

A. The base of the upper cloud layer is at 600 m altitude and extends 1,200 m upward.
B. The top of the lower cloud layer is at 1,202 m altitude.
C. The air temperature is higher than the dew point at 1,200 m altitude.
D. The dew point is above 80°F in both the upper and the lower cloud layers.

254. A *ceilometer* bounces a light beam off the base of a cloud layer and measures how long it takes the light to make the trip up and back. The scientists who made the measurements plotted in Figures 1–4 most likely used the ceilometer to determine which of the following data?

   F. The average air temperature at the top of the cloud layers at Cities A–D

   G. The average dew point of the air at the top of the cloud layers at Cities A–D

   H. The average altitude of the bottom of the cloud layers at Cities A–D

   J. The average thickness of the cloud layers at Cities A–D

255. Assume that the cloud layer at City C extends from an altitude of 3,000 m up to an altitude of 4,000 m. Based on this assumption and the observed trends within cloud layers for the 4 cities, which of the following would be the best approximation of the air temperature and dew point in the cloud layer at an altitude of 3,600 m over City C ?

	Air temperature	Dew point
A.	26°F	36°F
B.	36°F	36°F
C.	38°F	45°F
D.	45°F	45°F

256. The table below shows the average July air temperatures and dew points at 0 m altitude for Miami, Florida, and for Phoenix, Arizona.

City	Average air temperature (°F)	Average dew point (°F)
Miami	85	70
Phoenix	95	36

Based on this information and the data in Figures 1–4, which of these 2 cities, on average, would have lower cloud bases in July?

   F. Phoenix, because it has a higher average air temperature than Miami.

   G. Phoenix, because the difference between the average air temperature and the average dew point is larger than in Miami.

   H. Miami, because it has a lower average air temperature than Phoenix.

   J. Miami, because the difference between the average air temperature and the average dew point is smaller than in Phoenix.

257. A certain city reported that the air temperature and the dew point at 0 m altitude measured at 8 A.M. on a given day were both 40°F. Given this information and the data provided, one could be most certain that clouds were present at which of the following altitudes at that city at 8 A.M. on that day?

   A. 0 m
   B. 600 m
   C. 1,200 m
   D. 2,400 m

Passage XLV

The amount of O_2 present in blood and tissues can be measured, in mm Hg, as the *partial pressure of O_2* (P_{O_2}). The *percent saturation of Hb* is the percent of hemoglobin in the blood that is bound with O_2. Figure 1 shows the relationship between percent saturation of Hb and P_{O_2} at normal body conditions.

Figure 1

Figure 2 shows the relationship between percent saturation of Hb and P_{O_2} at different pHs. The pH of blood is affected by the partial pressure of CO_2 (P_{CO_2}).

Figure 2

Figure 3 shows the relationship between percent saturation of Hb and P_{O_2} at different blood temperatures.

Figure 3

Figures adapted from Robert Carola, John P. Harley, and Charles R. Noback, *Human Anatomy and Physiology.* ©1990 by McGraw-Hill, Inc.

258. According to Figure 1, the greatest change in the percent saturation of Hb occurs within which of the following partial pressure ranges?

F.   0 mm Hg to 10 mm Hg
G.   20 mm Hg to 30 mm Hg
H.   40 mm Hg to 50 mm Hg
J.   60 mm Hg to 70 mm Hg

259. Based on Figures 2 and 3, if blood has a P_{O_2} of 40 mm Hg, the amount of oxygen bound to Hb would be greatest at which of the following sets of conditions?

   A.   Temperature = 10°C; pH = 7.6
   B.   Temperature = 10°C; pH = 7.2
   C.   Temperature = 43°C; pH = 7.6
   D.   Temperature = 43°C; pH = 7.2

260. A researcher has claimed that the ability of Hb to bind with O_2 at a given P_{O_2} will decrease as temperature is increased. Do the data in Figure 3 support his claim?

   F.   No; as the temperature increased, the percent saturation of Hb increased.
   G.   No; as the temperature increased, the percent saturation of Hb decreased.
   H.   Yes; as the temperature increased, the percent saturation of Hb increased.
   J.   Yes; as the temperature increased, the percent saturation of Hb decreased.

261. Which of the following tables represents the assumptions about temperature and pH that would have to be made to properly interpret the data in Figures 1–3 ?

A.

	Factors held constant
Figure 1	pH only
Figure 2	temperature only
Figure 3	temperature and pH

B.

	Factors held constant
Figure 1	pH only
Figure 2	temperature and pH
Figure 3	temperature only

C.

	Factors held constant
Figure 1	temperature and pH
Figure 2	pH only
Figure 3	temperature only

D.

	Factors held constant
Figure 1	temperature and pH
Figure 2	temperature only
Figure 3	pH only

262. Based on the data in Figure 2, which of the following statements best explains why P_{CO_2} affects the pH of blood? When CO_2 dissolves in blood, it:

   F.   forms an acid.
   G.   absorbs acids.
   H.   breaks down to form O_2.
   J.   reacts with O_2 to form Hb.

Passage XLVI

Figure 1 depicts some of the steps of protein synthesis in eukaryotes.

Figure 1

In yeast, the genes that are expressed at a given time depend on environmental conditions, such as the glucose concentration in the environment.

Saccharomyces cerevisiae, a type of yeast, was grown for 12 hours on a growth medium containing glucose. The transcription rates of 4 genes (Genes 1–4) were determined. The *relative transcription rate* (*RTR*) of each gene was then calculated using the following formula:

$$RTR = \frac{\text{the gene's transcription rate at a given time}}{\text{the gene's transcription rate at time} = 0 \text{ hr}}$$

The results appear in Figure 2.

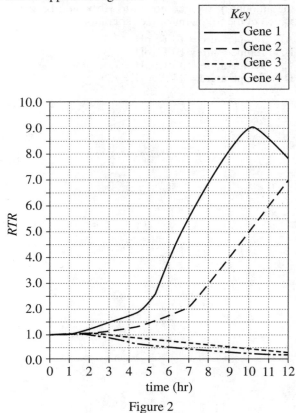

Figure 2

Figure 3 shows the glucose concentration of the medium during the experiment.

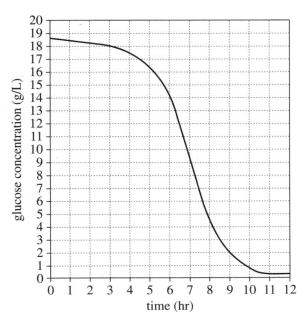

Figure 3

Figures 2 and 3 adapted from Joseph L. DeRisi, Vishwanath R. Iyer, and Patrick O. Brown, "Exploring the Metabolic and Genetic Control of Gene Expression on a Genomic Scale." ©1997 by the American Association for the Advancement of Science.

263. At which of the following times was the transcription rate of Gene 2 the greatest?

   A. Time = 0 hr
   B. Time = 2 hr
   C. Time = 4 hr
   D. Time = 6 hr

264. At which of the following times was the transcription rate of Gene 2 closest to 2 times the transcription rate of Gene 2 at time = 0 hr ?

   F. Time = 5 hr
   G. Time = 7 hr
   H. Time = 9 hr
   J. Time = 10 hr

265. Which of the following cellular components is most directly involved in Step 3 in Figure 1 ?

   A. Cell membrane
   B. Chloroplasts
   C. Lysosomes
   D. Ribosomes

266. Based on Figure 1, which of the following best describes what happens to introns during gene expression?

   F. Introns are transcribed and then translated.
   G. Introns are translated and then transcribed.
   H. Introns are transcribed, but not translated.
   J. Introns are translated, but not transcribed.

267. According to Figures 2 and 3, when the glucose concentration of the medium was 12 g/L, the *RTR* of Gene 4 was closest to which of the following?

   A. 0.1
   B. 0.5
   C. 0.9
   D. 1.3

Passage XLVII

Some students experimentally determined g, the acceleration due to gravity.

In each trial, the students suspended a spring from a stand and measured the spring's length, L. They attached a mass to the suspended spring, allowed the spring-mass system to come to rest, and measured the length, y, of the extended spring (see Figure 1).

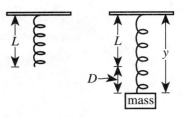

Figure 1

Then they calculated the distance $D = y - L$.

Next, they pulled the mass down to the release point, R, and released it, allowing the mass and spring to oscillate. Using a sensor and a computer, they plotted the distance of the mass from Point R over time (see Figure 2).

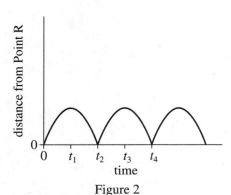

Figure 2

The measured period, P, of the spring-mass system equaled the time that elapsed from the moment the mass left Point R until the moment the mass returned to Point R. Finally, the students used D and P to calculate g.

Study 1

In Trial 1, the students tested Spring 1 with a 0.50 kg mass. (Spring 1 had a *spring constant* [stiffness], k, of 100 newtons/meter, N/m.) In Trials 2 and 3, the students replaced the 0.50 kg mass with a 1.00 kg mass and a 1.50 kg mass, respectively. The results are shown in Table 1.

Table 1				
Trial	Mass (kg)	D (m)	P (sec)	g (m/sec^2)
1	0.50	0.049	0.444	9.8
2	1.00	0.098	0.628	9.8
3	1.50	0.146	0.767	9.8

Study 2

The students followed the procedure from Study 1, except that they substituted Spring 2 (k = 200 N/m) for Spring 1. The results are shown in Table 2.

Table 2				
Trial	Mass (kg)	D (m)	P (sec)	g (m/sec^2)
4	0.50	0.025	0.315	9.9
5	1.00	0.049	0.444	9.8
6	1.50	0.073	0.544	9.7

Study 3

The students followed the procedure from Study 1, except that they substituted Spring 3 (k = 300 N/m) for Spring 1. The results are shown in Table 3.

Table 3				
Trial	Mass (kg)	D (m)	P (sec)	g (m/sec^2)
7	0.50	0.016	0.257	9.6
8	1.00	0.033	0.363	9.9
9	1.50	0.049	0.443	9.9

268. According to Figure 2, each mass was at Point R at which of the following 2 times?

    F. t_1 and t_2
    G. t_1 and t_3
    H. t_2 and t_3
    J. t_2 and t_4

269. Based on Trials 7–9, which of the following graphs best represents the relationship between mass and D ?

A.

C.

B.

D.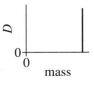

270. If, in Study 1, an additional trial had been conducted with a mass of 0.75 kg, P would most likely have been:

    F.   less than 0.444 sec.
    G. between 0.444 sec and 0.628 sec.
    H. between 0.628 sec and 0.767 sec.
    J.   greater than 0.767 sec.

271. Based on the introductory information, when D was equal to 0, what was the relationship between y and L ?

    A. $y = L$
    B. $y = 2 \times L$
    C. $y = \frac{L}{2}$
    D. $y = \frac{L}{4}$

272. In each trial, 2 forces acted on the mass: the force due to gravity and the force due to the spring. At the moment the spring was released at Point R, which of these forces must have been stronger?

    F.   The force due to gravity, because the mass moved upward from Point R.
    G. The force due to gravity, because the mass moved downward from Point R.
    H. The force due to the spring, because the mass moved upward from Point R.
    J.   The force due to the spring, because the mass moved downward from Point R.

273. Based on the 3 studies, if the students had suspended a 1.50 kg mass from a spring with $k = 400$ N/m, D would most likely have been:

    A. less than 0.049 m.
    B. between 0.049 m and 0.073 m.
    C. between 0.073 m and 0.146 m.
    D. greater than 0.146 m.

Passage XLVIII

As human life expectancy increases, people are becoming more familiar with the complex signs of aging; however, scientists still do not completely understand what causes aging at the molecular level.

Three scientists propose models to explain the human aging process.

Scientist 1

Aging is caused by the shortening of *telomeres*, specialized DNA sequences at the ends of chromosomes. Telomeres play an important role in protecting and replicating chromosome ends. Each time a cell replicates its DNA and divides, its telomeres become shorter. Eventually, the telomeres become too short to perform their necessary roles, and the cell is no longer able to divide, ultimately causing defects in cell structure and function that result in aging.

Scientist 2

Aging is caused by random DNA damage that accumulates over the lifetime of *somatic* (nonreproductive) cells. As humans age, the DNA in their somatic cells accumulates damage that is not repaired. This results in mutations that cause defects in proteins and in gene expression, leading to aging. Most DNA damage is caused by *free oxygen radicals* (oxygen species containing oxygen atoms with unpaired electrons) formed during metabolic processes. Thus, the accumulation of DNA damage can be slowed by decreasing the rate of metabolism. Although telomeres do become shorter each time a cell divides, this occurs too slowly to affect the aging process.

Scientist 3

Aging is caused by mutations present in each human at birth that usually produce defects after an individual is too old to reproduce. Because individuals with these mutations reproduce, the mutations can be passed on to the next generation and maintained in the population. Thus, aging is caused by the mutations that humans inherit from their parents. This is why closely related individuals tend to have similar life expectancies. Telomere shortening occurs too slowly to affect the aging process, and DNA damage from free oxygen radicals is easily repaired.

274. Based on the passage, would Scientist 1 or Scientist 3 be more likely to argue that the process of cell division contributes directly to aging, and why?

F. Scientist 1, because according to Scientist 1, telomeres become shorter each time a cell divides.
G. Scientist 1, because according to Scientist 1, telomeres become longer each time a cell divides.
H. Scientist 3, because according to Scientist 3, telomeres become shorter each time a cell divides.
J. Scientist 3, because according to Scientist 3, telomeres become longer each time a cell divides.

275. How does Scientist 2's model differ from Scientist 3's model? Scientist 2 claims that the mutations that cause aging:

A. are due to telomere shortening, whereas Scientist 3 claims that the mutations that cause aging are present at birth.
B. accumulate throughout a human's life span, whereas Scientist 3 claims that the mutations that cause aging are due to telomere shortening.
C. accumulate throughout a human's life span, whereas Scientist 3 claims that the mutations that cause aging are present at birth.
D. are present at birth, whereas Scientist 3 claims that the mutations that cause aging accumulate throughout a human's life span.

276. Scientist 1's model would be most weakened if which of the following observations were made?

F. Telomeres are the same length in both young cells and old cells.
G. The telomeres in a baby's cells are longer than the telomeres in an adult's cells.
H. More free oxygen radicals are produced by young cells than by old cells.
J. More free oxygen radicals are produced by old cells than by young cells.

277. All 3 scientists would most likely agree with which of the following statements about telomeres?

A. Telomeres become shorter as a human ages.
B. Telomeres remain the same length throughout a human's life span.
C. Telomeres become longer as a human ages.
D. Changes in telomere length are responsible for aging.

278. Scientist 3 proposes that the mutations that eventually cause aging are:

    F. produced when telomeres shorten.
    G. produced by metabolic products.
    H. present only in old cells.
    J. present in both young cells and old cells.

279. Scientist 2's model would be best supported by which of the following observations?

    A. There are fewer mutations in old cells than in young cells.
    B. There are fewer mutations in young cells than in old cells.
    C. Free oxygen radicals do not cause DNA damage.
    D. Telomere shortening influences the aging process.

280. Suppose studies show that consuming fewer calories can slow the aging process. How would Scientist 2 explain this result? Scientist 2 would most likely argue that consuming fewer calories:

    F. increases the rate of metabolism and increases the production of free oxygen radicals.
    G. increases the rate of metabolism and decreases the production of free oxygen radicals.
    H. decreases the rate of metabolism and increases the production of free oxygen radicals.
    J. decreases the rate of metabolism and decreases the production of free oxygen radicals.

Passage XLIX

A river's *discharge* is the volume of river water flowing past a location in the river in a given amount of time. Discharge is affected by several factors, including the area of the river's *drainage basin* (the land surface that delivers the rainwater that falls on it into the river) and the spatial relationship of the river to other rivers.

Two studies examined the discharge in 3 rivers—the North River, the Jones River, and the Calm River—following a rainfall event. As shown in Figure 1, the drainage basin of the North River and the drainage basin of the Jones River are within the drainage basin of the Calm River. The area of each river's drainage basin is given in kilometers².

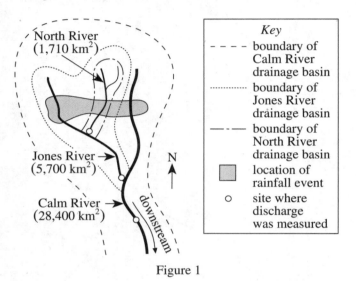

Figure 1

Study 1

The rainfall event produced 25 mm of rain. As rainwater drained into the 3 rivers, the discharges of the rivers increased. The maximum discharge measured immediately after a rainfall event is called a *flood*.

Over the 12 days following the rainfall event, as the flood caused by the rainfall moved downstream, the discharge was continuously measured, in m³/sec, at the 3 sites shown in Figure 1. The results are shown in Figure 2. (Note: No rainfall event occurred in the Calm River drainage basin during those 12 days.)

Study 2

The *normalized discharge* over the 12 days following the rainfall event was calculated for each of the 3 rivers. The normalized discharge values allowed the flood to be studied as if the 3 rivers had identical drainage basin areas of 1 km². Each normalized discharge value was calculated using the following equation:

$$\text{normalized discharge} = \frac{\text{river discharge (m}^3\text{/sec)}}{\text{river drainage basin area (km}^2)}$$

The value of the numerator, the river discharge, was obtained from Figure 2. The results are shown in Figure 3.

Figure 2

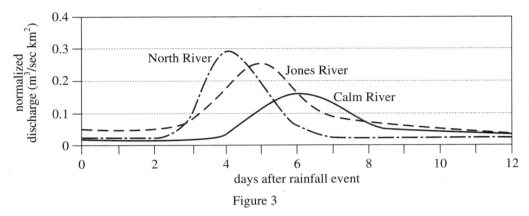

Figure 3

Figures 2 and 3 adapted from George Hornberger et al., *Elements of Physical Hydrology*. ©1998 by The Johns Hopkins University Press.

281. According to Figure 2, the maximum discharge in the Jones River after the rainfall event was closest to which of the following?

A. 500 m³/sec
B. 1,000 m³/sec
C. 1,500 m³/sec
D. 2,000 m³/sec

282. According to Study 1, the Jones River and Calm River discharges were closest to the same value at which of the following times after the rainfall event?

F. 0.5 day
G. 2 days
H. 3.5 days
J. 5 days

283. The *tributary* (a smaller stream flowing into a larger stream) of the North River shown in Figure 1 would most likely have a drainage basin area of:

A. less than 1,710 km².
B. between 1,710 km² and 5,700 km².
C. between 5,700 km² and 28,400 km².
D. greater than 28,400 km².

284. A student predicted that the river with the greatest maximum discharge would also have the greatest maximum normalized discharge. Based on Figures 2 and 3, is the student's prediction correct?

F. Yes, because the North River had both the greatest maximum discharge and the greatest maximum normalized discharge.
G. Yes, because the Calm River had both the greatest maximum discharge and the greatest maximum normalized discharge.
H. No, because the North River had the greatest maximum discharge but the Calm River had the greatest maximum normalized discharge.
J. No, because the Calm River had the greatest maximum discharge but the North River had the greatest maximum normalized discharge.

285. Based on Figures 1 and 2 and the description of Study 2, the normalized discharge of the Calm River 5 days after the rainfall event was most likely calculated using which of the following expressions?

A. 3,000 km² ÷ 28,400 m³/sec
B. 3,000 m³/sec ÷ 28,400 km²
C. 28,400 km² ÷ 3,000 m³/sec
D. 28,400 m³/sec ÷ 3,000 km²

286. Suppose that discharge in the Jones River had been measured at a site north of the area where the rainfall event occurred, instead of at the site indicated in Figure 1. How would the discharge data recorded after the rainfall event have differed from that shown in Figure 2 ?

F. No flood would have been recorded in the data for the North River.
G. No flood would have been recorded in the data for the Jones River.
H. The flood recorded in the data for the North River would have been greater than 700 m³/sec.
J. The flood recorded in the data for the Jones River would have been greater than 1,500 m³/sec.

Passage L

A *binary phase diagram* (BPD) shows how the phases of a mixture of 2 chemicals vary with temperature and composition at 1 atmosphere (atm) of pressure. The phases include the solid (*s*) phase of each chemical and the liquid (*l*) solution phase of the 2 chemicals. The eutectic is the point where all 4 regions of the BPD intersect. It indicates the conditions at which all the phases represented in the 4 regions exist in equilibrium. When a mixture is at equilibrium, no net phase change occurs. Figure 1 is a BPD for durene and biphenyl. Figure 2 is a BPD for durene and naphthalene.

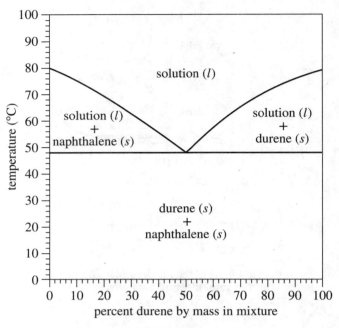

Figure 2

Figures adapted from Jürgen Gallus et al., "Binary Solid-Liquid Phase Diagrams of Selected Organic Compounds." ©2001 by Division of Chemical Education, Inc., American Chemical Society.

Figure 1

287. According to Figure 2, at 1 atm, solid will NOT be present in a durene-naphthalene mixture at 55°C that contains which of the following percents durene by mass?

A. 30%
B. 50%
C. 70%
D. 90%

288. According to Figure 1, at 1 atm, a durene-biphenyl mixture that is 70% durene by mass at 50°C will be a:

   F. liquid solution only.
   G. mixture of a liquid solution and solid biphenyl.
   H. mixture of a liquid solution and solid durene.
   J. mixture of solid durene and solid biphenyl.

289. Consider a durene-biphenyl mixture at 1 atm that is 40% durene by mass. According to Figure 1, solid durene, solid biphenyl, and a liquid solution will all be present in equilibrium at a temperature closest to which of the following?

   A. 42°C
   B. 52°C
   C. 69°C
   D. 79°C

290. A durene-biphenyl mixture that is 60% durene by mass at 90°C was slowly cooled to 20°C, then slowly heated to 70°C (all at 1 atm). Based on Figure 1, at the end of this procedure the mixture consisted of:

   F. liquid solution only.
   G. liquid solution and solid biphenyl.
   H. liquid solution and solid durene.
   J. solid durene and solid biphenyl.

291. Based on Figures 1 and 2, the melting point of durene is closest to which of the following?

   A. 19°C
   B. 39°C
   C. 59°C
   D. 79°C

Passage LI

Students studied the rates at which various heated, solid aluminum spheres cooled in air.

The spheres were allowed to cool over the next 30 min while the temperature of the air was kept constant at 20°C. A graph of the central temperature of each sphere versus time over the 30 min cooling period is shown in Figure 2. For each sphere, the *cooling rate* at a given time equals the graph's slope at that time.

Figure 2

Experiment 1

The students tested 3 solid aluminum spheres, A, B, and C, having different radii. The volume, V, in cm³, and the ratio of surface area to volume, $\frac{S}{V}$, in cm⁻¹, for each sphere are shown in Table 1.

Table 1		
Sphere	V (cm³)	$\frac{S}{V}$ (cm⁻¹)
A	3.9	3.1
B	31	1.5
C	490	0.6

Each of the spheres was fitted with a thermocouple to measure the *central temperature* (the temperature at the center) of the sphere. Then the 3 spheres were simultaneously heated. Once the temperature throughout each sphere was 100°C, the 3 spheres were immediately suspended at time = 0 min in air that was at a temperature of 20°C (see Figure 1).

Experiment 2

The students tested 2 solid aluminum spheres, X and Y, that were identical in size. Sphere X was painted with Coating X, and Sphere Y was painted with Coating Y. Each of the spheres was fitted with a thermocouple as in Experiment 1, and then the 2 spheres were simultaneously heated. Once the temperature throughout each sphere was 120°C, the 2 spheres were immediately suspended at time = 0 min in air that was at a temperature of 20°C. The spheres were allowed to cool over the next 55 min while the temperature of the air was kept constant at 20°C. A plot of the central temperature of each sphere versus time over the 55 min cooling period is shown in Figure 3.

Figure 1

Figure 3

292. A student stated that spheres that are the same in size but that are made of different metals will cool at different rates. Do the results of Experiment 1 verify this statement?
    F. Yes, because all the spheres tested in Experiment 1 were made of the same metal.
    G. Yes, because all the spheres tested in Experiment 1 were made of different metals.
    H. No, because all the spheres tested in Experiment 1 were made of the same metal.
    J. No, because all the spheres tested in Experiment 1 were made of different metals.

293. Based on Figures 2 and 3, the unit of measurement for the cooling rate was which of the following?
    A. °C/min
    B. °C/cm^3
    C. min/°C
    D. cm^3/°C

294. Suppose that Sphere A had been allowed to continue cooling until the central temperature of the sphere stopped decreasing with the passage of time. Based on the information given, once the temperature stopped decreasing, the central temperature of the sphere would most likely have been:
    F. 15°C.
    G. 20°C.
    H. 22°C.
    J. 30°C.

295. Based on the results of Experiment 1, a solid aluminum cylinder having which of the following values for $\frac{S}{V}$ will cool the fastest?
    A. 0.5 cm^{-1}
    B. 1.0 cm^{-1}
    C. 1.5 cm^{-1}
    D. 2.0 cm^{-1}

296. In Experiment 1, to adjust the temperature throughout each sphere before the 3 spheres were suspended and allowed to begin cooling, the students most likely immersed the spheres in:
    F. air at 20°C.
    G. boiling water.
    H. dry ice.
    J. molten aluminum.

297. During the 55 min cooling period of Experiment 2, the central temperature of Sphere Y reached 40°C how much sooner or later than the central temperature of Sphere X reached 40°C ?
    A. 13 min sooner
    B. 13 min later
    C. 17 min sooner
    D. 17 min later

Passage LII

Volcanoes put sulfur into the troposphere and the stratosphere, where the sulfur reacts to form sulfate *aerosols* (liquid droplets suspended in air). For locations at 50°N latitude, aerosols present at altitudes below 11 km scatter incoming solar energy, resulting in cooler air, while aerosols present at higher altitudes absorb incoming solar energy, warming the air.

Figure 1 shows the air temperature deviation at the surface of, and at 2 different altitudes above, a particular volcano (located at 50°N latitude), before and after it erupted. Figure 2 shows the maximum surface air temperature deviation associated with the specific mass of sulfate aerosols formed in the stratosphere after each of 8 volcanoes erupted.

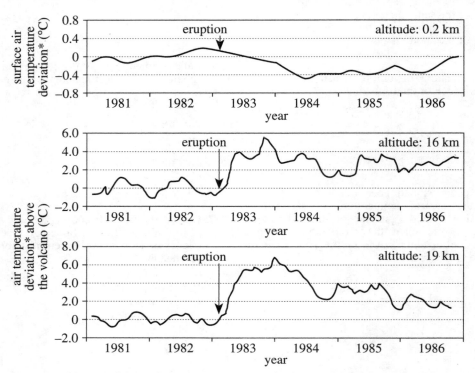

Note: A tick mark on the x-axis indicates Jan. 1 of a given year.

*air temperature deviation at a given altitude = [measured air temperature at the given altitude] −[average air temperature at the given altitude]

Figure 1

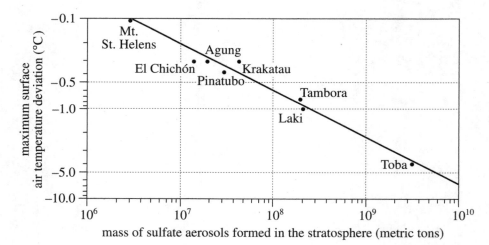

mass of sulfate aerosols formed in the stratosphere (metric tons)

Figure 2

Figure 1 adapted from Haraldur Sigurdsson, "Evidence of Volcanic Loading of the Atmosphere and Climate Response." ©1990 by Elsevier Science Publishers.

Figure 2 adapted from Michael Rampino, "Supereruptions as a Threat to Civilizations on Earth-like Planets." ©2002 by Elsevier Science (USA).

298. According to Figure 1, after the eruption, the greatest air temperature deviation at an altitude of 19 km was closest to which of the following?

   F.   5°C
   G. 6°C
   H. 7°C
   J.   8°C

299. Consider the equation provided in Figure 1 and the data point for Toba in Figure 2. After Toba erupted, the surface air temperature, when at its most extreme, was approximately:

   A.   4°C above average.
   B.   4°C below average.
   C. 10°C above average.
   D. 10°C below average.

300. According to Figure 1, after the eruption, the air temperature at 16 km altitude stayed more than 1°C above average for:

   F.   less than 1 year.
   G. between 1 year and 2 years.
   H. between 2 years and 3 years.
   J.   more than 3 years.

301. Consider the volcano whose data are shown in Figure 1. Suppose that the average air temperature 16 km above that volcano is −60.0°C. Based on Figure 1, on January 1, 1984, the measured air temperature 16 km above that same volcano would have been closest to which of the following?

   A. −64.0°C
   B. −60.0°C
   C. −56.0°C
   D. − 4.0°C

302. In Figure 1, a value of zero for the air temperature deviation at a given altitude indicates that the measured air temperature at that altitude equaled the:

   F.   maximum air temperature deviation at that altitude.
   G. average air temperature deviation at that altitude.
   H. maximum air temperature at that altitude.
   J.   average air temperature at that altitude.

12

Chapter 12: Answers and Explanations

Check your answers to the questions in chapter 11 with the following answer key. If you missed a question, review the answer explanations on the following pages.

Answer Key

1.	B	52.	F	103.	C
2.	F	53.	A	104.	G
3.	A	54.	J	105.	D
4.	G	55.	A	106.	G
5.	A	56.	H	107.	B
6.	J	57.	D	108.	J
7.	B	58.	J	109.	D
8.	G	59.	B	110.	F
9.	A	60.	F	111.	C
10.	H	61.	C	112.	F
11.	D	62.	G	113.	A
12.	J	63.	A	114.	J
13.	B	64.	J	115.	B
14.	G	65.	B	116.	J
15.	C	66.	G	117.	B
16.	F	67.	C	118.	H
17.	A	68.	H	119.	C
18.	H	69.	B	120.	J
19.	D	70.	F	121.	D
20.	G	71.	C	122.	F
21.	B	72.	H	123.	B
22.	H	73.	A	124.	H
23.	C	74.	F	125.	D
24.	G	75.	C	126.	J
25.	D	76.	J	127.	D
26.	F	77.	B	128.	F
27.	C	78.	J	129.	A
28.	H	79.	A	130.	H
29.	D	80.	F	131.	C
30.	J	81.	B	132.	J
31.	A	82.	F	133.	A
32.	J	83.	A	134.	J
33.	D	84.	H	135.	B
34.	J	85.	D	136.	H
35.	C	86.	G	137.	C
36.	G	87.	D	138.	G
37.	A	88.	F	139.	B
38.	J	89.	C	140.	J
39.	D	90.	G	141.	A
40.	J	91.	C	142.	G
41.	B	92.	H	143.	D
42.	J	93.	D	144.	G
43.	D	94.	G	145.	C
44.	J	95.	B	146.	F
45.	B	96.	F	147.	D
46.	G	97.	A	148.	G
47.	D	98.	J	149.	B
48.	F	99.	A	150.	H
49.	C	100.	J	151.	D
50.	J	101.	C	152.	J
51.	C	102.	H	153.	A

154.	H
155.	B
156.	F
157.	B
158.	F
159.	D
160.	J
161.	B
162.	G
163.	D
164.	H
165.	A
166.	H
167.	B
168.	G
169.	C
170.	H
171.	A
172.	F
173.	D
174.	H
175.	B
176.	F
177.	A
178.	G
179.	C
180.	J
181.	A
182.	F
183.	D
184.	G
185.	A
186.	G
187.	D
188.	J
189.	B
190.	J
191.	C
192.	J
193.	B
194.	H
195.	A
196.	H
197.	B
198.	F
199.	C
200.	J
201.	D
202.	H
203.	C
204.	G

205.	A
206.	H
207.	B
208.	H
209.	A
210.	F
211.	A
212.	H
213.	A
214.	F
215.	B
216.	J
217.	D
218.	F
219.	B
220.	F
221.	C
222.	H
223.	B
224.	H
225.	C
226.	F
227.	A
228.	H
229.	B
230.	G
231.	D
232.	F
233.	B
234.	H
235.	D
236.	J
237.	A
238.	J
239.	B
240.	H
241.	D
242.	J
243.	D
244.	G
245.	A
246.	G
247.	B
248.	H
249.	C
250.	F
251.	A
252.	G
253.	C
254.	H
255.	B

256.	J
257.	A
258.	G
259.	A
260.	J
261.	D
262.	F
263.	D
264.	G
265.	D
266.	H
267.	B
268.	J
269.	C
270.	GE
271.	A
272.	H
273.	A
274.	F
275.	C
276.	F
277.	A
278.	J
279.	B
280.	J
281.	C
282.	H
283.	A
284.	J
285.	B
286.	G
287.	B
288.	H
289.	A
290.	F
291.	D
292.	H
293.	A
294.	G
295.	D
296.	G
297.	D
298.	H
299.	B
300.	J
301.	C
302.	J

Explanatory Answers

Passage I

1. **The best answer is B.** According to Figure 1, the only site with *E. coli* levels above 400 colonies per 100 mL was Day 30 at Site 1. **A** is incorrect; the *E. coli* level on Day 1 at Site 1 was 101 colonies formed per 100 mL. **B** is correct; the *E. coli* level on Day 30 at Site 1 was 708 colonies formed per 100 mL. **C** is incorrect; the *E. coli* level on Day 1 at Site 2 was 16 colonies formed per 100 mL. **D** is incorrect; the *E. coli* level on Day 30 at Site 2 was 173 colonies formed per 100 mL.

2. **The best answer is F.** According to Figure 1, the *E. coli* levels were much higher at Site 1 than Site 2 on 3 of the five days measured and nearly the same on the other two days measured, indicating that the average *E. coli* levels were higher at Site 1 than at Site 2 over the collection period. According to Figure 2, the water flow was greater for Site 1 than Site 2 on all five days that measurements were taken, indicating that the average water flow was higher for Site 1 than Site 2 over the collection period. **F** is correct; both the water flow and *E. coli* levels were greater for Site 1 than Site 2. **G, H,** and **J** are incorrect.

3. **The best answer is A.** According to Table 1, the better the water quality rating, the greater the value for BI. Therefore, **A** is correct. **B, C,** and **D** are incorrect; biotic index is neither independent of water quality nor does it increase as water quality degrades.

4. **The best answer is G.** According to Table 2, the average BI for Site 1 was 6.3, indicating that the water quality rating for Site 1 was excellent. The average BI for Site 2 was 2.5, indicating that the water quality rating for Site 2 was fair. One would expect more stone fly larvae at the site with the higher water quality, which is Site 1. The results are consistent with the students' hypothesis. **F** is incorrect; Site 1 had a water quality rating of excellent, and Site 2 had a water quality rating of fair. **G** is correct. **H** and **J** are incorrect; Site 1 had a better water quality rating.

5. **The best answer is A.** According to the passage, *E. coli* levels above 100 colonies formed per 100 mL indicate reduced water quality. According to Figure 1, on Days 1 and 30, Site 1 had *E. coli* levels above 100 colonies formed per 100 mL. **A** is correct; Figure 1 contains the information about *E. coli* levels. **B** is incorrect; Figure 2 contains information about water flow, and no relationship is given between water flow and water quality. **C** is incorrect; Table 1 shows how water quality rating varies with BI. Table 1 contains no information about Sites 1 or 2. **D** is incorrect; according to Table 2, Site 1 has a higher water quality rating than does Site 2.

6. **The best answer is J.** In order to answer this item, the examinee must know that the introduction of large amounts of fertilizer may cause eutrophication, leading to reduction in water quality. A higher BI corresponds to a higher water quality rating. A reduction in water quality after the introduction of the fertilizer would therefore cause a decrease in the BI. **F** and **G** are incorrect; the BI will decrease, not increase. **H** is incorrect; the water quality will decrease. **J** is correct.

Passage II

7. **The best answer is B.** According to Table 1, AWP 2 produced 21 mL of H_2 by Day 2, 187 mL by Day 4, 461 mL by Day 6, and 760 mL by Day 8. **A** is incorrect; this figure shows the production of more than 200 mL of H_2 by Day 4. **B** is correct. **C** and **D** are incorrect; both show a decrease in the volume of H_2 over time.

8. **The best answer is G.** According to Table 1, AWP 1 produced 4 mL of H_2 in the first 2 days, 29 mL of H_2 in the next 2 days, 48 mL of H_2 in the next 2 days, and 52 mL of H_2 in the last 2 days. If the volume had been measured on Day 10, it is likely that the additional amount of H_2 produced would have been no more than 50–60 mL. This would have resulted in a total volume of no more than 200 mL H_2 produced. **F** is incorrect; 133 mL of H_2 had been produced by Day 8. **G** is correct. **H** and **J** are incorrect; a total volume of H_2 greater than 461 mL would require the formation of 328 mL from Day 8 to Day 10, which is very unlikely based on the rate of H_2 formation seen in Days 2–8.

9. **The best answer is A.** According to Table 1, 133 mL of H_2 was produced by AWP 1 on Day 8, and 81 mL of H_2 was produced by AWP 1 on Day 6. The amount produced between those measurements was $133 - 81 = 52$ mL. **A** is correct. **B**, **C**, and **D** are incorrect; 52 mL of H_2 was produced.

10. **The best answer is H.** In order to answer this item, the examinee must have a basic understanding of chemical equations. H_2 is one of the reaction products and is formed at half the rate that $Al(OH)_3$ is formed. Measuring the volume of H_2 that forms would therefore give information about the rate of formation of $Al(OH)_3$. **F** and **G** are incorrect; H_2O and Al are both reactants and are not converted into one another. **H** is correct; Al is converted to $Al(OH)_3$. **J** is incorrect; Al is converted to $Al(OH)_3$.

11. **The best answer is D.** In order to answer this item, the examinee must understand that a base will increase the pH of water (and realize that the passage states that AWPs are water-based). The passage states that DMEA is an AWP ingredient that increases pH. Therefore, DMEA is a base. **A**, **B**, and **C** are incorrect; DMEA is a base because it increases pH. **D** is correct.

12. **The best answer is J.** According to Table 1, on Day 2 the AWP 3 sample had produced 121 mL of H_2. According to Figure 1, the sample containing EDTA produced 121 mL of H_2 on approximately Day 10. **F** and **G** are incorrect; the volume of H_2 was not greater than 100 mL until Day 7. **H** is incorrect; only 100 mL of H_2 had been produced on Day 7. **J** is correct; on Day 10 approximately 121 mL of H_2 had been produced.

Passage III

13. **The best answer is B.** Figure 4 shows that for Trial 5 both scales had equal readings, indicating that the weight was equally distributed. **A** is incorrect; in Trial 4, Scale B had a higher reading than did Scale A. **B** is correct; in Trial 5, both scales had equal readings. **C** is incorrect; in Trial 6, Scale A had a higher reading than did Scale B. **D** is incorrect; the weight was equally distributed in Trial 5.

14. **The best answer is G.** Figure 2 (Trial 1) shows that Scale A caused the hand on Scale B to move ¼ of the way around the dial. Figure 2 (Trial 2) shows that a 5.0 N weight causes the hand on Scale A to move ¼ of the way around the dial. Scale B has a weight of 5.0 N. **F**, **H**, and **J** are incorrect; the scales have a weight of 5.0 N. **G** is correct.

15. **The best answer is C.** In order to answer this item, the examinee must know that as a spring is compressed, the potential energy stored in the spring increases. The stored potential energy would therefore be greatest when the spring is compressed the most, and the spring would be compressed the most when the heaviest weight is placed on the scale. In Trial 1, there is no weight on Scale A; thus the spring would not be compressed at all. In Trial 3, there is a 10.0 N weight on Scale A, and the spring would be compressed. **A** and **B** are incorrect; the potential energy stored in the spring of Scale A would be greater in Trial 3. **C** is correct. **D** is incorrect; the amount of weight was greater in Trial 3.

16. **The best answer is F.** According to Figure 2, the weight of Scale A is 5.0 N (the hand on the scale moves ¼ of the way around the dial). Scale B should read 5.0 N whether Scale A is right side up or upside down. When Scale A is upside down, the spring in Scale A is also compressed by the weight of Scale A; therefore, Scale A should also read 5.0 N. **F** is correct; both scales read 5.0 N with the hands ¼ of the way around the dials. **G** is incorrect; Scale B reads 10.0 N with the hand ½ of the way around the dial. **H** is incorrect; Scale A reads 10.0 N with the hand ½ of the way around the dial. **J** is incorrect; both scales read 10.0 N.

17. **The best answer is A.** The description of Study 2 states that the distance between Scale B and the 10.0 N weight was measured from the pencil to the weight. Therefore, the pencils were most likely intended to be used as a convenient visual reference from which to measure distance, so **A** is correct. **B** is incorrect; any side-to-side motion of the board would have been contrary to the design of Study 2. **C** is incorrect; the students intentionally zeroed out the weights of the pencils and the board. **D** is incorrect; air pressure would have been equal above and below each platform regardless of whether the pencils had been included or not.

18. **The best answer is H.** According to Figure 4, when the distance between the weight and the pencil on Scale B was 0.10 m, Scale B read approximately 7.5 N. When the distance between the weight and the pencil was 0.20 m, Scale B read 5.0 N, and when the distance was 0.30 m, Scale B read 2.5 N. As the distance increased, the amount of force exerted on Scale B decreased. **F, G,** and **J** are incorrect. **H** is correct.

19. **The best answer is D.** In Trials 4–6, pencils were placed on each scale and a board was placed on top. In order to measure only the amount of force exerted by the weight and not the force exerted by the pencils and the board, the scales were zeroed. **A** is incorrect; setting the dial readings to zero would not add in the weights of the scales. **B** is incorrect; the weights of the board and pencils were subtracted, not added. **C** is incorrect; setting the dial readings to zero would not subtract the weights of the scales. **D** is correct; the students were interested only in the force exerted by the weight and not the pencils and board.

Passage IV

20. **The best answer is G.** According to the passage, the EOR is the minimum octane number of a fuel required for an engine to operate without becoming damaged. According to Table 2, as engine speed increases the EOR decreases. **F, H,** and **J** are incorrect. **G** is correct.

21. **The best answer is B.** According to Table 2, as the engine speed increases, the octane numbers for each fuel decrease. At an engine speed of 2,000 rpm, the octane number for Fuel A was 96.6, and the octane number for Fuel B was 96.1. At an engine speed of 2,500 rpm, the octane number for Fuel A was 95.0, and the octane number for Fuel B was 95.4. At an engine speed of 2,200 rpm the octane number for Fuel A should be between 95.0 and 96.6, and the octane number for Fuel B should be between 95.4 and 96.1. **A** is incorrect; the octane numbers for both fuels should be higher. **B** is correct. **C** and **D** are incorrect; the octane numbers for both fuels should be lower.

22. **The best answer is H.** According to Table 1, the octane number is equal to the percent isooctane in the mixture. The percent isooctane for a given mixture is:

$$\frac{\text{volume of isooctane}}{\text{volume of isooctane} + \text{volume of heptane}} \times 100$$

F is incorrect; taking the first entry in the table as an example, $100 \div 0 \neq 0$. **G** is incorrect; taking the first entry in the table as an example, $0 \div 100 \neq 100$. **H** is correct; taking the first entry in the table as an example, $(100 \div 100) \times 100 = 100$. **J** is incorrect; taking the first entry in the table as an example, $(0 \div 100) \times 100 \neq 100$.

23. **The best answer is C.** Based on the information in Table 1, a mixture containing 100 mL of heptane and 900 mL of isooctane would have an octane number of 90. According to the results of Experiment 2, adding 4 mL of TEL to 1,000 mL of isooctane increased the octane number from 100 to 125. One would predict that adding 3 mL of TEL to the heptane/isooctane mixture would increase the octane number to some value greater than 90 but less than 125. **A** and **B** are incorrect; the octane number would be increased to a value greater than 90. **C** is correct. **D** is incorrect; upon addition of the TEL, the octane number of pure isooctane was increased to 125; the octane number of the mixture containing 90% isooctane would not be greater than 125.

24. **The best answer is G.** According to the passage, the minimum octane number of a fuel required for an engine to run without being damaged is the EOR. The best fuel would be that which has an octane number greater than the EOR at all engine speeds between 1,500 rpm and 3,500 rpm. Fuel A has an octane number greater than the EOR at all engine speeds. The octane number for Fuel B at 1,500 rpm is 96.7, and the EOR is 97.4. Fuel A would be the best choice. **A** is incorrect; the octane number for Fuel A is higher than the EOR at each engine speed tested. **G** is correct. **H** and **J** are incorrect; the octane number for Fuel B at 1,500 rpm is lower than the EOR.

25. **The best answer is D.** In order to answer this item, the examinee should understand solution properties. According to Table 1, the octane number decreases as the percentage of isooctane in the mixture decreases. A solution containing 80% isooctane should have an octane number between those of a solution containing 90% isooctane (90) and 75% isooctane (75). **A**, **B**, and **C** are incorrect; the octane number should be between 75 and 90. **D** is correct; a solution that is 80% isooctane would have an octane number of 80.

26. **The best answer is F.** The results of Experiment 2 indicate that adding 1 mL of TEL to 1,000 mL of isooctane increased the octane number from 100 to 115. It is reasonable to predict that if 1 mL of TEL were added to 1,000 mL of heptane, the octane number would likewise increase. However, because Table 1 indicates that pure heptane has an octane number of zero, the addition of such a small volume of TEL is unlikely to increase the octane number to 115 or greater. Therefore, it is most reasonable to predict that a mixture of 1 mL of TEL and 1,000 mL of heptane would have an octane number that is higher than that of pure heptane but lower than 115. **F** is correct. **G, H,** and **J** are incorrect; it is unlikely that adding 1 mL of TEL to 1,000 mL of heptane would result in the octane number either decreasing to less that of pure heptane or increasing to greater than 115.

Passage V

27. **The best answer is C.** Scientist B argues that short-period comets were once long-period comets. **A** is incorrect; Scientist B claims that long-period comets do become short-period comets. **B** is incorrect; Scientist B does not discuss whether or not short-period comets can become long-period comets. **C** is correct. **D** is incorrect; Scientist B agrees that both long-period and short-period comets orbit the Sun.

28. **The best answer is H.** Scientist A states that the KB is 30 AU to 50 AU from the Sun and has a small inclination with respect to the ecliptic plane. Scientists should search this region of space for objects in the KB. **F** is incorrect; this region would be too far away to find objects in the KB. **G** is incorrect; the region at smaller angles with respect to the ecliptic plane should be searched. **H** is correct. **J** is incorrect; Scientist A does not suggest that the region surrounding Jupiter would be part of the KB.

29. **The best answer is D.** According to the introduction, the orbital planes of short-period comets have inclinations of 30° or less with respect to the ecliptic plane. **A, B,** and **C** are incorrect; one would expect short-period comets to have orbital planes with inclinations of 30° or less with respect to the ecliptic plane. **D** is correct; one would not expect the orbital plane of a short-period comet to be as large as 45° with respect to the ecliptic plane.

30. **The best answer is J.** In order to answer this item, the examinee should know that Saturn is one of the "giant planets" of our solar system. Scientist B states that the orbits of long-period comets are affected by the gravitational fields of the giant planets. **F, G,** and **H** are incorrect; these are smaller planets and may not be large enough to affect the orbits of the long-period comets. **J** is correct; Saturn is a giant planet.

31. **The best answer is A.** According to the introduction, short-period comets have orbital periods of 200 years or less. Scientist B claims that short-period comets were once long-period comets. The introduction states that long-period comets originate in the Oort Cloud. Scientist B would most likely agree that Comet Halley is a short-period comet that originated in the Oort Cloud. **A** is correct. **B** is incorrect; Scientist B claims that the KB does not exist. **C** is incorrect; because the orbital period of Comet Halley is less than 200 years, it is a short-period comet. **D** is incorrect; Comet Halley is a short-period comet, and Scientist B claims that the KB does not exist.

32. **The best answer is J.** Scientist A states that the icy bodies in the KB with diameters between 10 km and 30 km are too small to be seen with telescopes on Earth's surface. The much larger icy bodies must have diameters greater than 30 km. **F, G**, and **H** are incorrect; the diameters should be greater than 30 km. **J** is correct.

33. **The best answer is D.** The two scientists do not dispute the presence of the Oort Cloud around our solar system. The absence of a spherical shell similar to the Oort Cloud near a similar star would not affect either viewpoint. **A, B**, and **C** are incorrect. **D** is correct.

Passage VI

34. **The best answer is J.** The plant in question has a height of only 21 cm, and it produced no fruit. According to the results of the experiment, these properties are most consistent with the data shown for the L4 plants that were grown in a nutrient solution containing 120 g of NaCl. The L2 and L4 plants grown in nutrient solutions containing 60 g of NaCl had both greater average plant heights and non-zero average fruit masses. Likewise, for the L2 plants grown in a nutrient solution containing 120 g of NaCl. Therefore, **F, G**, and **H** are incorrect. **J** is correct.

35. **The best answer is C.** In order to answer this item, the examinee must know that the cell membrane separates the cell's cytoplasm from the environment. According to the passage, the H_2O moved between the cytoplasm of the plants' cells and the environment. If the H_2O was passing from the cell to the environment, then it passed through the cell membrane. **A, B**, and **D** are incorrect; in order for water to pass between the cytoplasm into the environment, it must pass through the cell membrane. **C** is correct.

36. **The best answer is G.** In order to answer this item, the examinee must know that NaCl is a salt. According to Tables 1, 2, and 3, as the amount of NaCl added to the nutrient solution increased, the plant mass decreased. **F** is incorrect; the mass did not increase. **G** is correct. **H** and **J** are incorrect; the plant mass decreased only.

37. **The best answer is A.** The researchers controlled which lines received the *AtNHX1* gene. **A** is correct. **B** is incorrect; only tomato plants were used, so this was not a variable. **C** is incorrect; the plant mass was a dependent variable. **D** is incorrect; the plant height was a dependent variable.

38. **The best answer is J.** In order to answer this item, the examinee must understand the concept of an allele and the relationship between homozygosity and genotype. The passage indicates that two identical alleles of the *AtNHX1* gene were incorporated into L1's genome. An organism that has two identical alleles for a given gene is homozygous for that gene. Therefore, **F**, **G**, and **H** are incorrect. **J** is correct.

39. **The best answer is D.** According to the information in Tables 1, 2, and 3, as the height decreased, the mass decreased. A plot of this data would result in a line with a positive slope. **A** and **B** are incorrect; the line would have a slope because the mass changed as the height changed. **C** is incorrect; the line would have a positive slope because the mass increased as the height increased. **D** is correct.

40. **The best answer is J.** L1, L2, and L3 all had *AtNHX1* introduced. L4 did not have *AtNHX2* introduced; L4 was the control. **F**, **G**, and **H** are incorrect; L1, L2, and L3 all contained different genotypes for *AtNHX1*. **J** is correct; L4 was not altered.

Passage VII

41. **The best answer is B.** Figure 1 shows a model describing the relative proportions of a plume. In Figure 1, the head of the plume has a diameter of approximately 500 km, and the tail of the plume has a diameter of approximately 250 km. If the model is typical of all mantle plumes, then the heads of plumes are approximately twice the diameter of the tails.

    The best answer is NOT:

    A, **C**, or **D** because in Study 1, the head of the plume was approximately twice the diameter of the tail of the plume.

42. **The best answer is J.** The scientists hypothesized that the larger the volume of lava produced, the larger the number of marine organisms that would become extinct. If larger lava volumes resulted in a larger number of marine organisms becoming extinct, then the plateau with the largest lava volume would result in the largest number of marine organisms becoming extinct. According to Table 1, Plateau D has the largest lava volume. So, based on the scientists' hypothesis, the formation of Plateau D caused the largest number of marine organisms to become extinct.

    The best answer is NOT:

    F, G, or **H** because Plateau D has the largest lava volume, so the formation of Plateau D most likely caused the largest number of marine organisms to become extinct.

43. **The best answer is D.** Table 1 shows that as the length of time that lava was produced increased, lava volume increased. According to Table 1, Plateau D produced lava for 1.7 Myr and had a lava volume of 2,125,000 km^3. Based on these results, if a flood basalt plateau produced lava for 1.8 Myr, then the lava volume associated with this plateau would likely exceed 2,125,000 km^3.

    The best answer is NOT:

    A, B, or **C** because the lava volume would exceed 2,125,000 km^3.

44. **The best answer is J.** According to Table 1, the age of Plateau A is 60 Myr; of Plateau B, 67 Myr; of Plateau C, 135 Myr; and of Plateau D, 192 Myr. The length of time lava was produced at Plateau A is 1.6 Myr; at Plateau B, 1.3 Myr; at Plateau C, 1.2 Myr; and at Plateau D, 1.7 Myr. For these data, there is no apparent relationship between the age of a plateau and the length of time lava was produced.

    The best answer is NOT:

    F because as the age of a plateau increases, the length of time lava was produced does not increase only. Initially it decreases.

    G because as the age of a plateau increases, the length of time lava was produced does not decrease only. It increases after it decreases.

    H because as the age of a plateau increases, the length of time lava was produced does not increase and then decrease. It decreases, and then increases.

45. **The best answer is B.** For each of the four plateaus, an ordered pair can be determined using Table 1, which relates the age of the plateau and the rate of lava production. If the x-value corresponds to the age of a plateau in Myr and the y-value corresponds to the rate of lava production in km^3/yr, then the ordered pair for Plateau A is (60,1.25); for Plateau B, (67,1.2); for Plateau C, (135,1.2); and for Plateau D, (192,1.25). The graph in B best represents these four ordered pairs.

The best answer is NOT:

A because the y-value should decrease between 60 Myr and 67 Myr, remain constant between 67 Myr and 135 Myr, and then increase between 135 Myr and 192 Myr. In **A**, the y-value remains constant between 67 Myr and 192 Myr.

C because the y-value should exceed 1.0 km^3/yr. However, in **C** the y-value is less than 1.0 km^3/yr.

D because the y-value should decrease between 60 Myr and 67 Myr, remain constant between 67 Myr and 135 Myr, and then increase between 135 Myr and 192 Myr. In **D**, the y-value increases between 60 Myr and 67 Myr, remains constant between 67 Myr and 135 Myr, and then decreases between 135 Myr and 192 Myr.

46. **The best answer is G.** The scientists in Study 3 hypothesized that the production of large amounts of lava and gases in the formation of plateaus may have contributed to large extinctions of marine organisms. They cite large extinctions associated with the formation of Plateaus A, B, and C. Based on their hypothesis, a large extinction of marine organisms also occurred when Plateau D was formed, about 192 Myr ago.

The best answer is NOT:

F, H, or **J** because there is no evidence of the production of large amounts of lava and gases at 77 Myr ago, 250 Myr ago, and 314 Myr ago, respectively.

Passage VIII

47. **The best answer is D.** Figure 1 shows the net productivity of plants on abandoned farmland along the vertical axis and successional time along the horizontal axis. At Year 50, net productivity was between 1,000 $g/m^2/yr$ and 1,200 $g/m^2/yr$.

The best answer is NOT:

A, B, or **C** because 1,125 $g/m^2/yr$ is closer to the value at Year 50 than are 15 $g/m^2/yr$, 50 $g/m^2/yr$, and 425 $g/m^2/yr$, respectively.

48.   **The best answer is F.** Figure 1 shows how net productivity changed over the 200 years studied. During this time, net productivity increased from 0 g/m^2/yr to about 1,200 g/m^2/yr. Figure 2 shows how biomass changed over the 200 years studied. During this time, biomass increased from 0 kg/m^2 to about 35 kg/m^2. These data show that both net productivity and biomass increased over the 200 years studied.

The best answer is NOT:

G or **H** because biomass did not decrease.

J because net productivity did not decrease.

49.   **The best answer is C.** According to Figure 1, net productivity increased by less than 100 g/m^2/yr from the end of Year 2 to the end of Year 4, from the end of Year 4 to the end of Year 14, and from the end of Year 50 to the end of Year 200. In contrast, from the end of Year 14 to the end of Year 50, net productivity increased by about 700 g/m^2/yr.

The best answer is NOT:

A because net productivity increased more from the end of Year 14 to the end of Year 50 than it did from the end of Year 2 to the end of Year 4.

B because net productivity increased more from the end of Year 14 to the end of Year 50 than it did from the end of Year 4 to the end of Year 14.

D because net productivity increased more from the end of Year 14 to the end of Year 50 than it did from the end of Year 50 to the end of Year 200.

50.   **The best answer is J.** Figure 1 shows the net productivity of plants on abandoned farmland along the vertical axis and successional time along the horizontal axis. Successional time is subdivided into three stages—herb, shrub, and tree-based on the types of plants that were dominant at different times. According to Figure 1, net productivity was lowest when herbs were the dominant plants and highest when trees were the dominant plants.

The best answer is NOT:

F because net productivity was not lowest when shrubs were the dominant plants. Net productivity was lowest when herbs were the dominant plants.

G because net productivity was not lowest when trees were the dominant plants. Net productivity was lowest when herbs were the dominant plants.

H because net productivity was not highest when herbs were the dominant plants. Net productivity was highest when trees were the dominant plants.

51. **The best answer is C.** Table 1 shows the bird species on plots of abandoned farmland in Georgia. Based on Table 1, if a plot of abandoned farmland in Georgia supported eastern meadowlarks, yellowthroats, and field sparrows at a density of at least one pair per 10 acres, then the successional time for that farmland would most likely be approximately 15 years. At a successional time of 15 years, shrubs were the dominant plants.

The best answer is NOT:

A, B, or **D** because the presence of eastern meadowlarks, yellowthroats, and field sparrows at a density of at least one pair per 10 acres indicates that successional time was approximately 15 years. At a successional time of 15 years, shrubs were the dominant plants. Thus, weeds, grasses, and pines, respectively, were not the dominant plants.

Passage IX

52. **The best answer is F.** Figure 2 shows the rise of liquid in the capillary tube. As the level of liquid in the capillary tube increased, the volume of liquid increased. All the liquids had the same volume when the level of each liquid was the same. This occurred when the temperature of the water bath was 20°C.

The best answer is NOT:

G, H, or **J** because the height of ethanol in the capillary tube was greater than the height of glycerine and of water in the capillary tube at 30°C, 40°C, and 50°C, respectively.

53. **The best answer is A.** Figure 3 shows how the volume of the three gases varied with temperature. For each of the three gases, as temperature increased from 20°C to 100°C, the volume of each gas increased from about 20 mL to about 25 mL. The constant slope over this temperature interval indicates that the increase in volume was linear. These results support the hypothesis that as the temperature of a gas is increased at a constant pressure, the volume of the gas will also increase.

The best answer is NOT:

B because the volume of air increased as the temperature increased.

C because as the temperature increased from 20°C to 100°C, the volume of each gas increased from about 20 mL to about 25 mL.

D because the volumes of nitrogen and methane increased as the temperature increased.

54. **The best answer is J.** Figure 1 shows the linear expansion of the four metals when the metals were stretched. At each of the four temperatures used in Experiment 1, aluminum had the greatest linear expansion and nickel had the smallest linear expansion. Because the engineer needs a wire that is resistant to stretching, the engineer should use the metal with the smallest linear expansion.

    The best answer is NOT:

    F, G, or **H** because the linear expansions of aluminum, brass, and iron, respectively, were greater than that of nickel.

55. **The best answer is A.** If a balloon is placed on the surface of a heated water bath, the temperature of the gases within the balloon will increase. Figure 3 shows that the volume of air increases as the temperature of the air increases. Thus, the volume of the balloon would increase.

    The best answer is NOT:

    B or **C** because the volume of the balloon would increase only; it would not decrease.

    D because the volume of the balloon would increase only; it would not remain the same.

56. **The best answer is H.** In Experiment 1, each of the wires had the same initial length. After the wires were stretched in the apparatus, the final length of each wire was directly proportional to its linear expansion. According to Figure 1, at 80°C, the linear expansion of aluminum was 0.20 mm; of brass, 0.14 mm; of iron, 0.08 mm; and of nickel, 0.04 mm.

    Because the linear expansion of the copper wire at 80°C was 0.12 mm, the copper wire would be shorter than the brass wire and longer than the iron wire. Thus, the order of the wires from the longest wire to the shortest wire would be as follows: nickel, iron, copper, brass, and aluminum.

    The best answer is NOT:

    F or **G** because the nickel wire would be the shortest wire, not the longest wire.

    J because the copper wire would be shorter than the brass wire.

57. **The best answer is D.** If a heavier weight were used, the linear expansion would be greater, because the force exerted by the weight on the wire would be greater. Figure 1 shows that linear expansion increases as temperature increases. The correct figure should show linear expansion increasing with temperature and a greater linear expansion when the heavier weight was used.

    The best answer is NOT:

    A because in this figure, linear expansion decreases as temperature increases with the original weight. Linear expansion should increase as temperature increases.

    B because in this figure, linear expansion decreases as temperature increases with the heavier weight. Linear expansion should increase as temperature increases.

    C because in this figure, linear expansion is greater with the original weight than with the heavier weight. However, linear expansion should be greater with the heavier weight than with the original weight.

Passage X

58. **The best answer is J.** The figure shows the upper boundary of the troposphere, stratosphere, and mesosphere. It does not, however, show the upper boundary of the thermosphere.

    The best answer is NOT:

    F, G, or **H** because the figure does not indicate that the upper boundary of the thermosphere is located at 150 km, 200 km, and 250 km, respectively. Thus, one cannot conclude that the upper boundary of the thermosphere is located at any of these altitudes.

59. **The best answer is B.** According to the figure, radiation with wavelengths between 2,000 Å and 3,000 Å is absorbed at an altitude of about 35 km. This absorption occurs within the stratosphere. If the ozone layer absorbs radiation with wavelengths between 2,000 Å and 3,000 Å, then the ozone layer must be located within the stratosphere.

    The best answer is NOT:

    A because the figure does not indicate that radiation with wavelengths between 2,000 Å and 3,000 Å is absorbed at altitudes between 0 km and 17 km (troposphere).

    C because the figure does not indicate that radiation with wavelengths between 2,000 Å and 3,000 Å is absorbed at altitudes between 52 km and 82 km (mesosphere).

    D because the figure does not indicate that radiation with wavelengths between 2,000 Å and 3,000 Å is absorbed at altitudes greater than 82 km (thermosphere).

60. **The best answer is F.** Absorption of radiation within an atmospheric layer affects the air temperature of that layer. The troposphere absorbs radiation with wavelengths between 3,000 Å and 1,000,000 Å. Radiation with wavelengths outside this range will be less likely to affect the air temperature of the troposphere than will radiation with wavelengths within this range.

The best answer is NOT:

G because the troposphere absorbs radiation with wavelengths between 3,000 Å and 1,000,000 Å, including radiation with a wavelength of 4,500 Å. Because the troposphere absorbs radiation with a wavelength of 4,500 Å but does not absorb radiation with a wavelength of 1,500 Å, air temperature in the troposphere is less likely to be influenced by radiation with a wavelength of 1,500 Å than by radiation with a wavelength of 4,500 Å.

H because the troposphere absorbs radiation with wavelengths between 3,000 Å and 1,000,000 Å, including radiation with a wavelength of 6,000 Å. Because the troposphere absorbs radiation with a wavelength of 6,000 Å but does not absorb radiation with a wavelength of 1,500 Å, air temperature in the troposphere is less likely to be influenced by radiation with a wavelength of 1,500 Å than by radiation with a wavelength of 6,000 Å.

J because the troposphere absorbs radiation with wavelengths between 3,000 Å and 1,000,000 Å, including radiation with a wavelength of 7,000 Å. Because the troposphere absorbs radiation with a wavelength of 7,000 Å but does not absorb radiation with a wavelength of 1,500 Å, air temperature in the troposphere is less likely to be influenced by radiation with a wavelength of 1,500 Å than by radiation with a wavelength of 7,000 Å.

61. **The best answer is C.** The figure shows that atmospheric pressure increases as altitude decreases. For example, at an altitude of 100 km, atmospheric pressure is less than 0.001 millibar. At an altitude of 50 km, atmospheric pressure is between 0.1 millibar and 1 millibar. At an altitude of 0 km, atmospheric pressure equals 1,000 millibars. In general, atmospheric pressure increases with decreasing altitude. This trend occurs within each atmospheric layer as well as between atmospheric layers. The figure also shows that the average atmospheric temperature varies with atmospheric pressure. As atmospheric pressure increases within the troposphere, average atmospheric temperature increases. However, as atmospheric pressure increases within the stratosphere, average atmospheric temperature decreases.

    The best answer is NOT:

    A or **B** because there is no simple relationship between atmospheric pressure in each atmospheric layer and average atmospheric temperature. In the troposphere, as atmospheric pressure increases, average atmospheric temperature increases. However, in the stratosphere, as atmospheric pressure increases, average atmospheric temperature decreases.

    D because the atmospheric pressure in each atmospheric layer increases with decreasing altitude, not with increasing altitude.

62. **The best answer is G.** If atmospheric boundaries are a higher than usual altitude above areas that get more direct solar radiation, then atmospheric boundaries are at a lower-than-usual altitude above areas that get less direct solar radiation. Thus, if Earth received less solar radiation, the tropopause, stratopause, and mesopause would decrease in altitude.

    The best answer is NOT:

    F because the tropopause, stratopause, and mesopause would decrease in altitude; they would not increase in altitude.

    H because the tropopause and stratopause would decrease in altitude; they would not increase in altitude.

    J because the stratopause and mesopause would decrease in altitude; they would not increase in altitude.

SCIENCE • EXPLANATORY ANSWERS

Passage XI

63. **The best answer is A.** According to Table 1, for vertically migrating shrimp species, the percent dry weight composed of protein exceeds 50% for each of the three species. The percent dry weight composed of lipid ranges from 14.7% to 23.8% for each of the three species. The percent dry weight composed of carbohydrate is less than 1% for each of the three species. Based on these data, vertically migrating shrimp have a higher percent content of protein than lipid.

    The best answer is NOT:

    B because vertically migrating shrimp have a higher percent content of protein than lipid.

    C because vertically migrating shrimp have a higher percent content of lipid than carbohydrate.

    D because vertically migrating shrimp have a higher percent content of protein than carbohydrate.

64. **The best answer is J.** According to Table 1, nonmigrating shrimp species are generally found at greater ocean depths than are vertically migrating shrimp species. According to Figure 1, at greater ocean depths, the water has a lower temperature and a lower oxygen partial pressure. Thus, Table 1 and Figure 1 support the conclusion that compared to vertically migrating shrimp species, nonmigrating shrimp species can tolerate lower oxygen partial pressures.

    The best answer is NOT:

    F because, according to Table 1, nonmigrating shrimp species tend to have slightly less water content than do vertically migrating shrimp species.

    G because, according to Table 1, nonmigrating shrimp species have a higher lipid content than do vertically migrating shrimp species.

    H because nonmigrating shrimp species are generally found at greater depths than are vertically migrating shrimp species. Because temperature decreases as depth increases, nonmigrating shrimp species are found at depths that have lower water temperatures than are vertically migrating shrimp species. Thus, it is likely that nonmigrating shrimp species cannot tolerate higher water temperatures than can vertically migrating shrimp species.

65.   **The best answer is B.** The passage notes that for vertically migrating shrimp species, most of the population are found at the top of their depth range at night. If the newly discovered species were captured at night at a depth of 200 m or lower, then the top of the species' range would most likely be at a depth of 200 m. According to Figure 1, the water temperature at this depth is about 7.5°C. Below 200 m, temperature decreases. Thus, if temperature limits the range of the species, then the maximum water temperature at which these shrimp could survive is most likely 7.5°C.

The best answer is NOT:

A because the discovery of the shrimp species at a depth of 200 m indicates that the species can tolerate temperatures as high as 7.5°C. If they could not tolerate temperatures as high as 7.5°C, then they would be found at lower depths, where temperatures are lower.

C or D because the passage indicates that for vertically migrating shrimp species, most of the population are found at the top of their depth range at night. If temperature limits the range of the species, then the species cannot tolerate temperatures found at depths of less than 200 m. The temperature at 200 m is about 7.5°C. Therefore, 7.5°C is most likely the maximum water temperature at which these shrimp can survive.

66.   **The best answer is G.** According to Table 1, the protein:lipid ratios for the four species listed in the four options are: 53.4:16.4 for vm 2, 60.5:14.7 for vm 3, 36.9:36.1 for nm 1, and 35.8:49.0 for nm 3. The question indicates that shrimp that are stronger swimmers tend to have a higher protein:lipid ratio than do shrimp that are weaker swimmers. Based on this information, the shrimp with the highest protein:lipid ratio are most likely the strongest swimmers.

The best answer is NOT:

F because vm 3 has a higher protein:lipid ratio (60.5:14.7) than does vm 2 (53.4:16.4).

H because vm 3 has a higher protein:lipid ratio (60.5:14.7) than does nm 1 (36.9:36.1).

J because vm 3 has a higher protein:lipid ratio (60.5:14.7) than does nm 3 (35.8:49.0).

67. **The best answer is C.** According to Figure 1, oxygen partial pressure is greater than or equal to 25 mm Hg at depths of approximately 400 m or less. At depths greater than 400 m, oxygen partial pressure is less than 25 mm Hg. If only oxygen partial pressure limits the range of a species, then failure to observe a species at depths greater than 400 m would support the hypothesis that the species is unable to tolerate oxygen partial pressures below 25 mm Hg. According to Table 1, the depth range of vm 2 is 10–400 m and the depth range of vm 3 is 75–400 m. Thus, vm 2 and vm 3 are not observed at depths greater than 400 m.

The best answer is NOT:

A because temperatures above 10°C occur at depths of less than approximately 100 m. At these depths, oxygen partial pressures are above 80 mm Hg. Therefore, the inability of a species to tolerate temperatures above 10°C does not suggest that the species is unable to tolerate oxygen partial pressures below 25 mm Hg.

B because no evidence is provided that relates water content and the ability to tolerate specific oxygen partial pressures.

D because depths above 100 m have oxygen partial pressures that are above 80 mm Hg. An inability to survive in depths above 100 m would suggest that these species are unable to survive in oxygen partial pressures that are above 80 mm Hg. However, it would not indicate that these species are unable to survive in oxygen partial pressures that are below 25 mm Hg.

Passage XII

68. **The best answer is H.** According to Student 1, gases from burning wood are less dense than the air that surrounds the fireplace.

The best answer is NOT:

F because, according to Student 1, gases from burning wood are hotter than the surrounding air and the molecules of hotter gases have a higher average speed than do the molecules of cooler gases.

G because, according to Student 1, gases from burning wood are hotter than the surrounding air and the average distance between molecules is greater for hotter gases than for cooler gases.

J because, according to Student 1, gases from burning wood are hotter than the surrounding air. Thus, they have a higher temperature.

69. **The best answer is B.** Both Students 1 and 2 assert that as chimney height increases, efficiency increases. Therefore, according to both students, if Chimneys X and Y have the same temperature difference between the inside and the outside and Chimney Y is more efficient than Chimney X, then Chimney Y must be taller.

    The best answer is NOT:

    A because both students would conclude that Chimney Y is taller.

    C because Student 1 would conclude that Chimney Y is taller.

    D because Student 2 would conclude that Chimney Y is taller.

70. **The best answer is F.** According to Student 2, smoke rises because wind blows across the top of the chimney. If the air at the top of the chimney is not moving, then the smoke from burning wood will not rise up the chimney. In contrast, Student 1 does not suggest that air movement above a chimney affects the rising of smoke. Student 1 asserts that smoke rises because of the buoyant force on hot gases inside the chimney. The buoyant force will be present whether or not wind blows across the chimney.

    The best answer is NOT:

    G or **H** because Student 2 would not predict that smoke from burning wood will rise up the chimney from a fireplace on a day when the air at the top of the chimney is not moving.

    J because Student 1 would predict that smoke from burning wood will rise up the chimney from a fireplace on a day when the air at the top of the chimney is not moving.

71. **The best answer is C.** According to Student 1, gases from burning wood rise because they are less dense than the air that surrounds the fireplace. Student 1 also asserts that the gases from burning wood are less dense than the air that surrounds the fireplace because the gases from the burning wood are hotter than the air that surrounds the fireplace. Thus, Student 1 would likely predict that if the air in the fireplace rises, then this air is less dense than the air that surrounds the fireplace. Student 1 would also conclude that the air in the fireplace is less dense than the air that surrounds the fireplace because the air in the fireplace is hotter than the air that surrounds the fireplace.

The best answer is NOT:

A because although Student 1 argues that the gases from the burning wood are hotter than the air that surrounds the fireplace, Student 1 does not suggest that other gases (air) in the fireplace must be hotter than the gases from the burning wood.

B or D because Student 1 argues that hotter gases rise. Thus, cooler gases do not rise.

72. **The best answer is H.** Student 1 argues that heating a parcel of air makes it less dense. As the density of the parcel decreases, the buoyant force on the parcel increases. If the upward buoyant force exceeds the downward gravitational force, the parcel rises. Based on this line of reasoning, if the air inside a hot-air balloon cooled, then the density of the air would increase. As a result, the upward buoyant force on the balloon and its inside air would decrease.

If the downward gravitational force exceeded the upward buoyant force, the balloon and its inside air would descend.

The best answer is NOT:

F or J because the buoyant force is upward and the force of gravity is downward.

G because for the balloon to descend, the downward force of gravity acting on the balloon and its inside air must be greater than the upward buoyant force on the balloon and its inside air.

73. **The best answer is A.** According to Student 1, the average speed of the molecules that make up a gas increases as the average temperature of the gas increases. In addition, as the average speed of gas molecules increases, the average distance between adjacent gas molecules increases. As a result, the density of the gas decreases. Thus, if the temperature of a gas decreases, then the density of the gas increases, the average speed of the gas molecules decreases, and the average distance between adjacent gas molecules decreases.

The best answer is NOT:

B because the temperature of the gases decreases as the gases lose heat.

C because the average speed of the gas molecules decreases as the gases lose heat.

D because the average distance between adjacent gas molecules decreases as the gases lose heat.

74. **The best answer is F.** According to Student 2, the gases inside a chimney rise because air blowing over the top of the chimney results in a lower pressure at the top of the chimney than at the bottom of the chimney. Likewise, if the air on top of a wing moves faster than the air below the wing, the pressure above the wings is less than the pressure below the wings. As a result, there is an upward force on the wings, keeping the airplane up in the air.

The best answer is NOT:

G because if the air moves at a higher speed below the wings than above the wings, then the pressure above the wings will be greater than the pressure below the wings. As a result, there will be a downward force on the wings, forcing the airplane down.

H or J because Student 2's explanation does not provide a means for evaluating the relative impact of the speed of the air in front of the wings and the speed of the air behind the wings.

Passage XIII

75. **The best answer is C.** Figure 1 shows that the corrected absorbance was directly proportional to the concentration of NO_2^-. Thus, if the concentration of NO_2^- doubled, the corrected absorbance doubled. For example, as the concentration of NO_2^- increased from 4.0 ppm to 8.0 ppm, the corrected absorbance increased from 0.6 to 1.2.

The best answer is NOT:

A, B, or D because the corrected absorbance was directly proportional to the concentration of NO_2^-. Thus, a doubling of the NO_2^- concentration will result in a doubling of the corrected absorbance.

76. **The best answer is J.** In Experiment 1, the corrected absorbance was directly proportional to the concentration of NO_2^-. Therefore, the meat with the highest corrected absorbance had the highest concentration of NO_2^- and the meat with the lowest corrected absorbance had the lowest concentration of NO_2^-. According to the information provided, the corrected absorbance of bacon was 0.773; of pastrami, 0.603; and of bologna, 0.561.

The best answer is NOT:

F, G, or H because bacon had the highest corrected absorbance, so bacon has the highest concentration of NO_2^-. Therefore, bacon should be listed before pastrami and bologna.

77. **The best answer is B.** According to Table 1, an NO_2^- concentration of 1.0 ppm resulted in a corrected absorbance of 0.153 and an NO_2^- concentration of 2.0 ppm resulted in a corrected absorbance of 0.302. Thus, an NO_2^- concentration of 1.5 ppm should result in a corrected absorbance greater than 0.153 and less than 0.302. In addition, Table 1 shows that the corrected absorbance was directly proportional to the concentration of NO_2^-. Based on this trend, the corrected absorbance for an NO_2^- concentration of 1.5 ppm should be about halfway between 0.153 and 0.302, or approximately 0.228.

The best answer is NOT:

A because 0.23 is closer to 0.228 than is 0.15.

C because 0.23 is closer to 0.228 than is 0.30.

D because 0.23 is closer to 0.228 than is 0.36.

78. **The best answer is J.** According to the passage, a colorimeter is a device that measures how much light of a selected wavelength is absorbed by a sample. The colorimeter is typically set so that the wavelength measured corresponds to the wavelength associated with the color of the solution. If the color of the solution differed, then the wavelength measured would have to be changed. Apart from changing the wavelength measured, all other experimental procedures would be held constant.

The best answer is NOT:

F because the coloring agent must be added to the sample solutions before the absorbance of each solution can be determined. If the coloring agent is not added to the sample solutions, then all of the sample solutions would have the same absorbance and the NO_2^- concentration could not be determined.

G because the question supposes that Experiments 1 and 2 were repeated using a different coloring agent. Thus, the original coloring agent would not be added to the blank solution or to the samples.

H because the absorbances were corrected by subtracting the absorbance of the blank solution from each measured absorbance. This ensures that the corrected absorbance only reflects the concentration of the colored compound that is formed between the NO_2^- and the coloring agent.

79. **The best answer is A.** Table 1 indicates that the measured absorbances of the NO_2^- solutions were higher than the corrected absorbances. To get the corrected absorbance, the absorbance of the blank was subtracted from each measured absorbance. Similarly, the absorbance for the blank is subtracted from each of the measured absorbances for the meats. So the measured absorbance is always higher than the corrected absorbance.

The best answer is NOT:

B, C, or D because for each of the meats, to get the corrected absorbance, the absorbance of the blank was subtracted from the measured absorbance. Because the absorbance of the blank was greater than zero, the measured absorbance was higher than the corrected absorbance. Thus, the measured absorbance would not be lower than or the same as the corrected absorbance for any of the meats.

80. **The best answer is F.** If the water-soluble substances absorbed light at the wavelength being measured, then the measured absorbance would be higher. This would occur because the water-soluble substances would absorb light. As a result, the solution would appear to contain more NO_2^- than had actually been present in the solution. Therefore, the measured NO_2^- concentration would be higher than if the solution did not contain the water-soluble substances.

The best answer is NOT:

G or **J** because the water-soluble substances would increase the absorbance. Therefore, the measured NO_2^- concentration would be higher than the actual NO_2^- concentration for each of the meats. The measured NO_2^- concentration would not be lower than the actual NO_2^- concentration for any of the meats.

H because the water-soluble substance would increase the absorbance. Therefore, the measured NO_2^- concentration would be higher than the actual NO_2^- concentration for each of the meats. The measured NO_2^- concentration would not be the same as the actual NO_2^- concentration for any of the meats.

Passage XIV

81. **The best answer is B.** Table 2 lists the weekly average air temperatures in each of the three greenhouse sections. According to Table 2, the highest weekly average air temperature recorded was 21.13°C. This weekly average air temperature occurred in Section 1 during Week 6.

The best answer is NOT:

A because 18.47°C is lower than 21.13°C.

C or **D** because 120.7°C and 314.9°C, respectively, do not correspond to any of the weekly average air temperatures in Table 2.

82. **The best answer is F.** Table 2 lists the weekly average air temperatures. The values were recorded to the second decimal place. For example, in Section 1 during Week 1 the weekly average air temperature was 19.68°C. Therefore, weekly average air temperatures were recorded to the nearest 0.01°C.

The best answer is NOT:

G, H, or **J** because the weekly average air temperatures were recorded with greater precision than 0.1°C, 1.0°C, and 10°C, respectively.

83. **The best answer is A.** According to Table 1, in Section 1, the weekly average light intensity for Week 1 was 289.3; for Week 2, 305.5; for Week 3, 313.4; for Week 4, 314.9; for Week 5, 304.5; and for Week 6, 311.1. According to Table 2, in Section 1, the weekly average air temperature, in °C, for Week 1 was 19.68; for Week 2, 20.12; for Week 3, 20.79; for Week 4, 20.98; for Week 5, 21.04; and for Week 6, 21.13. The weekly average light intensity and the weekly average air temperature for each of the six weeks correspond to the six ordered pairs that must be plotted. For example, during Week 1, the weekly average light intensity was 289.3 and the weekly average air temperature was 19 .68°C. Thus, a plot of the data must include a point at 289.3 on the horizontal axis and 19.68 on the vertical axis. Likewise, during Week 2, the weekly average light intensity was 305.5 and the weekly average air temperature was 20.12°C. Thus, a plot of the data must include a point at 305.5 on the horizontal axis and 20.12 on the vertical axis. A is the only graph that has each of the six ordered pairs plotted correctly.

    The best answer is NOT:

    B, C, or **D** because the figures in these options do not contain the six ordered pairs. For example, none of the figures in **B**, **C**, and **D** has a point for the ordered pair that corresponds to a weekly average light intensity of 289.3 and a weekly average air temperature of 19.68°C.

84. **The best answer is H.** According to Table 2, in Section 1, the weekly average air temperature, in °C, for Week 1 was 19.68; for Week 2, 20.12; for Week 3, 20.79; for Week 4, 20.98; for Week 5, 21.04; and for Week 6, 21.13. Thus, from week to week, the weekly average air temperature always increased.

    The best answer is NOT:

    F because the weekly average air temperature did not decrease between Weeks 4 and 6.

    G because the weekly average air temperature did not decrease between Weeks 1 and 3.

    J because the weekly average air temperature did not always decrease.

85. **The best answer is D.** Efficiency of illumination is defined as the intensity of light absorbed by the plants divided by the intensity of light provided to the plants. Weekly average light intensities are listed in Table 1. However, the passage provides no information about the intensity of light absorbed by the plants. Without this information, the efficiency of illumination cannot be determined.

The best answer is NOT:

A because it is not possible to determine the efficiency of illumination based solely on the level of illumination. To determine the efficiency of illumination, the intensity of light absorbed must also be determined.

B because the amount of light not absorbed by the plants in Section 1 was not determined.

C because the amount of light absorbed by the plants in Section 1 was not determined.

Passage XV

86. **The best answer is G.** Table 1 lists the results from Experiment 1. According to Table 1, at -9°C (the only temperature measured) and at a given time after starting, the percent of CO in the exhaust was greater for the 1978 cars than for the 1996 cars. For example, one minute after starting, the percent of CO in the exhaust of the 1978 Model X car was 3.5% and the percent of CO in the exhaust of the 1978 Model Y car was 3.2%. In contrast, the percent of CO in the exhaust of the 1996 Model X car was 1.2% and the percent of CO in the exhaust of the 1996 Model Y car was 0.3%. Similar comparisons for each of the other seven times after starting indicate that both of the 1996 cars had a lower CO percent than did either of the 1978 cars. The results support the hypothesis that the exhaust of newer cars contains lower percents of CO than does the exhaust of older cars.

The best answer is NOT:

F because the 1996 Model Y car did not have the highest percent of CO.

H or J because the results of Experiment 1 support the hypothesis.

87. **The best answer is D.** The student was concerned that the presence of CO_2 in the exhaust may have affected the measurement of CO in the exhaust. To explore this issue, one could test the gas chromatograph with samples containing known amounts of CO_2 and CO. This would provide a means of determining whether the chromatograph is accurately reporting the amount of CO in a sample, even as the amount of CO_2 in the sample varies.

    The best answer is NOT:

    A because filling the bag with CO_2 before making measurements would not provide a means of determining whether the chromatograph was correctly reporting the CO in the sample, unless the percent of CO in the sample was already known.

    B because collecting the exhaust from additional cars would merely provide more data like that in Tables 1 and 2 and would not address the relationship between the presence of CO_2 in a sample and the measurement of CO in the sample.

    C because injecting air into the gas chromatograph would not help one determine whether the presence of CO_2 affects the measurement of CO by the gas chromatograph.

88. **The best answer is F.** The results of Experiments 1 and 2 show that for each of the four cars, at any given time after starting, the percent of CO in the exhaust was greater at -9°C than at 20°C. These results are consistent with the hypothesis that the percent of CO in the exhaust of a car increases as temperature decreases. The question indicates that Minneapolis has a lower average temperature during January than do Pittsburgh, Seattle, and San Diego. Together, this information supports the conclusion that cars in Minneapolis would most likely contribute a greater amount of CO to the atmosphere in January than would cars in any of the other cities listed (Pittsburgh, Seattle, and San Diego).

    The best answer is NOT:

    G because the average temperature for Pittsburgh is greater than the average temperature for Minneapolis.

    H because the average temperature for Seattle is greater than the average temperature for Minneapolis.

    J because the average temperature for San Diego is greater than the average temperature for Minneapolis.

89. **The best answer is C.** Some of the cars used in Experiment 1 were made in 1978 and some were made in 1996. That is, the year in which the cars were made varied.

    The best answer is NOT:

    A because the method of sample collection did not vary across the different trials and samples in Experiment 1.

    B because the volume of exhaust that was tested was always 1 mL in Experiment 1.

    D because the temperature at which the engine was started was always -9°C.

90. **The best answer is G.** For the four cars used in Experiment 1, the maximum values for percent of CO in the exhaust were obtained at either 5 min or 7 min after starting. For the four cars used in Experiment 2, the maximum values for percent of CO in the exhaust were obtained at 5 min, 7 min, and 9 min after starting. In Experiment 2, the maximum occurred at 9 min only once (1978 Model Y); however, for this car, the same maximum value was found at 7 min after starting. The data support the conclusion that the maximum value for percent of CO in the exhaust is typically reached between 5 min and 7 min after starting.

    The best answer is NOT:

    F because the percent of CO in the exhaust was greater between 5 min and 7 min than it was between 1 min and 3 min.

    H because the percent of CO in the exhaust was greater between 5 min and 7 min than it was between 9 min and 11 min.

    J because the percent of CO in the exhaust was greater between 5 min and 7 min than it was after 13 or more min.

91. **The best answer is C.** If the syringe contents were contaminated with air that did not contain CO, then the syringe would contain proportionately less CO than would a sample that had not been contaminated with CO-free air. This would occur because the amount of CO in the sample would remain constant, but the amounts of other gases in the sample would increase. As a result, the percent of CO would decrease. This effect would occur both at −9°C and at 20°C.

    The best answer is NOT:

    A or **B** because the measured percent of CO in the exhaust would be lower than the actual percents, rather than higher than the actual percents. This would be true for the measurements performed both at −9°C and at 20°C.

    D because the measured percent of CO in the exhaust would be lower than the actual percents, rather than the same as the actual percents. This would be true for the measurements performed both at −9°C and at 20°C.

Passage XVI

92. **The best answer is H.** The object viewed during Activity 2 had a length of 0.1 mm. The passage explains that magnification (M) can be calculated using the formula M = image size ÷ object size. If the image size was 30 mm, then M = 30 mm ÷ 0.1 mm = 300.

    The best answer is NOT:

    F, G, or **J** because, according to the formula provided, M = 300.

93. **The best answer is D.** According to the passage, magnification (M) equals image size divided by object size. Therefore, image size equals M times object size. Table 2 lists the magnification associated with each objective lens. These values can be used to calculate the image size of each of the lines described in the four options. The question asks for the line with the greatest image size. In D, image size = 400 × 0.4 = 160 mm, which is the greatest image size yielded by the answer choices.

    The best answer is NOT:

    A because image size = 40 × 0.7 mm = 28 mm, which is less than the value in D.

    B because image size = 100 × 0.6 mm = 60 mm, which is less than the value in D.

    C because image size = 200 × 0.5 mm = 100 mm, which is less than the value in D.

94. **The best answer is G.** Table 1 indicates whether the two lines appeared separate or whether the lines blurred together. For Slide C, the lines appeared separate with Objective Lenses 3 and 4. The lines appeared blurred with Objective Lenses 1 and 2. Based on Table 1, when viewing Slide C in Activity 1, the student was able to discern two distinct lines with two of the objective lenses.

    The best answer is NOT:

    F, H, or J because the student was able to discern two distinct lines with exactly two of the object lenses.

95. **The best answer is B.** According to the passage, R (in nm) can be calculated using the formula $R = \lambda \div 2(NA)$. According to Table 3, for Objective Lens 2, the NA (numerical aperture) equals 0.25. The question requires that R be calculated for light with a wavelength (λ) of 425 nm. The correct equation for determining R is $R = \lambda \div 2(NA) = 42.5 \div 2(0.25)$.

    The best answer is NOT:

    A because NA for Objective Lens 2 is 0.25, not 0.10.

    C or D because the equations used in these options do not correspond to the equation given in the passage. As noted above, $R = \lambda \div 2(NA)$. In C and D, an NA is being divided by two times the wavelength of the light (425 nm).

96. **The best answer is F.** The equation used to calculate resolution R indicates that R is directly proportional to wavelength and inversely proportional to NA. In Activity 3, calculations were based on a wavelength of 550 nm. Thus, variability in R reflected variability in NA. Specifically, as NA decreased, R increased. R for Objective Lenses 1 and 2 equaled 2,750 nm and 1,100 nm, respectively. For the fifth objective lens, R equaled 1,830 nm. Based on these results, the NA of the fifth lens was greater than the NA of Lens 1 (0.10) and less than the NA of Lens 2 (0.25).

    The best answer is NOT:

    G because 0.25 is the NA that resulted in an R = 1,100 nm.

    H or J because each of these values corresponds to an NA that would result in an R < 1,100 nm.

97. **The best answer is A.** In Activity 1, the student used four different slides (A, B, C, and D). In Activity 2, the student used a single prepared slide.

    The best answer is NOT:

    B because in both Activity 1 and Activity 2, four different objective lenses were used.

    C because the same light source was used in Activities 1 and 2.

    D because the microscope magnified each image, so image sizes were greater than object sizes in both Activity 1 and Activity 2.

Passage XVII

98. **The best answer is J.** The figure shows that as the blackbody temperature increases, the area under the blackbody curve increases. The question indicates that as the area under a blackbody curve increases, the rate at which energy is emitted also increases. This information supports the conclusion that 1 m^2 of the blackbody with the highest temperature emits the greatest amount of energy per second at the wavelengths shown. This information also supports the conclusion that 1 m^2 of the blackbody with the lowest temperature emits the least amount of energy per second at the wavelengths shown. The correct order is 500 K, 400 K, 300 K.

    The best answer is NOT:

    F or **G** because the blackbody with the lowest temperature emits the least amount of energy per second at the wavelengths shown, not the greatest amount of energy per second at the wavelengths shown.

    H because the blackbody with the highest temperature emits the greatest amount of energy per second at the wavelengths shown. Therefore, more energy will be emitted at 500 K than at 400 K.

99. **The best answer is A.** According to the figure, at a temperature of 300 K and a wavelength equal to or greater than 11×10^{-6} m, brightness decreases as wavelength increases. The maximum wavelength included in the figure is 25×10^{-6} m. At this wavelength, brightness is about 1×10^6 watts per m^3. Thus, for longer wavelengths, such as 30×10^{-6} m, brightness will be less than 1×10^6 watts per m^3.

    The best answer is NOT:

    B, C, or **D** because all of the values for brightness in each of the ranges listed are greater than 5×10^6 watts per m^3.

100. **The best answer is J.** The figure shows that the area under a blackbody curve increases as the temperature of the blackbody increases. The figure also shows that the wavelength with the maximum brightness for a blackbody increases as the temperature of the blackbody decreases. Of the four options, only **J** shows both of these characteristics.

   The best answer is NOT:

   F or **H** because in these options, the area under the blackbody curve decreases as the temperature of the blackbody increases.

   G because in this option, the wavelength with the maximum brightness for a blackbody decreases as the temperature of the blackbody decreases.

101. **The best answer is C.** In the figure, the maximum of the blackbody curve increases as the temperature of the blackbody increases. At 300 K, the blackbody had a maximum brightness of about 10×10^6 watts per m³ At 400 K, the blackbody had a maximum brightness of about 42×10^6 watts per m³. At 500 K, the blackbody had a maximum brightness of about 128×10^6 watts per m³. The temperature associated with a maximum brightness of 75×10^6 watts per m³ can be determined through interpolation. This temperature must fall between 400 K and 500 K.

   The best answer is NOT:

   A or **B** because at 400 K, the blackbody had a maximum brightness of about 42×10^6 watts per m³. Thus, if the blackbody has a maximum brightness of 75×10^6 watts per m³, it must have a temperature greater than 400 K.

   D because at 500 K, the blackbody had a maximum brightness of about 128×10^6 watts per m³. Thus, if the blackbody has a maximum brightness of 75×10^6 watts per m³ it must have a temperature less than 500 K.

102. **The best answer is H.** According to the question, the frequency of radiation increases as the wavelength of the radiation decreases. In the figure, for each of the three temperatures, as wavelength decreases, the brightness of the blackbody increases, then decreases. Because frequency is inversely proportional to wavelength, as the frequency of the radiation from a blackbody increases, the brightness increases, then decreases.

   The best answer is NOT:

   F because as the frequency of the radiation from a blackbody increases, the brightness does not increase only.

   G because as the frequency of the radiation from a blackbody increases, the brightness does not decrease only.

   J because as the frequency of the radiation from a blackbody increases, the brightness increases before it decreases, not the other way around.

Passage XVIII

103. **The best answer is C.** In Experiment 1, at 20°C, the vapor pressure of 2-butanone was 75 mm Hg; of ethyl acetate, 70 mm Hg; of hexane, 110 mm Hg; of methanol, 90 mm Hg; and of 2-propanol, 35 mm Hg. Only the figure in C shows relative bar heights for the liquids that correctly correspond to these values.

    The best answer is NOT:

    A or **D** because the vapor pressure of hexane should be greater than the vapor pressure of methanol.

    B because the vapor pressure of methanol should be greater than the vapor pressure of 2-butanone.

104. **The best answer is G.** Before the liquid was added, the forces exerted by the gases in the two sections of the tubing were equal. As a result, the heights of the Hg in the two sections of the tubing were the same. When the liquid was added to the flask, some of the liquid evaporated. This increased the vapor pressure of the gases in the section of the tubing that was connected to the flask (the left side of the tubing in the figures). As a result, the force exerted by these gases increased, pushing down the column of Hg in the left side of the tubing. The correct figure should show the levels of Hg within the two sections of the tubing at the same height before the liquid was added and the level of Hg within the left section of the tubing lower than the level of Hg within the right section of the tubing after the liquid was added.

    The best answer is NOT:

    F because the figure shows the level of Hg within the left section of the tubing as being higher than the level of Hg within the right section of the tubing after the liquid was added.

    H or **J** because the figures show the levels of Hg within the two sections of the tubing at different heights before the liquid was added.

105. **The best answer is D.** The liquids used in Experiment 2 can be ordered based on their boiling points at a given external pressure. For example, if the liquids are ordered from the liquid with the lowest boiling point to the liquid with the highest boiling point at 760 mm Hg, the correct sequence is as follows: methanol, hexane, ethyl acetate, 2-butanone, and 2-propanol. Similarly, if the liquids are ordered from the liquid with the lowest boiling point to the liquid with the highest boiling point at 400 mm Hg, the correct sequence is as follows: hexane, methanol, ethyl acetate, 2-butanone, and 2-propanol. At 100 mm Hg, the correct sequence is as follows: hexane, methanol, 2-butanone, ethyl acetate, and 2-propanol. If these same liquids are ordered from the liquid with the lowest molecular weight to the liquid with highest molecular weight, the correct sequence is as follows: methanol, 2-propanol, 2-butanone, hexane, and ethyl acetate. These orderings are inconsistent with the hypothesis that at a given external pressure, the higher a liquid's molecular weight, the higher the boiling point of the liquid. The results are consistent with the conclusion that there is no relationship in these data between boiling point and molecular weight.

The best answer is NOT:

A or **B** because the data do not support the hypothesis. For example, hexane has one of the highest molecular weights, but its boiling point is lower than the boiling points of most of the other liquids. Likewise, ethyl acetate has the highest molecular weight, but it has an intermediate boiling point compared with the other liquids.

C because liquids with higher molecular weights do not have lower boiling points. For example, ethyl acetate has the highest molecular weight, but its boiling point is higher than the boiling point of both hexane and methanol at each of the three external pressures.

106. **The best answer is G.** In Experiment 2, for each liquid, as the external pressure increased, the boiling point of the liquid increased. For example, at external pressures of 100 mm Hg, 400 mm Hg, and 760 mm Hg, the boiling points of 2-butanone were 25.0°c, 60.0°C, and 79.6°C, respectively. Likewise, at external pressures of 100 mm Hg, 400 mm Hg, and 760 mm Hg, the boiling points of ethyl acetate were 27.0°C, 59.3°C, and 77.1°C, respectively.

The best answer is NOT:

F, **H**, or **J** because as the external pressure increased, the boiling points never decreased. For each of the five liquids used in Experiment 2, the highest boiling point was obtained at a pressure 760 mm Hg and the lowest boiling point was obtained at a pressure of 100 mm Hg.

107. **The best answer is B.** For Experiment 2, the apparatus was described as a test tube containing a thermometer. This test tube was heated in an oil bath. Of the four figures, only the figure in **B** shows a thermometer inside a test tube, which sits in an oil bath.

The best answer is NOT:

A because the test tube does not contain a thermometer.

C because the apparatus does not have a thermometer.

D because the apparatus does not have a test tube.

108. **The best answer is J.** In Experiment 1, the procedure states that the manometer was connected five minutes after the flask was placed in an H_2O bath. This procedure indicates that the experimenter wanted the air in the flask to reach the temperature of the H_2O bath. The procedure is also consistent with the experimental design. For a gas, pressure varies with temperature. So the procedure helped to ensure that changes in pressure within the flask were due to the addition of the liquid added and not simply due to changes in air temperature.

The best answer is NOT:

F because at the temperatures that were used in the experiment, five minutes would not be enough time to remove all of the H_2O vapor from the flask.

G because the liquid was not added to the flask until after the manometer was connected to the flask.

H because at this point in the experiment, the manometer had not been connected to the flask.

Passage XIX

109. **The best answer is D.** According to the passage, all proteins have primary structures. In addition, proteins with lower-energy shapes are more stable than proteins with higher-energy shapes. Because of this, proteins with lower-energy shapes tend to maintain their shapes. In contrast, proteins with higher-energy shapes tend to denature. If a protein is almost completely denatured, it is a random coil and has a relatively high-energy shape.

The best answer is NOT:

A because random coils have relatively high-energy shapes.

B because all proteins have primary structures.

C because proteins with relatively low energy shapes tend to maintain their shapes. Therefore, they do not tend to become denatured.

110. **The best answer is F.** The passage explains that the primary structure of a protein is the sequence of amino acids in each polypeptide of that protein. Because a protein is composed of a sequence of amino acids, it must have a primary structure. Otherwise, the protein does not exist. Higher levels of structure—secondary, tertiary, and quaternary—are all associated with the spatial relationships between different parts of the amino acid sequence. When a protein becomes a random coil, these relationships are destroyed. Thus, when a protein denatures, it loses its original secondary, tertiary, and quaternary structure.

The best answer is NOT:

G, H, or **J** because a protein that is completely denatured lacks its original secondary structure, tertiary structure, and quaternary structure, respectively.

111. **The best answer is C.** Scientist 1 states that the active shape of a protein is always identical to the protein's lowest-energy shape. This shape is determined by the primary structure of the protein. Scientist 2 also states that the active shape of a protein is dependent upon the protein's primary structure. However, according to Scientist 2, a protein's active shape may also depend on its process of synthesis, the order (in time) in which the amino acids were bonded together as the protein was created. Both scientists believe that the active shape of a protein is dependent on the sequence of amino acids in the protein, but only Scientist 2 believes that the process of synthesis influences the active shape of the protein.

The best answer is NOT:

A because many proteins do not have quaternary structures. Only proteins with more than one polypeptide have quaternary structures.

B because both Scientists 1 and 2 believe that a protein's active shape is partially determined by its amino acid sequence.

D because Scientist 2 believes that a protein's active shape is determined by its primary structure and by its process of synthesis. Tertiary folding patterns are determined by these two factors.

112.   **The best answer is F.** The student selected 15 colored balls from a pool of 100 balls and aligned the 15 balls in a row. This is analogous to the primary structure of a protein, because the primary structure of a protein corresponds to the sequence of amino acids in the protein. Additional levels of structure reflect folding patterns between different parts of a polypeptide or between two or more polypeptides. These levels of structure do not correspond to the alignment of 15 balls into a row.

The best answer is NOT:

G because the secondary structure of a protein is the local folding patterns within short segments of each polypeptide. Because the balls lack a folding pattern, their arrangement does not correspond to the secondary structure of a protein.

H because the tertiary structure of a protein is the folding patterns that result from interactions between amino acid side chains. Because the balls lack a folding pattern, their arrangement does not correspond to the tertiary structure of a protein.

J because the quaternary structure of a protein is the result of the clustering between more than one folded polypeptide. The balls correspond to a single polypeptide, so their arrangement does not correspond to a structure that arises due to the clustering of more than one polypeptide.

113.   **The best answer is A.** Suppose a protein is almost completely denatured and then is allowed to renature so that the protein has its lowest-energy shape. According to Scientist 1, the protein will still be in its active shape, because the active shape is identical to the lowest-energy shape. Scientist 2 disagrees. According to Scientist 2, the active shape may be identical to the lowest-energy shape, but it also may not be identical to the lowest-energy shape. So if a protein is almost completely denatured and then is allowed to renature so that the protein is in its lowest-energy shape, the protein may, or may not, be in its active shape.

The best answer is NOT:

B because, according to Scientist 1, each protein will be in its active shape.

C because, according to Scientist 2, the active shape may be identical to the lowest-energy shape, but it also may not be identical to the lowest-energy shape. Thus, some of the proteins will not have their active shapes.

D because, according to Scientist 2, the active shape may be identical to the lowest-energy shape, but it also may not be identical to the lowest-energy shape. Thus, some of the proteins will have their active shapes.

114.   **The best answer is J.** According to the passage, the most stable shape of a protein corresponds to the protein's lowest-energy shape. The passage also explains that the randomly coiled shape is a high-energy shape. Therefore, in the correct figure, the randomly coiled shape should have a higher relative energy than does the most stable shape. In addition, Scientist 1 believes that the active shape is identical to the lowest-energy shape, while Scientist 2 believes the active shape of a protein may differ from the lowest-energy shape. Scientist 2's view is consistent with a higher relative energy for the active shape than for the most stable shape.

The best answer is NOT:

F or G because the randomly coiled shape should have a higher relative energy than do the active shape and the most stable shape.

H because it is consistent with Scientist 1's assertion that the active shape is identical with the lowest-energy shape and that this shape has a lower relative energy than the randomly coiled shape.

115.   **The best answer is B.** According to Scientist 2, the secondary structure of a protein can correspond to stable, local structures that are associated with a moderately high energy shape rather than the lowest-energy shape. If, as B suggests, energy barriers that maintain the stability of these local structures could be overcome, the secondary structure of the protein would change such that the protein would no longer be trapped in a moderately high-energy shape, but would instead exist in its lowest-energy shape.

The best answer is NOT:

A because it is consistent with Scientist 2's viewpoint that during protein synthesis, stable local structures can form that are associated with a moderately high-energy shape. These stable, local structures correspond to the protein's secondary structure, which is formed prior to the formation of the tertiary structure.

C because it is consistent with Scientist 2's viewpoint that the secondary structure of a protein begins to form as the protein is constructed. That is why the active shape of the protein is affected by the protein's process of synthesis. The tertiary structure, however, corresponds to folding patterns that generally occur across greater distances than those associated with the secondary structure. Therefore, these folding patterns lag the formation of the secondary structure. Thus, according to Scientist 2, the secondary structure is determined before the tertiary structure is formed.

D because proteins that lose their tertiary structures or quaternary structures are no longer in their active shapes. Thus, proteins that lose their tertiary structure or quaternary structure also lose their biological functions. This observation is not inconsistent with Scientist 2's viewpoint, so it could not be used to counter Scientist 2's argument.

Passage XX

116. **The best answer is J.** Figure 2 shows that at depths below 4.5 km the seafloor is typically covered with red clay sediment and at depths above 4.5 km the seafloor is typically covered with calcareous ooze. If the Arctic Ocean seafloor has an average depth of 4.9 km, it is likely that a majority of the seafloor will be at a depth of 4.5 km or greater. As a result, the Arctic Ocean seafloor will be covered with more red clay than calcareous ooze. Figure 3 is consistent with this view. As average depth increases, the relative proportion of the seafloor that is covered with red clay increases. In addition, in the Pacific Ocean, which has an average depth of 4.30 km, a greater proportion of the seafloor is covered with red clay than with calcareous ooze.

    The best answer is NOT:

    F, G, or **H** because a majority of the Arctic Ocean seafloor will be at a depth of more than 4.5. km. Thus, a greater proportion of the Arctic Ocean seafloor will be covered with red clay than with calcareous ooze.

117. **The best answer is B.** Figure 2 shows that calcareous oozes composed mainly of thin-shelled organisms cover areas of the seafloor having depths up to 1.8 km. Between a depth of 1.8 km and a depth of 4.5 km, the seafloor is covered with calcareous oozes composed mainly of thick-shelled organisms. Therefore, calcareous oozes composed mainly of thick-shelled organisms are found at greater depths than those composed mainly of thin-shelled organisms.

    The best answer is NOT:

    A or **C** because calcareous oozes composed mainly of thick-shelled organisms are found at greater depths than those composed mainly of thin-shelled organisms.

    D because calcareous oozes composed mainly of thick-shelled organisms are found at greater depths than those composed mainly of thin-shelled organisms. Thus, calcareous oozes composed mainly of thick-shelled organisms would occur in different locations than would calcareous oozes composed mainly of thin-shelled organisms.

118.   **The best answer is H.** Figure 1 shows that seawater in shallow areas (less than 1 km deep) is supersaturated with respect to $CaCO_3$. This means that the seawater contains more dissolved $CaCO_3$ than would be expected based simply on the solubility of $CaCO_3$ in seawater. When seawater is supersaturated with respect to $CaCO_3$, the $CaCO_3$ tends to precipitate out of the seawater.

The best answer is NOT:

F because in areas where the seawater is shallow (less than 1 km deep), the seawater is supersaturated with respect to $CaCO_3$; it is not undersaturated with respect to $CaCO_3$.

G because in areas where the seawater is shallow (less than 1 km deep), the seawater is supersaturated with respect to $CaCO_3$; it is not saturated with respect to $CaCO_3$.

J because in areas where the seawater is shallow (less than 1 km deep), the seawater is supersaturated with respect to $CaCO_3$; therefore, this seawater contains $CaCO_3$.

119.   **The best answer is C.** Figure 1 shows that seawater is supersaturated with respect to $CaCO_3$ between depths of 0 km and 4.0 km. At a depth greater than 4.0 km, seawater is undersaturated with $CaCO_3$. At a depth of 4.0 km, seawater is saturated with $CaCO_3$. Thus, 4.0 km is the maximum depth above which all the seawater is supersaturated with respect to $CaCO_3$.

The best answer is NOT:

A or B because at depths less than 4.0 km, seawater is supersaturated with respect to $CaCO_3$ Therefore, there are depths greater than 3.0 km and 3.5 km that are saturated with respect to $CaCO_3$.

D because at a depth of 4.5 km, the seawater is not supersaturated with respect to $CaCO_3$.

120. **The best answer is J.** Figure 1 shows the rate at which $CaCO_3$ dissolves in seawater. From a depth of 3.5 km to a depth of 4.0 km, the increase in the rate at which $CaCO_3$ dissolves is relatively small. That is, the rate at which $CaCO_3$ dissolves in seawater at a depth of 3.5 km is similar to the rate at which $CaCO_3$ dissolves in seawater at a depth of 4.0 km. Likewise, from a depth of 4.0 km to a depth of 4.5 km, and from a depth of 4.5 km to a depth of 5.0 km, the increase in the rate at which $CaCO_3$ dissolves is relatively small. However, from a depth of 5.0 km to a depth of 5.5 km, the increase in the rate at which $CaCO_3$ dissolves is relatively large. Of the 4 options provided, the rate at which $CaCO_3$ dissolves increases the most between depths of 5.0 km and 5.5 km.

    The best answer is NOT:

    F because the change in the rate at which $CaCO_3$ dissolves in seawater between depths of 3.5 km and 4.0 km is less than the change in the rate at which $CaCO_3$ dissolves in seawater between depths of 5.0 km and 5.5 km.

    G because the change in the rate at which $CaCO_3$ dissolves in seawater between depths of 4.0 km and 4.5 km is less than the change in the rate at which $CaCO_3$ dissolves in seawater between depths of 5.0 km and 5.5 km.

    H because the change in the rate at which $CaCO_3$ dissolves in seawater between depths of 4.5 km and 5.0 km is less than the change in the rate at which $CaCO_3$ dissolves in seawater between depths of 5.0 km and 5.5 km.

Passage XXI

121. **The best answer is D.** Table 1 lists R for each of the four initial speeds. At an initial speed of 20 mi/hr, $R = 22$ ft. At an initial speed of 80 mi/hr, $R = 88$ ft. Compared to R at an initial speed of 20 mi/hr, R at an initial speed of 80 mi/hr is four times as great.

    The best answer is NOT:

    A because compared to R at an initial speed of 20 mi/hr, R at an initial speed of 80 mi/hr is four times as great, not one-fourth as great.

    B because compared to R at an initial speed of 20 mi/hr, R at an initial speed of 80 mi/hr is four times as great, not one-half as great.

    C because compared to R at an initial speed of 20 mi/hr, R at an initial speed of 80 mi/hr is four times as great, not two times as great.

122.   **The best answer is F.** Table 1 lists R, B, and D. At 20 mi/hr, $R = 22$ ft, $B = 20$ ft, and $D = 42$ ft. At 40 mi/hr, $R = 44$ ft, $B = 80$ ft, and $D = 124$ ft. At 60 mi/hr, $R = 66$ ft, $B = 180$ ft, and $D = 246$ ft. At 80 mi/hr, $R = 88$ ft, $B = 320$ ft, and $D = 408$ ft. So, for each initial speed, $D = R + B$.

The best answer is NOT:

G because $D \neq R - B$.

H because $D \neq R \times B$. Note that if $D = R \times B$, the unit of measure for D would be ft. However the unit of measure for D is ft^2.

J because $D \neq R + B$. Note that if $D = R + B$, then D would not have a unit of measure. However, the unit of measure for D is ft.

123.   **The best answer is B.** In Figure 1, the two methods give the same value for D where the two curves intersect. The curves intersect at an initial speed of about 37 mi/hr. Of the speeds listed in the four options, 37 mi/hr is closest to 40 mi/hr.

The best answer is NOT:

A because at 20 mi/hr, Method 2 yields a larger value for D than does Method 1.

C or **D** because at 60 mi/hr and 80 mi/hr, respectively, Method 1 yields a larger value for D than does Method 2.

124.   **The best answer is H.** According to Method 2, the total stopping distance (D) equals the initial speed in ft/sec multiplied by 2 sec. The question specifies that the initial speed is 60 mi/hr, which, according to Table 1, is 88 ft/sec. So, $D = 88$ ft/sec $\times$ 2 sec = 176 ft, as given in Table 1. The answer can also be determined using Figure 1. In Figure 1, along the curve for Method 2, an x-value of 60 mi/hr corresponds to a y-value of approximately 176 ft for D.

The best answer is NOT:

F or **G** because the car would travel more than 58 ft and 118 ft, respectively, during the 2-sec interval.

J because the car would travel less than 234 ft during the 2-sec interval.

125. **The best answer is D.** According to Table 1, for every 20 mi/hr increase in the initial speed, *D* increases approximately 60 ft. Because an initial speed of 90 mi/hr represents a 10 mi/hr increase over an initial speed of 80 mi/hr, *D* for an initial speed of 90 mi/hr must be about 30 ft longer than *D* for an initial speed of 80 mi/hr. Based on this analysis, *D* for an initial speed of 90 mi/hr is 236 ft + 30 ft = 266 ft. In Figure 1, note that the slope of the straight line representing Method 2 is approximately equal to 150 ft per 50 mi/hr, or 3 ft per 1 mi/hr. For an initial speed of 80 mi/hr, *D* is greater than 230 ft. For an initial speed of 90 mi/hr, *D* will be greater than 230 ft + (10 mi/hr × 3 ft per mi/hr) = 260 ft.

    The best answer is NOT:

    A, **B**, or **C** because, as noted above, for an initial speed of 90 mi/hr, *D* will be greater than 260 ft, not less than 260 ft.

Passage XXII

126. **The best answer is J.** The urine sample with the highest water content per milliliter will most likely be the urine sample with the lowest concentration of suspended solids. In addition, because the specific gravity of a urine sample equals the density of the urine sample divided by the density of water, the urine sample with a specific gravity closest to 1.0 is the urine sample with the highest water content per milliliter. According to Tables 1 and 2, of the four options provided, the urine sample from Student D at 8:00 P.M. had the lowest concentration of suspended solids and had a specific gravity closest to 1.0.

    The best answer is NOT:

    F because the urine sample from Student D at 8:00 P.M. had a lower concentration of suspended solids and a specific gravity closer to 1.0 than did the 8:00 A.M. urine sample from Student A.

    G because the urine sample from Student D at 8:00 P.M. had a lower concentration of suspended solids and a specific gravity closer to 1.0 than did the 8:00 A.M. urine sample from Student B.

    H because the urine sample from Student D at 8:00 P.M. had a lower concentration of suspended solids and a specific gravity closer to 1.0 than did the 8:00 P.M. urine sample from Student C.

127. **The best answer is D.** Table 1 shows that as the urine volume increases from 100 mL to 385 mL, the color value decreases from 8 to 2. The note in the table indicates that the values for color range from 0 for very pale urine to 10 for very dark urine. These data do not support the conclusion that as urine volume increases, urine color darkens. Table 2 shows that as the urine volume increases from 150 mL to 400 mL, the color value decreases from 7 to 0. These data do not support the conclusion that as urine volume increases, urine color darkens. The urine samples with the greatest volume had the lightest color (for example, Student D at 8:00 A.M. and Student D at 8:00 P.M.).

The best answer is NOT:

A or **B** because the data do not support the conclusion that as urine volume increases, urine color darkens.

C because in each of the two tables the urine sample with the greatest volume had the lowest color value, not the highest color value. For example, in Table 2 the 8:00 P.M. urine sample from Student D had the greatest volume and the lowest color value.

128. **The best answer is F.** If the urine samples are listed in order from the sample with the lowest concentration of suspended solids (Student D at 8:00 P.M.) to the sample with the highest concentration of suspended solids (Student A at 8:00 A.M.), then the urine samples will also be ordered from the urine sample with the lowest specific gravity to the urine sample with the highest specific gravity. This result supports the conclusion that as the concentration of suspended solids in urine increases, the specific gravity of the urine increases.

The best answer is NOT:

G, H, or **J** because as the concentration of suspended solids in the urine samples increases, the specific gravity of the urine samples never decreases.

129. **The best answer is A.** If one of the four students experienced a net fluid loss prior to providing urine samples, then this student would most likely have urine samples of low volume. In addition, compared to the other urine samples, these urine samples would have higher specific gravities, because they would contain higher concentrations of suspended solids. For both sets (8:00 A.M. and 8:00 P.M.) of urine samples, Student A's urine sample had the lowest volume and the highest specific gravity.

The best answer is NOT:

B, C, or **D** because for both sets of urine samples, Student A's urine sample had a lower volume and a higher specific gravity than did Student B's urine sample, Student C's urine sample, and Student D's urine sample, respectively.

130. **The best answer is H.** If volume is held constant across urine samples, then the urine sample with the greatest density will weigh the most. Because the specific gravity of a urine sample equals the density of the urine sample divided by the density of water, the urine sample with the highest specific gravity will have the highest density. Of the four options provided, the urine sample with the highest specific gravity was the 8:00 P.M. urine sample from Student A. Therefore, per unit volume, this urine sample weighed the most.

The best answer is NOT:

F, G, or J because the 8:00 P.M. urine sample from Student A had a higher specific gravity than did the 8:00 A.M. urine sample from Student B, the 8:00 A.M. urine sample from Student D, and the 8:00 P.M. urine sample from Student C, respectively.

Passage XXIII

131. **The best answer is C.** Table 2 shows that the boiling point of an NaCl solution made with 100 g of H_2O increases by 1°C for every 0.1 moles of NaCl in the solution. Because the boiling point of pure H_2O is 100°C, if the solution boils at 104°C, the solution must contain 0.4 moles of NaCl.

The best answer is NOT:

A because a solution containing 100 g of H_2O and 0.2 moles of NaCl will boil at 102°C.

B because a solution containing 100 g of H_2O and 0.3 moles of NaCl will boil at 103°C.

D because a solution containing 100 g of H_2O and 0.5 moles of NaCl will boil at 105°C.

132. **The best answer is J.** In Experiment 2, the student kept the amount of H_2O constant at 100 g, kept the substance added (NaCl) the same in each trial, and intentionally varied the amount of NaCl added in each trial, while measuring the boiling point of the resulting solutions. Thus, boiling point was not directly controlled. (Boiling point was the dependent variable.)

The best answer is NOT:

F because the student always added NaCl to the solution.

G because the student always used 100 g of H_2O to make each solution.

H because the student determined the amount of solute added to the H_2O by controlling the amount of NaCl added to the H_2O.

133.   **The best answer is A.** The passage explains that each mole of NaCl dissolves to produce 2 moles of solute particles. So, as the amount of NaCl dissolved increases, the number of solute particles increases. Table 2 shows that as the amount of NaCl dissolved in the H_2O increased, the boiling point increased. This information supports the hypothesis that as the number of solute particles increases, the boiling point of a solution increases.

The best answer is NOT:

B because more solute particles resulted in a higher boiling point.

C because as the concentration of NaCl was varied, the concentration of solute particles varied. Thus, a hypothesis *can* be made about the relationship between the number of solute particles in a solution and the boiling point of the solution.

D because as the number of solute particles increases, the boiling point of a solution increases. Thus, the number of solute particles *does* affect the boiling point of the solution.

134.   **The best answer is J.** Solutions 4 and 12 each contained 0.2 mole of NaCl and 100 g of H_2O. The NaCl resulted in a 6.9°C decrease in the freezing point (from 0°C for H_2O to −6.9°C for Solution 4) and a 2.0°C increase in the boiling point (from 100°C for H_2O to 102.0°C for Solution 12). Thus, the freezing point was lowered more than the boiling point was raised.

The best answer is NOT:

F or **G** because the freezing point was lowered.

H because the freezing point was lowered more than the boiling point was raised.

135.   **The best answer is B.** According to the passage, each mole of NaCl dissolved to form a mole of sodium ions and a mole of chloride ions. Accordingly, as the amount of NaCl increased, the number of sodium particles and chloride particles in solution also increased. In addition, Table 1 shows that as the amount of NaCl increased, the freezing point decreased. Thus, as the number of sodium particles and chloride particles in solution increased, the freezing point decreased.

The best answer is NOT:

A or **C** because as the number of sodium particles and chloride particles in solution increased, the freezing point decreased only.

D because as the number of sodium particles and chloride particles in solution increased, the freezing point did not remain the same.

136. **The best answer is H.** The passage states that each mole of NaCl produces 2 moles of solute particles. Because each mole of $CaCl_2$ produces 3 moles of solute particles, the addition of 0.1 mole of $CaCl_2$ will result in 0.3 mole of solute particles. Solution 3 contained 0.2 mole of solute particles. Solution 4 contained 0.4 mole of solute particles. Because $CaCl_2$ affects the freezing point of H_2O in the same way that NaCl affects the freezing point of H_2O, the effect of 0.3 mole of $CaCl_2$ will be greater than the effect of 0.2 mole of NaCl and less than the effect of 0.1 mole of NaCl. That is, 0.1 mole of $CaCl_2$ will decrease the freezing point by more than 3.4°C and less than 6.9°C. As a result, the freezing point will be less than −3.4°C and more than −6.9°C.

The best answer is NOT:

F or **G** because 0.1 mole of $CaCl_2$ will decrease the freezing· point by more than 3.4°C. Thus, the freezing point· will be lower than −3.4°C.

J because 0.1 mole of $CaCl_2$ will decrease the freezing point by less than 6.9°C. Thus, the freezing point will be greater than −6.9°C.

Passage XXIV

137. **The best answer is C.** According to Figure 1, the average air temperature was −26°C for January and −16°C for March. The average air temperature was −16°C for March and −5°C for September. The average air temperature was −5°C for May and −5°C for September. The average air temperature was −10°C for October and −24°C for December.

The best answer is NOT:

A, B, or **D** because the average air temperatures in the Arctic were identical in May and September. For each of the other pairs of months, the average air temperatures in the Arctic were not identical.

138. **The best answer is G.** Figure 1 shows that from January to July, the average monthly air temperature increased and $\delta^{18}O$ increased. Figure 1 also shows that from July to December, the average monthly air temperature decreased and $\delta^{18}O$ decreased. In general, Figure 1 is most consistent with the conclusion that as the average monthly air temperature increased (from January to July), then decreased (from July to December), $\delta^{18}O$ increased, then decreased.

The best answer is NOT:

F because as the average monthly air temperature increased, then decreased, $\delta^{18}O$ did not increase only.

H because as the average monthly air temperature increased, then decreased, $\delta^{18}O$ did not decrease only.

J because as the average monthly air temperature increased, then decreased, $\delta^{18}O$ did not decrease, then increase.

139. **The best answer is B.** The passage explains that the scientists wanted to examine $\delta^{18}O$ in glacial ice. The Arctic and Antarctic were chosen because many locations in the Arctic and Antarctic have had glaciers for thousands of years. Thus, ice cores could be collected from these locations.

The best answer is NOT:

A because Figure 1 shows that the Arctic does not have average monthly air temperatures below −25°C year round.

C because the experimenters wanted to collect precipitation during each month so they could calculate $\delta^{18}O$.

D because though it may be true that the sites had large areas of bare soil and rock present, the researchers were doing studies on areas where glaciers were present. The areas of bare soil and rock would not provide a reason to choose these locations for the studies.

140. **The best answer is J.** Figure 2 shows $\delta^{18}O$ along the bottom of the graph and climate along the top of the graph. As the climate warms, $\delta^{18}O$ increases. In Figure 2, at depths between 150 and 200 m, $\delta^{18}O$ ranges from -17.5 to -10.0. The $\delta^{18}O$ value at the surface (a depth of 0 m) corresponds to the present-day climate. The $\delta^{18}O$ values for the portion of the ice cores at depths of 150 m and 200 m are all higher than the value for the present day. This indicates that compared to the present-day climate, the climate was warmer at the time the ice that is currently located at depths of 150 m to 200 m was forming.

The best answer is NOT:

F or **G** because compared to the present-day climate, the climate was warmer at the time the ice that is currently located at depths of 150 m to 200 m was forming.

H because Study 2 did not examine ice cores from the Antarctic.

141. **The best answer is A.** The ice cores in Studies 2 and 3 correspond to 100,000 years of glacial ice accumulation. If 100,000 years resulted in 500 m of ice in the Arctic and 300 m of ice in the Antarctic, then the rate of ice accumulation was greater in the Arctic (0.005 m/year) than in the Antarctic (0.003 m/year).

The best answer is NOT:

B or **C** because 100,000 years resulted in more glacial ice accumulation in the Arctic than in the Antarctic. Thus, the rate of glacial ice accumulation was greater in the Arctic than in the Antarctic.

D because the rate could be determined by dividing the ice core length by the time of accumulation.

142. **The best answer is G.** Based on the formula provided in the passage, $\delta^{18}O$ equals zero if and only if the $^{18}O/^{16}O$ of the sample equals the $^{18}O/^{16}O$ of the standard. When this occurs, the numerator equals zero, so $\delta^{18}O$ equals zero.

The best answer is NOT:

F, H, or **J** because each of these options results in a nonzero numerator. If the numerator in the formula is nonzero, then $\delta^{18}O$ is also nonzero.

SCIENCE • EXPLANATORY ANSWERS

Passage XXV

143. **The best answer is D.** In zone A you can see the largest population of mice at 300. The larvae/mouse ratio is 50 which is the second highest value. However if you look at zone D, which has the second lowest mice population, you see that it has the highest larvae/mouse ratio. There is no distinct trend between the zones so the correct answer is that it varied but that there is no specific pattern by which it varied.

   The best answer is NOT:

   A since there is no distinct increasing pattern. B because there is no distinct decreasing pattern. C because there is no specific pattern to the ratio.

144. **The best answer is G.** Figure 1 shows that the life cycle begins in the top left corner and then traces in a spiral clockwise several times. There are several points at which other organisms play a role in continuing the tick life cycle. In two of the boxes there are several organisms that act as a feeding host for the tick. However, in the first box the only organism mentioned is mice. That makes it essential as there is no other pathway for the spread of bacteria to continue without mice. Therefore, **G** is correct.

   The best answer is NOT:

   F because deer are not the only pathway where the bacteria can be maintained. Even though deer are preferred, humans and domestic animals can also transmit the bacteria, so deer are not essential. The same applies to **H** and **J** as well. Neither humans nor domestic animals are the sole pathway by which the bacteria can be maintained at any point in the life cycle.

145. **The best answer is C.** This relatively straightforward question asks you to determine the average percentage of households with at least 1 infected person. To do this, look at Table 1 and find the average of the 5 values given to you. If you add $75 + 62 + 54 + 38 + 36$ you get 265. Divide this by 5 and the average is 53%. Then choose the closest value answer choice, which is **C.**

   The best answer is NOT:

   A, B, and D 60% is close to 53% but 50% is closest so make sure you pick the best and most accurate answer.

146. **The best answer is F.** 75% of households in Zone A have at least 1 infected person. This percentage is higher than any of the other zones. If more data about the total number of deer tick larvae is determined, you can assume the greatest number of infected larvae would be present in the zone with the greatest percentage of infected people. Choice **F**, Zone A, is correct because the percentage of households inhabited by at least 1 infected person is higher than any of the other zones.

    The best answer is NOT:

    G, H, and J, because they all have lower percentages than Zone A.

147. **The best answer is D.** August and November do not have the same total cases, so **D** is correct. The graph presents new cases with and without a bull's-eye rash but that doesn't matter in this question. The only thing you need to look at is the height of the column for each month.

    The best answer is NOT:

    A and C because their columns are exactly the same height. B because there were no new cases reported in either month.

Passage XXVI

148. **The best answer is G.** Look at the patterns you see as the temperature shown in Table 1 is increased. You can see that the OFC1 value is cut almost exactly in half every time you increase the temperature by 20°. This means that if you have a temperature of 150° you can expect the answer to be between 442 and 218.

    The best answer is NOT:

    F and J because the answer should be between 442 and 218. If you continue you can also see a decreasing trend in OFC2 as you increase temperature. This means that you would expect a value between 301 and 133 at 150°. This rules out choice **H** since 442 is outside that range.

149.   **The best answer is B.** Look at the induction period for each compound shown in Table 2. Though Experiment 2 doesn't specifically mention decomposition you can look at the initial explanation provided to you and the explanation provided in Experiment 1 and you see that this experiment looks at the rate of decomposing of OFC1 and 2 under different conditions. The induction rate is being used as a way to measure the rate of decomposition. Knowing that, you can then look back to Table 2 and determine which chemical compound had the fastest induction rate. This would correspond to the fastest decomposition rate of OFC1. Choice **B**, FeF_3, has by far the fastest induction period and is the correct answer.

The best answer is NOT:

Choices **A**, **C**, and **D** because they all have slower induction periods than choice B.

150.   **The best answer is H.** If you look at both experiments you will see that Experiment 1 varies the temperature from 100° to 220°. In Experiment 2 the temperature is constant at 180.

The best answer is NOT:

F because OFC 1 and 2 are studied in Experiment 1 and only OFC 1 is studied in Experiment 2. **G** because OFC 1 and 2 were studied in Experiment 1. **J** because it is the opposite of the correct answer. Temperature is varied in Experiment 1 but not Experiment 2.

151.   **The best answer is D.** This question requires you to read the description provided about Experiment 1. You can see that the induction period measures how long it takes for the pressure to rise from 0.01 atm to 0.20 atm. At 100° the induction time for OFC2 was 998 sec. This corresponds to the time it took for the pressure to rise from 0.01 atm to 0.20 atm which makes **D** the correct answer.

The best answer is NOT:

A because the pressure is increasing, not decreasing. **B** because going from 0.01 atm to 0.20 atm is an increase in pressure not a decrease. C because 0.20 atm to 0.01 atm is not an increase, nor is it the correct range of increase.

152. **The best answer is J.** You can determine this answer by looking at the induction rates of OFC1 and OFC2 at different temperatures as shown in Table 1. At every temperature range between 100° and 220° OFC1 had a longer induction period than OFC2. This means that OFC1 broke down slower than OFC2 every time.

The best answer is NOT:

F because OFC2 was less than OFC1. **G** because the answer should say Yes, not No. The wording of the answer states correctly that OFC1 has a greater induction period than OFC2 but it begins by saying No so that makes it incorrect. **H** because even though it says Yes, it incorrectly states OFC1 was less than OFC2 in every trial.

153. **The best answer is A.** You need to determine how to identify the correct formula. Read the passage introduction and you will see in the very first sentence "*Oxyfluorocarbons* (OFCs) are oils composed of only carbon (C), fluorine (F), and oxygen (O)." Once you know this, you simply need to look at the chemical formulas in the answer choices and determine which one is made exclusively of C, F, and O. **A** is the only formula which is comprised of only C, F, and O. so it is the correct answer.

The best answer is NOT:

B because it has hydrogen (H), **C** because it has chlorine (Cl), and **D** because it has hydrogen (H) in it.

Passage XXVII

154. **The best answer is H.** You need to examine Experiment 2 and understand the design of it and what it is controlling for. Experiment 2 states that mesh bags were used which excluded insects but allowed for wind. Student 2's hypothesis states that insect and wind each account for 50% of pollination occurring. Since Experiment 2 is excluding insects, the correct percentage should be 50%, choice **H**.

The best answer is NOT:

F because both insects and wind would need to be removed to achieve 0. **G** because the question concerns Student 2's hypothesis and not Student 1's. **J** since you would need to include both wind and insects to achieve a 99% rate.

155.   **The best answer is B.** Student 2 specifically states that female cones create air currents that facilitate the horizontal movement of pollen into the cones, so **B** is correct.

   The best answer is NOT:

   C and **D** as they start by saying male cones which invalidates them. **A** because it states that, though female, the air currents decrease the likelihood of pollen entering, which is not what Student 2 states.

156.   **The best answer is F.** If insects and wind were both excluded from pollination, then, according to Student 1, there is no other means of pollination. That means the percentage of ovule pollination would be 0%. There is no need to think too hard about this question or go into more depth than that.

   The best answer is NOT:

   G, H, and **J** because each corresponds to a percentage greater than 0% which is not possible, according to Student 1, if all means of pollination is removed.

157.   **The best answer is B.** Student 1 believes that wind only accounts for 10% of the zamia ovule pollinations and states that Zamia pollen is large and heavy, and this would not allow for the wind to carry it very far. This makes answer **B** correct.

   The best answer is NOT:

   Answers **A** and **C** because Student 1 clearly states that male Zamia release pollen, not the females. **D** because since the student states that pollen is large and heavy, not smaller than pollen found in most plants.

158.   **The best answer is F.** Both students agree that insect and wind pollination contribute to the overall percentage of ovule pollination. The option that allows for both wind and insects to reach the cones without any interference would be the option resulting in the highest pollination rate. That is choice **F,** where the cones are not covered by anything.

   The best answer is NOT:

   Choice **G** because as it would exclude insects and both Students 1 and 2 agree that insects contribute to pollination. The rate at which they contribute differs but the students still agree on the fact that they do. The same goes for **H** excluding wind—both agree it contributes, just at different rates. Choice **J** because as both would agree that it would result in zero pollination due to there being no insects or wind.

159. **The best answer is D.** Experiment 1 describes how female Zamia cones are covered with plastic bags that exclude insects and wind from coming into contact with them. This, according to both students, should completely limit pollination to those Zamia cones since it reduces the ability for both insects and wind to pollinate. A control group in an experiment is one that has nothing altered, so it can used as a comparison to the experimental group, in this case the covered female Zamia cones. Since female Zamia cones are covered, the control group would be uncovered female Zamia cones.

   The best answer is NOT:

   Choices **A** and **B** because both involve male Zamia cones. Choice **C** involves female Zamia cones but it is incorrect because there is a change made to the cones. A mesh bag covers them.

160. **The best answer is J.** Student 2 states they believe that wind and insect pollination are each responsible for 50% of pollination events in Zamia ovules. For this to be proven true, you need to have a result focused specifically on the pollination rates of just wind and another result focusing on insect pollination. If both of those experimental results turned out to have an equal effect on pollination, it would confirm Student 2's hypothesis. In this case Experiment 2 looks at wind pollination exclusively and Experiment 3 looks at insect pollination exclusively which makes choice **J** correct.

   The best answer is NOT:

   F and **G** because they both deal with Experiment 1 which doesn't look at wind or insect pollination separately. **H** refers to only Experiment 2 and doesn't address insect pollination at all so it is incorrect.

Passage XXVIII

161. **The best answer is B.** In Table 1 in Study 1 you can see that the percentage of clay in the soil increases as you go from soil A to B to C. You can also see a clear increase in the water content percentage as you go from A to B to C. This supports the hypothesis that a higher clay content in soil will result in more water content in the soil.

   The best answer is NOT:

   A because its rationale is wrong. The water content didn't decrease. **C** and **D** because they both say the hypothesis is incorrect regardless of the rationale given.

162. **The best answer is G.** You need to determine where the fourth soil presented in the question would fall in the range of soils given in Table 1 in Study 1. Take a look at the values given to you for sand, silt, and clay. They clearly fit in between Soils A and B. This means that the water content % should be between the values given for A and B, 2.9% to 6.8%. So, choice **G** is correct.

   The best answer is NOT:

   F, H, and **J** because they do not give the correct range.

163. **The best answer is D.** This question asks you to look at both Study 1 and Study 3. Study 3 is saturating the soil in water for 24 hours. That is a key piece of information. Then, look at Table 1 in Study 1 and examine the water content shown for soil C. The water content of the soil when randomly sampled initially as described in Study 1 was 21.3%. Given the answer choices in this question it would make sense that after soaking in water for 24 hours the soil would be at least as saturated as was when initially sampled. This means that the only viable answer is **D**.

   The best answer is NOT:

   A, B, and **C** all give water content values below the minimum that you would expect soil C to have.

164. **The best answer is H.** Look at the "no sand added" column found in Table 2 in Study 2. The threshold wind speed for each sand was either 0.31 or 0.30. These values are close to one another. Then determine which answer choice best supports this observation. Only **H** states correctly that all three were almost the same.

   The best answer is NOT:

   F says that A is twice as high which doesn't match the data. **G** says that C was twice as high which again doesn't match the data. **J** says that all three soils had a threshold speed of 0 m/sec which doesn't match the data.

165. **The best answer is A.** Compare the "no sand added" and "sand added" columns in Table 2 in Study 2 to see how the threshold speeds changed between the two columns. The "sand added" column is approximately 2/3 the value of the "no sand added" column. This makes choice **A** the correct answer. You can also determine the answer through elimination of the other answers.

   The best answer is NOT:

   The answer clearly isn't the same as described in **B**, it isn't half of the values as described in **C**, and it isn't twice as high as described in **D**.

166.   **The best answer is H.** Look at the "sand added" column in Table 2 in Study 2. The question says you will be mixing Sand A and B and then basically repeating Study 2 again with the mixed sand. You would expect that the "sand added" column for this mix of A and B would have the average value of sand A and B. In this case their values are basically the same—only a very minor difference—so you don't even need to calculate the average. You can just look at the answer choices and see which provides you with a correct range that encompasses 0.21 and 0.22. In this case that answer choice is **H.**

   The best answer is NOT:

   F, G, and **J** do not contain the possible average from mixing sand A and B together.

Passage XXIX

167.   **The best answer is B.** The question says you should follow the values as the voltage across the plates increases and the capacitance decreases. Look at Table 1. You can see that as the voltage increases and capacitance decreases as you move down the table the plate separation increases.

   The best answer is NOT:

   A because as the surface area remains constant. **C** because the plate separation increases, not decreases. **D** because number K is discussed in Experiment 3 and has no bearing on Experiment 1.

168.   **The best answer is G.** This question asks you to look at what varies during Experiment 3. The first sentence in the description clearly says that "three pairs of square copper plates, each pair having a different surface area, were tested." This indicates that surface area is being varied and choice **G** is the correct answer. For further confirmation look at Table 2 and you can see that the surface area of each plate is what is varied.

   The best answer is NOT:

   F because Number K of the plates is not mentioned in Experiment 2. **H** because plate separation is not varied in Experiment 2, only in Experiment 1. **J** as the material is not varied in Experiment 2, only in Experiment 3.

169.   The best answer is C. Look at all three experiments since each experiment investigated one of the things asked for in the question: plate separation, surface area, and material. In Experiment 1 the maximum capacitance corresponded to a plate separation of 1×10^{-4} m. In Experiment 2 the maximum capacitance corresponded to a surface area of 5×10^{-3} m^2. In Experiment 3 the maximum capacitance corresponded to titanium oxide as a material. Find the answer choice that best matches these options.

The best answer is NOT:

Choices **A** and **D** because both have a material that is not titanium dioxide. Choices **B** and **C** are similar in that they both have the maximum separation value and the correct material for maximum capacitance. However, their surface area values are different and do not correspond directly to the values given in the table. Use the trend shown in Experiment 2—as surface area increases, the capacitance also increases. Thus, **C** is the correct answer because its surface area is larger than choice **B**.

170.   The best answer is H. This question says that as K decreases a material's suitability for use between the plates of a capacitor decreases. It then asks you to list the three materials in order of decreasing ability, from greatest to least K value. In this case choice **H** lists the materials in the correct order for K with titanium dioxide having the greatest value, water being in the middle, and mica having the lowest K value.

The best answer is NOT:

Answer choices **F, G,** and **J** because they do not list the materials in the correct order from most suitable to least suitable, making them incorrect.

171.   The best answer is A. The answer can be found in the initial passage description before you even read about the individual experiments. It doesn't specifically state what the charge on Plate A is after the switch is opened, but it does tell you the information you need to figure this out. The passage states that each plate contained an equal number of positive charges and negative charges. When the switch was closed, negatively charged electrons flowed from Plate A to Plate B. The switch was reopened when the total negative charge that has flown through is equal to -1×10^{-8} coulombs. Keeping in mind that the plates contained equal parts negative and positive charges, you can determine that the positive charge remaining on Plate A was equal to the charge that just went to Plate B. So in this case it is simply the same number value but with a positive instead of negative charge. This is why choice A, 1×10^{-8} coulombs is correct.

The best answer is NOT:

Choices **B, C,** and **D** because the charge listed for each of them is not equal to the charge that will flow through to plate A when the switch is opened.

172. **The best answer is F.** You need to look carefully at the diagrams presented in the answer choices. The only differences between them are the arrows indicating the direction of electron flow along the circuit diagram. The introduction to the passage states that "when the switch in the circuit was closed, electrons (negatively charged particles) flowed from Plate A of the capacitor through the ammeter, resistor, and battery to Plate B." You simply need to find the arrows that support this pathway as described. Choice **F** shows the arrows moving from switch to Plate B to Plate A to ammeter. This is the correct path so it is the correct answer.

    The best answer is NOT:

    Choice **G** because it shows the arrows both flowing out from Plate A and B in opposite directions. Choice **H** because it shows the electrons flowing in the opposite direction of the correct path. Choice **J** because it shows electrons flowing into Plate A and Plate B.

Passage XXX

173. **The best answer is D.** You need to look at the graphs shown in Figure 2 and Figure 3. Look at each temperature given as a point in Figure 2 and see if any of them match to the corresponding solubility and temperature shown in Figure 3. None of them do—none are even close—so the only possible correct answer is **D**.

    The best answer is NOT:

    A, B, and **C** because the temperatures given do not have their solubilities in Figures 2 and 3.

174. **The best answer is H.** This question states that you mix Compound A and Compound B into a solution. It states that you have 1 mole/L of compound A and 0.5 mole/L of Compound B. It then asks you to compare the number of molecules of each compound present in the solution. The relationship is: 1 mole/L of Compound A is twice the 0.5 mole/L of Compound B.

    The best answer is NOT:

    Choice **G** as the molecules are clearly not equal. Choice **J** because 1 is not 4 times as large as 0.5. Choice **F** is because it asks you to compare Compound **B** to Compound **A**.

175. **The best answer is B.** Refer to all three figures. First, look at Figure 1 to determine which compound dissolves exothermically. Figure 1 shows that Compound B dissolving is exothermic. Then look at Figure 3 to see how Compound B's solubility changes with temperature. As the temperature of Compound B increases, the solubility decreases.

The best answer is NOT:

A is not the correct choice because though it answers Yes, it describes Compound A instead of Compound B. **C** and **D** because they both say No, which is incorrect based on the chemist's hypothesis.

176. **The best answer is F.** The key to determining this question is entirely presented in Figure 1. You don't need to have an in-depth understanding of what the delta H values mean or even what endothermic and exothermic mean. The key information you need is under endothermic and exothermic for Compounds A and B. Compound B indicates that it is exothermic, meaning heat is given off to the solution. When heat is given off, that will not result in freezing. Compound A is said to be endothermic meaning that heat is absorbed from the solution. When heat is absorbed from a solution that solution will become colder and eventually freeze. That means that Compound A is the most likely thing the chemist added to the water, making **F** the correct answer.

The best answer is NOT:

Choices **G, H,** and **J.** Be sure you pay attention to the second portion of the answers for **F** and **G. G** indicates that the delta H for Compound A is negative which is incorrect. In Figure 1 it is positive.

177. **The best answer is A.** If ammonium nitrate has a positive delta H it will absorb heat from the solution just like Compound A does. Both are endothermic. The delta H value given for ammonium nitrate is less than Compound A's value of 59.8 KJ/mole. That means that Compound A absorbs more heat than ammonium nitrate. Choice **A** is correct because it says that ammonium nitrate will absorb less heat than Compound A.

The best answer is NOT:

Choice **B** because it says ammonium nitrate will absorb more heat than Compound A. **C** and **D** because they both state that ammonium nitrate will give off heat to the solution instead of absorbing heat.

Passage XXXI

178. **The best answer is G.** The first graph in Figure 2 has a semimajor axis of 1.5×10^8 km, so that is the graph to use. You are looking for an eccentricity of 0.10 which corresponds to the solid dark line on the graph. You are looking at a range of degrees from 0 to 359, which means you are essentially looking at the entire length of the graph on the x-axis since the values go from 0 degrees to 360 degrees. Then determine how many times the dark line, representing the planet, crosses the y-axis at 30 km/sec. You can see it does this twice, at 90 degrees (between 60 and 120) and 270 degrees (between 240 and 300). Therefore, the correct answer is **G**.

    The best answer is NOT:

    F, H, and **J.**

179. **The best answer is C.** Perihelion can be found at 0 degrees for every graph and aphelion can be found at 180 degrees for every graph shown in Figure 2. When a planet moves beyond 180 degrees it is continuing in its orbit and moving back towards perihelion. On the graphs in Figure 2 you will be looking at them from left to right to determine how the speed, shown on the y-axis, changes. Any of the three graphs can be used to answer the question. The trend is clear in every graph showing that, as you move from left to right towards 180 degrees (aphelion), the speed of the planet slows. Once that 180 degrees point is reached and it continues back towards 360 degrees (perihelion), the speed of the planet begins to increase again. This corresponds to answer **C**.

    The best answer is NOT:

    A because the planet slows down before it speeds up again. **B** because it does not speed up first—it slows down first. **D** because it speeds up in the second half of its orbit.

180. **The best answer is J.** This question is about interpreting the information you find on a graph. Look at the first graph since it identifies the semimajor axis of the planet as being 1.5×10^8 km. The solid black line gauges the speed of the planet since it says the eccentricity is 0.10. Perihelion is found at 0 degrees which is the beginning of the graph on the x-axis. (The definition of perihelion can be found in the passage's introductory material.) The speed found on the graph is about 33 km/sec, which is well below the escape velocity of 44.2 km/sec stated in the question. **J** is correct because it correctly states that at the given semimajor axis and eccentricity the planet's escape velocity at perihelion will not be high enough to escape the solar system.

    The best answer is NOT:

    F and **G** because the velocity of the planet does not go above escape velocity so they should say No. **H** because even though it says No, its reasoning is incorrect. Specifically, the planets orbital speed at perihelion is *not* greater than escape velocity.

181.   **The best answer is A.** This question asks you to consider the different eccentricities of orbit shown in Figure 2. In each figure there is a clear trend: as the eccentricity of the orbit decreases the variation of the speed of the planet decreases as well. The closer the graphed line is to straight, the closer the speed of the planet is to constant. If you had an eccentricity of 0, as proposed in choice **A,** it can be predicted that the speed of the planet would be near constant. This makes **A** the correct choice.

The best answer is NOT:

B, C, and **D** because they all have a higher eccentricity which corresponds to greater variation in speed change by the planet.

182.   **The best answer is F.** Find the graph shown in Figure 2 that has a semimajor axis of 3.0×10^8 km. This is the second graph down. The question states the eccentricity of the orbit is 0.05 which is below any of the given values shown in the graph. You need to then predict the speed at 0 degrees based on what you see in the graph. There is a clear trend that as the eccentricity of the orbit decreases, the speed of the planet also decreases. From that trend you can predict that the speed of the planet with a lower eccentricity of 0.05 will be slower than anything shown in the graph. The lowest value given in the answer choices is **F,** less than 23 km/sec.

The best answer is NOT:

G, H, and **J** because they are all higher than that value.

183.   **The best answer is D.** Figure 1 shows a map of several genes on chromosomes. Chromosome 13 specifically shows it has a ribosomal RNA gene. Since the question specifically states that this is "according to Figure 1 and Table 1," you must find ribosomal RNA gene in Table 1, which is in the protein synthesis section. You may be tempted to rely on prior knowledge that ribosomes are involved in protein synthesis, but for questions that include "according to" the information is available in the data presentations listed.

The best answer is NOT:

A, B, and **C** because each of the given biological processes do not involve the ribosomal RNA gene which is present on Chromosome 13.

Passage XXXII

184.   **The best answer is G.** The introduction to this passage states that linked genes are found on the same chromosome. For the tRNA proline gene and the hexokinase gene to be linked both need to be found on the same chromosome in Figure 1, which they are not. The tRNA proline gene is found on Chromosome 14 and the hexokinase gene is found on Chromosome 10. This means they are not linked.

The best answer is NOT:

Choice **F** because its reasoning is wrong. If the genes were found on the same chromosome, then they would be linked. Choices **H** and **J** because the genes are not found on the same chromosome and are not linked so the correct answer should be No.

185.   **The best answer is A.** Table 1 shows the three genes related to digestion are the amylase gene, the trypsin gene, and the chymotrypsin gene. The amylase gene is found on Chromosome 1 and has no other genes shown on the chromosome meaning nothing is linked to it according to Figure 1. The trypsin gene is found on Chromosome 7 and has no genes linked to it either. Finally, the chymotrypsin gene is found on Chromosome 16 and has the hemoglobin α chain gene linked with it. The hemoglobin α chain gene is associated with respiration according to Table 1. From all of this information, you can conclude that the three genes associated with digestion are not found on the same chromosome and are not all linked to immune response or respiration. This makes answer choice **A** the correct answer as all three genes are on different chromosomes.

The best answer is NOT:

Choice **B** because the genes are not found on the same chromosome. Choice **C** because none of the genes are linked with any genes associated with immune response. Two of the genes are not linked to any other genes, while one gene is linked with a gene associated with respiration. Although one of the genes is linked with a gene associated with respiration, the other two are not. **D** because the question specifically asks about all three genes.

186. **The best answer is G.** Linked genes, as stated in the passage introduction, are genes found on the same chromosome. However, in this case, neurofibromatosis is not found on any chromosome in Figure 1 because it is not a specific gene. Instead, neurofibromatosis is a genetic disease, as shown in Table 2, and is associated with Chromosome 17. Looking at Chromosome 17 in Figure 1 shows the growth hormone gene is present. This makes answer choice **G** correct.

The best answer is NOT:

F, H, and **J** because they occur on chromosomes other than the neurofibromatosis Chromosome 17: amylase, Chromosome 1; myoglobin, Chromosome 22; rhodopsin, Chromosome 3.

187. **The best answer is D.** Human males and human females have a different chromosomal configuration. Human males have an XY chromosome pairing while human females have an XX chromosome pairing. This means that any gene found on a Y chromosome will typically present in human males but not in human females. In the chromosome map shown in Figure 1, the TSPY gene is the only gene listed on the Y chromosome. This means the TSPY gene will present in human males but not in human females making choice **D** the correct answer.

The best answer is NOT:

A, B, and **C** because none of those genes are found on the Y chromosome. There is no other information given to you in Figure 1 or Tables 1 or 2 that would indicate any of those genes as being present in males but not females. You may be tempted by the X-linked recessive choices from Table 2 that include X-linked recessive traits because they are more prevalent in males, but none of the these are "typically present" in human males.

Passage XXXIII

188. **The best answer is J.** Table 2 shows the results of Experiment 2 and the different concentrations and percentages of tocopherol in each of the strains. Be careful when reading the question to make sure that you are identifying where the greatest amount of γ-tocopherol specifically per kilogram of plant material is found. The S4 strain has the greatest percentage of γ-tocopherol present according to Table 2, so this makes **J** the correct answer.

The best answer is NOT:

F, because although strain S1 had a greater tocopherol concentration overall and a greater α-tocopherol, the question specifically asks about the amount of γ-tocopherol present. Choices **G** and **H,** S2 and S3, because they do not have the greatest amount of γ-tocopherol present as shown in Table 2.

189. **The best answer is B.** If a strain of *A. thaliana* used in Experiment 2 was genetically identical to one of the strains from experiment 1, it should show the same tocopherol results. To determine this you need to examine Table 1 and Table 2. Look at the two tables to see which strain from Table 2 had the same results as a trial in Table 1. Table 1 shows the tocopherol concentration of all lines to be 360 mg/kg. This eliminates all strains in Table 2 except S2, which has the same concentration result. In the γ-tocopherol and α-tocopherol results of S2, the results specifically match the results of line L2. This confirms that S2 is likely genetically identical to L2, making choice **B** the correct answer.

    The best answer is NOT:

    A because S1's results do not match anything in Table 1. **C** because S3's results do not match anything in Table 1. Choice **D** because S4's results, while they match L5 and L6 regarding α-tocopherol and γ-tocopherol, do not match the tocopherol concentration result.

190. **The best answer is J.** Each of the lines investigated in Experiment 1 had a different initial treatment given to it. Lines L1–L4 had the vector + a cloned gene exposed to each. L5 was exposed only to the vector but no cloned gene. Line L6 was left untreated completely and was exposed to nothing. L6 can be the control group of this experiment—it can be used to compare with the treatment groups results. To see whether only the vector affected tocopherol concentration one needs to look at the line that has only the vector, L5, and compare it to the untreated control group, L6. This makes **J** the correct answer.

    The best answer is NOT:

    Choice **F** because comparing L1 and L2 shows how genes TMT1 and TMT2 interact with the vector to affect tocopherol concentration. Choice **G** because comparing L2 and L4 does not indicate how the vector alone affected concentration. Choice **H** because comparing the result of L3 and L4 tells you nothing about only the vector. Each of the lines, L1–L4, was treated with the vector and a different gene. They tell you nothing about the vector alone.

191.   **The best answer is C.** The introduction to this passage states that the enzyme used in these experiments helps *A. thaliana* convert γ-tocopherol to α-tocopherol. The question poses the idea that one of the enzymes produced by a gene used was far less effective than the others. A less effective enzyme would likely result in less α-tocopherol than the more efficient enzymes. This means the line showing the highest concentration of γ-tocopherol among the four genes tested produced a less efficient enzyme. Table 1 shows that line L3 has a γ-tocopherol % of 51 in comparison to results for L1, L2, and L5 of 3%, 3% and 2% respectively. Clearly L3 was less efficient, making choice **C** the correct answer.

The best answer is NOT:

A, B, and **D** because they have a much lower concentration of γ-tocopherol, meaning they were more efficient in their conversion.

192.   **The best answer is J.** The TMT gene is being introduced into the *A. thaliana* to help the plant convert γ-tocopherol to α-tocopherol. If a gene transfer was unsuccessful in Experiment 2, the results should show that little to no γ-tocopherol was converted to α-tocopherol. You can see strain S4 has the highest percentage of γ-tocopherol at 99%. The next highest strain, S3, only has 9%. The other strains, S1 and S2, have even lower percentages of γ-tocopherol indicating the genes worked very well in facilitating the conversion. Clearly, the gene transferred to S4 did not work, as almost no γ-tocopherol was converted to α-tocopherol. This makes choice **J**, S4, the correct answer.

The best answer is NOT:

F, G, and **H** because those genes worked as described above resulting in a much lower γ-tocopherol percentage and a much higher percentage of α-tocopherol.

193. **The best answer is B.** The introduction to this passage indicates that the *G. soja* plant produces γ-tocopherol and then converts some of it to α-tocopherol using the TMT enzyme. The *A. thaliana* plant produces γ-tocopherol but struggles to convert γ-tocopherol to α-tocopherol because it lacks the ability to produce the TMT enzyme. The scientist in this passage wanted to see if introducing the TMT enzyme from the *G. soja* plant to the *A. thaliana* plant would help it convert γ-tocopherol to α-tocopherol. This makes choice **B** the correct answer. The scientist wanted to increase the amount of α-tocopherol produced by some of the *A. thaliana* plants. Both experiments involve exposing *A. thaliana* plants to different forms of the TMT gene and then measuring the concentration and percentages of γ-tocopherol and α-tocopherol.

The best answer is NOT:

A because the *G. soja* already has the ability to convert γ-tocopherol to α-tocopherol. Nothing was done to the *G. soja* plant. **C** because there was no experimentation done to the *G. soja* plant. There were no experimental groups that included the plant. **D** because the goal of the experiment was to increase the amount of α-tocopherol produced by transferring the TMT gene, not decrease the production.

Passage XXXIV

194. **The best answer is H.** Examine both Figure 2 and Figure 3. Figure 2 indicates the results when the sphere rolls. The X value at a height (H) of 1.5 m is indicated with an x for each data point. As the θ increases from 5° to 45° there is an initial increase in value followed by a decrease. It peaks around 30° and then begins to decrease. Figure 3 indicates the results when the sphere slides. The X value at a height (h) of 1.5 m for each point on this Figure is indicated with a small square. From 5° to 45° there is an initial increase followed by a decrease in the X value just as Figure 2 shows. In Figure 3, the peak of the increase is at 25° and then the decrease begins. Since both figures agree, answer choice **H** is correct. There is an initial increase in each graph followed by a decrease.

The best answer is NOT:

F because there is an increase initially but then there is a decrease after the peak. **G** because there is an initial increase before the decrease begins. **J** because initially there is an increase, not a decrease.

195.   **The best answer is A.** The data associated with the sliding sphere is in Figure 3. This graph shows that as θ increases there is an initial rise and then a slow decrease in the value of X which is the horizontal distance, in m, from the bottom of the inclined plane. The key relationship to see in this graph, for this question, is the relationship of the different values for height, H. For every data point recorded on the graph, the lowest H value had the lowest X value. That means the lower the height from the floor, the shorter the sliding sphere traveled. If an H value of 0.5 m was used, that would be the lowest H value in the experiment. The lowest H value should correspond to the lowest X value in Figure 3. The current lowest H value at θ = 10° is approximately 0.56 m. The only answer choice to indicate a lower X value is choice **A**, less than 0.56 m, making it the correct answer.

   The best answer is NOT:

   B, C, and **D** because they all indicate an X value greater than 0.56 m.

196.   **The best answer is H.** The data associated with the sliding sphere can be found in Figure 3. In this graph, the symbol that matches an H value of 2.0 m is the star. The question is effectively asking where the highest possible value is on this chart with an H value of 2.0 m. However, the question says that measurements were taken every 2.5° instead of 5° as shown on Figure 3. So you need to find a hypothetical point between each measurement along with the star points already shown in Figure 3. The highest X value for H = 2.0 m can be found between 25° and 30°. This matches with answer choice **H**, 27.5°, making it correct.

   The best answer is NOT:

   Answer choice **F** because it would have a much lower X value than choice **H**. Choices **G** and **J** because though they have a large X value, relative to the rest of the data, they are still not the highest X value present.

197.   **The best answer is B.** The data associated with the rolling sphere can be found in Figure 2. An H value of 2.0 in Figure 2 corresponds with star data points. Be sure not to get the X value of distance confused with the X data point marker on Figure 2. The X data points on Figure 2 correspond with an H value of 1.5 m instead of 2.0 m and do not apply to this question. The current data points given in Figure 2 end at θ = 45°. This question asks what the next measurement would be if a value of θ = 50° was used. At θ = 45° the X value, looking at the circles, is right around 0.75 – 0.800 m and there is a clear downward trend being shown in the data. It is not a dramatic decrease but at θ = 50° the value of X should be a bit lower than 0.75-0.80 m. The only answer choice that matches that general trend is 0.65 m, choice **B**.

   The best answer is NOT:

   A because it is much too low and does not match the trend shown on the graph. Choices **C** and **D** because they indicates an increase in X which does not match the trend.

198. **The best answer is F.** Kinetic energy, simply put, is a measure of energy related to the motion of an object. The greater the motion, meaning the faster the object is moving, the more kinetic energy the object will have. The kinetic energy of the sphere, as it begins at the top of the incline, is 0. Once the sphere is released, the kinetic energy will slowly increase as the sphere begins to roll down the incline and pick up speed. The only answer choice that supports this is choice **F.** Choice **F** shows the kinetic energy beginning at 0 for time 0 and then a gradual increase in kinetic energy as time progresses, indicating the sphere is rolling down the incline. The other three answer choices are invalidated immediately as none of them show a kinetic energy of 0 at the origin of the graph.

The best answer is NOT:

G, H, and **J** because they all show varying values of kinetic energy above zero which is not possible if the sphere is stationary.

Passage XXXV

199. **The best answer is C.** Study 4 states the data shown in Table 4 is related to the copper test wire used in Study 1. This question asks what the temperature of the test wire was in Study 1. However, no temperature values are given in Study 1. Instead, there are multiple temperature possibilities shown in Table 4 for the copper wire. To determine which temperature was used in Study 1, match the volt and ohm values for copper in Table 1 with the same values in Table 4 and determine which temperature matches with those values. Table 1 shows the copper test wire had a value of 0.11 volts and 0.14 ohms this corresponds to a temperature of 20°C making choice **C** the correct answer.

The best answer is NOT:

A, B and **D** because they are not the correct temperature.

200. **The best answer is J.** This question presents multiple graphs showing the relationship of cross-sectional area and R (ohms) in Study 3. Table 3 displays the results of Study 3. As cross-sectional area increases down the table, the value of R decreases. It is as simple as that. There is no need to do any math to determine the exact amount the ohms value decreases as cross-sectional area increases—the concept that as one increases the other decreases is enough. Choice **J** is the correct answer as it shows this relationship. In choice **J**, as cross-sectional area increases on the graph, the R value of ohms decreases as you move along the x-axis in an inverse relationship.

The best answer is NOT:

Choice **F** because it shows that as cross-sectional area increases the R value increases at the same rate, which is not true. Choice **H** because it shows that the R value does not vary depending on cross sectional area, which is not true. Choice **G** because it shows that as cross-sectional area increases the R value increases dramatically, which is not true.

201. **The best answer is D.** The introduction to the passage states in the first sentence that electrical resistance is represented in these studies as R, ohms. The greater the R value, the greater the electrical resistance. To answer this question, look at Table 1 and order the different metals used for the wire in order from lowest to greatest resistance, R. Copper is the lowest with an R of 0.14, followed by tungsten with an R of 0.44, followed by platinum with an R of 0.83, and finally the greatest resistance is lead with an R of 1.7. This makes answer choice **D** correct. If you are pressed for time, you could eliminate the incorrect answers. All four answer choices list copper as the wire with the least resistance but three of the four choices have a different wire listed as the highest resistance. Table 1 identifies the wire with the greatest resistance, which is lead. Then you know immediately that **D** is the correct answer choice because it is the only choice that has lead as the wire with the greatest resistance.

The best answer is NOT:

A, B, C because you can assume that the other two wires are listed in the correct order, as there would be no correct answer if they are not listed correctly.

202. **The best answer is H.** Study 2 can be used, in Table 2, to observe the relationship between wire length and V. As wire length increases, the V value also increases. More specifically, as the length of the wire doubles, the V value increases by at least double. At a length of 50 cm, the V was 0.05 volts and at 100 cm the V was 0.11 volts. When the length was doubled again to 200 cm the V value doubled to 0.22 volts. Using this information, find copper wire in Figure 4 of Study 4 at 60° C—the V value is initially 0.13 volts. If the length of the wire is doubled from 100 cm to 200 cm this results in a doubling of the V value from 0.13 volts to 0.26 volts. This matches answer choice **H**, making it the correct answer.

   The best answer is NOT:

   F and **G** because they are too low and do not match with what will happen when increasing length. **J** because, although it is greater voltage, the increase is too dramatic and does not match the trend as shown in Table 2.

203. **The best answer is C.** This question asks for the wire conditions, specifically length and cross-sectional area, that lead to the greatest electrical resistance, which is represented by the value of R. Table 2 shows how length affects the R value of a wire. The greater the length of the wire, the greater the R value. This means comparing 20 cm and 40 cm of length as seen in the answer choices, 40 cm is going to have a greater R value. This eliminates choices **A** and **B**. Next, Table 3 shows that as cross-sectional area increases the R value of a wire decreases. Therefore, the smaller cross-sectional area will lead to the highest resistance. This means the correct answer choice overall is choice **C**. It has the longest length and the smallest cross-sectional area.

   The best answer is NOT:

   D because it has the longest length, but a larger cross-sectional area.

SCIENCE • EXPLANATORY ANSWERS

204. **The best answer is G.** An assumption was made by the students regarding the ammeter positioning in Figure 1. The ammeter is being used to measure the electrical current until it reaches a specific value of 0.80 amp. Upon reaching this value, the voltage (V) across the test wire is measured and this measurement, along with the amperage, is then used to calculate the R value. The key assumption the students made is that all of the current is flowing through the test wire. If the current were not flowing through the test wire, none of their calculations would be accurate and the experiment would not work. This makes choice **G** correct.

The best answer is NOT:

F because the voltmeter is being used to measure the voltage across the test wire only. **H** because if none of the current went through the test wire than there would be no experiment because nothing would be measured across the test wire. **J** because if none of the current went through the rheostat it would be impossible to control the amperage of the experiment which needs to remain at 0.8 amps as stated in the passage. Students familiar with voltmeters could use prior knowledge: Voltmeters are high-resistance devices hooked up in parallel because so that they draw almost no current; however, ammeters are very low-resistance devices hooked in series because they cause almost no voltage drop.

Passage XXXVI

205. **The best answer is A.** In Figure 1, oceanic basalt is represented by the trend line with stars used to mark the data points and continental basalt is represented by the line with squares to mark the data points. The correct answer to this question can be determined by seeing at which REE those trend lines are at maximum distance apart. As the atomic number of the REE increases, the square and star points initially are very close together but slowly and then increasingly move apart. The difference in concentration of REE is greatest in Figure 1 for oceanic basalt and continental basalt at the REE with the highest atomic number. Of the answer choices given, cerium has the highest atomic number according to Figure 1. Lanthanum actually is shown to have the greatest difference in concentration but that is not an answer choice. This makes cerium, **A,** the correct answer.

The best answer is NOT:

B, **C,** and **D** because each of those REEs has a lesser difference in concentration than cerium between the two rocks.

206. **The best answer is H.** This question provides three specific relative concentration data points related to specific REEs. First identify which of the rock types shown in Figure 1 matches the concentration data points. Identify which symbol is represented at each of these given data points. A relative concentration value of 91 for lanthanum has a triangle symbol. In the Key to Figure 1, the triangle corresponds to granite. Europium with a concentration of 11 and ytterbium with a concentration of 10 both also match the relative concentration of REE for granite. This makes answer choice **H** correct.

The best answer is NOT:

F, G and **J** because none of the other rock types have the exact relative concentrations of REE's for the specific elements that match what is given in the question.

207. **The best answer is B.** Choice **B** is correct because Table 1 shows that for all rock types neodymium is present at a higher average concentration than samarium.

The best answer is NOT:

A because it states the opposite of the above indicating that samarium should have a greater concentration in each rock type. **C** and **D** because they state there is some level of variation in the average concentration of neodymium and samarium in relation to one another. That is inaccurate according to Table 1. Every rock type has a greater concentration of neodymium in comparison to samarium.

208. **The best answer is H.** Limestone is not mentioned in the passage. You should know that limestone is a common sedimentary rock. Figure 1 does not specifically discuss limestone, but it does provide a potential range of REE concentrations for sedimentary rock indicated by a broad gray line in Figure 1. Even if you didn't already know that limestone was a sedimentary rock you could use the process of elimination to solve this question. Eliminate every other rock shown in the key for Figure 1. None of them is limestone. The only possible data given in Figure 1 that could be useful for solving this problem is the sedimentary line graph. This line shows that the relative concentration of terbium, for sedimentary rock, would likely be between 15 and 20. This matches with answer choice **H** making it the correct answer.

The best answer is NOT:

F and **G** because the values they show are lower than the correct range for terbium. **J** because it is higher than the correct range for terbium.

209. **The best answer is A.** Figure 1 shows the relative concentration of different REE in relation to the atomic number. This question asks for the rock which shows the smallest range in relative concentration. This means it wants to know which of the rock types showed the smallest difference in concentrations among all of the relative concentrations. Since the graph has a non-uniform scale, it is important to find the ranges for each rock type listed and not rely only on visual cues. The X-scale increases dramatically as the concentration value increases. Specifically, it goes from 10 to 20 but then the next graduations are 20 to 50 then 50 to 100, etc. … This means that though a line might appear relatively straight, or having not much variation, it depends on the exact data points to determine the correct answer. Oceanic basalt has a range from approximately 8 to 19, or 11 percent.

The best answer is NOT:

B because continental basalt ranges from approximately 18 to 70, approximately 52 percent **C** because sodium granite ranges from approximately 3 to 250. **D** because sedimentary rocks range from approximately 12 to 130, which is also larger than oceanic basalt.

Passage XXXVII

210. **The best answer is F.** Scientist 2 states that large quantities of CO_2 continuously enter the atmosphere through long-term volcanic activity. This means the correct answer choice should show CO_2 being emitted from a volcano. This eliminates choices **G** and **J** as they both show CO_2 being absorbed by a volcano instead of emitted. Scientist 2 also states "Today, as in the past, much CO_2 is removed from the atmosphere as CO_2 becomes part of carbonates in rock and sediment on land." This indicates that the CO_2 produced by the volcanoes, as described earlier by Scientist 2, moves into the atmosphere and then eventually becomes a carbonate deposit in rock on land. Nowhere does Scientist 2 state that CO_2 accumulates in the ocean. This makes answer choice **F** correct as it shows CO_2 being emitted by a volcano, moving into the atmosphere, and then being deposited onto land.

The best answer is NOT:

H because it shows the CO_2 being deposited into the ocean, which does not match Scientist 2's statement. **G** and **J** because they show CO_2 being absorbed by the volcano which does not match Scientist 2's statement.

211. **The best answer is A.** Scientist 1 states that CH_4, methane, was abundant in the atmosphere 4 BYA. The passage states that it combined with molecular nitrogen gas to produce organic compounds that blocked much of the incoming UV radiation and kept NH_3 molecules intact. The question states that CH_4 is a greenhouse gas, so Scientist 1 would agree that a greenhouse gas helps to warm the earth's surface making choice **A** correct.

   The best answer is NOT:

   Choice **C** because Scientist 1 states that CH_4 likely helped keep NH_3 intact. Choice **D** because Scientist 1 states that CO_2 was removed by the ocean water and thus never accumulated in the atmosphere. Choice **B** because a greenhouse gas does not help to cool the surface. Both scientists agree that greenhouse gases increase temperatures.

212. **The best answer is H.** Scientist 2 states that the current concentration of CO_2 in Earth's atmosphere is 360 parts per million (PPM). The question states that it takes three times as much CO_2 in the atmosphere compared to NH_3 to trap equivalent amounts of heat. This means that if the current concentration of CO_2 in the atmosphere is 360 PPM, as described by Scientist 2, the equivalent amount of NH_3 concentration required to trap a similar amount of heat would be 1/3 that of 360 ppm. This equates to a concentration of 120 ppm NH_3 making answer choice **H** correct.

   The best answer is NOT:

   Choices **F** and **G** because they are too small and do not match the relationship between CO_2 and NH_3 as stated in the question. Choice **J** because it is not a 1-to-1 equivalent ratio of CO_2 to NH_3, so the value of 360 ppm is incorrect.

213. **The best answer is A.** The key statement in the question is that the sun was 30% dimmer 4 BYA than today. That means less heat energy was hitting the earth and warming it. Regardless of which gas it was, to maintain a temperature above freezing, more greenhouse gas—relative to the concentration today—would be required to hold the heat and maintain a temperature above freezing. This makes answer choice **A** correct.

   The best answer is NOT:

   B and **C** because if there were less greenhouse gas present in the atmosphere 4 BYA compared to today and the sun's output was 30% dimmer, the temperature of the earth's surface would have been below freezing. **D** because both Scientists 1 and 2 agree on the idea that greenhouse gases contributed to the warming of the Earth 4 BYA. This means both think there is some level of greenhouse gas concentration required to warm the Earth. If there were no greenhouse gases present 4 BYA, the Earth's surface temperature would not have been above freezing according to the initial information presented in the passage which states the earth's temperature would have been −15°C.

214.   **The best answer is F.** Scientist 1 states that CH_4 combined with molecular nitrogen to block UV radiation and keep NH_3 molecules present for much longer than 10 days. This indicates Scientist 1 thinks that CH_4 is a direct contributor to NH_3 being the most important greenhouse gas present in the atmosphere 4 BYA. Scientist 2 states that CH_4 did not exist in a large enough quantity 4 BYA to help preserve atmospheric NH_3, thus making NH_3 too short-lived to be an effective greenhouse gas. If volcanic activity was shown to produce large quantities of CH_4 4 BYA, it would directly support Scientist 1's statements and weaken Scientist 2's claims. Specifically, it would explain where the CH_4 came from to help preserve atmospheric NH_3. This makes choice **F** correct.

The best answer is NOT:

Choice **G** because the CH_4 helps to preserve NH_3 gas, but it is not responsible for it entering the atmosphere. Choices **H** and **J** because as they state the information strengthens Scientist 2's claims.

215.   **The best answer is B.** Incoming UV radiation comes from the sun's rays. For an organic compound to protect the greenhouse gas NH_3 from breaking down significantly it would have to have been located between NH_3 and the sun's rays. This means the organic compound would have been above or at the same elevation as the NH_3 in the earth's atmosphere. This makes answer choice **B** correct.

The best answer is NOT:

A because if the organic compound was below the NH_3 it would neither absorb the sun's rays nor protect the NH_3 in any way. **C** and **D** because if the organic compounds were located on the ocean floor or on land it would be impossible for them to protect NH_3 from the sun's rays.

216.   **The best answer is J.** Scientist 2 states in the first sentence that "Two carbon isotopes found in sedimentary rocks indicate a 75% higher concentration of CO_2 in Earth's atmosphere 4 BYA than the 360 parts per million (ppm) present today." This indicates the concentration of CO_2 4 BYA was greater than the current concentration of 360 PPM, specifically that it was 75% greater according to Scientist 2. In looking at the answer choices given, only one choice is greater than 360 PPM, making choice **J** correct.

The best answer is NOT:

F, G, and **H** as they are all at 360 PPM or below.

Passage XXXVIII

217. **The best answer is D.** To determine whether the water would mix when the barrier is removed, the density of the water at 10°C would be compared to the density of the water at 80°C. If the water at 80° is denser than the water at 10° it would remain at the bottom of the container and would not mix. However, if the 80° water is less dense, it would move upward causing the liquids to mix. To determine the density, examine the results of Experiments 1 and 2. Experiment 1 indicates that as the temperature of the water was heated, the density of the liquid decreased—the height of the water in the tubing increased in height as the temperature increased. Experiment 2 also confirms that as water decreased in temperature the density of the water increased until the temperature reached 4°C. This indicates that the 80° water is actually less dense than the 10° water and will rise to the surface. This makes choice **D** correct.

    The best answer is NOT:

    Choices **A** and **B** because mixing would occur. Choice **C** because though mixing would occur, the explanation of the lower water being denser is inaccurate.

218. **The best answer is F.** Experiment 1 indicates that boiling occurred at 100°C with no salt added to the water. Experiment 3 indicates that two solutions of salt water were observed and heated until boiling. Solution I contained a lesser concentration of salt and Solution II contained a greater salt concentration. Solution I boiled at 102° C and solution 2 boiled at 104°C. Both of these temperatures were higher than the 100° boiling point observed in Experiment 1. This indicates that less salt led to a lower boiling point in water with the lowest possible point being no salt added. This makes choice **F** correct, 0 g of salt added.

    The best answer is NOT:

    J because you need to remember that the question is asking about the lowest boiling temperature, not the highest. **G** and **H** because they both also involve adding salt to the water which would increase the temperature at which the water boils.

219. **The best answer is B.** The height of the water can be used to examine how the volume changed in relation to temperature. In Experiment 2, the flask was submerged in a cold bath of −6°C resulting in the temperature of the water inside the flask decreasing. As the temperature of the flask decreased, the height of the water in the column slowly dipped down indicating the volume was decreasing. At 4°C, this decrease stopped and the height of the water started to increase again as the temperature of the water continued to decrease. This makes answer choice **B** correct as it shows a decrease in volume along with temperature until 4°C at which point it shows that the volume increases as temperature continue to decrease.

    The best answer is NOT:

    Choice **A** because it shows the volume increasing until 4°C at which point the volume begins to decrease, which is the opposite of what is described. Choice **C** because it shows that volume directly increases as temperature increases. Choice **D** because it shows that volume increases as temperature decreases.

220. **The best answer is F.** The second portion of Experiment 3 submerged the flasks in a cold-water bath at a temperature of −6° as described in Experiment 2. Both solutions, 1 and 2, cooled until they reached −6°C with neither solution freezing. As it was designed, there was no way for Experiment 3 to show how much colder the water could have gotten. Both flasks reached the temperature of the surrounding water bath. The only way to provide more information about the effects of decreasing temperature on salt water would have been to use a water bath that is colder than the one described. That makes answer choice **F** correct as −13°C is colder than −6°C.

    The best answer is NOT:

    Choice **G** because −3°C is not colder than −6° and would provide no extra information. Choices **H** and **J** because the size of the flask and volume of the water used would not have an impact on the results of the experiment. The freezing point of water is an intensive property and does not depend on the amount of water present.

221. **The best answer is C.** Experiment 1 heated up distilled water until it began to squirt out the top of the flask at 100°C. Experiment 3 did the same thing to two saltwater solutions. Those solutions began squirting out of the tubing at temperatures of 102°C and 104°C. If those two solutions from Experiment 3 were mixed together and heated again until water squirted out the top of the tube, it would make sense that the boiling point, the temperature at which the liquid squirted out the top of the tube, should be somewhere between 102°C and 104°C. This makes answer choice **C** correct.

    The best answer is NOT:

    Choice **A** because saltwater boils at a temperature above 100°C. Choice **B** because the lowest boiling point possible for the mixture should be somewhere above 102°C based on the results of Experiment 3. Choice **D** because the highest boiling point possible for the mixture should be below 104°C based on the results of Experiment 3.

222. **The best answer is H.** Experiment 2 describes how, after the flask was submerged in a cold bath, the temperature of the water began to decrease, resulting in the height of the water in the tubing also decreasing. This decrease in tubing height indicated the volume of the water was being reduced and it indicated the density of the water was also being reduced. The mass of the water however, was not changed because the amount of water in the flask and tube did not change. Only the density and volume were being observed in Experiment 2. This makes choice **H** correct.

    The best answer is NOT:

    Answer choice **F** because although the volume was changing the density of the water was also changing. Choices **G** and **J** because the mass did not change at any point in time.

Passage XXXIX

223. **The best answer is B.** Scientist 2 states that the *Dimetrodon* sail absorbs heat from the side facing the sun but at the same time it also loses nearly as much from the side facing away from the sun. This supports choice **B** which says that there will be no increase in body temperature since the heat gained would be similar to the heat lost.

    The best answer is NOT:

    Choice **A** because there would not be enough heat gained to cause overheating. Choice **C** because it doesn't lead to an increase in the length of the sail spines. Choice **D** because the *Dimetrodons* regulated the blood supply to their sail to control the appearance of their skin.

224.   The best answer is H. Scientist 1 states that the *Dimetrodon's* body temperature was regulated by its sail. They specifically say that a model shows the body temperature of a reptile with a sail would increase in temperature three times as quickly as a reptile without a sail. If the *Dimetrodon* warms up quickly then it can be assumed that it would also cool off more quickly if the sail was exposed to colder temperatures, which supports choice **H.** Also, the comparison to elephants flapping their ears could be used to justify Choice **H.**

The best answer is NOT:

Choice **F** because it says it would warm the sail but also lower the body temperature. This is contradictory and also does not match what Scientist 1 says. Choice **G** is not contradictory but it still does not agree with what Scientist 1 says. Choice **J** because since it says it would remove heat, which is correct, but it then says that the body temperature would increase. The body temperature would not increase if heat was removed.

225.   The best answer is C. Scientist 2 states that male *Dimetrodons* control their appearance by regulating the supply of blood to their sail. Scientist 2 also states that modern lizards change their color or pattern to attract a mate, which is one of the reasons for the sail in Scientists 2's model. So, Choice **C** is correct for stating that it changes the sail's color or pattern.

The best answer is NOT:

Choice **A** because Scientist 2 does not state the blood supply has anything to do with the width of the spines. Choice **B** because the scientist does not say that the blood supply is used to reduce body temperature. Choice **D** because the blood supply does not raise or lower the sail specifically.

226.   The best answer is F. Choice **F** is correct because both scientists discuss modern-day animals and how they share characteristics in their statement on *Dimetrodons*. Specifically, Scientist 1 states "Today, elephants regulate their body temperature by flapping their large ears." and Scientist 2 states "Modern lizards change their skin color and pattern to attract a mate." Both of these statements support the idea that *Dimetrodons* share some similarities with modern animals.

The best answer is NOT:

Choice **G** because both scientists think that *Dimetrodons* share characteristics with modern animals. Choice **H** because there is no specific language anywhere in the passage stating what either scientist thinks in relation to the descendants of *Dimetrodons*. Choice **J** because again there is no specific language in either statement supporting the idea that modern animals look exactly like *Dimetrodons*.

227. **The best answer is A.** Scientist 1 states clearly that "A mathematical model shows that a reptile with a sail would reach the activity temperature 3 times faster than a reptile without a sail." This supports choice **A** as the correct answer. Specifically, if this reptile was the same size as a *Dimetrodon* but didn't have a sail it should heat up much slower and thus it would take longer to reach the activity temperature.

The best answer is NOT:

Choice **B** because without a sail the reptile would take longer to heat up, it wouldn't be quicker. Choice **C** because there is no way to determine that from what Scientist 1 says. Choice **D** because again there is no specific mention by Scientist 1 about how the presence of a sail would affect things preying upon *Dimetrodon*.

228. **The best answer is H.** Both scientists make statements specifically stating that *Dimetrodons* are able to control the flow of blood to their sails making choice H the correct answer. Scientist 1 states "Regulating the blood flow through these vessels during the heat of the day allowed the reptile to radiate heat away from its body and prevent overheating." Scientist 2 states "Similarly, *Dimetrodons* controlled the appearance of the skin on the sail by regulating the blood supply to the sail." This shows that both agree and makes choice **H** the correct answer.

The best answer is NOT:

Choice **F** and **G** because there is no mention of either of the things discussed in those choices. Choice **J** because, though the scientists discuss the regulation of temperature for the *Dimetrodon* they both do so regarding the sails present. There is no discussion of a *Dimetrodon* without a sail.

229. **The best answer is B.** Scientist 1 states that *Dimetrodon* needed to warm its body temperature to be able to hunt. To do this, Scientist 1 states that for *Dimetrodon* "this could be achieved most rapidly by turning the broad side of the sail toward the morning sun." The broad side of the sail means the longest part, which exposes the greatest area of the sail to the sun. So if *Dimetrodon* is turning its sail to face the sun to warm up then it would best orient itself to cool down, as asked in the question, with its sail having as little exposure as possible to the sun. Choice **B** shows *Dimetrodon* with the smallest cross-section of its sail facing the direction of the sun, meaning that its sail has the least exposure to the sun. This would minimize its heating the best.

The best answer is NOT:

A, because though it is close to that alignment, it still has some of the broadside of the sail exposed to the sun **C** and **D** have even more of the sail exposed, making them incorrect.

Passage XL

230. **The best answer is G.** In Table 1, you can see that as the temperature increases in each trial the reaction time, representing when the purple color disappears, decreases. There is not a single instance of the time increasing. This makes **G** correct since the time decreases with each temperature increase.

The best answer is NOT:

Choice **F** because the time does not remain the same. Choice **H** because since the time does not increase. Choice **J** because the temperature does not increase in any of the four trials; it decreases.

231. **The best answer is D.** In Table 2, you can observe that as the temperature is increased for each trial the reaction time decreases. If the reaction time of the new trial is only 6 sec, that is lower than any of the other trials. That should correlate, based on the data you see in the table, to a higher temperature than any of the trials since higher temperature equals lower reaction time based on what you can observe in Table 2. This means the temperature must be greater than 55° C, making choice **D** the correct answer.

The best answer is NOT:

A, B, and C since they all indicate temperatures lower than 55° C.

232. **The best answer is F.** The designs of Experiment 1 and 2 are similar but there is one very specific difference. Experiment 2 is conducted with a catalyst present, which is a substance that can speed up the rates of the reaction. It is stated that the catalyst used in Experiment 2 is $MnSO_4$. Experiment 1 has no mention of a catalyst or $MnSO_4$. This makes choice **F** correct.

The best answer is NOT:

G, H, and J since Experiment 2 states clearly "The procedure from Experiment 1 was repeated in every way except" for the addition of $MnSO_4$.

233. **The best answer is B.** This question is looking for the factor that was not investigated in the experiments. This makes **B** correct since there is no mention in any experiment about changing the solvent used during the reaction.

The best answer is NOT:

A because this was investigated in Experiment 2 where it states that a catalyst was added. **C** because this was investigated in Experiment 1 and Experiment 2 as they both specifically change the temperature of the reaction during the different trials. Choice **D** because this was investigated in Experiment 3 where it clearly states and shows in Table 3 how different concentrations of $H_2C_2O_4$ were used.

234. **The best answer is H.** In this question, a student mixes two solutions together, one at 40° C and one at 45°C, and measures the reaction time. This would result in a final temperature of the solution that is somewhere between 40° C and 45° C. To predict the time, you need to determine how this solution's temperature would fit in Table 1. Based on the data, it should fit somewhere between Trials 2 and 3. This means that the reaction time would have a range between 48 sec and 105 sec which makes answer choice **H** correct.

The best answer is NOT:

F, G, and **J** because they do not predict the correct reaction time.

235. **The best answer is D.** If the student repeated Trial 9 with extra water present in the solution this would lead to the concentration of the solution being lowered. Knowing that, you can look at Table 3 and see that as the concentration of the solution increases the reaction time decreases. This means that if you lower the concentration present in Trial 9 you should see a larger reaction time. Therefore, **D** is right: it says that the time would likely be greater than 837 seconds.

The best answer is NOT:

Choices **A** and **B** because as they are both well below the correct reaction time predication. Choice **C** because even though it mentions that time could be equal to 837 seconds, the concentration of the solution would be lower, which means the time would have to be at least a small amount greater than 837 seconds.

Passage XLI

236. **The best answer is J.** There is a lot going on with this question, since you have to look at two separate charts, so it is important to stay focused on what you are asked. This question effectively asks which of the answer choices' eggs have the largest volume. It states that large volume ova tend to contain more nutrients and it then asks which of the following ova would most likely contain the greatest amount of nutrients. The question asks which of the choices has the largest volume. If you know that the volume of a sphere is equal to $\frac{4}{3}\pi r^3$, then the ova with the largest diameter (double the radius) will also have the largest volume. If you do not know this mathematical formula, then you will need to use both Figure 2 and Table 2. Figure 2 displays a trend that as surface area increases the volume of a sphere increases greatly. So the greater the surface area the greater the volume. Table 2 shows the surface area of several eggs, the largest surface area of the answer choices is Hen, choice **J**.

     The best answer is NOT:

     F, G, and **H** because all of those options have a lower surface area as shown in Table 2. Background knowledge from both math and science may be used to answer questions more efficiently.

237. **The best answer is A.** This question asks you to compare the columns of edge length and S/V in Table 1. You can see a trend that as edge length increases the S/V ratio decreases. You must determine which of the edge lengths given will have the largest S/V ratio so based on the trend the largest S/V ratio should correspond to the smallest edge length given as an answer choice. This makes choice **A** the correct answer.

     The best answer is NOT:

     B, C, and **D** because they all have a greater edge length than 20 mm.

238. **The best answer is J.** S/V is a ratio comparing the surface area of something to the volume. This is done by dividing the surface area of an object by its volume to determine the S/V ratio. But you can simply determine which answer choice labels the units correctly. Choice **J** is correct since the units are properly matched to their measurements.

     The best answer is NOT:

     Choice **F** because the units for volume are mm^3. Choice **G** because the units for surface area are mm^2 not mm and the units for surface area are mm^2 not mm^3. Choice **H** since the units for surface area are mm^2 not mm and the units for volume are mm^3 not mm^2.

239. **The best answer is B.** You are told that a spherical object has a diameter of 6 mm. So the object should fit exactly between the objects with a 4 mm diameter and an 8 mm diameter. You can estimate that the S/V ratio of this object, observing the downward trend as diameter increases, should be around 1 mm^{-1}. This makes answer choice **B** correct.

The best answer is NOT:

A, C, and **D** because they give values that do not follow the trend of decreasing S/V ratio and are incorrect.

240. **The best answer is H.** An edge length of 0.5 mm is not given in Table 1, but you can make a prediction of the S/V ratio based on the trend you see in the table. As the edge length increases, the S/V ratio decreases by exactly half each time in cube-shaped objects. If you reverse this trend that means that as edge length decreases, the S/V ratio should increase by exactly double each time. This means that if you decrease the edge length from 1 to 0.5 mm, the S/V ratio should double from 6 to 12 mm^{-1}. This makes answer choice **H** correct.

The best answer is NOT:

F and **G** as they do not match the trend shown for edge length and S/V. **J** since it shows too large of an increase in the S/V ratio.

Passage XLII

241. **The best answer is D.** Figure 1 in Experiment 2 shows that as the % $C_2H_6O_2$ (by mass) in H_2O increases the boiling point of the solution gradually shows an increase as well. For this question, you must predict what the boiling point of the solution would be if the % $C_2H_6O_2$ by mass in the solution was increased to 80%. The highest values shown on Figure 1 are 60% and 100% though, so this will require you to extrapolate and determine the likely boiling point of the 80% solution. The 60% solution appears to have a boiling point around 113°C and the 100% solution appears to have a boiling point around 198°C. From the trend shown on the graph it appears that an 80% solution should fall somewhere in between that range. Only **D** gives the correct option of the boiling point being greater than 115°.

The best answer is NOT:

A, B, and **C** because all state the boiling point would be at most 115°C which does not match the trend.

242.   **The best answer is J.** The first thing to notice is how the answer choices are given to you as % $C_2H_6O_2$ instead of grams $C_2H_6O_2$ as Table 1 shows. You can informally do some quick percentage calculations to determine which answer choices match the ones shown in Table 1. For example, each of the sample solutions has a total mass of 100. So if you have a mass of 20 g $C_2H_6O_2$, you can divide 20/100 × 100 to determine the percentage of $C_2H_6O_2$ in solution. In this case, the grams given for each solution match the % $C_2H_6O_2$ of each solution. The lowest temperature where the student lives was −31°C. For an antifreeze to not freeze in that location would require a freezing point below −31°C. Table 1 shows there were two possible solutions that contained enough $C_2H_6O_2$ to depress the freezing point below −31°C, 50 g and 60 g. This corresponds to either 50% or 60%. The highest % given in the answer choices is **J**, 50%, which is the correct answer.

The best answer is NOT:

F, G, and **H** because they all would result in a solution that would freeze.

243.   **The best answer is D.** Experiment 1 states: "The students found that as the concentration of $C_2H_6O_2$ increased the density of the solution increased." So, as more $C_2H_6O_2$ was added to the solution the density of that solution also increased. Based on that statement, and with volume constant at 10.00 mL as described in the problem, this shows that as the % $C_2H_6O_2$ increases, the mass of the solution should also increase. This can be determined by examining the density formula given to you in Experiment 1. If the volume of the solution does not change but the density increases, then the mass also must increase, according to the density formula. So **D** is the correct answer choice as it has the highest % of $C_2H_6O_2$ present.

The best answer is NOT:

A, B, and **C** because they have lower % $C_2H_6O_2$ and will result in a lower mass of the 10 mL solution.

244.   **The best answer is G.** Experiment 3 states that ice crystals are observed when the temperature of the bath reaches the freezing point of the mixture. Choice **G** is correct because it states that if no crystals are observed, the low-temperature bath's temperature must have been higher than the mixture's freezing point.

The best answer is NOT:

Choice **F** because if the temperature of the low-temperature bath was the same as the freezing point, crystals would have been observed. Choice **H** because if the bath had a lower temperature than the freezing point of the mixture crystals would have been observed. Choice **J** because there is no evidence given that the mixture will not freeze at any temperature measured.

245. **The best answer is A.** Experiment 2 shows that as more antifreeze is added to H_2O the boiling point of that mixture increases. A mixture of water and antifreeze always has a higher boiling point than pure H_2O, making **A** the correct answer.

The best answer is NOT:

Choice **B** because a mixture of antifreeze and water will always have a higher boiling point, not a lower boiling point. Choices **C** and **D** because they are discussing freezing points which are not mentioned by the question or Experiment 2 and have no bearing on why an antifreeze mixture is useful in hot weather.

246. **The best answer is G.** Experiment 2 shows that as you dissolve more $C_2H_6O_2$ into water, the boiling point of that solution increases. The initial introduction to this passage also states that students "knew that when a substance is dissolved in H_2O, the boiling points are elevated and the freezing points are lowered relative to H_2O." Based on the data from Experiment 2 and the passage, you can conclude that the more of a substance you have dissolved in water, the higher the boiling point will be for that resulting solution. **G** is correct because distilled water is pure H_2O. It has no dissolved solutes in it and thus would have the lowest boiling point of the choices given.

The best answer is NOT:

F because lake water has some dissolved solutes in it. You do not know exactly how much, but it has some solutes dissolved in it because lake water is not purely H_2O. Choice **H** because salt water has a large amount of salt dissolved in it and thus is not purely H_2O. **J** because tap water also has some dissolved solutes in it and is not purely H_2O.

Passage XLIII

247. **The best answer is B.** If the goal of a new experiment is to test if the rate of heat conduction depends on the type of wire material used, then all things in the experiment must be the same except for the type of wire material used. This makes **B** correct since it means all the wires need to be the same size to best make a determination as to how well they can transmit heat.

The best answer is NOT:

Choice **A** because though it describes how different wire materials would be used, it says that the size of these new wires would differ from the copper used in the initial experiments. The results of Experiments 1 and 2 both show that using copper wires of different sizes affects the efficiency of the heat conduction. See the example in Table 1 where a 10 cm length of wire compared to a 20 cm length of wire results in differing temperatures at all measurement times. Choices **C** and **D** because as they only discuss copper wire and make no mention of using different types of wire material.

248. **The best answer is H.** Thermal equilibrium is a point at which all heat transfer has stopped between two objects and they are the same temperature. To answer this question, you need to determine which trial in Table 1 or Table 2 results in the final temperature, at three minutes, being the same for Blocks A and B. **H** is the correct answer because after three minutes using a wire with a 1.4 mm diameter, the temperature of Block A and Block B is 40°C. Since they are at the same temperature, they are in thermal equilibrium.

   The best answer is NOT:

   Choices **F, G,** and **J** because after three minutes none of those trials resulted in Blocks A and B having the same temperature, so they never reached thermal equilibrium.

249. **The best answer is C.** Experiments 1 and 2 show that as you increase the length of the wire the temperature of Block A increases. This can be observed in both Tables 1 and 2. For example, in Table 2 with a 10 cm wire the temperature of Block A after 1 minute is 61 °C, with a 20 cm wire the temperature of Block A after 1 minute is 79 °C, and with a 30 cm wire the temperature of Block A after 1 minute is 85 °C. This trend can be observed at the 2- and 3-minute time measurements in Table 2 and all the time measurements in Table 1 as well. So, as wire length increases the temperature of Block A also increases. Choice **C** is correct because it shows temperature increasing as wire length is increased.

   The best answer is NOT:

   Choice **A** because shows temperature decreasing and then remaining constant based on the length of wire. Choice **B** because it shows temperature remaining constant regardless of wire length. Choice **D** because it shows that wire length was not varied at all which is not true for either experiment.

250. **The best answer is F.** If brass was used in place of copper for these experiments, it would result in less heat being transferred out of Block A due to brass' lower thermal conductivity as described in the question. If less heat is transferred out of Block A, then Block A will cool more slowly and retain a higher temperature with brass than with copper. This makes choice **F** the correct answer.

   The best answer is NOT:

   Choice **G** because brass and copper have different thermal conductivity values so Block A would not transfer heat at the same rate with both materials. Choice **H** because brass and copper have different thermal conductivity values so Block B would not gain heat at the same rate. Choice **J** because if brass was used, the heat transfer to Block B would slow down instead of speed up, due to brass' lower thermal conductivity compared to copper.

251. **The best answer is A.** These experiments measure how well heat can be transferred from Block A to Block B using a wire to connect them. However nowhere in the experiments does it say that Block A and B are perfectly insulated and that heat can go nowhere except from Block A to Block B. Heat is being lost from Block A to its surroundings. Blocks A and B are put on an insulated surface but they are not covered, so they are exposed to the air. This results in Block A losing some of its initial heat to the air before it can be fully transferred to Block B making choice **A** the correct answer.

 The best answer is NOT:

 Choice **B** because the copper wire is not losing heat, it is helping to transfer the heat from A to B. Choice **C** because Block B is colder than Block A and the flow of heat is moving from A to B. Block B is not losing heat back to the wire or Block A. Choice **D** because if the air lost heat to Block B, that would contribute to Block B absorbing more heat energy than Block A lost, which is the opposite of what the question states. The air temperature is not discussed in these experiments.

252. **The best answer is G.** Both experiments show the results of 3 minutes of heat transfer. This question requires you to predict the values at 4 minutes of heat transfer. A wire with a 1 mm diameter and length of 20 cm after 3 minutes results in a Block A temperature of 72°C and a Block B temperature of 19° C. If you follow the decreasing trend in Block A and the increasing trend in Block B you end up at 64°C in Block A and 23°C in Block B, making **G** the correct answer.

 The best answer is NOT:

 Choice **F** because at 10 cm of length and 1 mm diameter, the temperature of Block A after 3 minutes is already at 54 °C which is below 64°C and the temperature of block B is already at 31°C which is above 23°C. Choice **H** because a 1.4 mm diameter wire that is 10 cm long results in the temperature of Block B after 3 minutes being 35°C which is above 23°C. Choice **J** because a 1.4 mm diameter wire that is 20 cm long results in the temperature of Block A after 3 minutes being 53°C which is above 64°C and the temperature of block B is already at 35°C which is above 23°C.

Passage XLIV

253. **The best answer is C.** In the initial passage description, there is a statement describing how cloud layers form. It states: "When air cools to its dew point, the water vapor in the air can begin to condense and form clouds." This supports answer choice **C** as the correct answer. The question states there are cloud layers above and below 1,200 m but nothing specifically at the 1,200 m level at which the pilot is currently flying. This means the air temperature at 1,200 m must be higher than the dew point since there are no clouds.

The best answer is NOT:

Choice **A** because it says a cloud layer extends from 600 m upward, which contradicts the information in the question. Choice **B** because if the lower cloud layer was at 1,202 m, the pilot would be flying through clouds at 1,200 m. Choice **D** because it impossible to know if that is correct. Knowing the dew point alone does not indicate the temperature or altitude of the other cloud layers.

254. **The best answer is H.** Figures 1–4 show several measurements: the air temperature, the dew point, and the average cloud base altitude for each city. The only measurement a ceilometer takes is the average altitude of the cloud base for each city. As the question states, a ceilometer bounces light off the base of a cloud layer to measure the height of that cloud layer.

The best answer is NOT:

Choice **F** because a ceilometer does not measure air temperature. Choice **G** because a ceilometer does not measure dew point. Choice **J** because a ceilometer does not measure the thickness of a layer of clouds.

255.   **The best answer is B.** This question asks you to predict what the air temperature and dew point would be in Figure 3, City C, at 3,600 m. The graph only shows up to 3,000 m, so you need to predict (based on the air temperature and dew point trends you see in the other figures) what the most likely values for City C will be beyond 3,000 m. You can see in each of the other Figures A, B, and D that after the dew point and temperature lines intersect the dew point and air temperature stay the same for at least 600 m. Figures 1 and 4 show the same dew point and temperature for three measurements after intersection and Figure 2 shows they stay the same for at least one measurement after intersection. If 3,000 m is the intersection point, it is fair to predict that the dew point and temperature will be the same for the following measurement based on the other results. This makes choice **B** correct.

The best answer is NOT:

Choices **A** and **C** because the dew point and air temperature are not the same. **D** because even though the air temperature and dew point are the same they do not follow the decreasing trend shown in every figure including the temperature trend in Figure 3. 45°F is greater than the 43°F temperature shown at 3,000 m.

256.   **The best answer is J.** This question asks you to determine which city, Miami or Phoenix, will have the lowest average cloud base. You are provided with the average air temperature and the average dew point, so you can draw some comparison from the figures shown in the passage. Figure 3 has the largest difference in initial dew point and temperature and thus the average cloud base altitude is the highest of all the figures at 3,000 m. Figure 4 has the smallest different between initial air temperature and dew point and thus has the lowest average cloud-base altitude at 600 m. Figures 1 and 2 also show this trend by showing that the larger the initial separation of dew point and air temperature, the higher the average cloud base altitude will be. The difference between air temperature and dew point for Miami is 15. The difference between air temperature and dew point for Phoenix is 59. Miami has a much smaller difference between air temperature and dew point so it will have a lower cloud base.

The best answer is NOT:

Choices **F** and **G** because Phoenix is not the correct city. It has a larger difference between air temperature and dew point than Miami. Choice **H** because the reasoning it gives is not sufficient. Miami having a lower air temperature than Phoenix does not by itself correlate with having a lower average cloud base. The correct statement needs to account for the relationship between dew point and air temperature.

257. **The best answer is A.** The key piece of information provided in this question is that at 8 A.M., at 0 m of altitude the dew point and air temperature measured were both 40°F. When the dew point and air temperature are the same, clouds form. This can be observed in each figure shown in the passage. This means that clouds will form at 0 m of altitude in the example city. This makes answer choice **A** correct.

   The best answer is NOT:

   Choices **B, C,** and **D** because they all give higher altitudes. There is no way to say for sure that clouds would be present based on the data presented in the question. The only thing you can be certain of is that there will be clouds at 0 m based on the data given.

Passage XLV

258. **The best answer is G.** To answer this question, you must look at the slope of the trend line shown in Figure 1. The greatest change within a pressure range will have the steepest slope, or in simpler terms: It will be the range where the line is closest to vertical (straight up and down). The range given in choice **G,** 20 mm Hg to 30 mm Hg, is the correct answer. From 20 to 30 mm Hg the line has the sharpest upward slope.

   The best answer is NOT:

   F, 0 mm Hg to 10 mm Hg, because it has a sharp upward slope but it is not as great as choice **G. H,** 40 mm Hg to 50 mm Hg, because it has an upward slope as well but the curve is starting to level off there, so less change is evident **J,** 60 mm Hg to 70 mm Hg, because it shows the line starting to level off, so the slope is far lower than in any of the other choices.

259. **The best answer is A.** The amount of oxygen bound to Hb is measured on the Y axes of Figures 2 and 3 where it shows the percent saturation of Hb. The conditions showing the greatest amount of oxygen bound to Hb will be the ones resulting in the highest value on the y-axis at 40 mm Hg as measured on the x-axis. Choice **A** is correct because the pH with the highest level of saturation at 40 mm Hg is 7.6 and the temperature with the highest level of saturation is 10°C.

   The best answer is NOT:

   Choice **B** because a pH of 7.2 does not correspond to the highest level of oxygen saturation. Choice **C** because a temperature of 43°C corresponds to the lowest level of oxygen saturation instead of the highest. Choice **D** because a temperature of 43°C and pH of 7.2 both correspond to the lowest level of saturation rather than the highest.

260. **The best answer is J.** In Figure 3, higher temperatures lead to a lower percent saturation of Hb. You can see this when you compare the four trend lines on the graph. 43°C shows the lowest percent saturation of Hb at all pressures and 10°C shows the highest percent saturation at all pressures. This supports the scientist's claim that the ability of Hb to bind with O_2 at a given pressure decreases as temperature increases. This makes choice **J** the best answer.

The best answer is NOT:

Choices **F** and **G** because as temperature increases the ability of Hb to bind with O_2 decreases. Choice **H** because its reasoning is the percent saturation of Hb does not increase as temperature increases.

261. **The best answer is D.** Figure 1 shows the relationship between O_2 saturation of Hb and partial pressures of O_2. There is no mention of pH or temperature so it is assumed that those must be held constant. Figure 2 compares different pH levels regarding partial pressure of O_2 and the percent saturation of Hb. There is no mention of temperature in Figure 2 so it can be assumed that it is held constant. Figure 3 compares different temperature levels regarding partial pressure of O_2 and the percent saturation of Hb. It can be assumed that pH is held constant in all trials shown for Figure 3. That makes choice **D** correct.

The best answer is NOT:

Choice **A** because Figure 1 holds pH and temp constant, and Figure 3 holds only pH constant. Choice **B** because Figure 1 holds pH and temp constant, Figure 2 only holds temp constant, and Figure 3 holds pH constant. Choice **C** because Figure 2 holds temp constant and Figure 3 holds pH constant.

262. **The best answer is F.** Figure 2 shows that higher blood pH leads to a higher value of O_2 saturation of Hb at all partial pressure levels. A lower pH corresponds to a higher concentration of acid being present. The figure also shows that a high level of PCO_2 results in a lower percent saturation of Hb. A low level of PCO_2 results in a higher percent saturation of Hb at all partial pressures. Since low pH levels correspond to an acid being present it follows that increasing the amount of CO_2 present results in more acid being formed. This leads to the lower pH level and the lower percent saturation of Hb that is shown in Figure 2. Therefore, **F** is the correct answer.

The best answer is NOT:

Choice **G** because if CO_2 was absorbing acid it would actually raise the pH level. Choice **H** because if CO_2 broke down to form O_2 you would see a high PCO_2 resulting in a higher percent saturation of Hb, which is not present in Figure 2. This would have no impact on the pH of blood. Choice **J** because CO_2 reacting with O_2 to form Hb would have no impact on the pH of blood. pH is impacted by the addition or subtraction of acids or bases to a solution. Students may know that non-metal oxides, like CO_2, dissolve in water to form acids, like H_2CO_3.

Passage XLVI

263. **The best answer is D.** The RTR graphed in Figure 2 vs time is the rate of transcription this question is asking about. Figure 2 shows the RTR of four genes so be sure to specifically look at Gene 2's plotted line based on the key shown above the graph. The figure shows a slow then faster increase in RTR as time progresses. Compare the specific RTR values at each of the given time points and determine which is highest. Choice **D**, 6 hr, has the highest RTR value around 1.75 making it the correct answer.

The best answer is NOT:

Choices **A, B,** and **C** because the values at 0.2. and 4 hours are all less than 1.8, which is the approximate value at 6 hours.

264. **The best answer is G.** The transcription rate of Gene 2 at time 0 hr is 1. This question asks at which of the given times was the transcription rate of Gene 2 double that value, or 2. Choice **G** is correct because the transcription rate was almost exactly 2 at 7 hr.

The best answer is NOT:

Choice **F** because the transcription rate at 5 hrs was 1.5. Choice **H** because the transcription rate at 9 hrs was 4. **J** because the transcription rate at 10 hr was 5.

265. **The best answer is D.** Figure 1 depicts the general steps of protein synthesis in eukaryotic cells. Step 3 in Figure 1 indicates that translation is taking place as the mRNA is processed into a protein. The answer choices are all different cellular organelles. Translation specifically occurs in the ribosome, making answer choice **D** the correct answer.

The best answer is NOT:

Choice **A** because the cell membrane does not serve a purpose in translation and instead acts as a barrier between the inside of the cell and the outside of the cell. Choice **B** because photosynthesis, not translation, takes place in chloroplasts. Lysosomes contain digestive enzymes that are used to break down excess, worn out cell parts or other non-organelle cellular waste and also sometimes to fight off cell-invading pathogens. They do not play a role in protein synthesis.

266. **The best answer is H.** In Figure 1, the gene contains both introns and exons. It then proceeds through the process of transcription, Step 1. After this process the primary transcript also contains introns and exons. After the primary transcript is processed in Step 2, all introns have been removed and only exons are left in the mRNA. This means that during Step 3, translation, introns are not included, since they have been removed during the previous processing phase. This makes choice **H** correct, as it states introns go through translation but not transcription.

The best answer is NOT:

Choice **F** because introns are transcribed but they are not translated as it says. Choice **G** because introns are not translated, nor is translation first in the process either. Choice **J** because introns are not translated first, they are transcribed. They are removed during processing and are not translated at all.

267. **The best answer is B.** Both Figures 2 and 3 need to be used to solve this problem. First, look at Figure 3 to determine what time showed a glucose concentration of 12 g/L as described in the problem. Figure 3 shows that a glucose concentration of 12 g/L can be found between 6 and 7 hrs. Then refer to Figure 2, specifically looking at Gene 4. Between 6 and 7 hrs on Figure 2 Gene 4 shows an RTR of 0.5. This makes choice **B** the correct answer.

The best answer is NOT:

A, C, and **D** because they list incorrect RTR values for Gene 4.

Passage XLVII

268. **The best answer is J.** Figure 2 shows the location of the mass in relation to Point R. The passage clearly states that a sensor plots the distance of the mass from Point R over time. This is the key phrase you need to understand Figure 2. Specifically, as the position increases on the y-axis the distance from Point R is increasing. The question asks you to identify when the mass was at Point R, which would occur when the distance from Point R is 0. On the graph, you observe the oscillation of the mass to see that it returns to 0 distance from Point R at t_2 and at t_4. This makes **J** the correct answer.

     The best answer is NOT:

     F because t_1 has a non-zero distance from Point R. **G** because t_1 and t_3 both show the mass being at maximum distance from Point R instead of at 0 distance from point R. **H** because t_3 is at maximum distance from Point R instead of 0.

269. **The best answer is C.** This question asks you to plot a relationship between mass and D as shown in trials 7–9 which can be found in Study 3. Numbers are not given on any of the answer choices besides the origin of the graph at 0,0 so instead of plotting the exact data, you need to identify the relationship between mass changes and D values. In Trial 7, mass was 0.5 kg and the D value was 0.016 m. Both of those values increased in Trial 8 with mass 1.00 kg and D 0.033 m. In Trial 9 these values both increased again, with mass 1.5 kg and D 0.049 m. This indicates that on the graph you should see a trend line showing both mass and D increasing. Choice **C** shows this increase and is the correct answer. Alternatively, you could simply look for the trend. The mass increased each time from Trials 7 through 9. The D value also increased from Trials 7 to 9. When both variables increase, the graph should have a positive slope which is only true of the graph in choice **C**.

     The best answer is NOT:

     Choice **A** because it shows an inverse relationship with D decreasing as mass increases. Choice **B** because it shows mass increasing while distance remains constant. Choice **D** because it shows distance increasing but the mass remaining constant.

270.   **The best answer is choice G.** Examine Table 1 and determine the relationship between mass and P. Mass increased from 0.5 kg in Trial 1, to 1.0 kg in Trial 2, and finally 1.50 kg in Trial 3. Based on this evidence, mass was increased from Trial 1 to Trial 3. P increased from 0.444 sec in Trial 1, to 0.628 sec in Trial 2, and finally to 0.767 sec in Trial 3. Based on this evidence, P increased from Trial 1 to Trial 3 as mass was increased. If another mass of 0.75 kg was used for an extra trial this mass value would fall between the values used in Trial 1 and Trial 2. Combining this knowledge with the fact that P increased in Study 1 as mass increased means the P value result should fall somewhere between the P values given for Trial 1 and 2 as well. Choice G is correct because it falls between the results of Trial 1 and 2.

The best answer is NOT:

H and **J** because the possible P values given are too high and above the possible range it could be. Choice **F** because it indicates P would be less than the result in Trial 1.

271.   **The best answer is A.** The initial value of L in any given experiment was the length of the spring before any mass is added. Once a mass was added the spring extends some distance towards the ground. When the spring stabilized, this new, longer distance is y. The y value will always be greater than the initial L value with a mass attached to the spring because the spring has the mass pulling it down and extending it. D is the difference in length between L and y. If D is 0, that would mean that L and y were the same length. You could assume that there is no mass on the spring also but that is outside what the question asks. Answer choice **A** is correct because it indicates that $y = L$ if D is 0.

The best answer is NOT:

Choice **B** because it indicates that y would be double the value of L, producing a positive value. Choice **C** because it indicates that y would be half of the L value, which would result in a negative value for D. Choice **D** because it indicates that y would be 1/4 the value of L which would also produce a negative value for D.

272. **The best answer is H.** The passage indicates the mass in each trial was pulled down to Point R, where it was then released. Figure 2 shows the distance of the mass from Point R over time. When the mass was released (t = 0), it moves quickly up and away from Point R, stops at t_1, and then returns to Point R at t_2. This indicates that the upward force of the spring was greater than the downward force of gravity pulling on it. This makes answer choice **H** correct.

The best answer is NOT:

Choice **F** because the force of gravity would make the mass move downwards, not upwards if it was stronger. Choice **G** because the mass did not move downward upon being released so gravity is not the stronger force. Choice **J** because the spring moved upward, not downward.

273. **The best answer is A.** k is a measure of the spring constant (stiffness) found in each spring. Study 1 examined a spring with k = 100 N/m. A mass of 1.5 kg (Trial 3) results in a D of 0.146 m. Study 2 examined a spring with k = 200 N/m. A mass of 1.5 kg (Trial 6) resulted in a D of 0.073 m. This is a smaller result. Study 3 examined a spring with k = 300 N/m. A mass of 1.5 kg (Trial 9) resulted in a D of 0.049 m. This is an even smaller result. Examine this trend and you can see that with a mass of 1.5 kg, as the k value increases, the D value decreases. If a spring with a k value of 400 N/m was used in another trial as speculated in the question, you would expect the D value, using a mass of 1.5 kg, to be even smaller than 0.049 as shown in Study 3. This makes answer choice **A** correct.

The best answer is NOT:

Choices **B, C,** and **D** because they all indicate a D value greater than 0.049, which is incorrect.

Passage XLVIII

274. **The best answer is F.** Scientist 1 states that aging is caused by the shortening of telomeres. This shortening occurs every time a cell divides. The more divisions a cell has undergone, the shorter the telomeres get. Eventually, the telomere is too short to facilitate the process of reproduction correctly, which results in aging. Scientist 3 states that aging is due to mutations inherited from parents. Scientist 3 says each human has mutations present at birth and that these mutations eventually are passed on to their eventual offspring as well. There is no mention of cellular division in Scientist 3's statement. Scientist 3 states telomeres do not play a role in aging because they shorten too slowly. This makes choice **F** correct because it agrees with Scientist 1 and it correctly indicates the aging takes place due to telomere shortening after cellular division.

The best answer is NOT:

Choice **G** because it says telomeres get longer after each division, which is incorrect. Choices **H** and **J** because they both indicate Scientist 3 thinks cell division contributes to aging, which is not true.

275. **The best answer is C.** Scientist 2 states that the mutations which cause aging accumulate throughout a person's life due to random DNA damage that occurs over time. They state this happens in non-reproductive cells which indicates they do not think that mutations are inherited or passed on in any way. Scientist 3 states that aging takes place due to mutations inherited from parents which are present at birth and not developed over time. This makes choice **C** correct as it best summarizes those two conflicting views.

The best answer is NOT:

Choice **A** because Scientist 2 states that telomere shortening is too slow to play a role in aging. Choice **B** because Scientist 3 states that telomere shortening is too slow to play a role in aging. Choice **D** because Scientist 2 and Scientist 3's opinions are flipped. Scientist 2 thinks mutations happen over a life span and Scientist 3 thinks they are present at birth.

276. **The best answer is F.** Scientist 1 states that aging occurs as telomeres shorten over the course of time and that this shortening is caused by repeated cellular division—as a person gets older, the telomeres should be shorter. Choice **F** is correct. It states telomere length is found to be the same in both young and old cells, which would weaken and invalidate Scientist 1's claim about telomere shortening. If telomere length was the same in old and young cells, then they clearly do not shorten over time and thus could not be the cause of aging as Scientist 1 states.

The best answer is NOT:

Choice **G** because it would support and strengthen Scientist 1's claim that telomeres shorten as aging takes place. Choices **H** and **J** because Scientist 1's model has nothing to do with free oxygen radicals and thus neither choice has any impact one way or the other on Scientist 1's model. **H** and **J** are instead related to Scientist 2's explanation.

277. **The best answer is A.** All three scientists have different views on the specific cause of aging. However, they all clearly state in their models that telomeres shorten as humans age. Scientist 1 states this shortening is the cause of aging. Scientists 2 and 3 agree that the shortening occurs but they believe the shortening occurs too slowly to impact aging. This makes choice **A** correct.

The best answer is NOT:

Choice **B** because none of the three models states that telomeres remain the same length. Choice **C** because all three models state that telomeres get shorter as aging takes place. Choice **D** because only Scientist 1 states that telomere length is responsible for aging. Scientists 2 and 3 do not agree with that conclusion.

278. **The best answer is J.** Scientist 3's model states that mutations that cause aging are inherited from parents and present at birth. This indicates that any mutations which would cause aging should exist in young cells and old cells alike—that there is no difference in the mutations present in young and old organisms. This makes choice **J** correct.

The best answer is NOT:

Choice **F** because Scientist 3 does not state that mutations are caused by telomere shortening. They state telomere shortening does not play a role in aging. Choice **G** because there is no mention of metabolic products in Scientist 3's model. Choice **H** because it contradicts Scientist 3's model. If mutations were present in only old cells but not new cells, the mutations would not be inherited and present at birth as Scientist 3 states.

279. **The best answer is B.** Scientist 2's model suggests that mutations develop as people age. The mutations that develop as a person gets older are what lead to aging. Choice **B** is correct, because if there were fewer mutations in young cells compared to older cells this would support the model that mutations accumulate over time.

The best answer is NOT:

Choice **A** because it contradicts the model that mutations develop over time. If choice **A** were true, then it would invalidate Scientist 2's model completely. Choice **C** because Scientist 2 states that free oxygen radicals are the major cause of the DNA damage that occurs leading to the mutations that lead to aging. If it were true that free oxygen radicals do not damage DNA, then their model would be weakened. Choice **D** because Scientist 2's model clearly states that telomere shortening takes place too slowly to impact aging. If this were true, it would weaken Scientist 2's model.

280. **The best answer is J.** Scientist 2 states that aging takes place over time due to mutations that occur from damage to DNA. Scientist 2's model argues this damage takes place due to free oxygen radicals formed during metabolic processes. Choice **J** is correct because it states that decreasing the rate of metabolism and decreasing the production of free oxygen radicals would lead to a slowing of the aging process. The presented scenario of reducing calories and hence metabolism matches Scientist 2's model exactly.

The best answer is NOT:

Choice **F** because increasing the rate of metabolism would lead to more free oxygen radicals. This would lead to more DNA damage and more mutations quickening the aging process. Choice **G** because increasing the rate of metabolism would increase free radical production, not decrease it. In any case, though, it would still speed the aging process making it incorrect. Choice **H** because lowering the rate of metabolism would slow aging if it also decreased the production of free radicals. However, Choice **H** states that this increases the production rate of free radicals, making it incorrect.

Passage XLIX

281. **The best answer is C.** Figure 2 shows a graph of discharge over time relative to a rainfall event for three different rivers. This question specifically asks about the Jones River, so make sure you are looking at the correct line according to the labels. You need to identify the maximum discharge present on the graph for the Jones River after a rainfall event. Find the highest point shown in Figure 2 for the Jones River. This point occurs on day 5 approximately midway between the 1,000 and 2,000 m^3/sec levels on the graph. This would indicate the correct answer is 1,500 m^3/sec making choice **C** correct.

   The best answer is NOT:

   Choices **A, B,** and **D** because none of them have the maximum discharge amount for the Jones River after a rainfall event as shown on Figure 2.

282. **The best answer is H.** This question refers you to Study 1 to compare the Jones River and Calm River discharges. However, the paragraphs discussing Study 1 do not contain the required information. They direct you to the results of the study as displayed in Figure 2. Once you see Figure 2, you find which answer choice best matches the point on the graph where the Jones River and Calm River lines intersect. In Figure 2 you can see that the lines intersect around 3.5 days and 4.25 days after the rainfall event. Choice **H** is correct because 3.5 days matches one of those intersections exactly.

   The best answer is NOT:

   Choices **F, G,** and **J** because none of them represent when the two discharges were closest in value.

283. **The best answer is A.** The key word in this question is *tributary* which is defined as a smaller stream flowing into a larger stream. Based on this information, the tributary must be smaller than the North River. So the key point is that the drainage basin of the tributary is smaller than the drainage basin of the North River. Based on Figure 1, the drainage basin of the North River is 1,710 km^2. The tributary drainage basin should be smaller than 1,710 km^2. This makes answer choice **A** correct.

   The best answer is NOT:

   Choices **B, C,** and **D** because all indicate drainage basin sizes that are greater than the size of the North River drainage basin.

284. **The best answer is J.** You need to use Figures 2 and 3 to determine this answer. Figure 2 shows the maximum discharge that occurred in each river after a rainfall event. Figure 3 shows the maximum normalized discharge that occurred in the same three rivers over the same time span. The student in the question predicted that both figures should show the same river having the highest peak. This prediction is not correct. Figure 2 shows the Calm River had the greatest maximum discharge. Figure 3 shows the North River had the greatest normalized discharge. This makes answer Choice **J** correct.

The best answer is NOT:

Choices **F** and **G** because the student's prediction is incorrect, so the statement must begin with No. Choice **H** because in the reasoning given supporting the answer of No, the two rivers are reversed. The Calm River had the greatest maximum discharge, and the North River had the greatest maximum normalized discharge.

285. **The best answer is B.** The formula for calculating the normalized discharge of a river, shown in Study 2, is relatively straightforward. It involves dividing the river discharge, in m^3/sec, by the river drainage basin area in km^2. The Calm River has a drainage basin area of 28,400 km^2. At day 5 after a rainfall event Figure 2 shows the discharge of the Calm River was 3,000 m^3/sec. This makes answer choice **B** correct.

The best answer is NOT:

Answer choice **A** because the units used for the discharge and basin area are switched. It should be 3,000 m^3/sec and 28,400 km^2. Answer choice **C** because it flips the numerical values in place. It displays drainage basin area / discharge rate instead of the correct formula as shown in Figure 1. Answer choice **D** because it uses the wrong units and also displays the calculation with the 28,400 and 3,000 flipped.

286. **The best answer is G.** The key to this question is identifying the location of the rainfall event on the map shown in Figure 1 and identifying which direction is downstream for the rivers. In this case, if the measurement of the discharge event was taken north of the rainfall event, that measurement would be upstream of the rain and not downstream. Rivers flow downstream, so the water from the rain moves downstream. This would lead to no increase in discharge and thus no flood because none of the rainfall would be flowing towards the measurement site, making **G** the correct answer.

The best answer is NOT:

Choice **F** because the Jones River was measured and not the North River. Choice **H** because the Jones River was measured and not the North River. Choice **J** because no flood would have occurred at all so there would be no discharge measured for the Jones River.

Passage L

287. **The best answer is B.** Figure 2 shows the phase of different compounds in a range of temperatures and percent durene by mass. At 55°C there are three potential regions of the graph to choose from, showing the phases of matter of each substance. The only one of the three that does not have a solid (*s*) present is the solution (*l*) which compromises the majority of the top of Figure 2. At 55° C, which is viewed on the y-axis, the only answer choice that would fall into the solution (*l*) area is 50% on the x-axis. This makes choice **B** correct.

The best answer is NOT:

Choice **A** because there you have the solution (*l*) + naphthalene (*s*). Naphthalene (*s*) is a solid, making this incorrect. Choices **C** and **D** because they have the solution (*l*) and durene (*s*).

288. **The best answer is H.** This question simply asks you to locate the point corresponding to 50°C on the y-axis and 70% durene by mass on the x-axis of the graph shown in Figure 1. Once you have located this, you can identify that the plotted location indicates you will have a solution (*l*) + durene (*s*). This makes choice **H** correct.

The best answer is NOT:

Choice **F** because not only is there a liquid solution, but also solid durene is present. Choice **G** because biphenyl is not the solid present. Choice **J** because a liquid solution needs to be present along with solid durene to be correct.

289. **The best answer is A.** This question asks for the temperature on the graph where the two chemicals and the liquid solution are present and exist at equilibrium. The eutectic is described in the introduction to the passage as the location on the graph where this occurs. That point specifically is where all of the lines intersect on the graph. According to the question, you must determine on the graph where there is 40% by mass durene. The intersection point can be found at the 40% by mass durene point right around 42° as shown in answer choice **A**.

The best answer is NOT:

Choices **B, C,** and **D** because at any temperature above 42° and 40% by mass durene the only substance present is the liquid solution.

290. **The best answer is F.** This question presents you with a mixture at 60% durene by mass initially at 90° C. Then the mixture is cooled 20°C and then then heated to 70°C. You need to focus only on the final temperature given. The first two do not matter as the question wants to know only what the mixture consisted of at the end of the procedure. In this case at 60% durene by mass and 70°C you will have a liquid solution only, making **F** the correct answer choice.

 The best answer is NOT:

 Choice **G** because 70° is above all the possible areas on the graph where solid biphenyl could exist. Choice **H** because again 70°C is above all areas on the graph where solid durene could exist. Choice **J** because 70°C is above all areas on the graph where solid durene or solid biphenyl could exist.

291. **The best answer is D.** In both Figures 1 and 2, solid durene only exists in certain areas of the graph. For 100% durene by mass (the far right of both figures) the highest temperature that contains solid durene is just below 80°C. Also, the equilibrium line between solid and liquid (the definition of melting point) for the 100% durene is about 80°C in both figures. The answer choice that best matches this is 79°C making choice **D** correct.

 The best answer is NOT:

 Choices **A, B,** and **C** because they indicate the melting point of durene as being too low.

Passage LI

292. **The best answer is H.** The first line in Experiment 1 states all three spheres used in Experiment 1 were solid aluminum metal. This makes the student's statement that the spheres are made of different metals incorrect. In addition, the spheres in Experiment 1 were not the same size. Therefore, **H** is the correct answer.

 The best answer is NOT:

 Choices **F** and **G** because the student's statement is not supported by Experiment 1. It does not examine spheres composed of different metals. Choice **J** because the spheres were not made of different metals as it states.

293.   **The best answer is A.** Cooling rate is defined in the passage as the slope of the graph so the unit of measurement should match the unit of the y-axis divided by the units of the x-axis. Both Figures 2 and 3 show a plot of the temperature of each sphere versus time over a given cooling period. The unit for the y-axis in each figure is °C and the unit for the x-axis is minutes (min). The cooling rate is the change in °C per minute. This makes the unit of measurement °C/min. Thus, **A** is the correct answer choice.

   The best answer is NOT:

   Choice **B** because it uses volume (cm^3) from Table 1 instead of time. Choice **C** because it reverses the units and has minutes over temperature. Choice **D** because it uses volume instead of time and it also has temperature in the wrong location.

294.   **The best answer is G.** The passage indicates that all of the spheres are kept in an environment with a constant air temperature of 20°C. Sphere A began at a temperature of 100°C and slowly cooled over the course of the 30 min cooling period to 25°C. If the sphere had been allowed to keep cooling beyond 30 minutes, eventually it would have reached equilibrium with the surrounding air temperature, 20°C. This would have been the final temperature of the sphere. Given enough time, objects reach thermal equilibrium. When thermal equilibrium is reached, the temperatures of the system (the sphere) and the surroundings (the air) are equal. Thus, choice **G** is correct.

   The best answer is NOT:

   Choice **F** because 15°C is lower than the temperature of the air surrounding the sphere. Choices **H** and **J** because they are above the temperature of the air surrounding the sphere.

295.   **The best answer is D.** This question asks you to look at Figure 2 and determine the relationship between the ratio of surface area to volume (S/V) and cooling rate. Figure 2 shows that at the end of 30 minutes sphere A was the coolest, having the lowest temperature of the three spheres. Sphere A also had the largest S/V ratio. Sphere B was the second coolest and it had the second largest S/V ratio. Sphere C also fit this trend. This implies the larger the S/V ratio, the faster the sphere will cool. The three data points validate the relationship: as the S/V ration increases, the cooling rate also increases. Therefore, the correct answer will have the largest ratio, which is choice **D**, 2.0 cm^{-1}.

   The best answer is NOT:

   Choices **A, B,** and **C** because they have a smaller S/V ratio than **D**.

296.   **The best answer is choice G.** In Experiment 1, each of the spheres was brought to a temperature of 100°C. For a student to get the spheres to that temperature they must have immersed the spheres in something that is at 100°C. Water boils at a temperature of 100°C making it the correct answer. So **G** is the correct answer.

   The best answer is NOT:

   Choice **F** because air at 20°C would not raise the temperature of the sphere at all. Choice **H** because dry ice has a temperature below 0°C and would would lower the temperatures of the spheres. Choice **J** because the spheres are made of aluminum and would melt if placed into molten aluminum.

297.   **The best answer is D.** From the information shown in Figure 3, Sphere X reached 40°C at 38 minutes. Sphere Y reached 40°C at 55 minutes. When you subtract 55 – 38, you calculate that Sphere Y reaches 40°C 17 minutes later than Sphere X, making **D** the correct answer.

   The best answer is NOT:

   Choice **A** because Y reaches the temperature later and it takes 17 minutes. Choice **B** because while it does happen later, 13 minutes is incorrect. Choice **C** because while it does take 17 minutes it happens later, not sooner.

Passage LII

298.   **The best answer is H.** This question asks you to look at Figure 1—specifically, the third graph showing the air temperature deviation at an altitude of 19 km. The line plotted on the graph shows the air temperature deviation above the volcano. The greatest air temperature deviation at 19 km is exactly between 6°C and 8°C of deviation. That makes the correct answer 7°C. This is the place on the graph where the plotted line peaks and achieves its maximum value. So **H** is the correct answer.

   The best answer is NOT:

   Choice **F** because 5°C is the greatest temperature deviation at 16 km, not 19 km. Choices **G** and **J** because neither is the best answer. The greatest temperature change is close to both, but the best answer is 7°C which matches the changes exactly.

299. **The best answer is B.** Figure 2 shows that the maximum surface air temperature deviation after Toba erupted was 4°C. This can be found by looking at the plotted points in Figure 2 and identifying the one labeled Toba. In addition, the y-axis shows the temperature deviation. It is not a straight scale, however, as the space between each value is not equal. Thankfully, there are graduations on the graph showing exactly where each measurement of the volcanoes falls. So you know Toba was 4°C. In addition, all of the values shown on the air temperature graph are negative values. This indicates the air temperature deviation above Toba was below the average value and not above. It would be positive if it was above average. Therefore, **B** is the correct answer.

The best answer is NOT:

Choice **A** because it indicates an above-average deviation despite showing the correct temperature. Choice **C** because it indicates above-average change which is wrong and shows the incorrect temperature deviation. Choice **D** because it indicates correctly that the change is below average, but it shows the wrong temperature value.

300. **The best answer is J.** Figure 1 shows the eruption occurred towards the beginning of the year 1983. Prior to the eruption, the air temperature deviation at 16 km stayed mostly below 1°C. However, after the eruption it increased quickly and remained in that increased state for quite some time. The plotted line never again returns below 1°C on the graph. This encompasses the remainder of the year 1983, and all of 1984, 1985, and 1986. That is more than three years and makes choice **J** correct.

The best answer is NOT:

Choices **F, G,** and **H** because they indicate that at some point on the graph, after the eruption, the plotted line dips down below 1°C but it never does.

301. **The best answer is C.** This question tells you that the average air temperature above the volcano at 16 km can be assumed to be −60°C. It then asks you to look at the air temperature deviation on January 1, 1984 in Figure 1. The note with the graphic states that a tick mark (vertical line) on the x-axis indicates January 1 of that year. On January 1, 1984, the air temperature deviation above the volcano was exactly 4°C. This indicates the air temperature above the volcano was 4°C above the average air temperature. So the air temperature should be 4 degrees above −60°C. Make sure when you answer this question that you pay attention to the fact that increasing a negative temperature means you actually lower the absolute value of the number. −56°C is 4 degrees warmer than −60°C. So, the correct answer is **C**.

The best answer is NOT:

Choice **A** because −64°C is actually a colder temperature, not a warmer temperature as shown in the graph. Choice **B** because there would be no deviation in temperature if that was true. Be careful when you see an answer choice like D, the temperature deviation is 4°C so it is easy to quickly jump to filling in the answer as −4°C without giving it much thought because the numbers match up with something you see in the passage. Choice **D** because −4°C is a much warmer temperature than the correct answer.

302. **The best answer is J.** The equation included in Figure 1 states the relationship between measured air temperature and average air temperature that results in the air temperature deviation. A zero value for air temperature deviation would require the measured air temperature and the average air temperature at a given altitude to be equal. This makes **J** the correct answer.

The best answer is NOT:

Choice **F** because the maximum air temperature is represented by the high point on each graph, not a measure of 0°. Choice **G** because the average air temperature deviation at that altitude is represented by the plotted line for each graph. Choice **H** because the maximum air temperature at each altitude is not shown on the graph.

NOTES